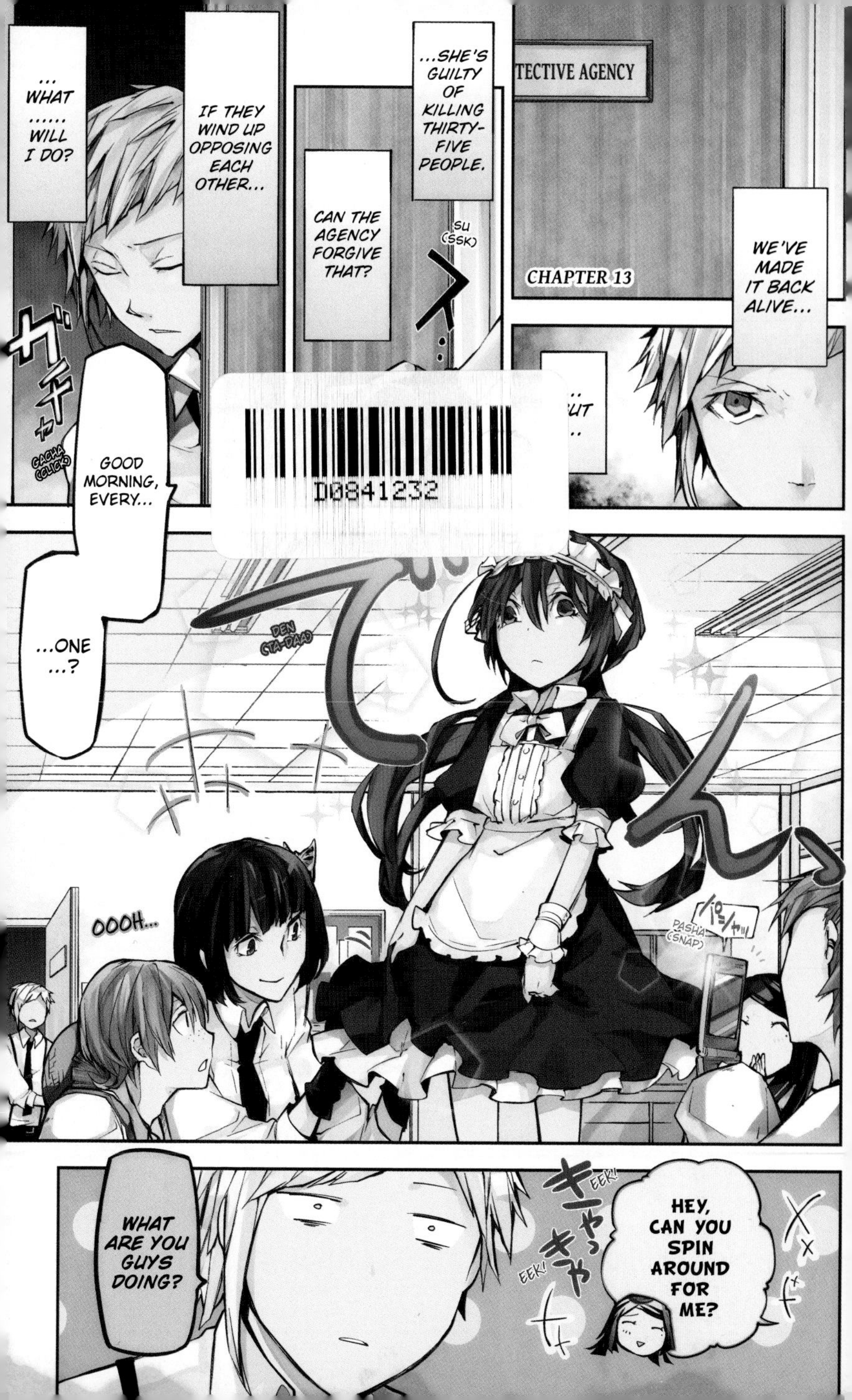TECTIVE AGENCY
CHAPTER 13
WE'VE MADE IT BACK ALIVE...
...SHE'S GUILTY OF KILLING THIRTY-FIVE PEOPLE.
SU (SSK)
CAN THE AGENCY FORGIVE THAT?
IF THEY WIND UP OPPOSING EACH OTHER...
...WHAT ...... WILL I DO?
GACHA (CLICK)
GOOD MORNING, EVERY...
...ONE ...?
DEN (TA-DAA)
PASHA (SNAP)
OOOH...
HEY, CAN YOU SPIN AROUND FOR ME?
EEK!
EEK!
WHAT ARE YOU GUYS DOING?

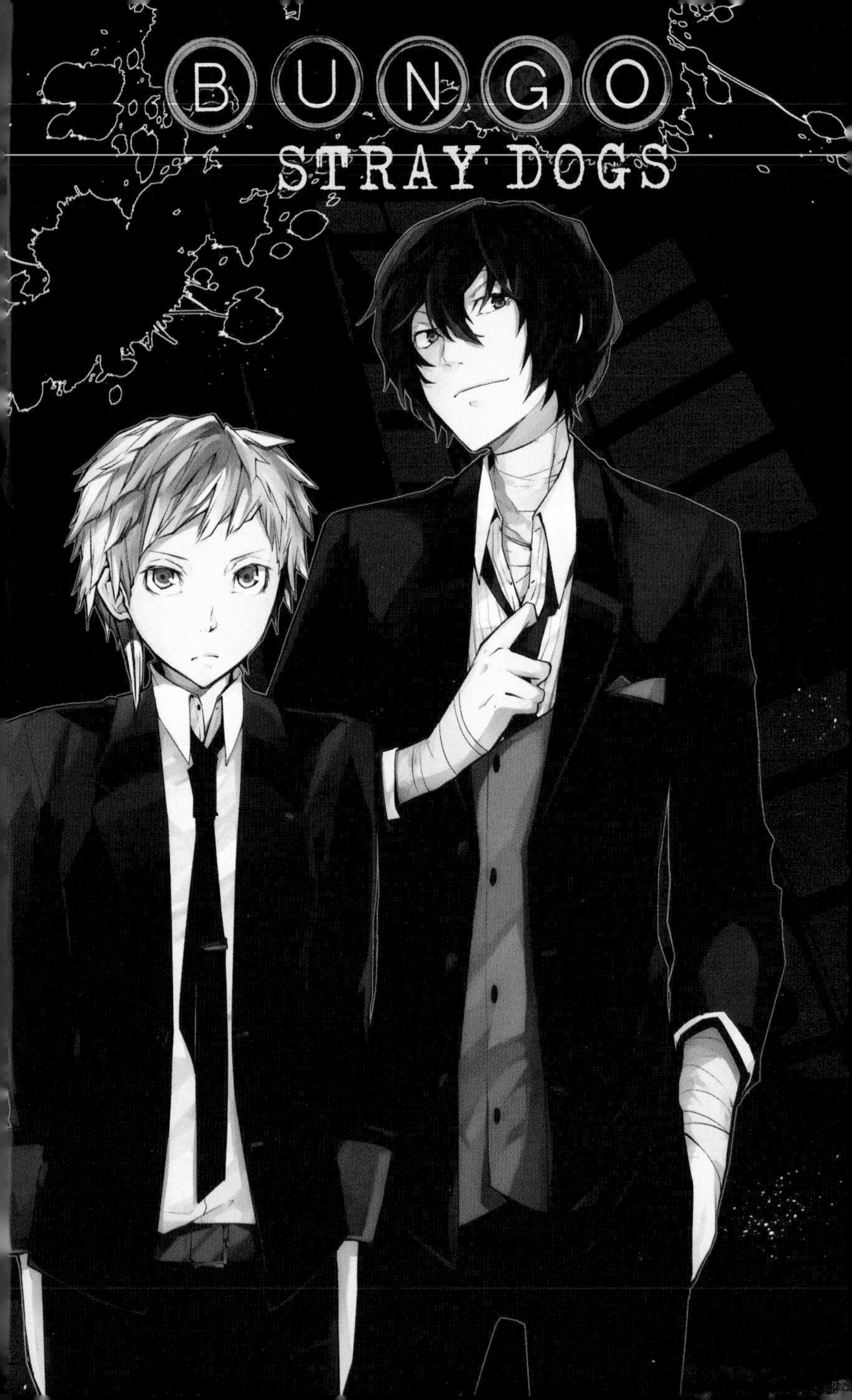
BUNGO
STRAY DOGS

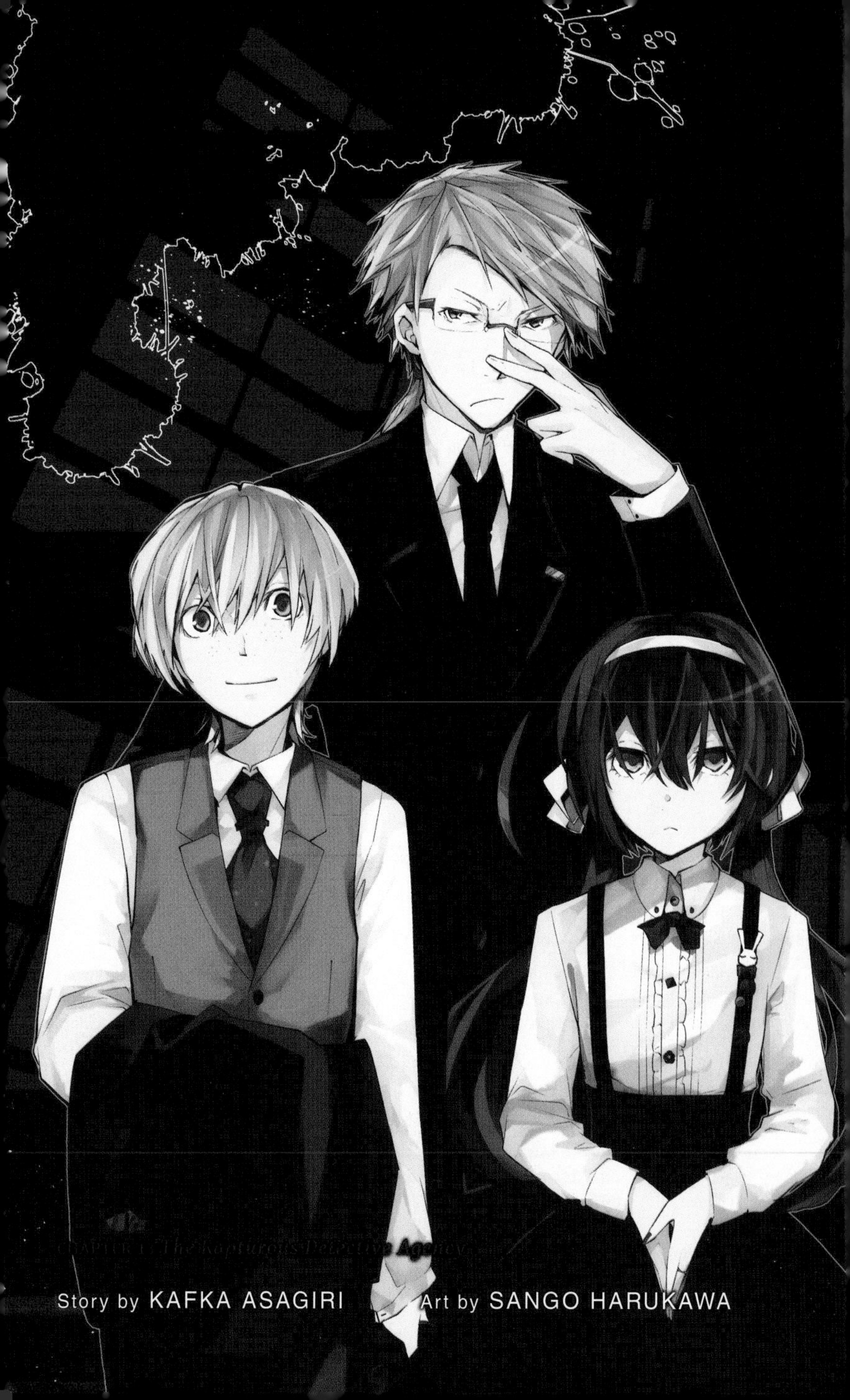
Story by KAFKA ASAGIRI
Art by SANGO HARUKAWA

TABLE of CONTENTS

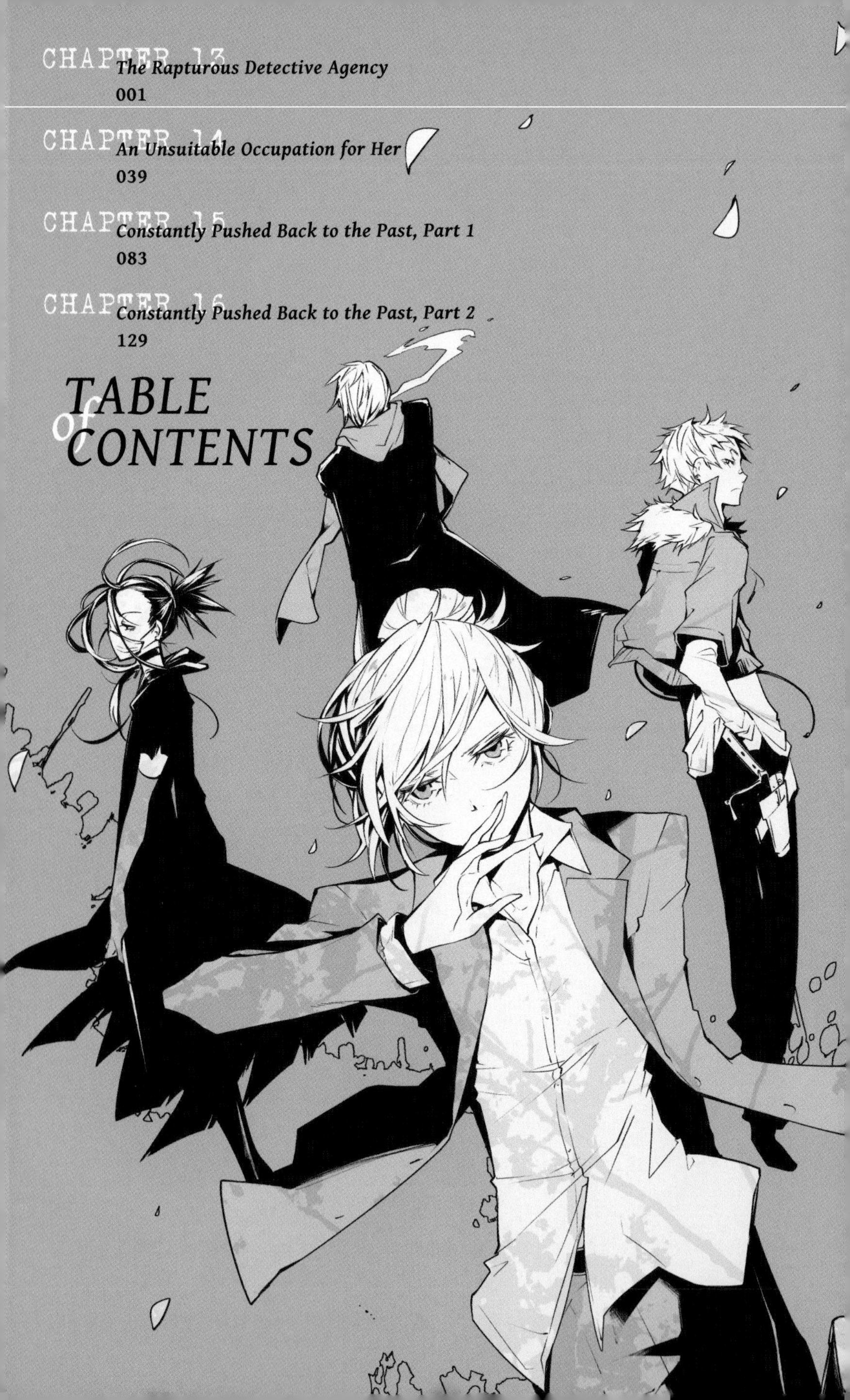

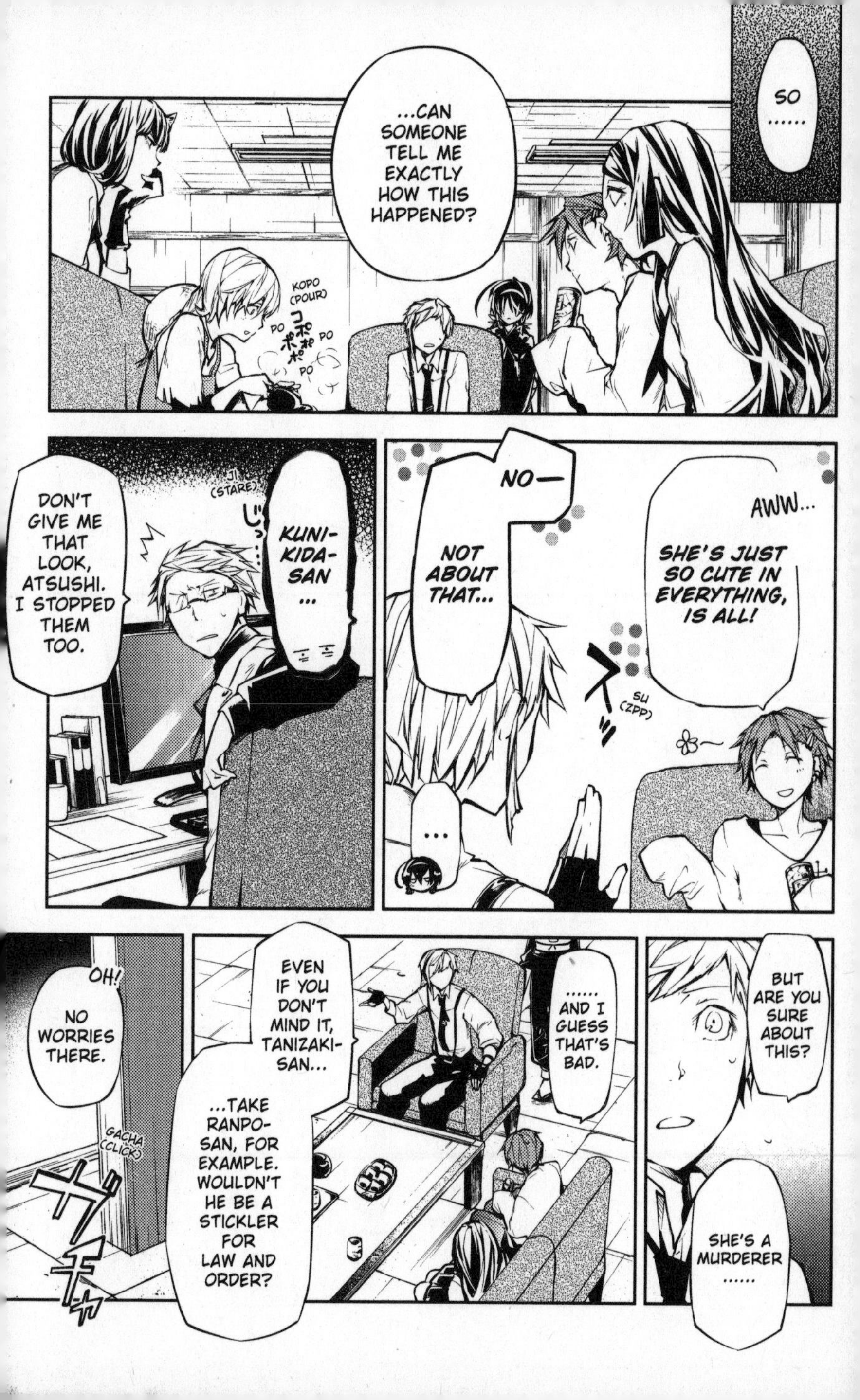
SO......
...CAN SOMEONE TELL ME EXACTLY HOW THIS HAPPENED?
KOPO (POUR)
PO PO PO
AWW...
SHE'S JUST SO CUTE IN EVERYTHING, IS ALL!
SU (ZPP)
NO—
NOT ABOUT THAT...
...
KUNI-KIDA-SAN...
JI (STARE)
DON'T GIVE ME THAT LOOK, ATSUSHI. I STOPPED THEM TOO.
BUT ARE YOU SURE ABOUT THIS?
SHE'S A MURDERER......
......AND I GUESS THAT'S BAD.
EVEN IF YOU DON'T MIND IT, TANIZAKI-SAN...
...TAKE RANPO-SAN, FOR EXAMPLE. WOULDN'T HE BE A STICKLER FOR LAW AND ORDER?
OH!
NO WORRIES THERE.
GACHA (CLICK)

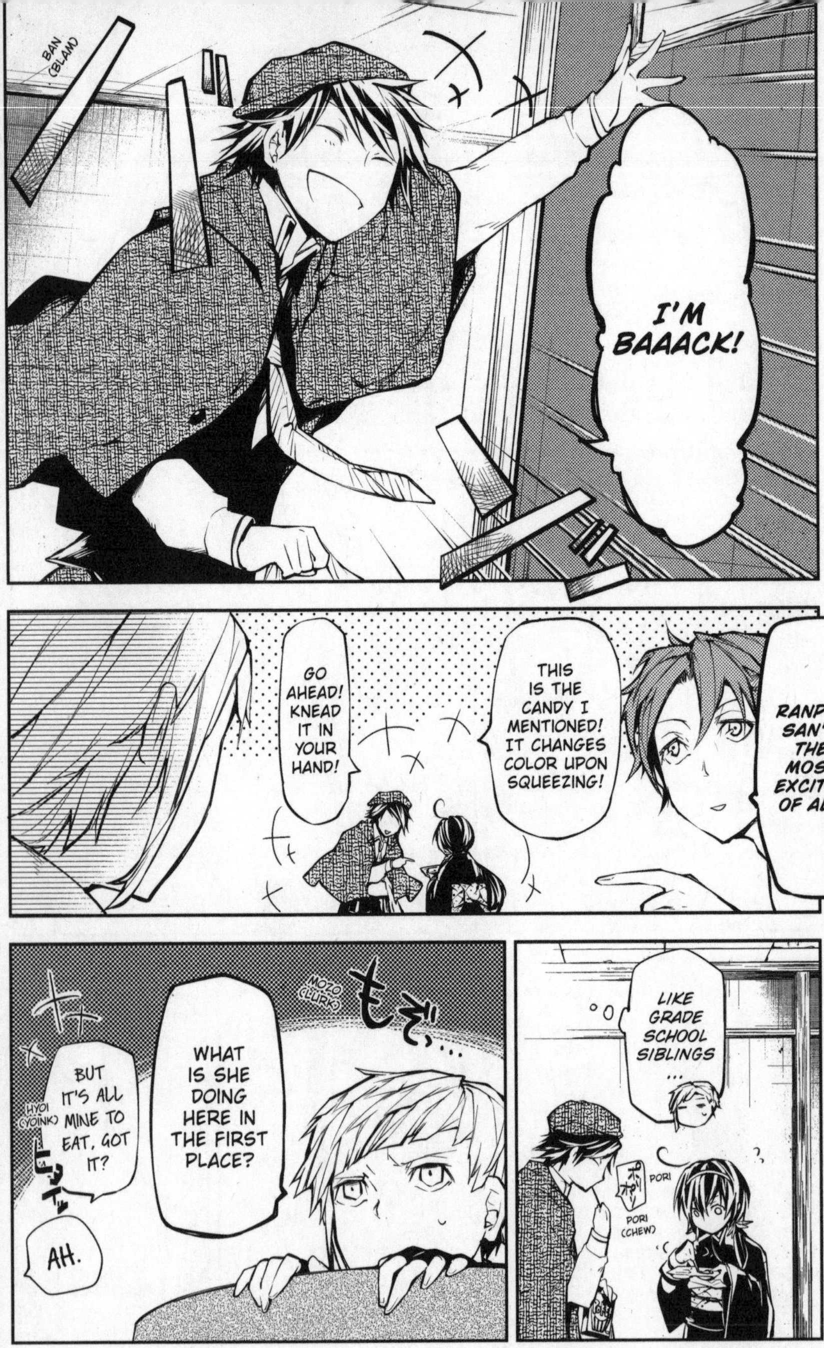
BAN (BLAM)
I'M BAAACK!
RANPO-SAN'S THE MOST EXCITED OF ALL.
THIS IS THE CANDY I MENTIONED! IT CHANGES COLOR UPON SQUEEZING!
GO AHEAD! KNEAD IT IN YOUR HAND!
LIKE GRADE SCHOOL SIBLINGS ...
PORI
PORI (CHEW)
MOZO (LURK)
もぞ…
WHAT IS SHE DOING HERE IN THE FIRST PLACE?
BUT IT'S ALL MINE TO EAT, GOT IT?
HYOI (YOINK)
AH.

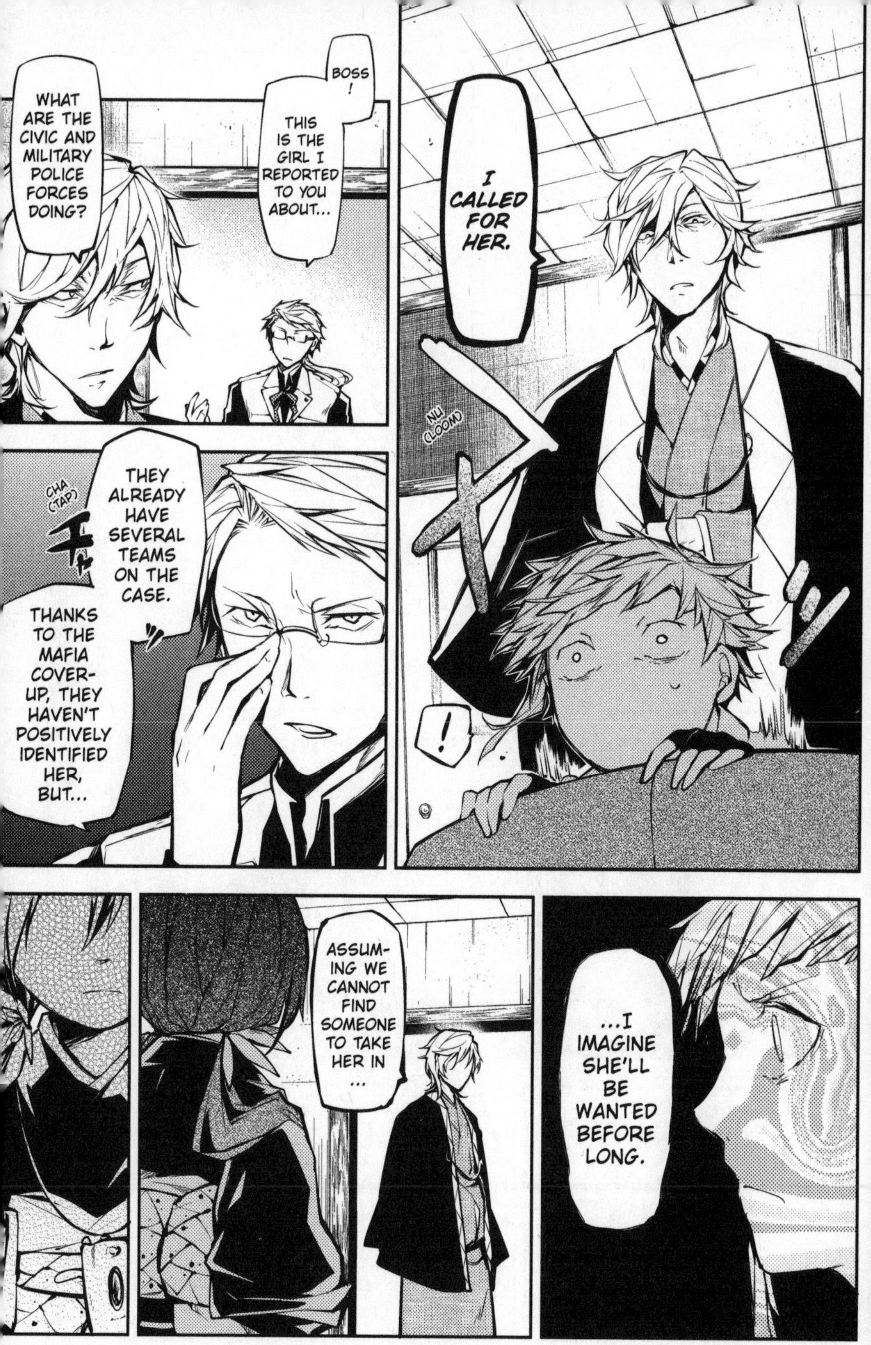
I CALLED FOR HER.
NU (LOOM)
!
BOSS!
THIS IS THE GIRL I REPORTED TO YOU ABOUT...
WHAT ARE THE CIVIC AND MILITARY POLICE FORCES DOING?
THEY ALREADY HAVE SEVERAL TEAMS ON THE CASE.
CHA (TAP)
THANKS TO THE MAFIA COVER-UP, THEY HAVEN'T POSITIVELY IDENTIFIED HER, BUT...
...I IMAGINE SHE'LL BE WANTED BEFORE LONG.
ASSUMING WE CANNOT FIND SOMEONE TO TAKE HER IN...

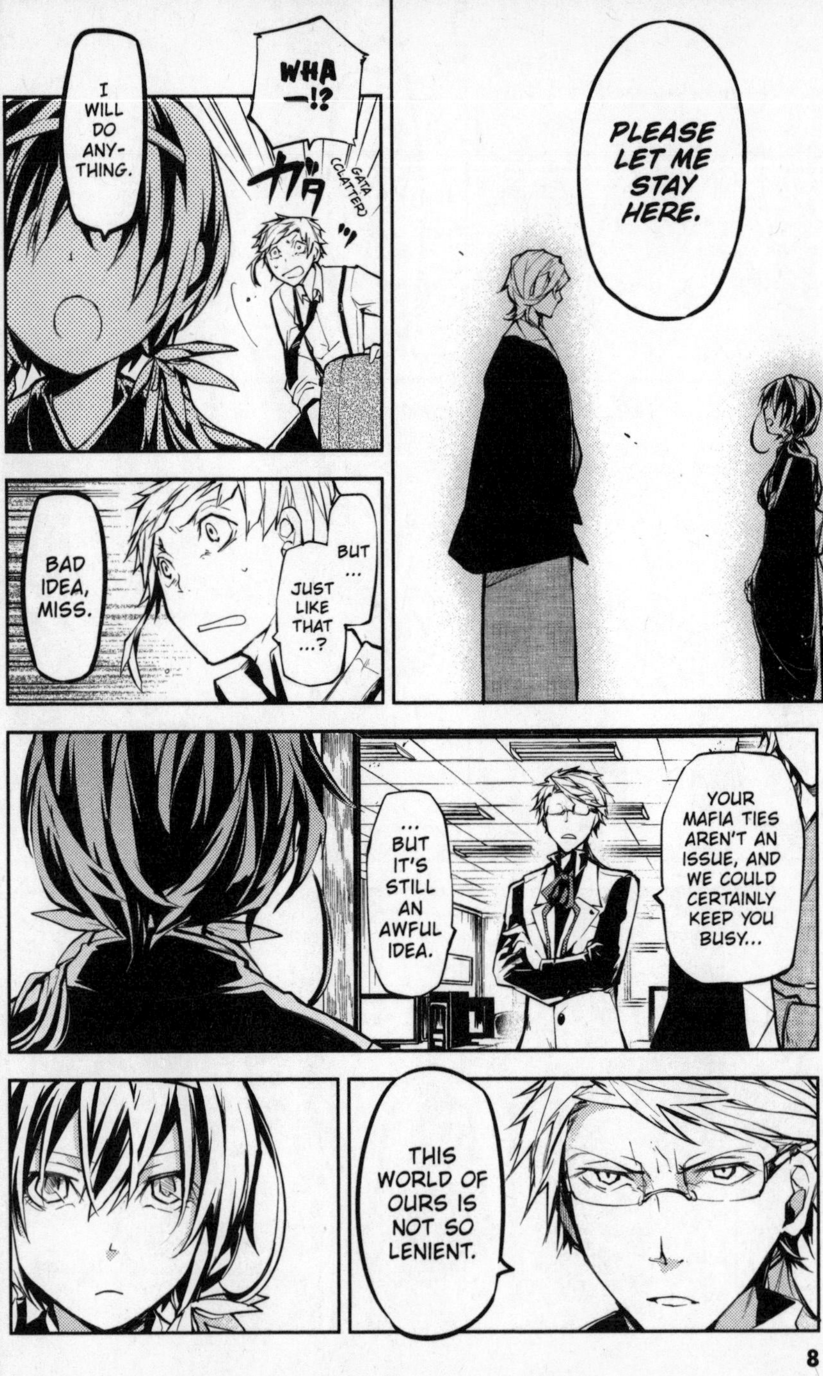
PLEASE LET ME STAY HERE.
WHA—!?
ガタ
GATA (CLATTER)
I WILL DO ANYTHING.
BUT ... JUST LIKE THAT ...?
BAD IDEA, MISS.
YOUR MAFIA TIES AREN'T AN ISSUE, AND WE COULD CERTAINLY KEEP YOU BUSY...
... BUT IT'S STILL AN AWFUL IDEA.
THIS WORLD OF OURS IS NOT SO LENIENT.

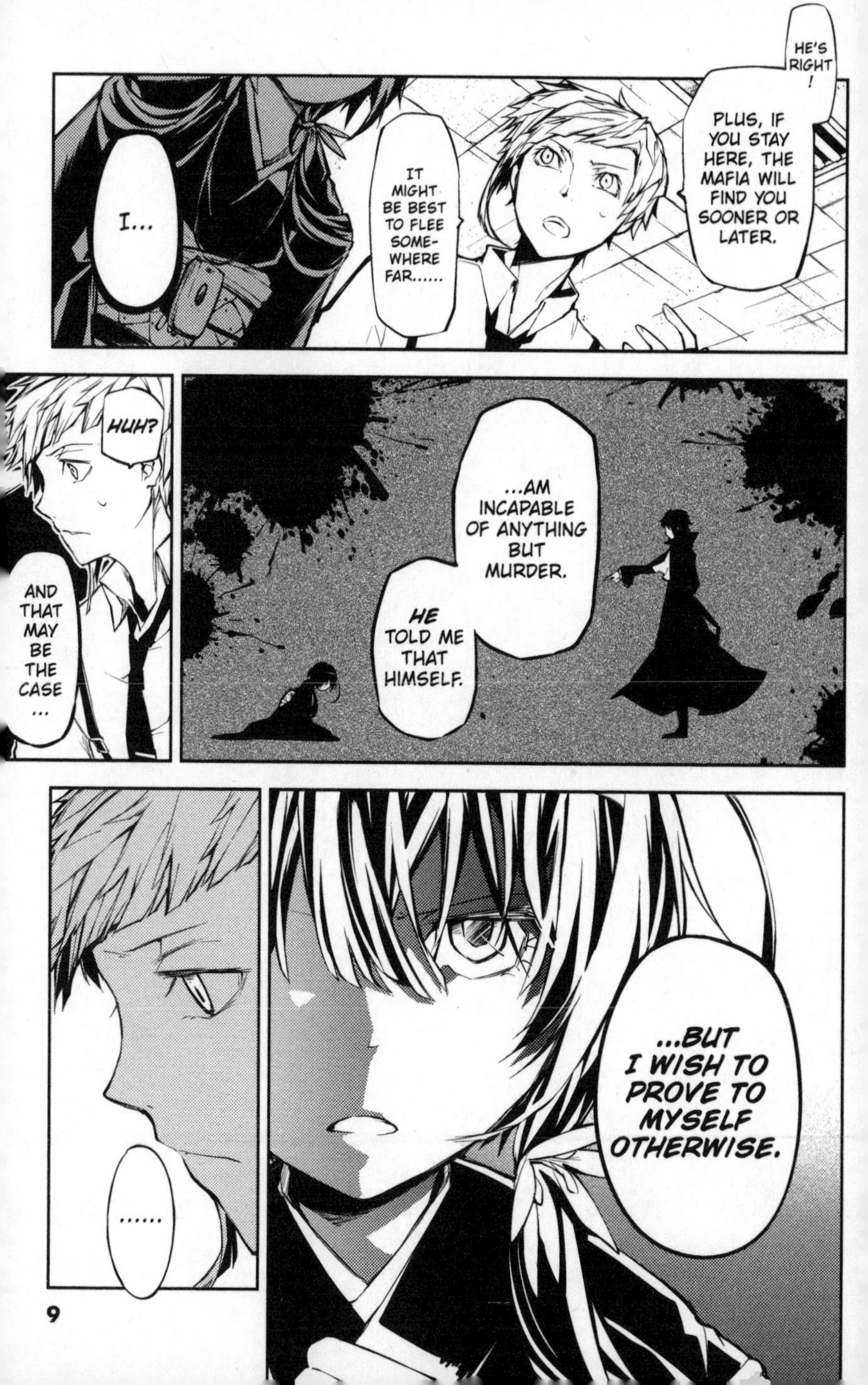
HE'S RIGHT!
PLUS, IF YOU STAY HERE, THE MAFIA WILL FIND YOU SOONER OR LATER.
IT MIGHT BE BEST TO FLEE SOMEWHERE FAR......
I...
...AM INCAPABLE OF ANYTHING BUT MURDER.
HE TOLD ME THAT HIMSELF.
HUH?
AND THAT MAY BE THE CASE...
...BUT I WISH TO PROVE TO MYSELF OTHERWISE.
......

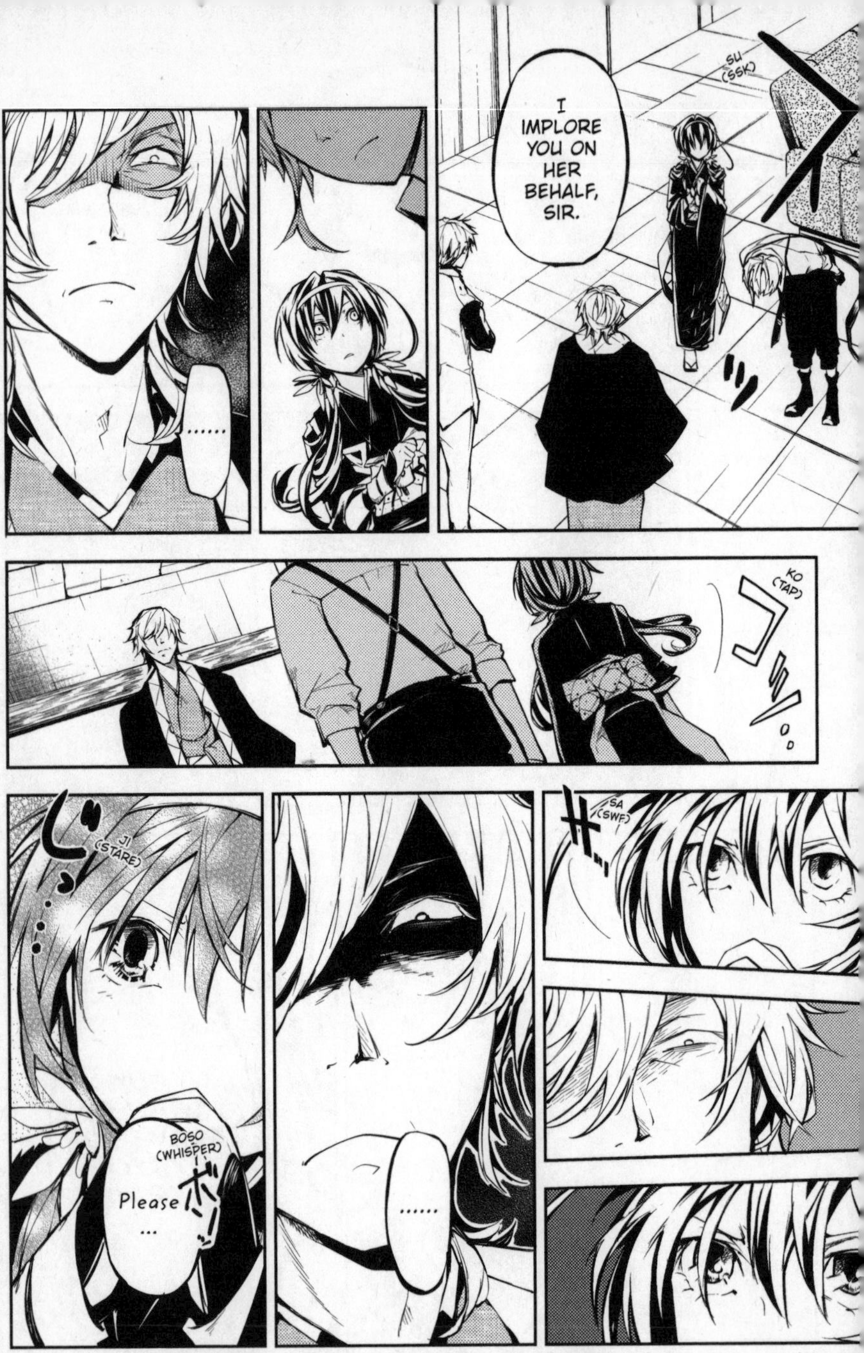
SU (SSK)
I IMPLORE YOU ON HER BEHALF, SIR.
......
KO (TAP)
SA (SWF)
......
JI (STARE)
BOSO (WHISPER)
Please ...

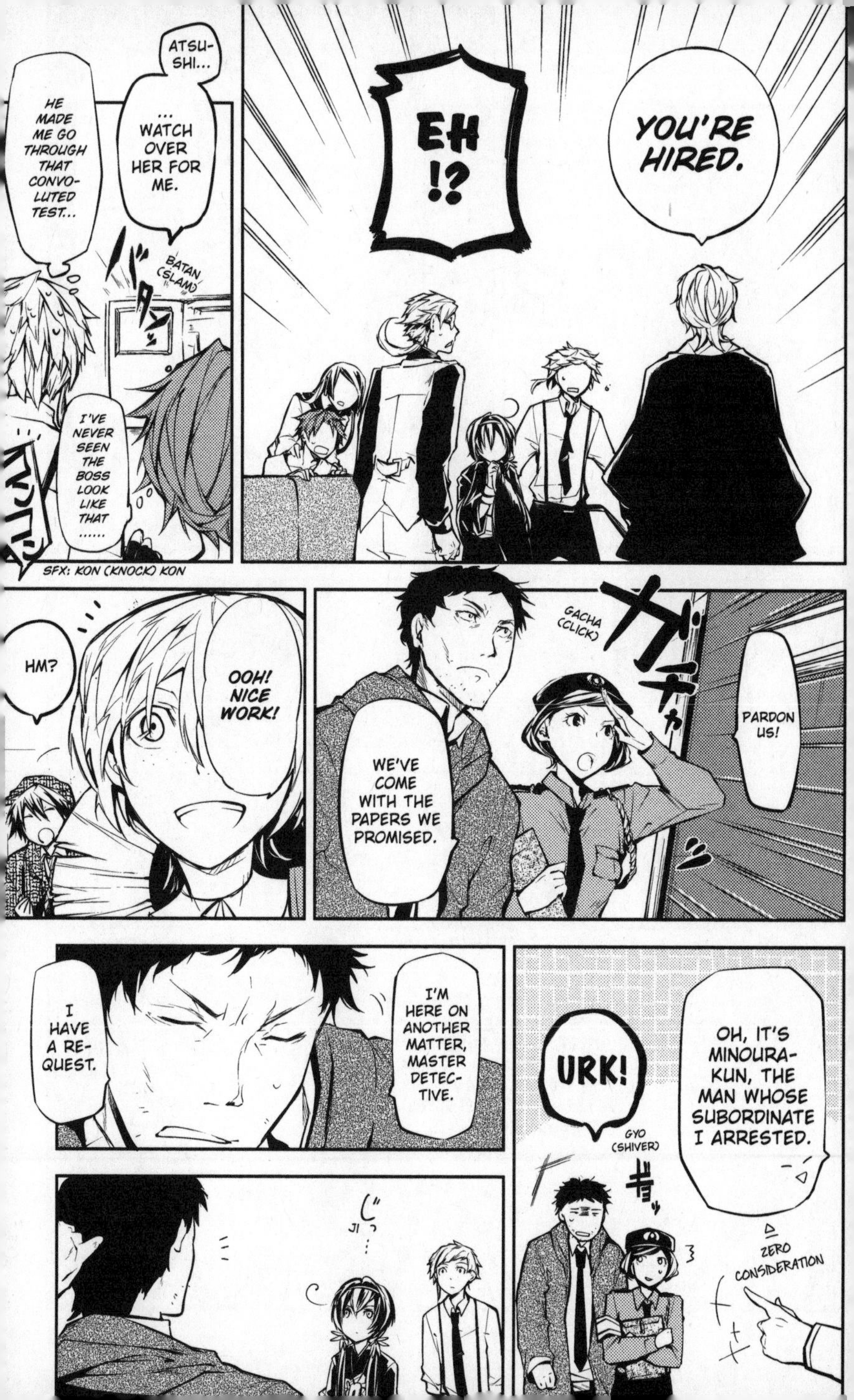
YOU'RE HIRED.
EH!?
ATSUSHI...
...WATCH OVER HER FOR ME.
HE MADE ME GO THROUGH THAT CONVOLUTED TEST...
BATAN (SLAM)
I'VE NEVER SEEN THE BOSS LOOK LIKE THAT......
SFX: KON (KNOCK) KON
GACHA (CLICK)
PARDON US!
WE'VE COME WITH THE PAPERS WE PROMISED.
OOH! NICE WORK!
HM?
OH, IT'S MINOURA-KUN, THE MAN WHOSE SUBORDINATE I ARRESTED.
URK!
GYO (SHIVER)
ZERO CONSIDERATION
I'M HERE ON ANOTHER MATTER, MASTER DETECTIVE.
I HAVE A REQUEST.
JI

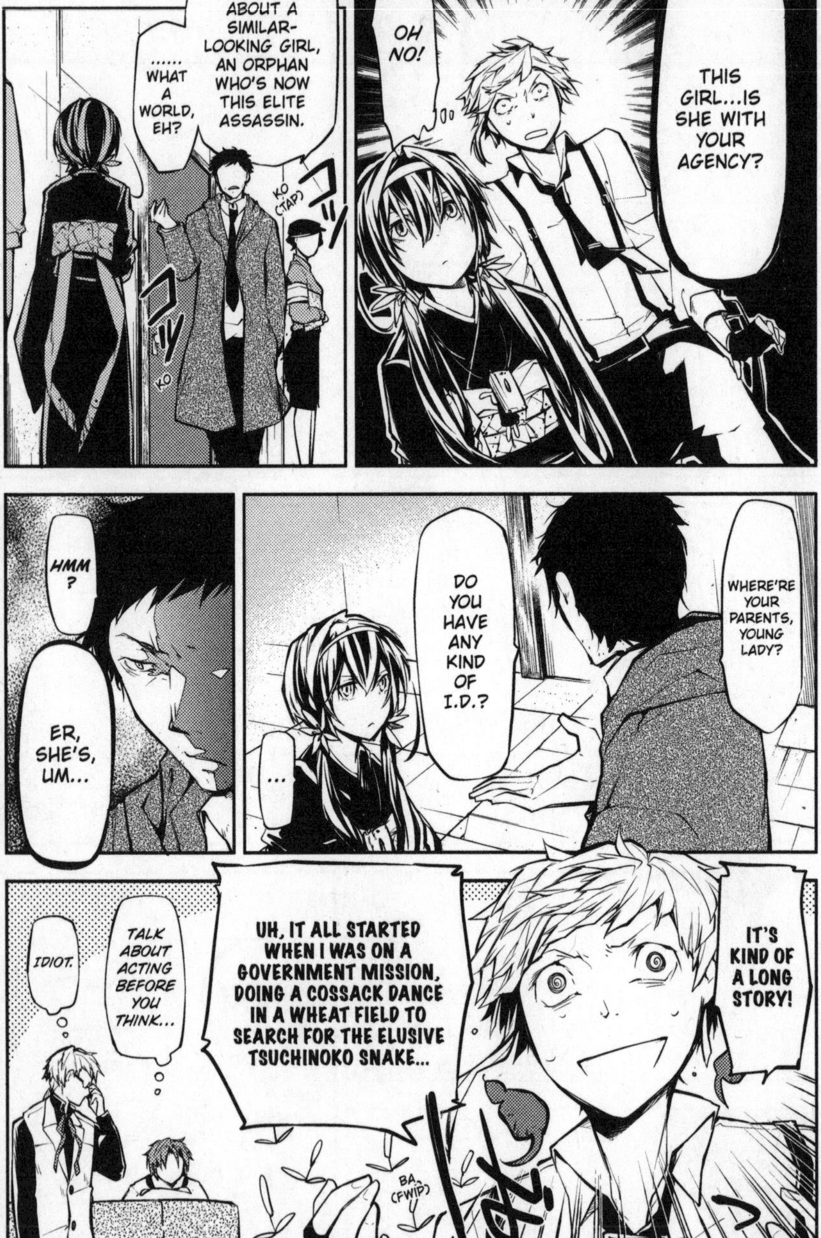
THIS GIRL...IS SHE WITH YOUR AGENCY?
OH NO!
I RECEIVED A BULLETIN ABOUT A SIMILAR-LOOKING GIRL, AN ORPHAN WHO'S NOW THIS ELITE ASSASSIN.
......WHAT A WORLD, EH?
KO (TAP)
KO
WHERE'RE YOUR PARENTS, YOUNG LADY?
DO YOU HAVE ANY KIND OF I.D.?
...
HMM?
ER, SHE'S, UM...
IT'S KIND OF A LONG STORY!
UH, IT ALL STARTED WHEN I WAS ON A GOVERNMENT MISSION, DOING A COSSACK DANCE IN A WHEAT FIELD TO SEARCH FOR THE ELUSIVE TSUCHINOKO SNAKE...
BA (FWIP)
TALK ABOUT ACTING BEFORE YOU THINK...
IDIOT.

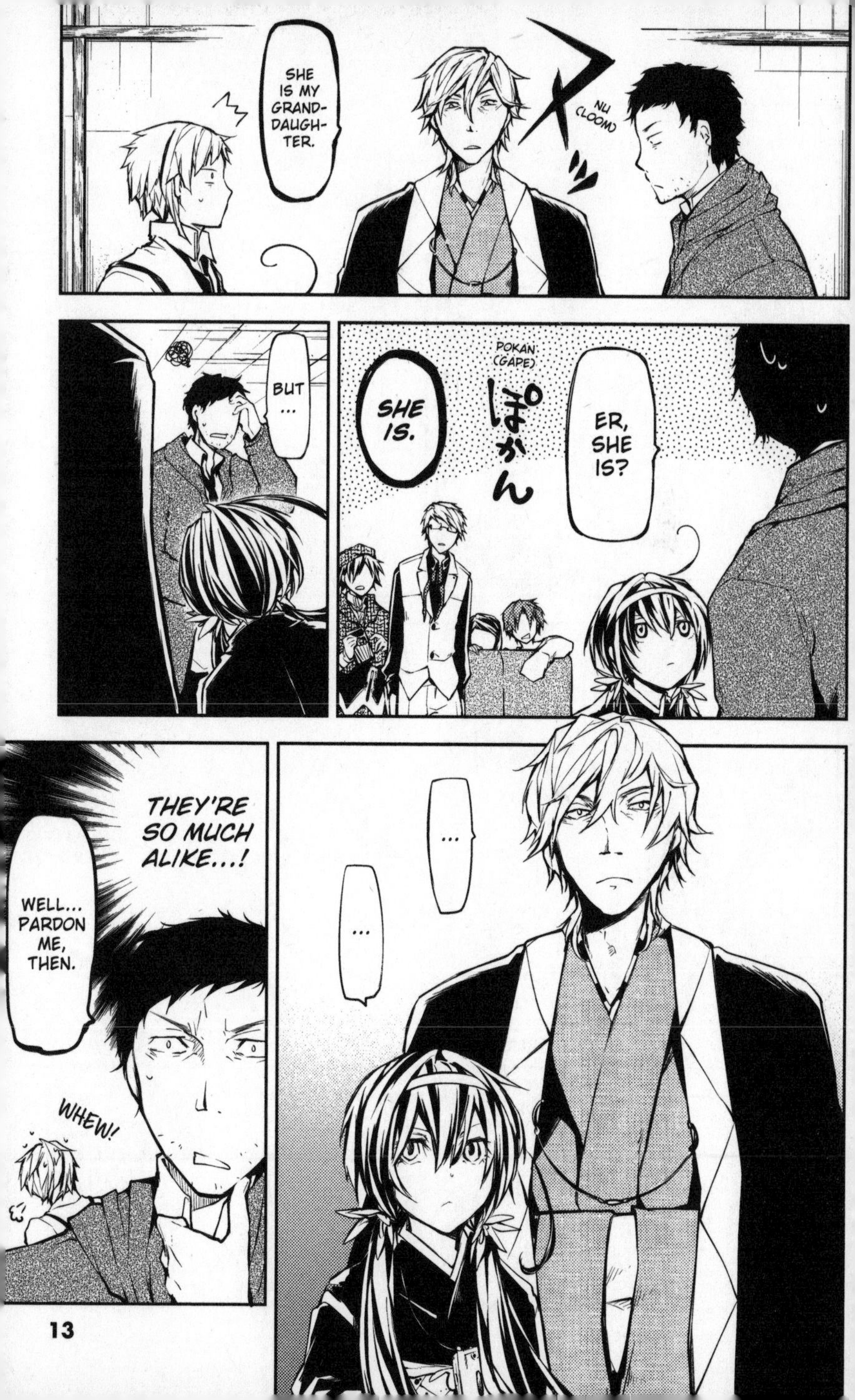
NU (LOOM)
SHE IS MY GRAND-DAUGH-TER.
ER, SHE IS?
ぽかん
POKAN (GAPE)
SHE IS.
BUT ...
...
...
THEY'RE SO MUCH ALIKE...!
WELL... PARDON ME, THEN.
WHEW!

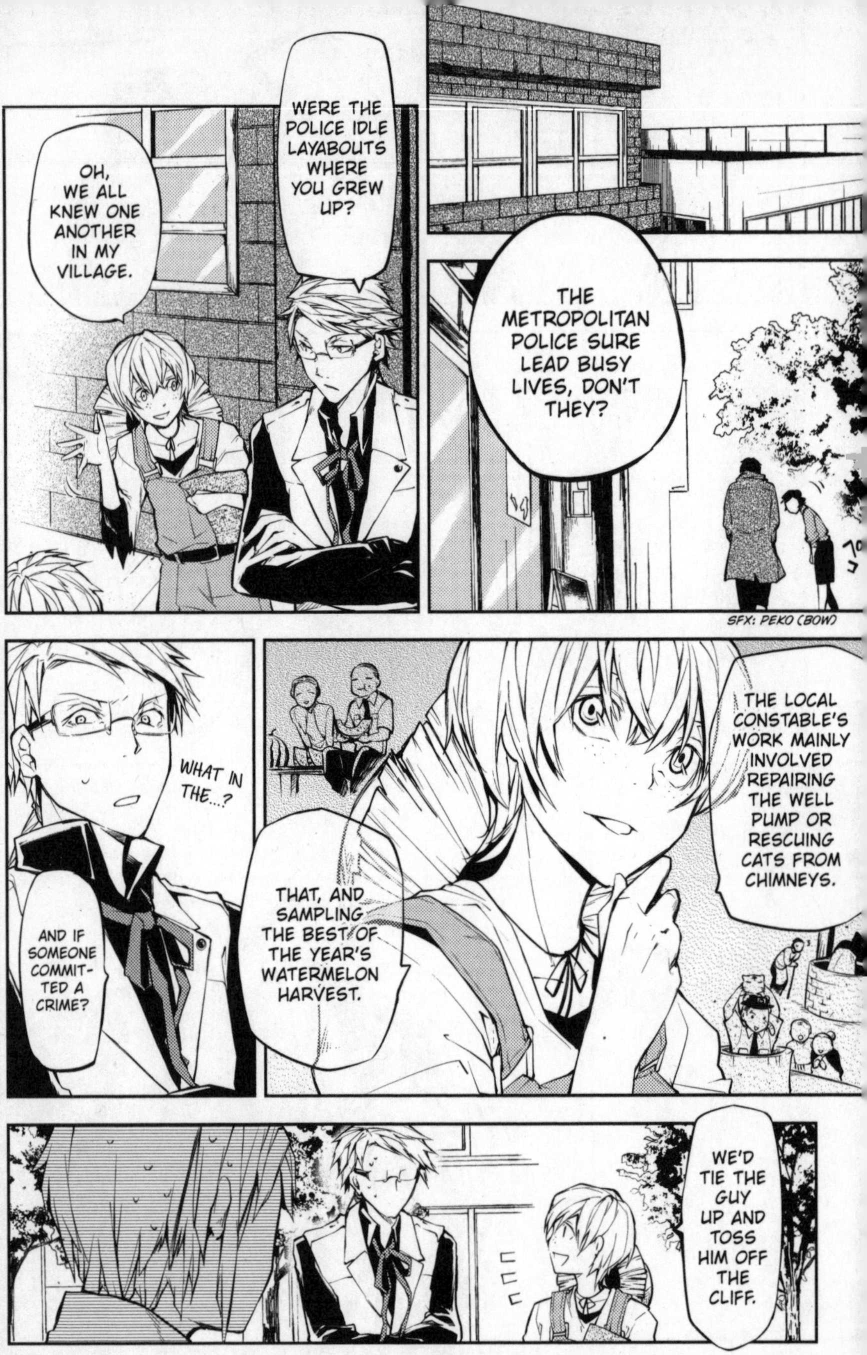
THE METROPOLITAN POLICE SURE LEAD BUSY LIVES, DON'T THEY?
SFX: PEKO (BOW)
WERE THE POLICE IDLE LAYABOUTS WHERE YOU GREW UP?
OH, WE ALL KNEW ONE ANOTHER IN MY VILLAGE.
THE LOCAL CONSTABLE'S WORK MAINLY INVOLVED REPAIRING THE WELL PUMP OR RESCUING CATS FROM CHIMNEYS.
THAT, AND SAMPLING THE BEST OF THE YEAR'S WATERMELON HARVEST.
WHAT IN THE...?
AND IF SOMEONE COMMIT-TED A CRIME?
WE'D TIE THE GUY UP AND TOSS HIM OFF THE CLIFF.

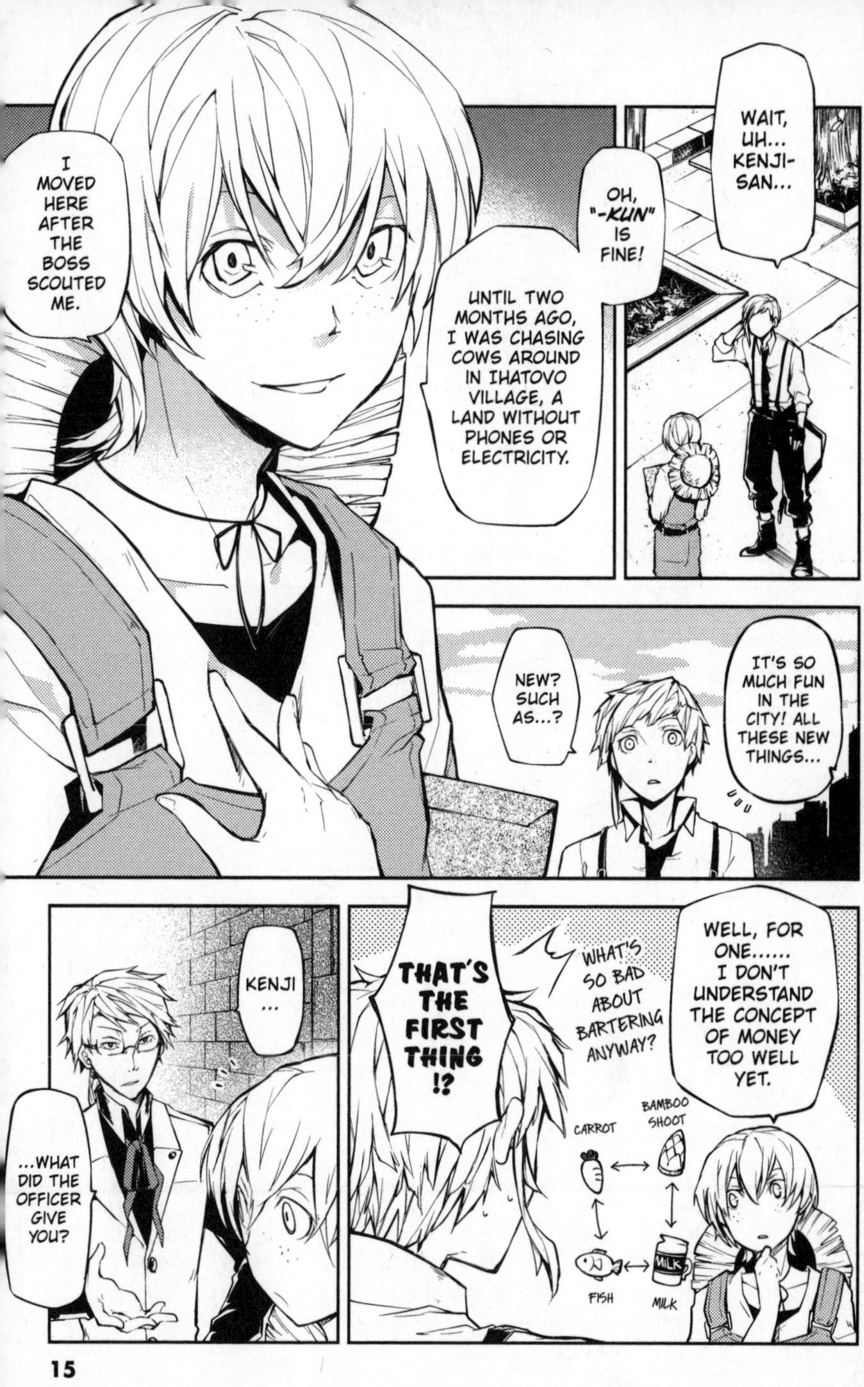
WAIT, UH... KENJI-SAN...
OH, "-KUN" IS FINE!
UNTIL TWO MONTHS AGO, I WAS CHASING COWS AROUND IN IHATOVO VILLAGE, A LAND WITHOUT PHONES OR ELECTRICITY.
I MOVED HERE AFTER THE BOSS SCOUTED ME.
IT'S SO MUCH FUN IN THE CITY! ALL THESE NEW THINGS...
NEW? SUCH AS...?
WELL, FOR ONE...... I DON'T UNDERSTAND THE CONCEPT OF MONEY TOO WELL YET.
BAMBOO SHOOT
CARROT
FISH
MILK
MILK
WHAT'S SO BAD ABOUT BARTERING ANYWAY?
THAT'S THE FIRST THING!?
KENJI...
...WHAT DID THE OFFICER GIVE YOU?

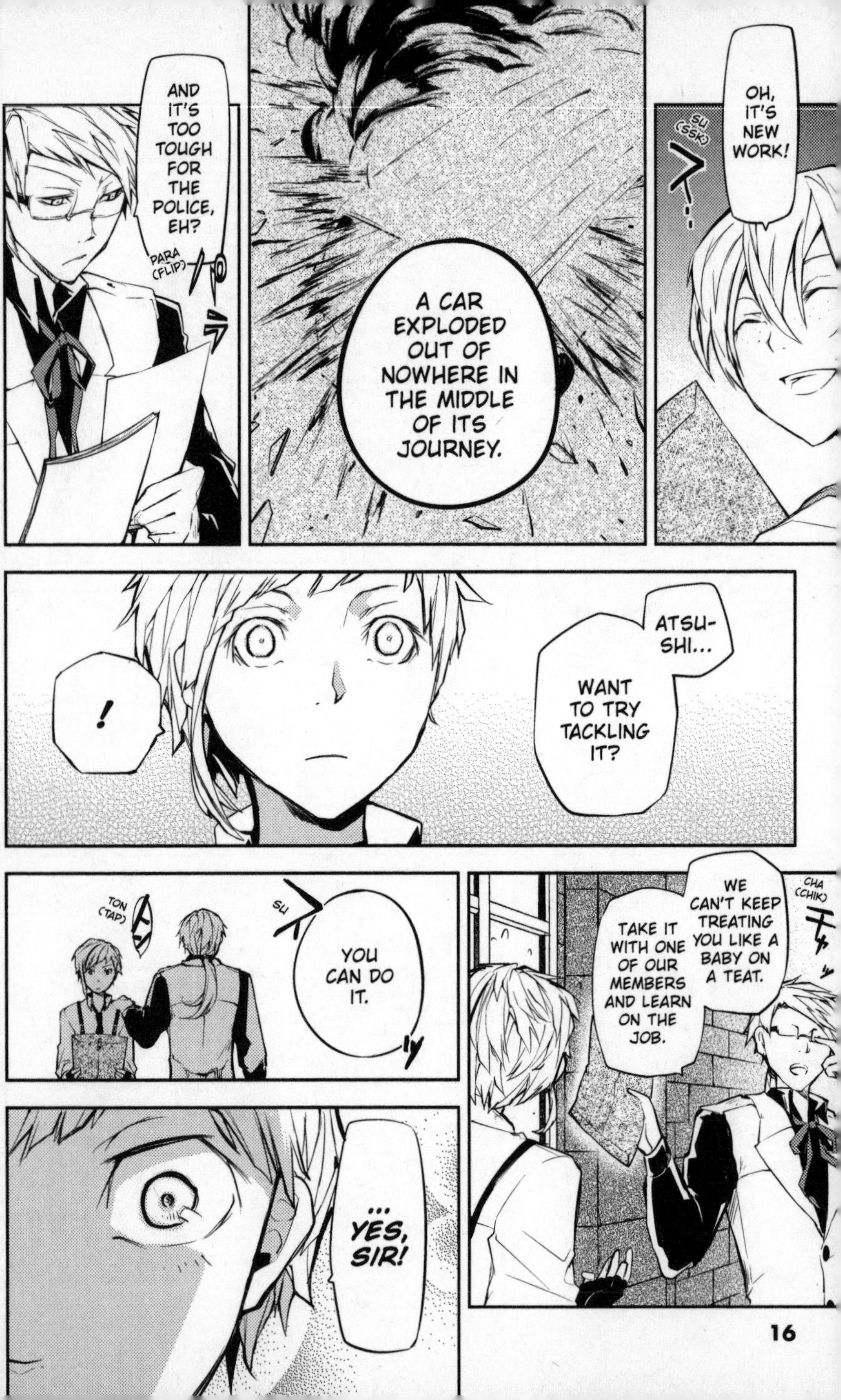
SU (SSK)
OH, IT'S NEW WORK!
A CAR EXPLODED OUT OF NOWHERE IN THE MIDDLE OF ITS JOURNEY.
AND IT'S TOO TOUGH FOR THE POLICE, EH?
PARA (FLIP)
ATSU-SHI...
WANT TO TRY TACKLING IT?
!
CHA (CHIK)
WE CAN'T KEEP TREATING YOU LIKE A BABY ON A TEAT.
TAKE IT WITH ONE OF OUR MEMBERS AND LEARN ON THE JOB.
SU
YOU CAN DO IT.
TON (TAP)
...YES, SIR!

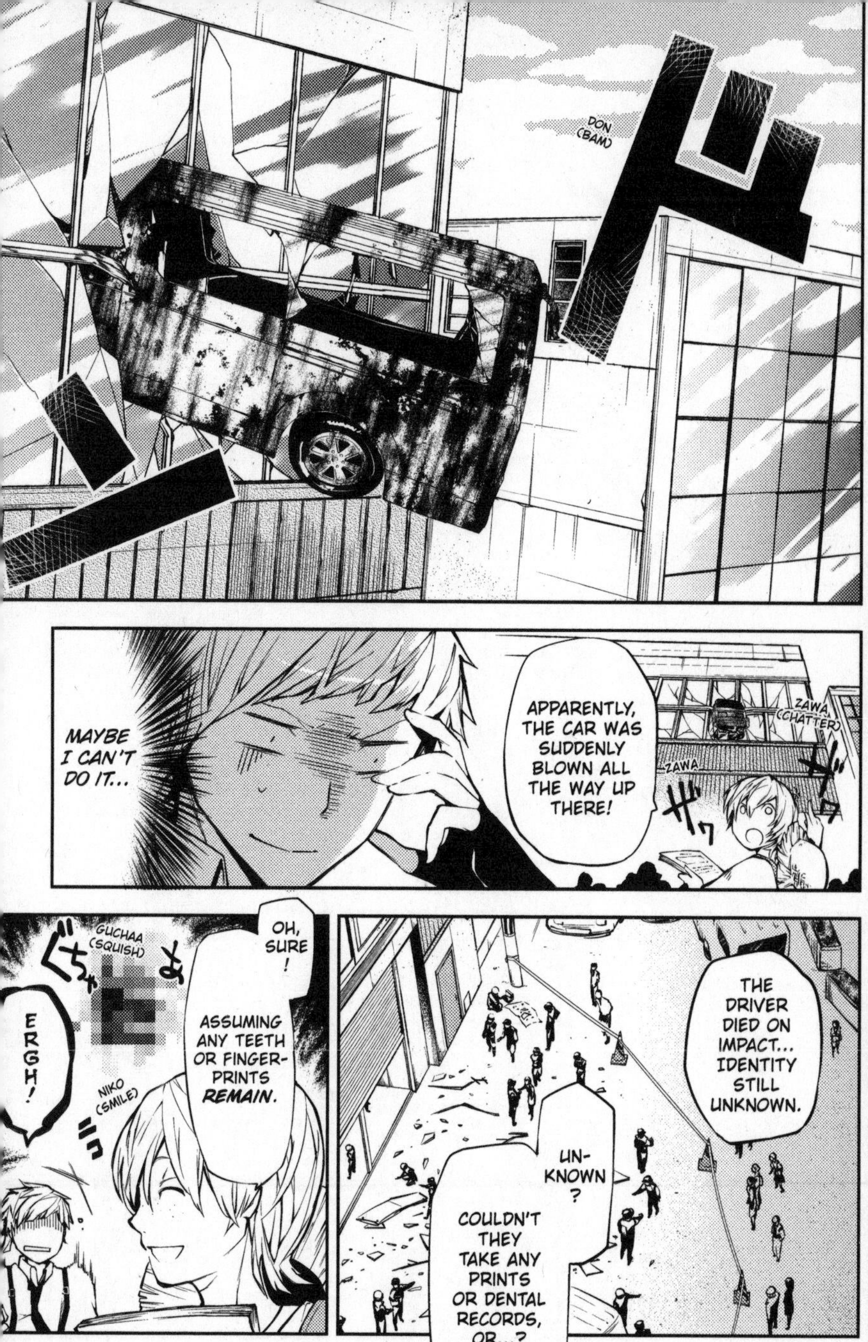
DON (BAM)
ZAWA (CHATTER)
APPARENTLY, THE CAR WAS SUDDENLY BLOWN ALL THE WAY UP THERE!
ZAWA
MAYBE I CAN'T DO IT...
THE DRIVER DIED ON IMPACT... IDENTITY STILL UNKNOWN.
UN-KNOWN?
COULDN'T THEY TAKE ANY PRINTS OR DENTAL RECORDS, OR...?
OH, SURE!
GUCHAA (SQUISH)
ASSUMING ANY TEETH OR FINGER-PRINTS *REMAIN*.
ERGH!
NIKO (SMILE)

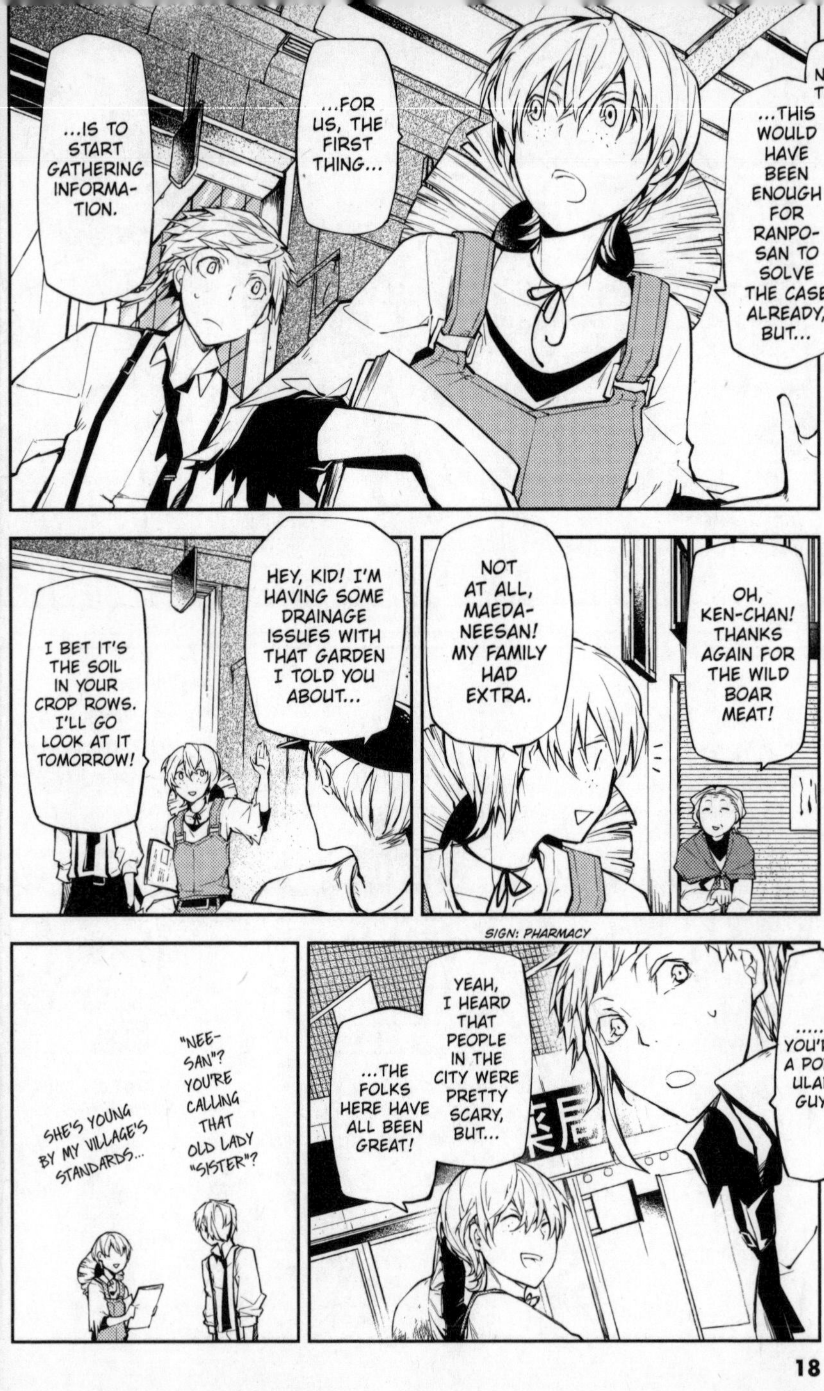
NOW, THEN ...THIS WOULD HAVE BEEN ENOUGH FOR RANPO-SAN TO SOLVE THE CASE ALREADY, BUT...
...FOR US, THE FIRST THING...
...IS TO START GATHERING INFORMATION.
OH, KEN-CHAN! THANKS AGAIN FOR THE WILD BOAR MEAT!
NOT AT ALL, MAEDA-NEESAN! MY FAMILY HAD EXTRA.
SIGN: PHARMACY
HEY, KID! I'M HAVING SOME DRAINAGE ISSUES WITH THAT GARDEN I TOLD YOU ABOUT...
I BET IT'S THE SOIL IN YOUR CROP ROWS. I'LL GO LOOK AT IT TOMORROW!
......YOU'RE A POPULAR GUY.
YEAH, I HEARD THAT PEOPLE IN THE CITY WERE PRETTY SCARY, BUT...
...THE FOLKS HERE HAVE ALL BEEN GREAT!
"NEE-SAN"? YOU'RE CALLING THAT OLD LADY "SISTER"?
SHE'S YOUNG BY MY VILLAGE'S STANDARDS...

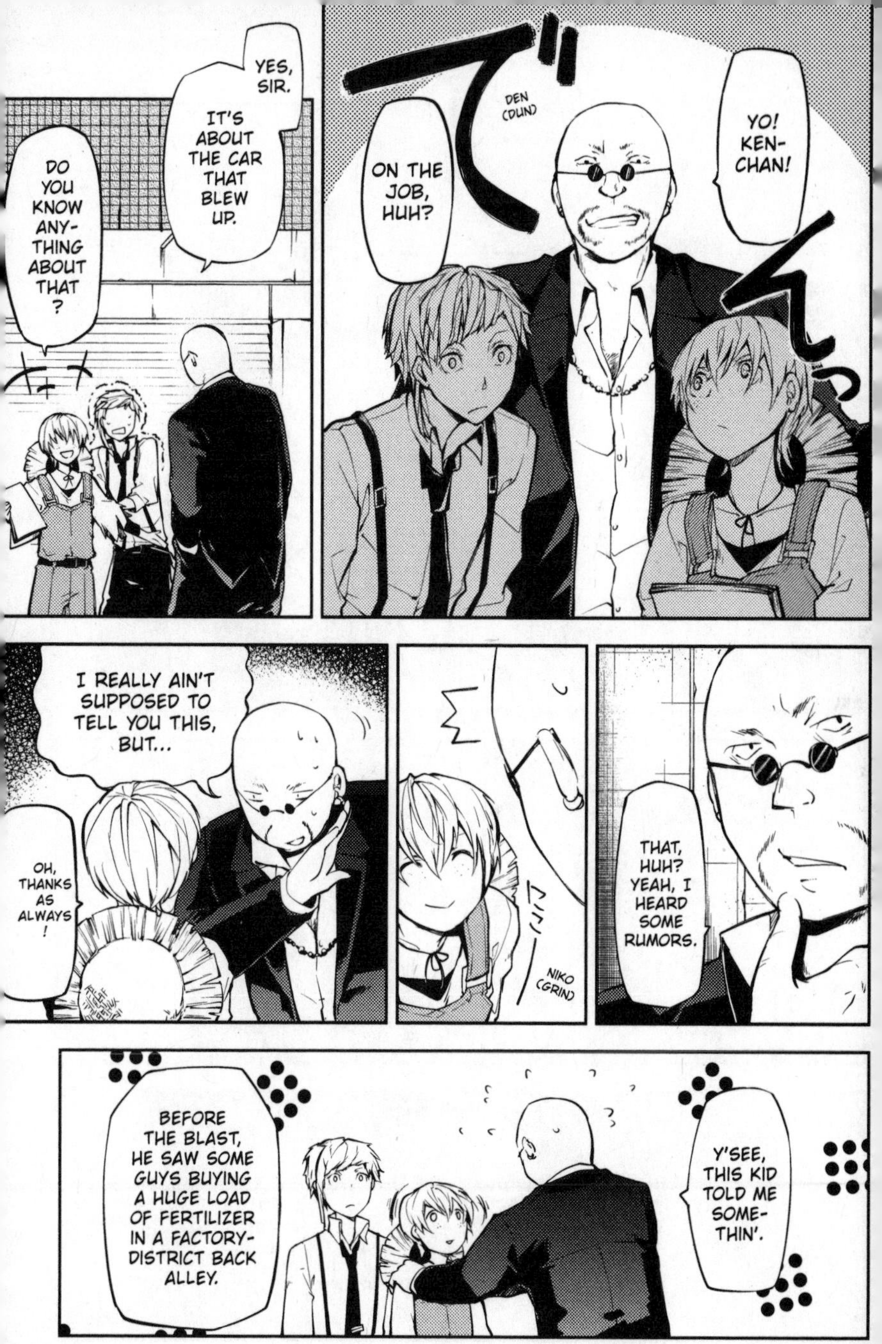
YO! KEN-CHAN!
DEN (DUN)
ON THE JOB, HUH?
YES, SIR.
IT'S ABOUT THE CAR THAT BLEW UP.
DO YOU KNOW ANY-THING ABOUT THAT?
THAT, HUH? YEAH, I HEARD SOME RUMORS.
NIKO (GRIN)
I REALLY AIN'T SUPPOSED TO TELL YOU THIS, BUT...
OH, THANKS AS ALWAYS!
Y'SEE, THIS KID TOLD ME SOME-THIN'.
BEFORE THE BLAST, HE SAW SOME GUYS BUYING A HUGE LOAD OF FERTILIZER IN A FACTORY-DISTRICT BACK ALLEY.

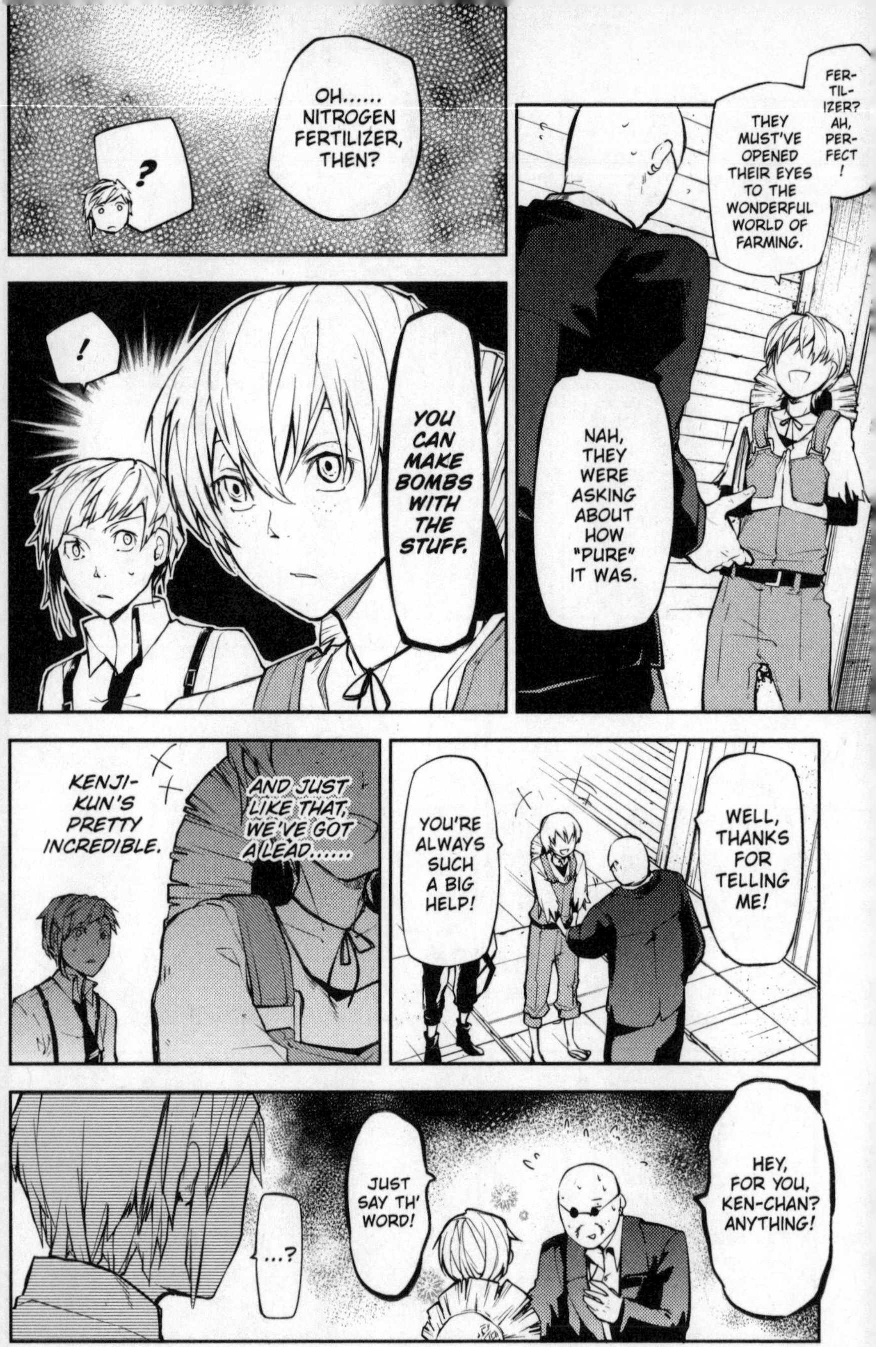
FER-TIL-IZER? AH, PER-FECT!
THEY MUST'VE OPENED THEIR EYES TO THE WONDERFUL WORLD OF FARMING.
NAH, THEY WERE ASKING ABOUT HOW "PURE" IT WAS.
OH...... NITROGEN FERTILIZER, THEN?
?
YOU CAN MAKE BOMBS WITH THE STUFF.
!
WELL, THANKS FOR TELLING ME!
YOU'RE ALWAYS SUCH A BIG HELP!
AND JUST LIKE THAT, WE'VE GOT A LEAD......
KENJI-KUN'S PRETTY INCREDIBLE.
HEY, FOR YOU, KEN-CHAN? ANYTHING!
JUST SAY TH' WORD!
...?

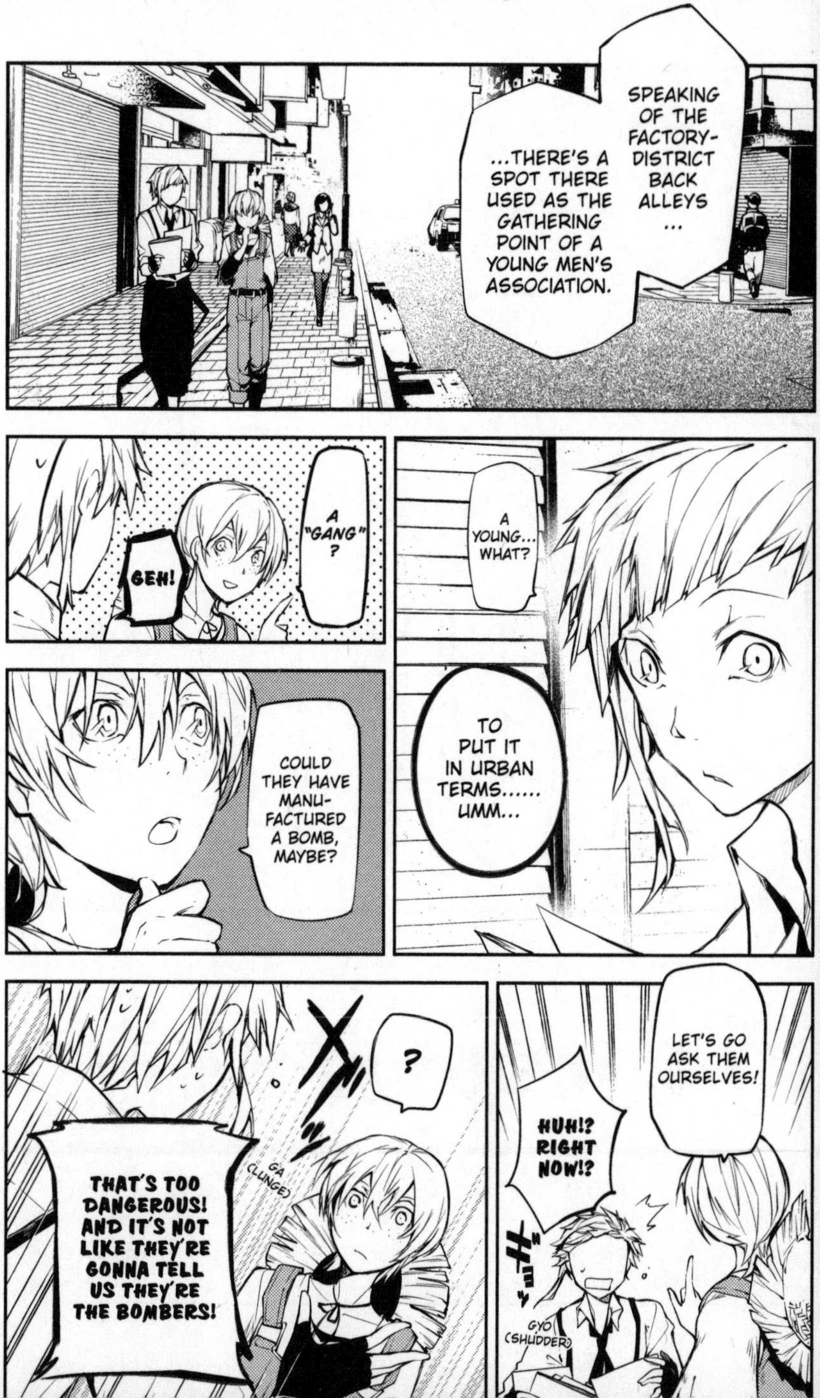
SPEAKING OF THE FACTORY-DISTRICT BACK ALLEYS ...
...THERE'S A SPOT THERE USED AS THE GATHERING POINT OF A YOUNG MEN'S ASSOCIATION.
A YOUNG... WHAT?
TO PUT IT IN URBAN TERMS...... UMM...
A "GANG"?
GEH!
COULD THEY HAVE MANU-FACTURED A BOMB, MAYBE?
LET'S GO ASK THEM OURSELVES!
HUH!? RIGHT NOW!?
GYO (SHUDDER)
?
GA (LUNGE)
THAT'S TOO DANGEROUS! AND IT'S NOT LIKE THEY'RE GONNA TELL US THEY'RE THE BOMBERS!

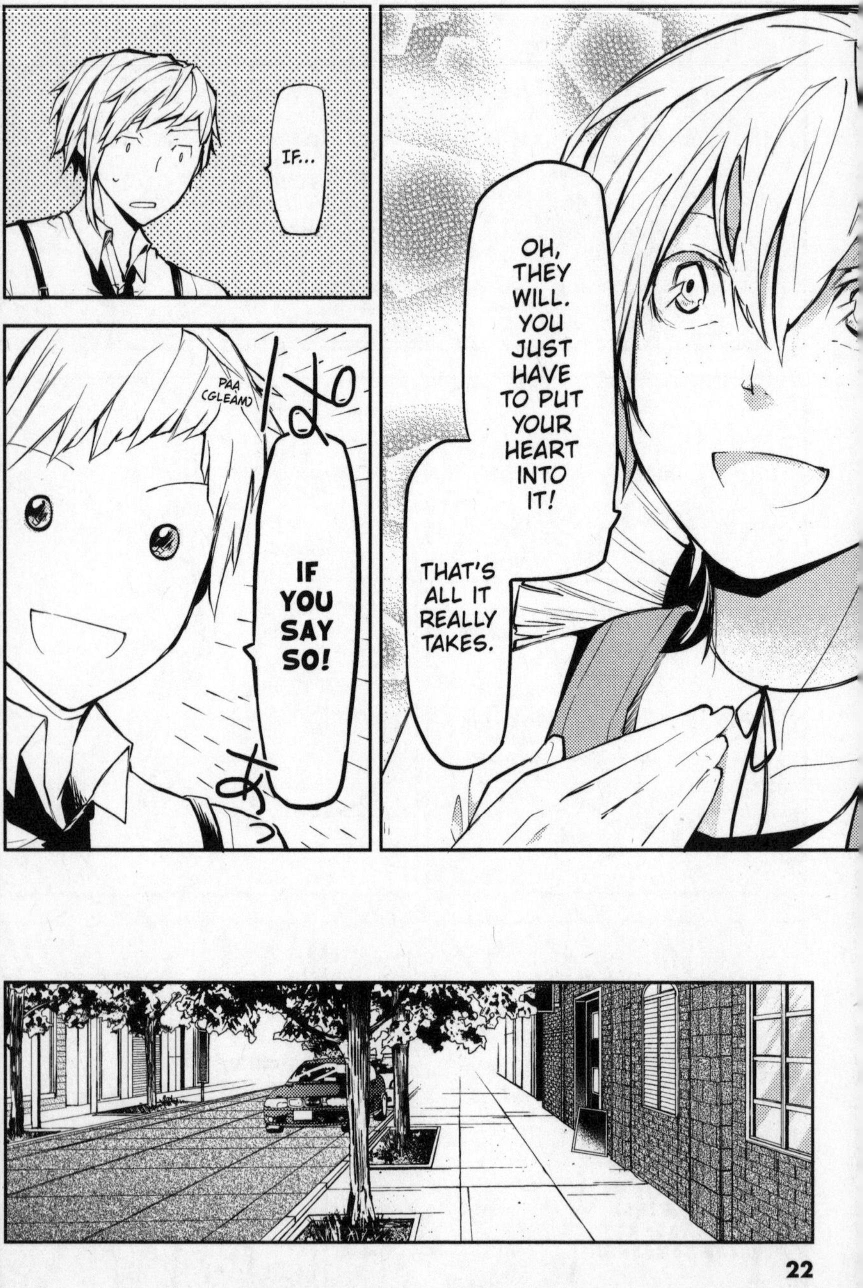
OH, THEY WILL. YOU JUST HAVE TO PUT YOUR HEART INTO IT!
THAT'S ALL IT REALLY TAKES.
IF...
PAA (GLEAM)
IF YOU SAY SO!

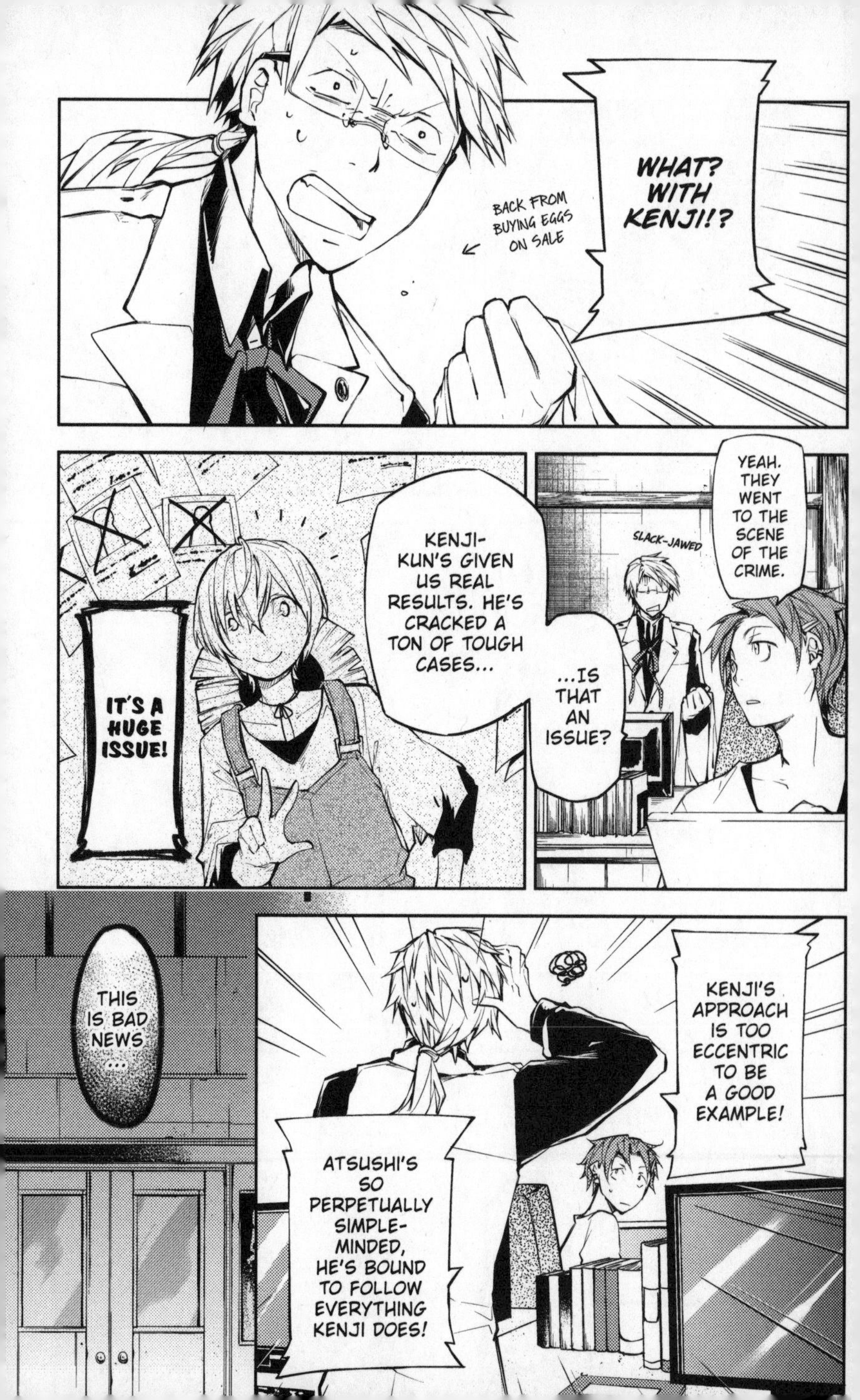
WHAT? WITH KENJI!?
BACK FROM BUYING EGGS ON SALE
YEAH. THEY WENT TO THE SCENE OF THE CRIME.
SLACK-JAWED
KENJI-KUN'S GIVEN US REAL RESULTS. HE'S CRACKED A TON OF TOUGH CASES...
...IS THAT AN ISSUE?
IT'S A HUGE ISSUE!
KENJI'S APPROACH IS TOO ECCENTRIC TO BE A GOOD EXAMPLE!
ATSUSHI'S SO PERPETUALLY SIMPLE-MINDED, HE'S BOUND TO FOLLOW EVERYTHING KENJI DOES!
THIS IS BAD NEWS...

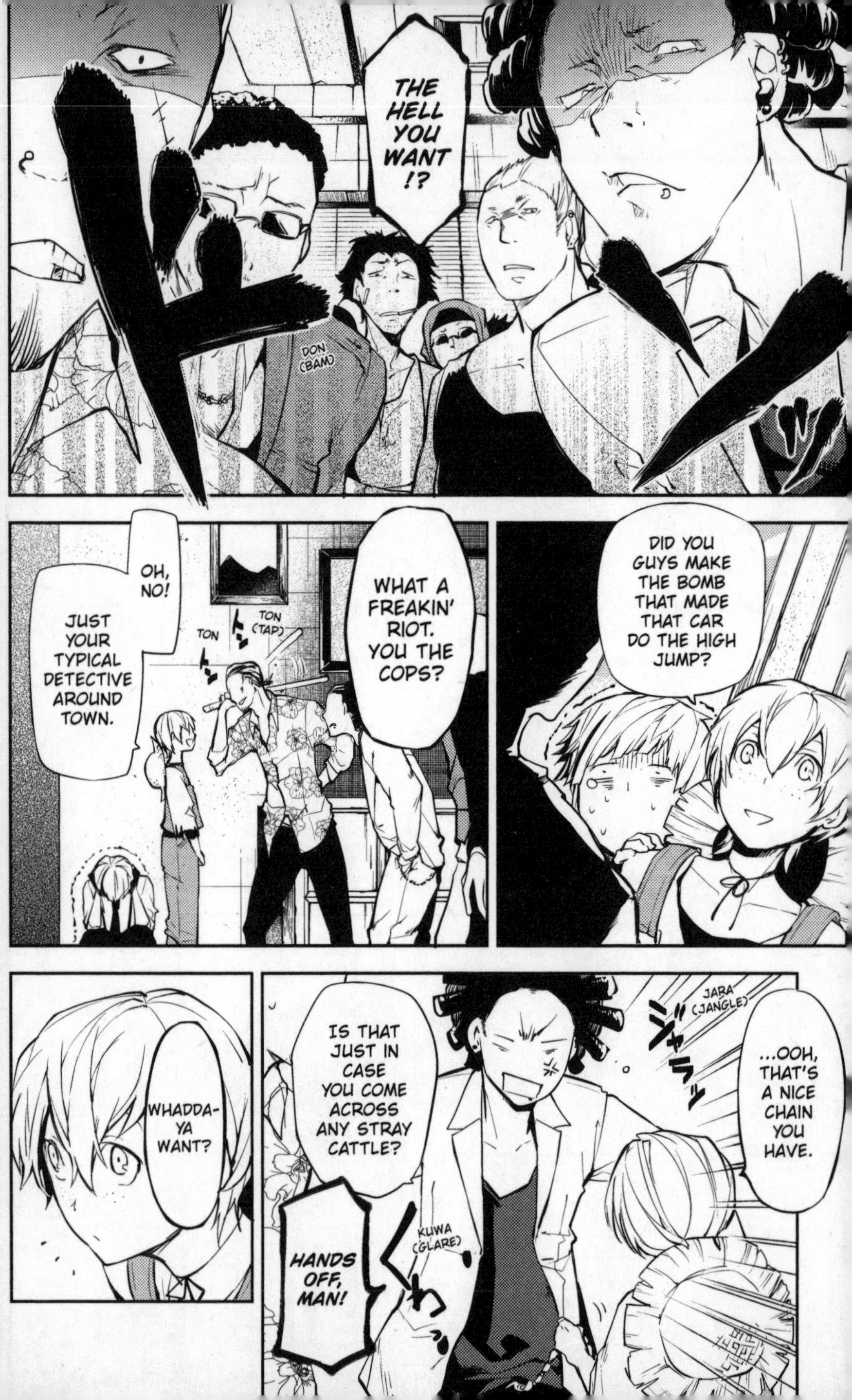
THE HELL YOU WANT!?
DON (BAM)
DID YOU GUYS MAKE THE BOMB THAT MADE THAT CAR DO THE HIGH JUMP?
WHAT A FREAKIN' RIOT. YOU THE COPS?
TON (TAP)
TON
OH, NO!
JUST YOUR TYPICAL DETECTIVE AROUND TOWN.
JARA (JANGLE)
...OOH, THAT'S A NICE CHAIN YOU HAVE.
IS THAT JUST IN CASE YOU COME ACROSS ANY STRAY CATTLE?
KUWA (GLARE)
HANDS OFF, MAN!
WHADDA-YA WANT?

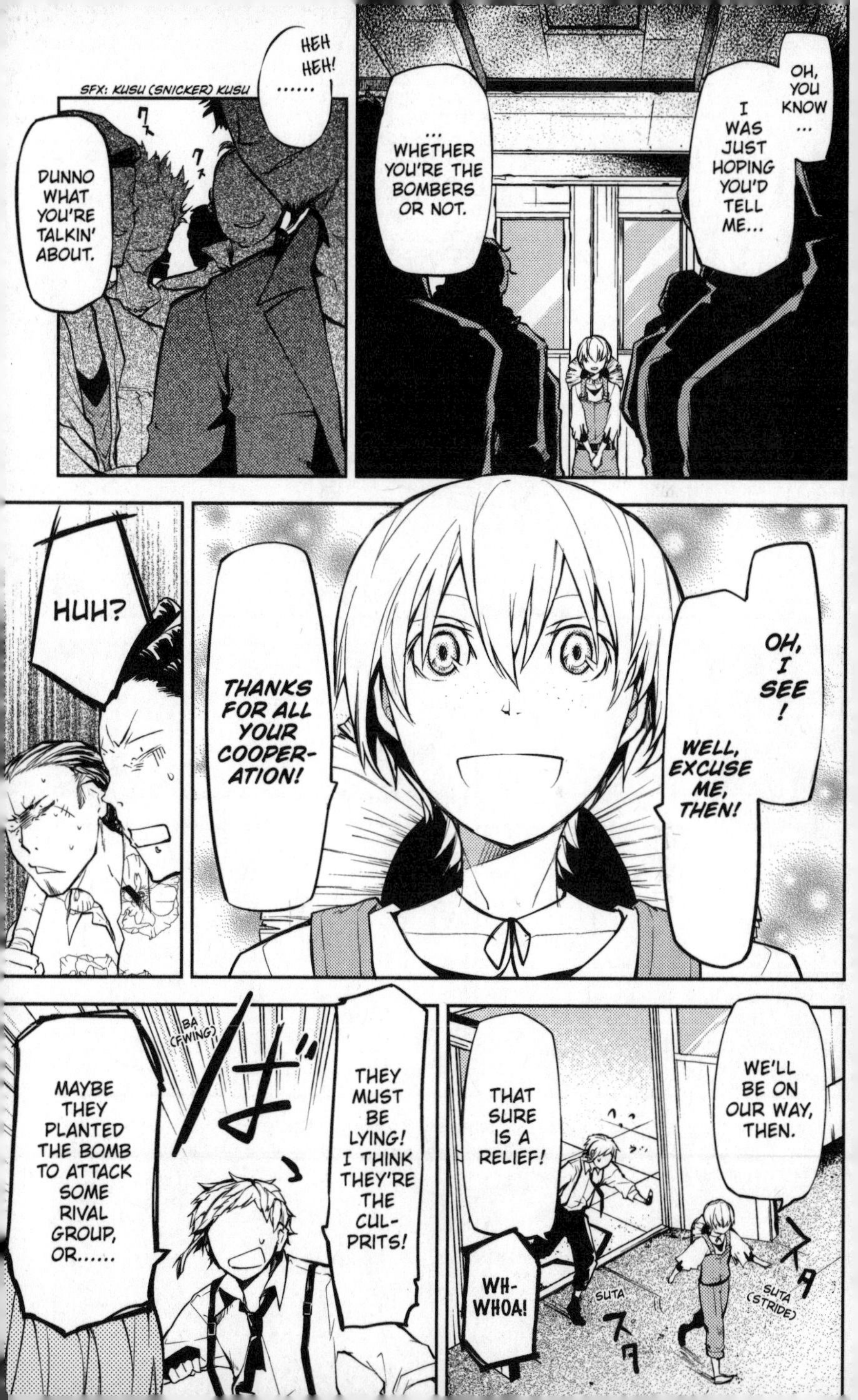

OH, YOU KNOW...
I WAS JUST HOPING YOU'D TELL ME...
...WHETHER YOU'RE THE BOMBERS OR NOT.
HEH HEH! ......
SFX: KUSU (SNICKER) KUSU
DUNNO WHAT YOU'RE TALKIN' ABOUT.
OH, I SEE!
WELL, EXCUSE ME, THEN!
THANKS FOR ALL YOUR COOPERATION!
HUH?
WE'LL BE ON OUR WAY, THEN.
SUTA (STRIDE)
SUTA
THAT SURE IS A RELIEF!
WH-WHOA!
THEY MUST BE LYING! I THINK THEY'RE THE CUL-PRITS!
BA (FWING)
MAYBE THEY PLANTED THE BOMB TO ATTACK SOME RIVAL GROUP, OR......

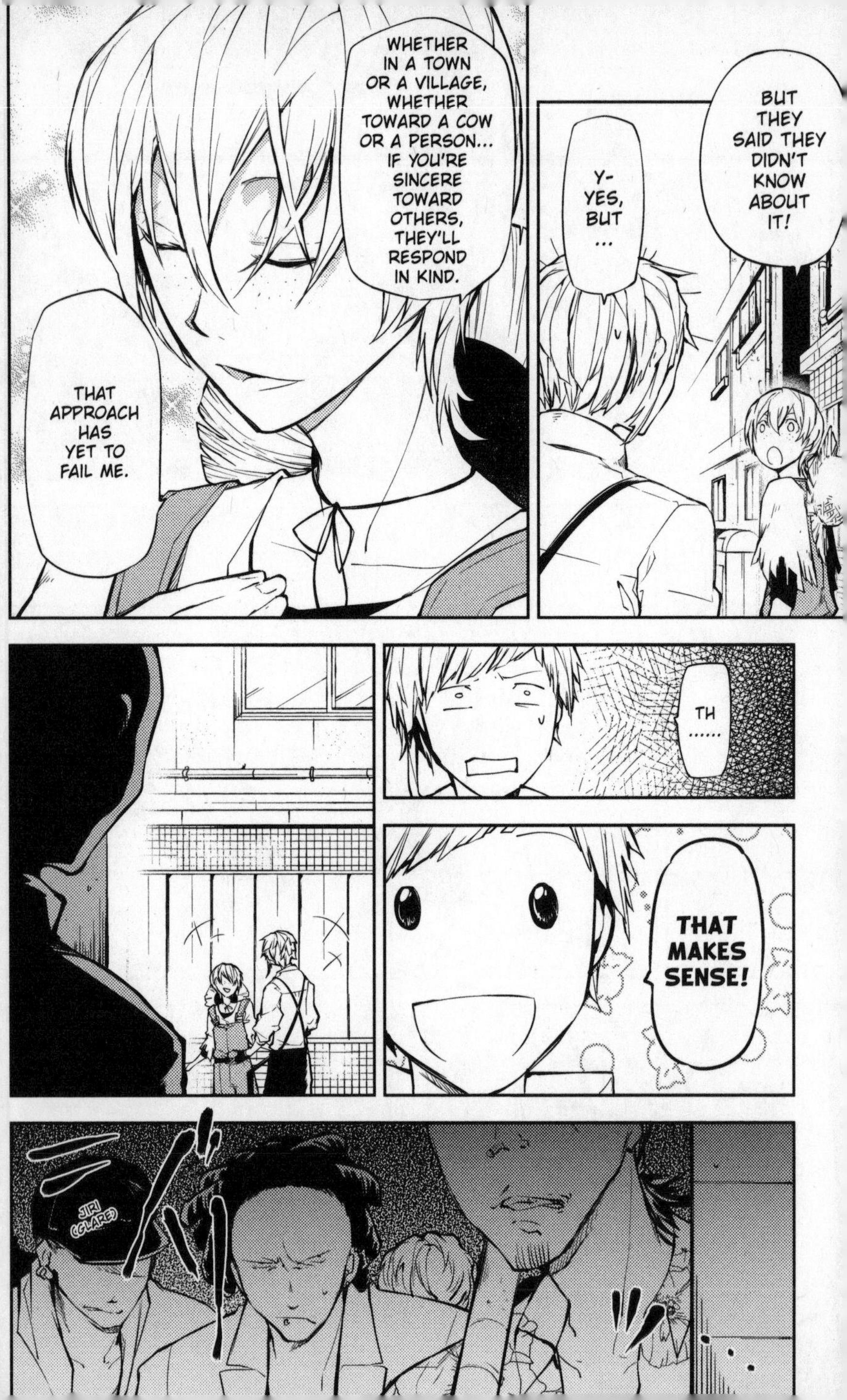
BUT THEY SAID THEY DIDN'T KNOW ABOUT IT!
Y-YES, BUT ...
WHETHER IN A TOWN OR A VILLAGE, WHETHER TOWARD A COW OR A PERSON... IF YOU'RE SINCERE TOWARD OTHERS, THEY'LL RESPOND IN KIND.
THAT APPROACH HAS YET TO FAIL ME.
TH ......
THAT MAKES SENSE!
JIRI (GLARE)

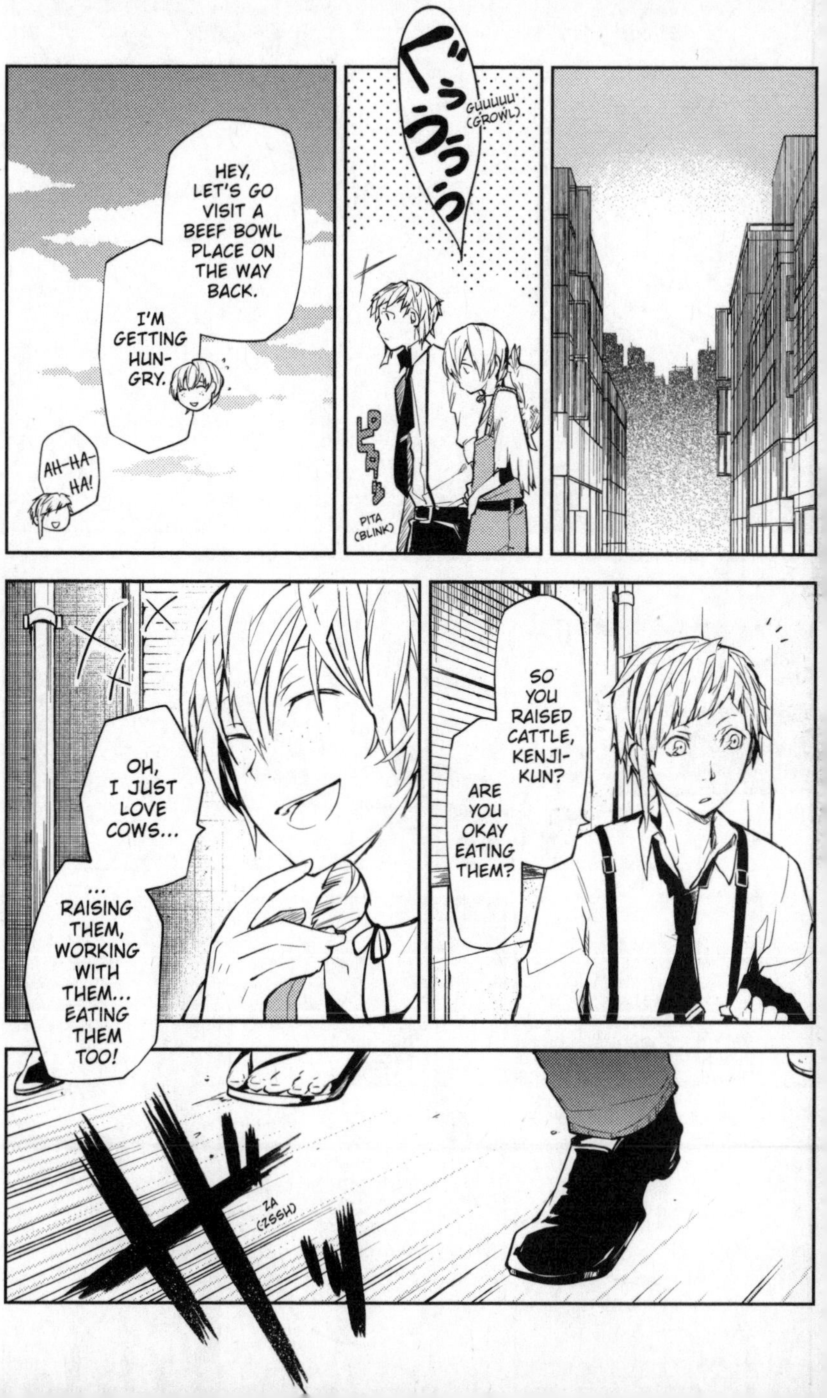
GUUUUU (GROWL)
PITA (BLINK)
HEY, LET'S GO VISIT A BEEF BOWL PLACE ON THE WAY BACK.
I'M GETTING HUN-GRY.
AH-HA-HA!
SO YOU RAISED CATTLE, KENJI-KUN?
ARE YOU OKAY EATING THEM?
OH, I JUST LOVE COWS...
...RAISING THEM, WORKING WITH THEM... EATING THEM TOO!
ZA (ZSSH)

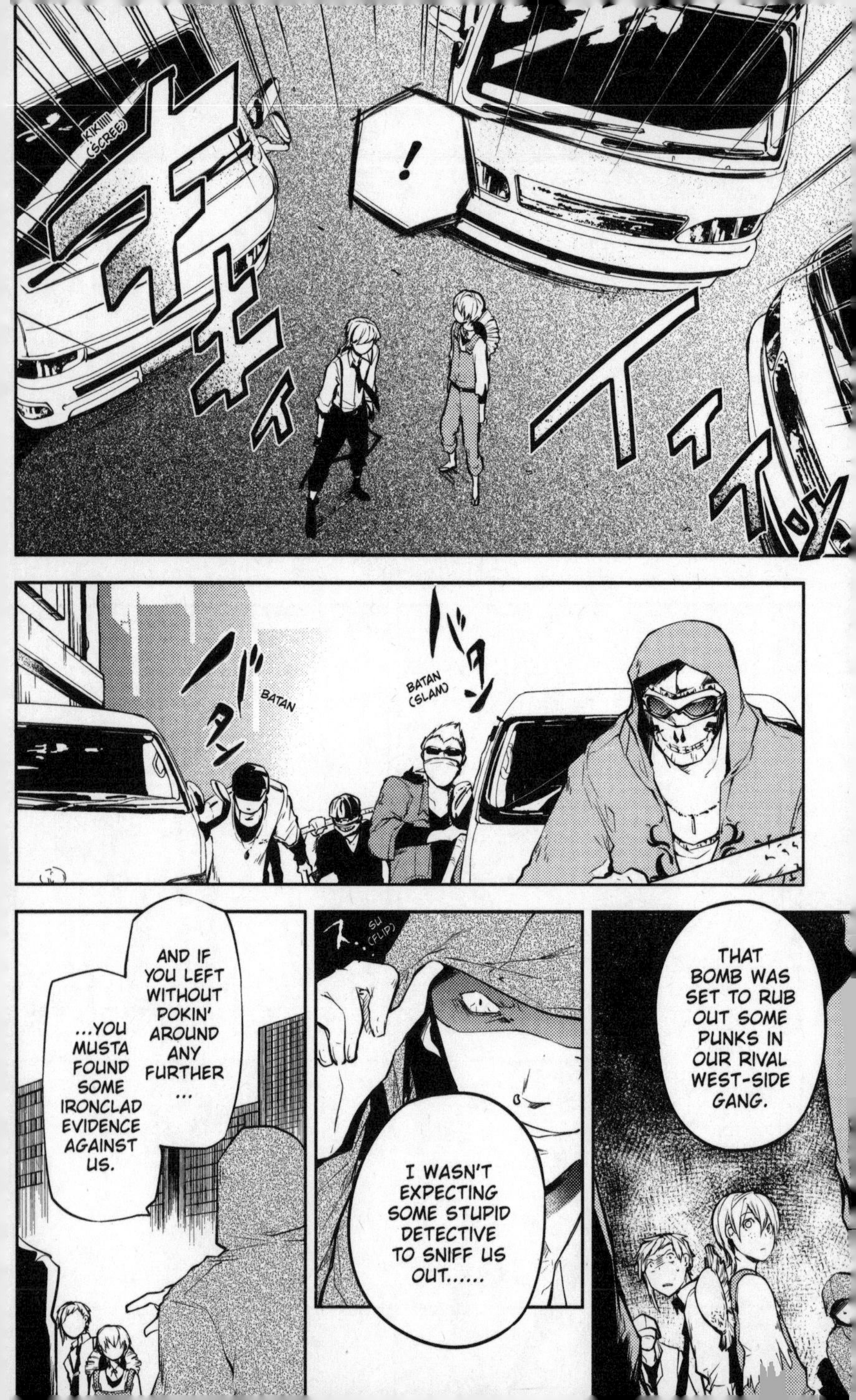
KIKIIIII (SCREE)
!
BATAN (SLAM)
BATAN
THAT BOMB WAS SET TO RUB OUT SOME PUNKS IN OUR RIVAL WEST-SIDE GANG.
SU (FLIP)
I WASN'T EXPECTING SOME STUPID DETECTIVE TO SNIFF US OUT......
AND IF YOU LEFT WITHOUT POKIN' AROUND ANY FURTHER...
...YOU MUSTA FOUND SOME IRONCLAD EVIDENCE AGAINST US.

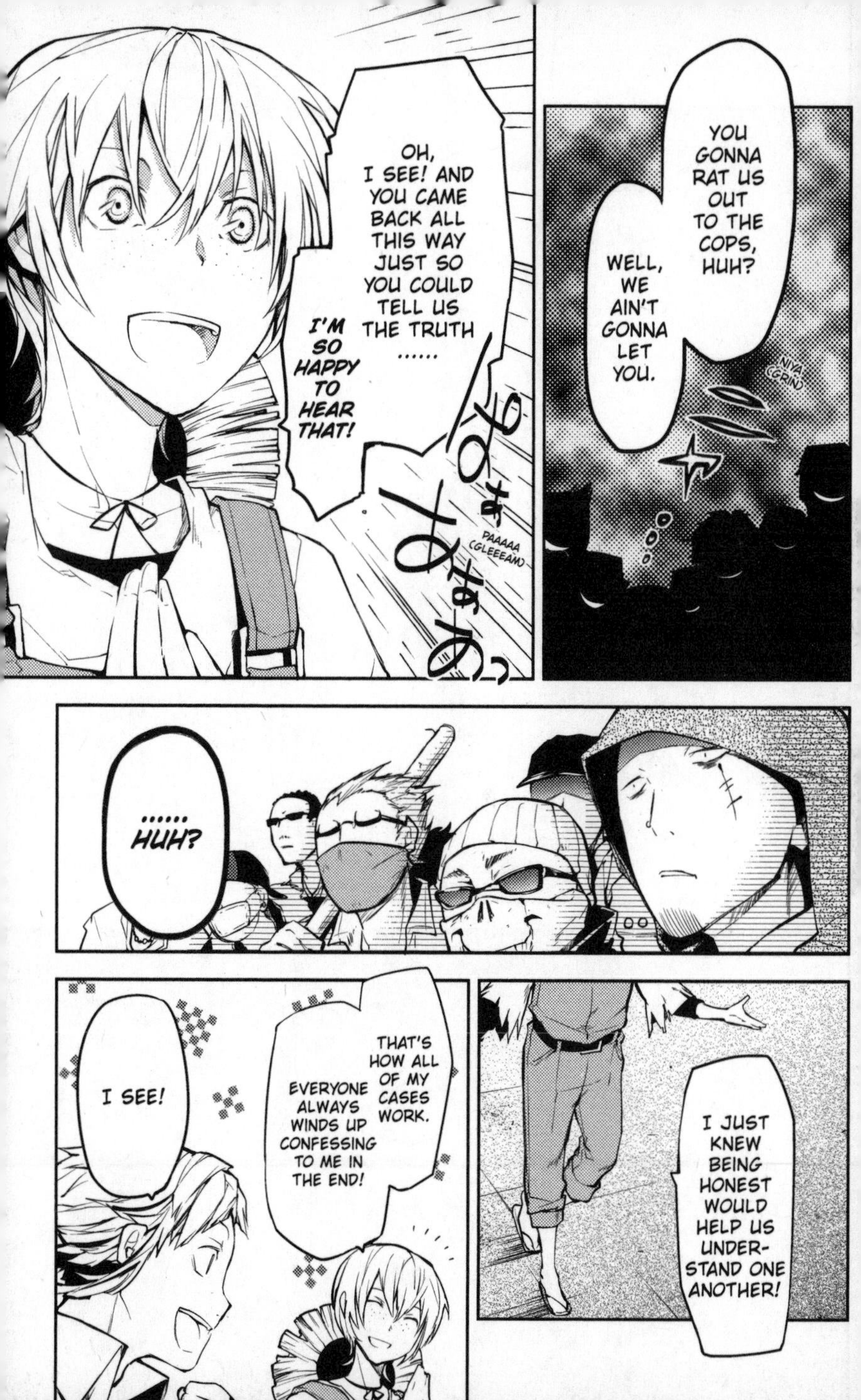
YOU GONNA RAT US OUT TO THE COPS, HUH?
WELL, WE AIN'T GONNA LET YOU.
NIYA (GRIN)
OH, I SEE! AND YOU CAME BACK ALL THIS WAY JUST SO YOU COULD TELL US THE TRUTH......
I'M SO HAPPY TO HEAR THAT!
PAAAAA (GLEEEAM)
......HUH?
I JUST KNEW BEING HONEST WOULD HELP US UNDER-STAND ONE ANOTHER!
THAT'S HOW ALL OF MY CASES WORK.
EVERYONE ALWAYS WINDS UP CONFESSING TO ME IN THE END!
I SEE!

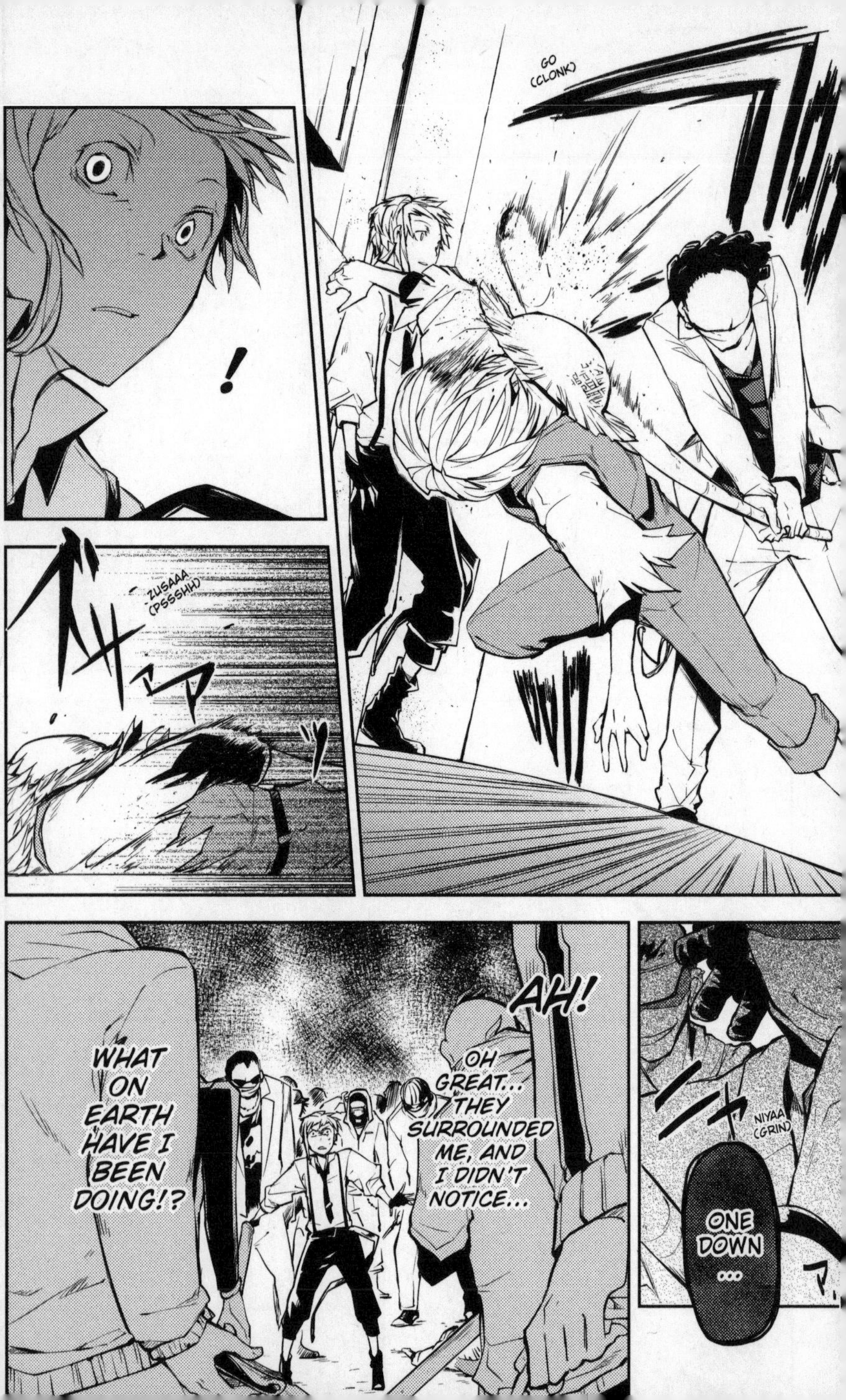
GO
(CLONK)
!
ZUSAAA
(PSSSHH)
NIYAA
(GRIN)
ONE DOWN...
AH!
OH GREAT... THEY SURROUNDED ME, AND I DIDN'T NOTICE...
WHAT ON EARTH HAVE I BEEN DOING!?

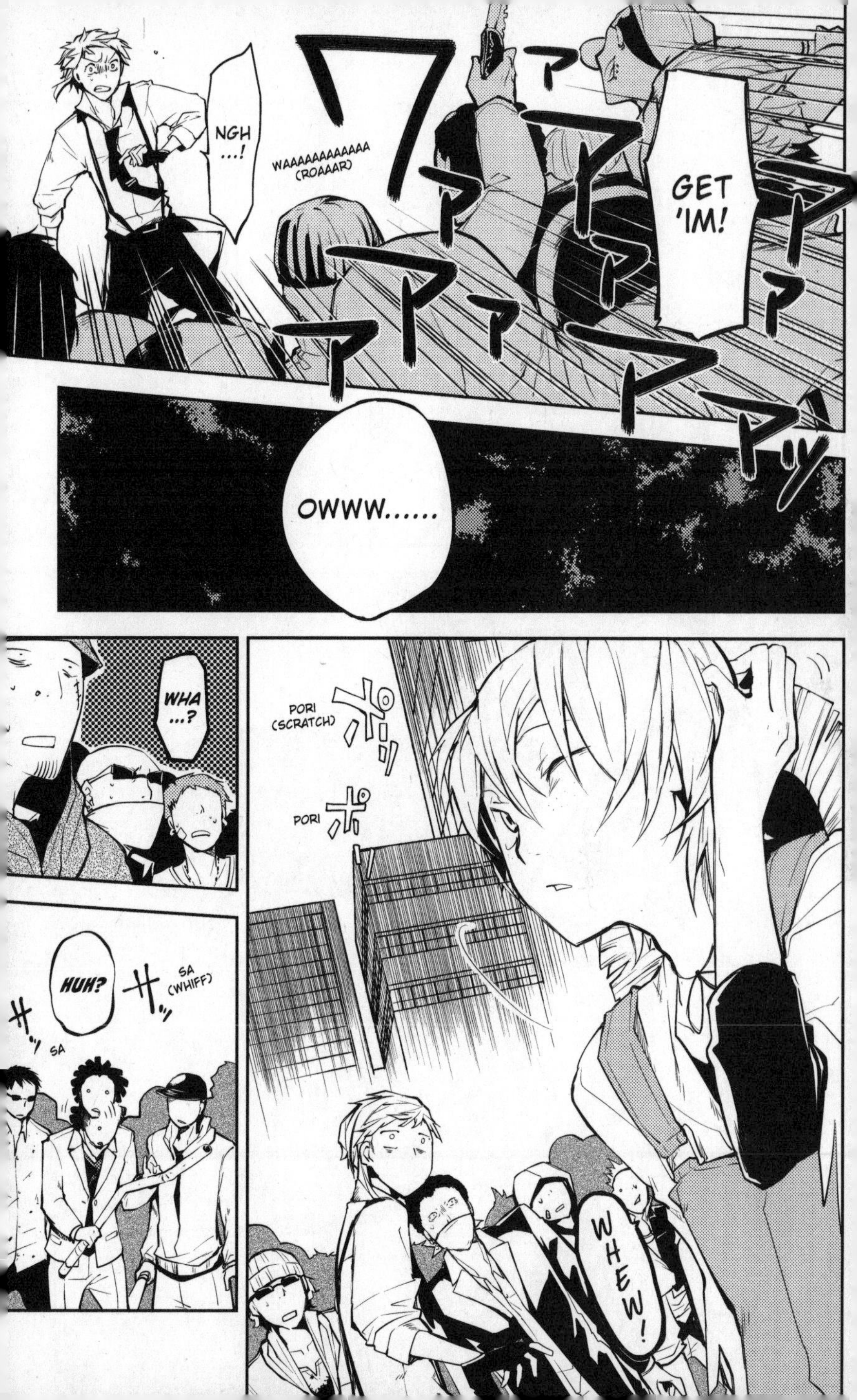
GET 'IM!
WAAAAAAAAAAAA (ROAAAR)
NGH ...!
OWWW......
PORI (SCRATCH)
PORI
WHEW!
WHA ...?
HUH?
SA (WHIFF)
SA

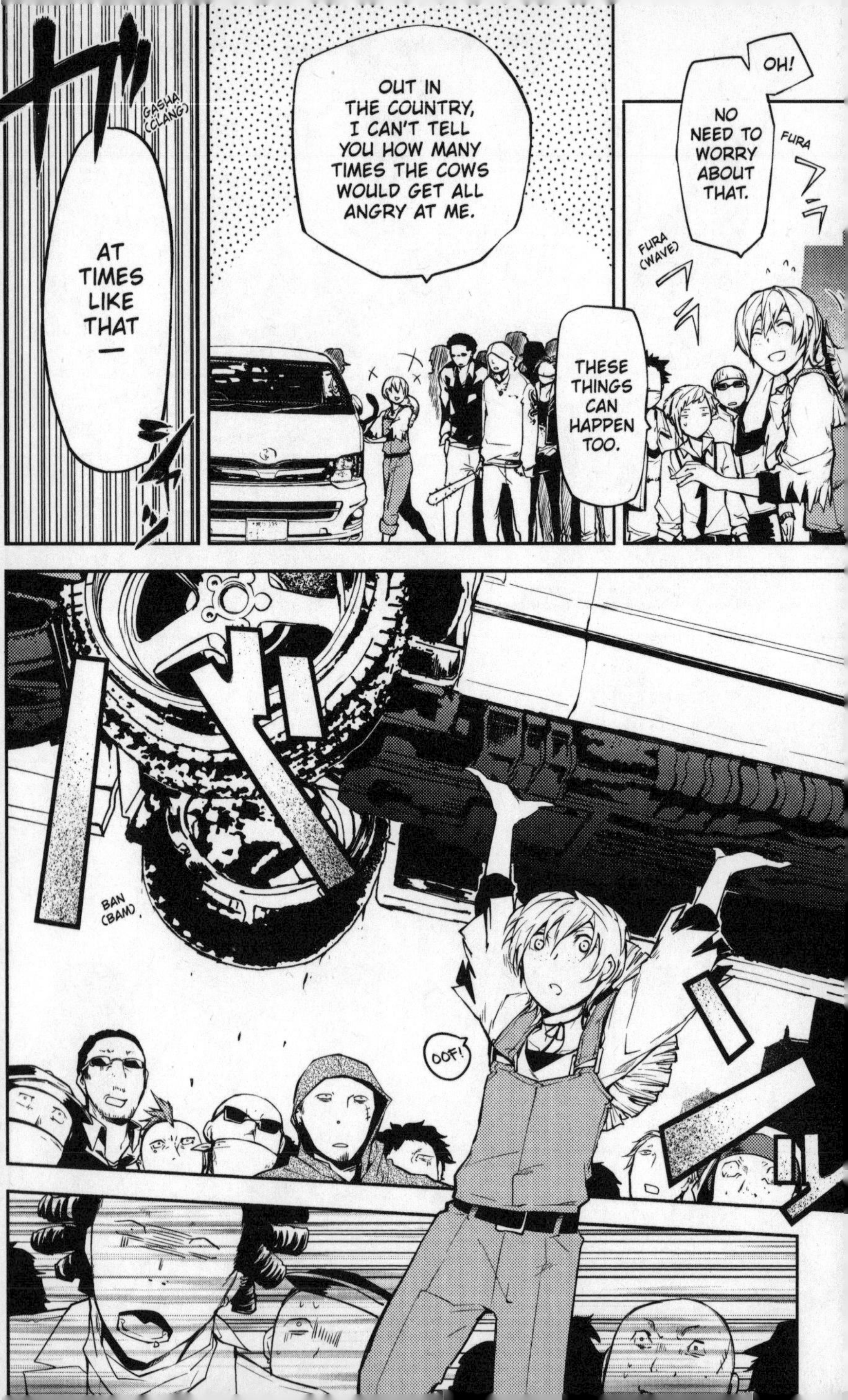
OH!
NO NEED TO WORRY ABOUT THAT.
FURA
FURA (WAVE)
THESE THINGS CAN HAPPEN TOO.
OUT IN THE COUNTRY, I CAN'T TELL YOU HOW MANY TIMES THE COWS WOULD GET ALL ANGRY AT ME.
GASHA (CLANG)
AT TIMES LIKE THAT—
BAN (BAM)
OOF!

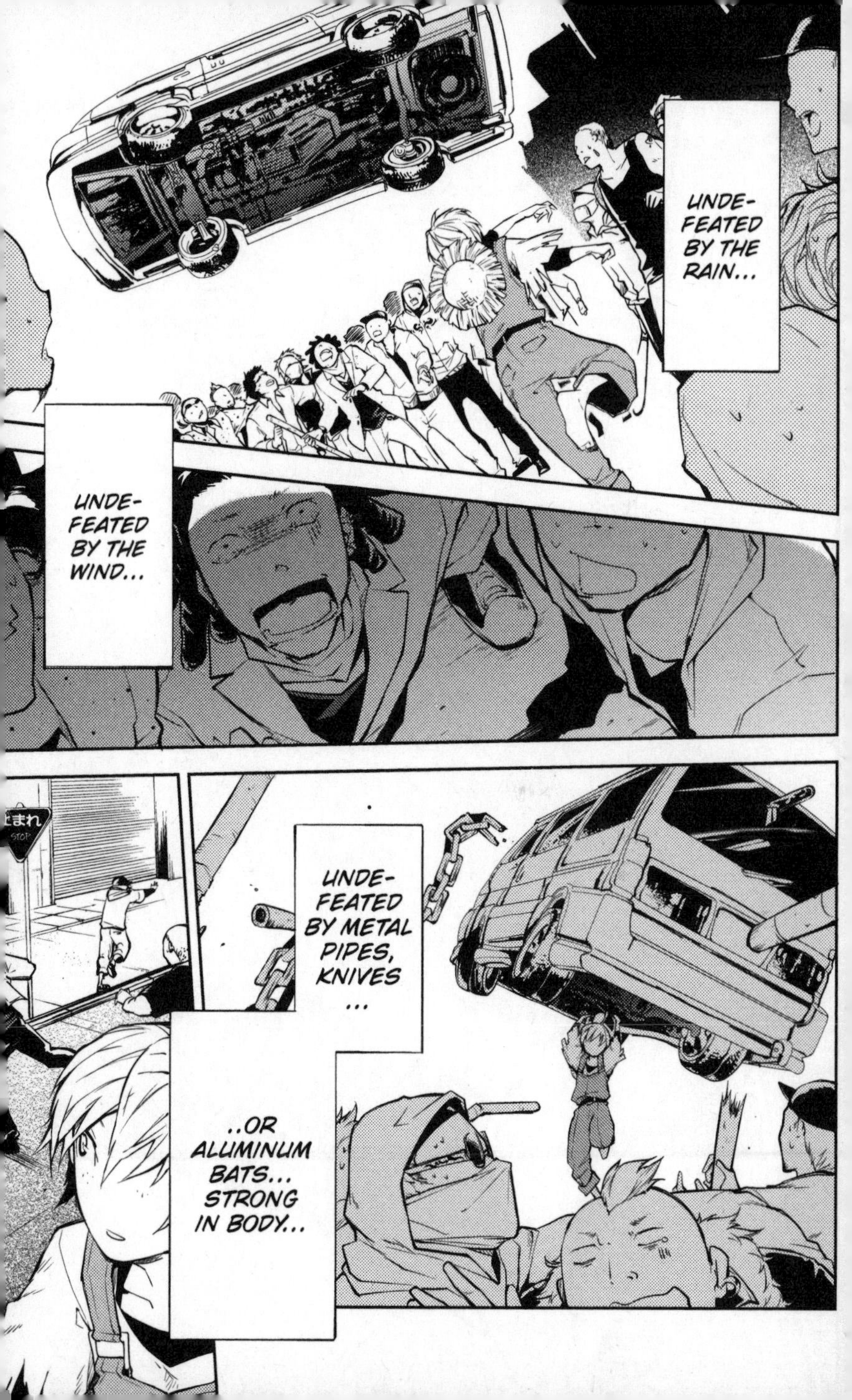
UNDE-
FEATED
BY THE
RAIN...
UNDE-
FEATED
BY THE
WIND...
UNDE-
FEATED
BY METAL
PIPES,
KNIVES
...
..OR
ALUMINUM
BATS...
STRONG
IN BODY...
とまれ
STOP

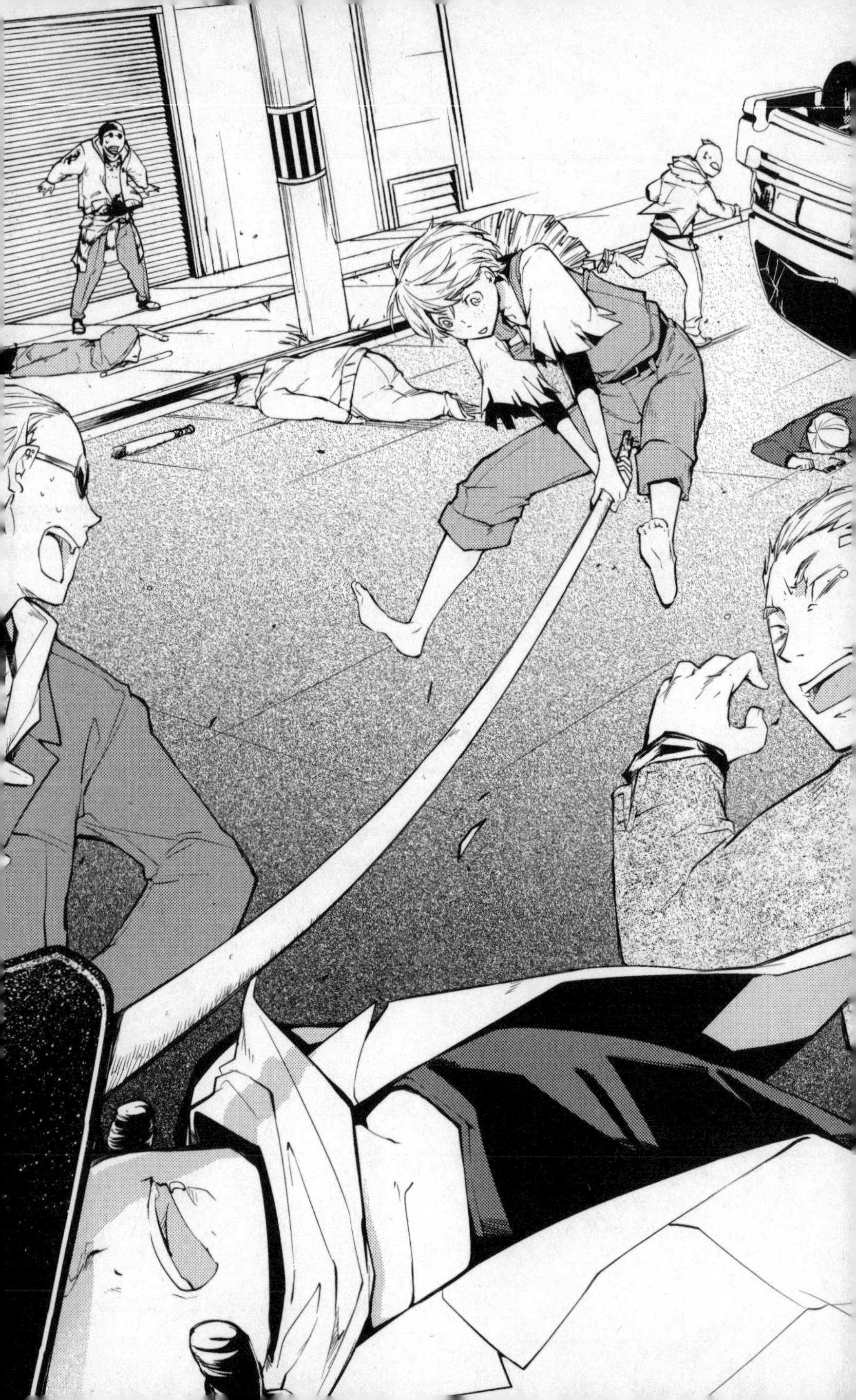

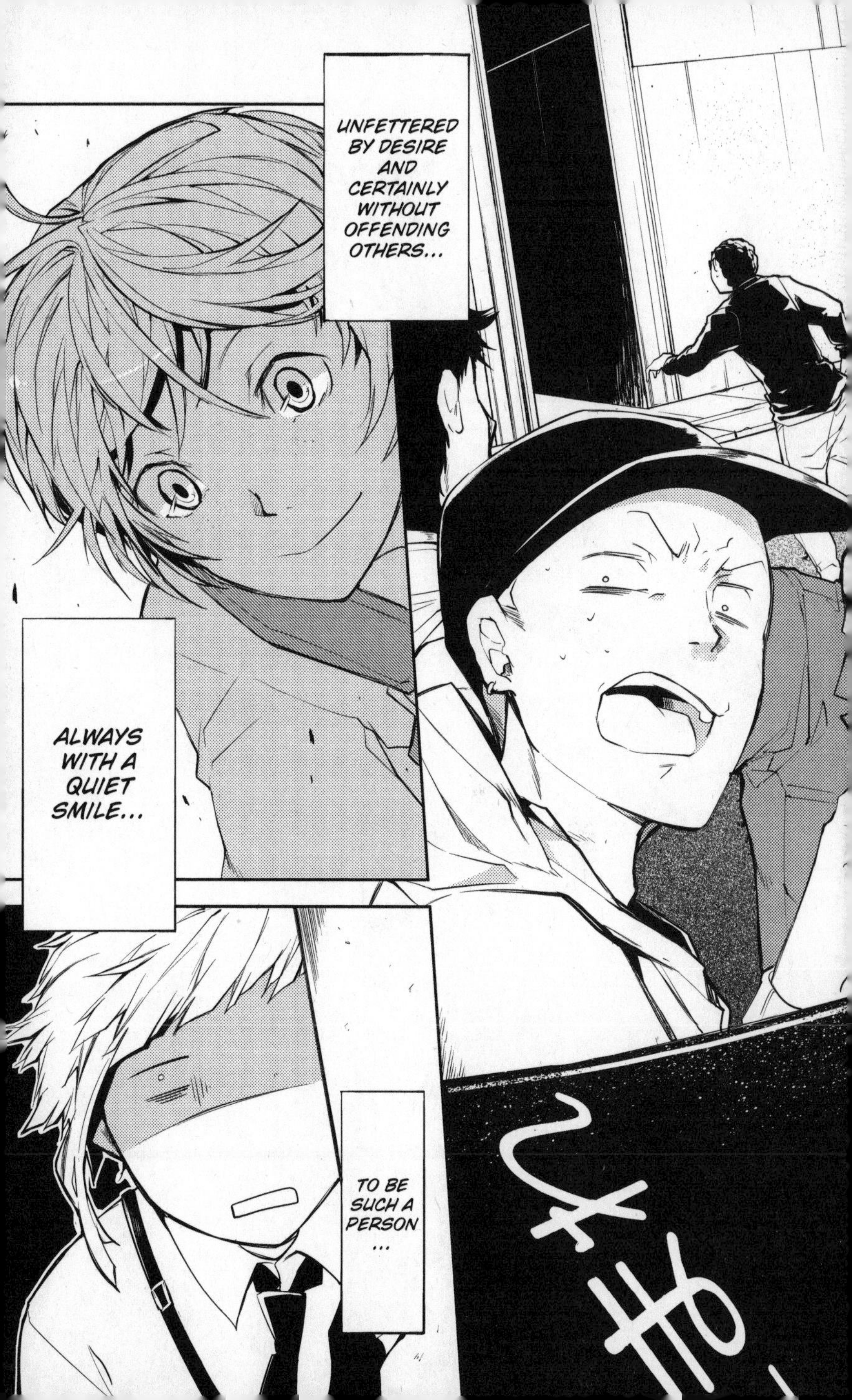
UNFETTERED BY DESIRE AND CERTAINLY WITHOUT OFFENDING OTHERS...
ALWAYS WITH A QUIET SMILE...
TO BE SUCH A PERSON ...

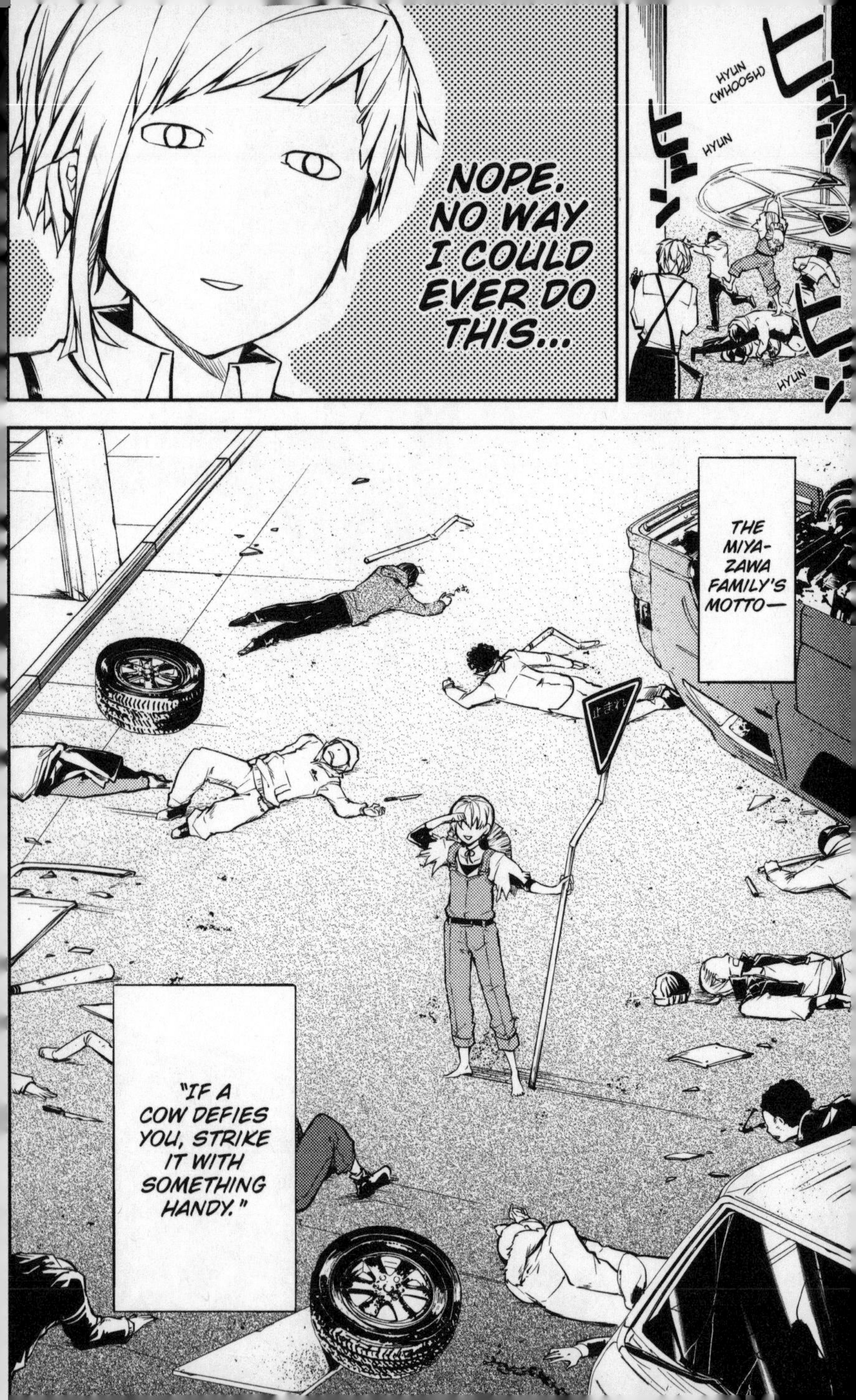
HYUN (WHOOSH)
HYUN
HYUN
NOPE. NO WAY I COULD EVER DO THIS...
THE MIYAZAWA FAMILY'S MOTTO—
"IF A COW DEFIES YOU, STRIKE IT WITH SOMETHING HANDY."

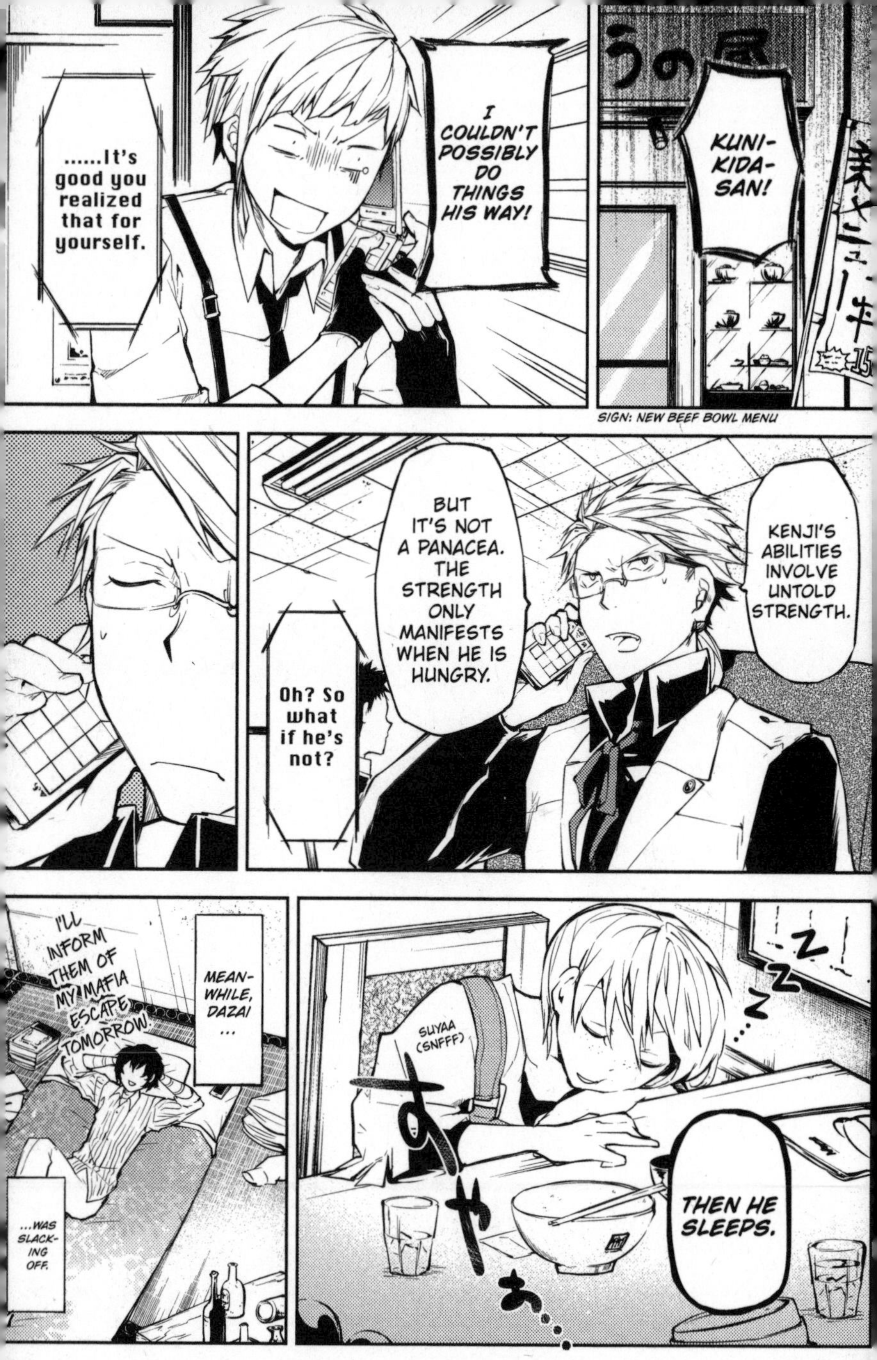
KUNI-KIDA-SAN!
SIGN: NEW BEEF BOWL MENU
I COULDN'T POSSIBLY DO THINGS HIS WAY!
......It's good you realized that for yourself.
KENJI'S ABILITIES INVOLVE UNTOLD STRENGTH.
BUT IT'S NOT A PANACEA. THE STRENGTH ONLY MANIFESTS WHEN HE IS HUNGRY.
Oh? So what if he's not?
Z Z Z
SUYAA (SNFFF)
THEN HE SLEEPS.
MEAN-WHILE, DAZAI ...
I'LL INFORM THEM OF MY MAFIA ESCAPE TOMORROW.
...WAS SLACKING OFF.

BUNGO STRAY DOGS

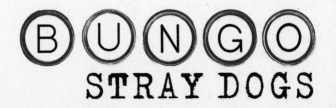

CHAPTER 14

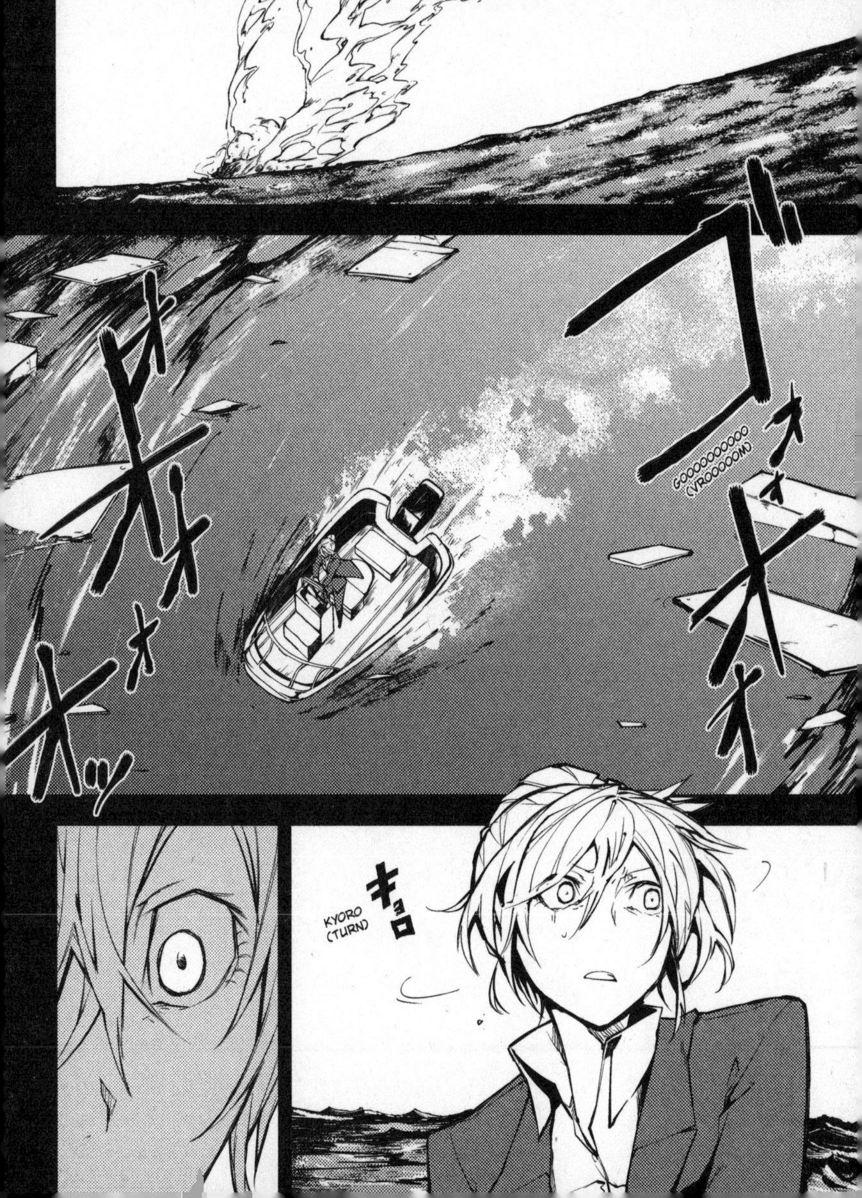
GOOOOOOOOOOO
(VROOOOOM)
KYORO
(TURN)

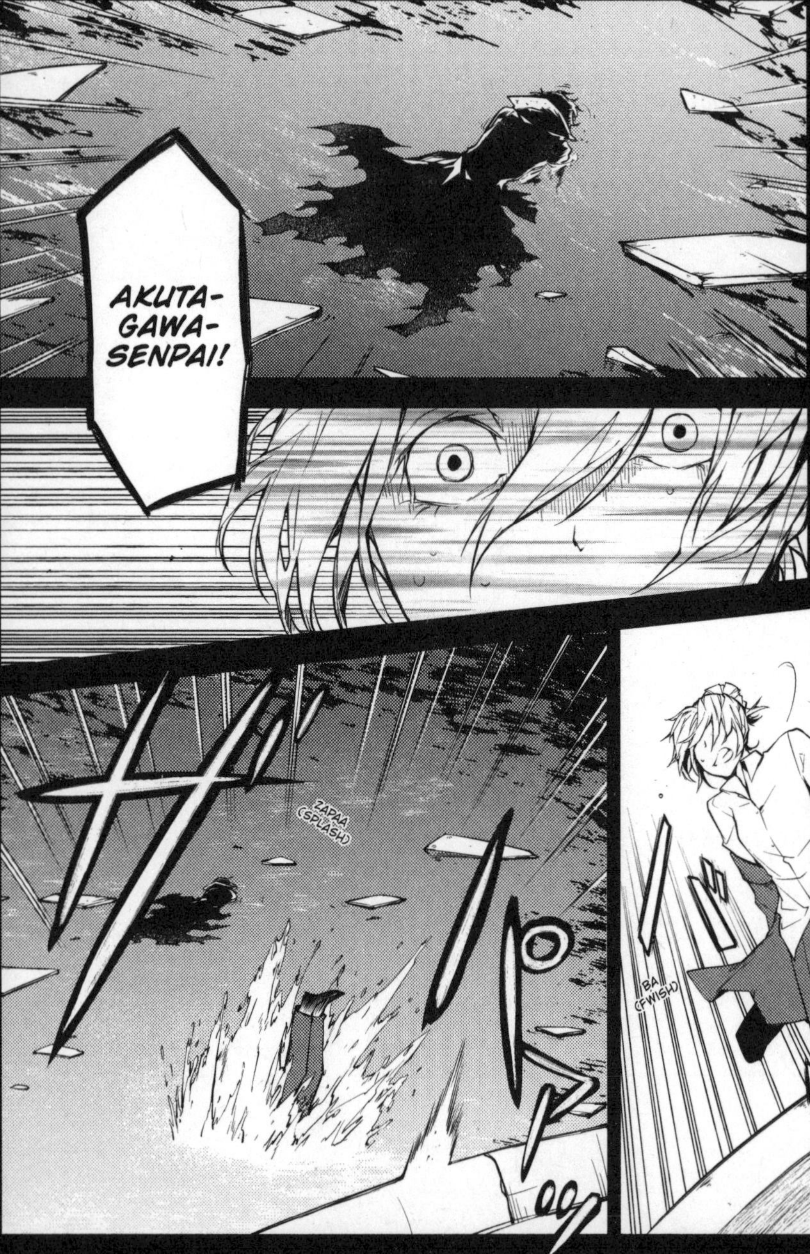
AKUTA-GAWA-SENPAI!
ZAPAA (SPLASH)
BA (FWISH)

CHAPTER 14
An Unsuitable Occupation for Her

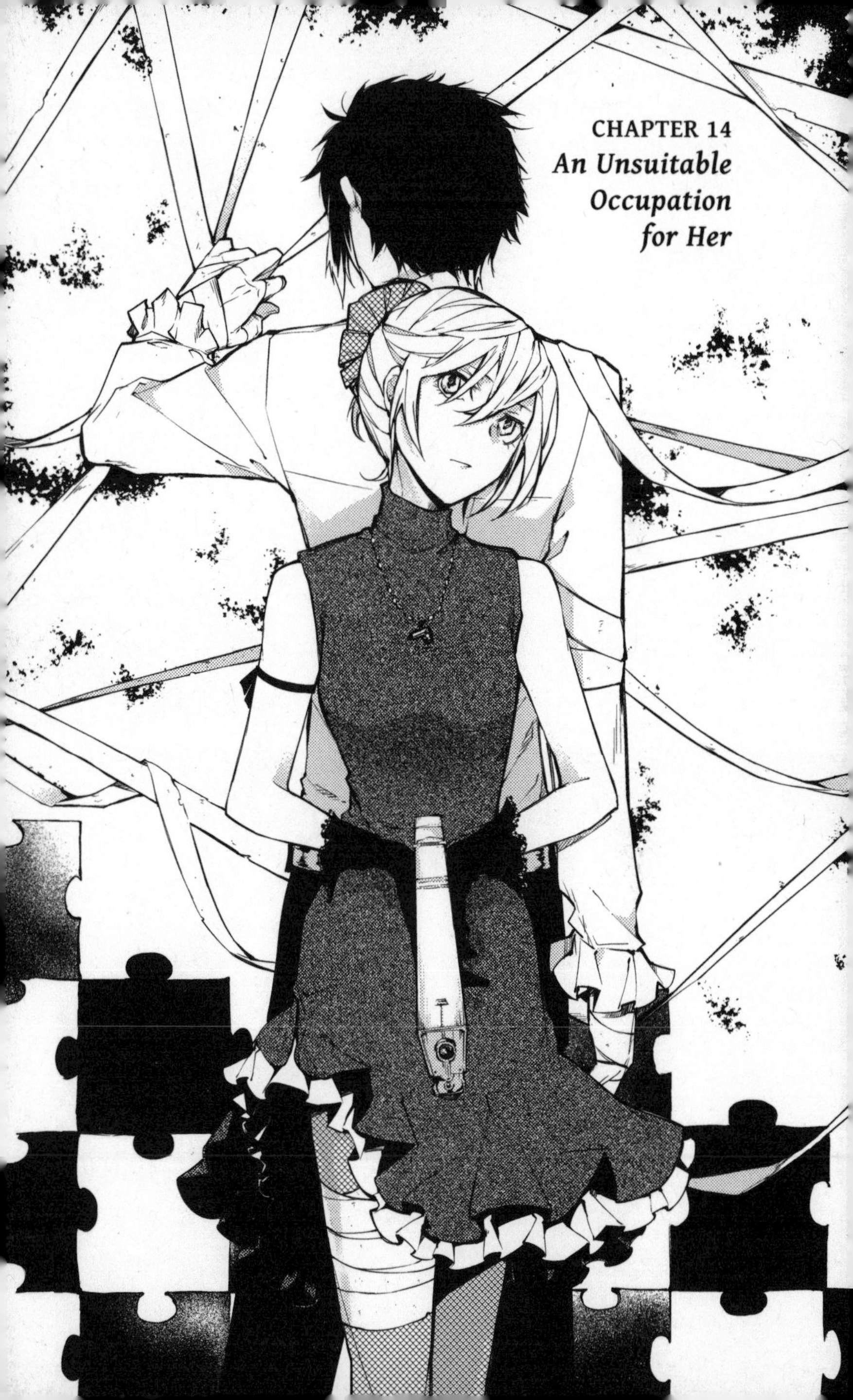

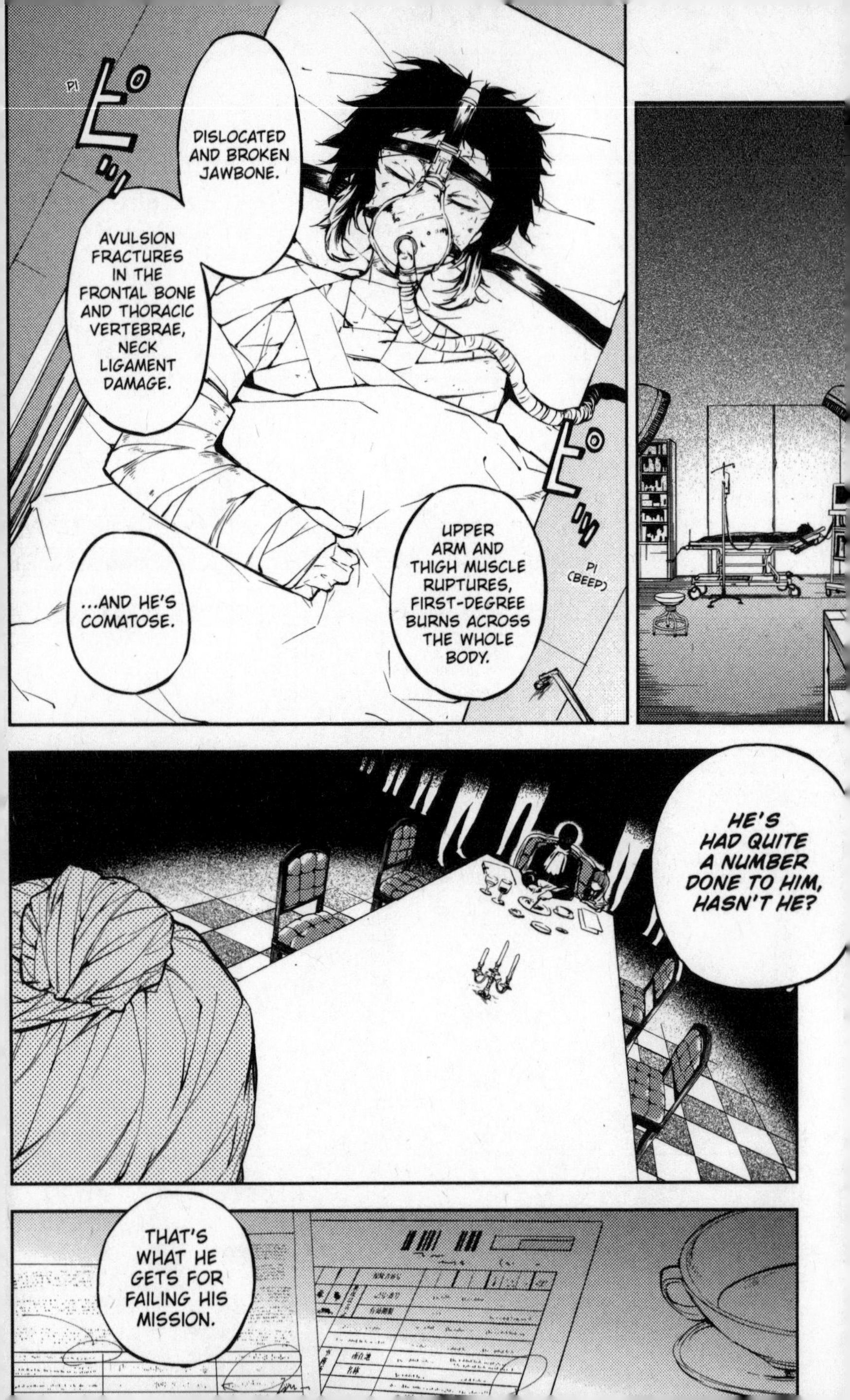
DISLOCATED AND BROKEN JAWBONE.
PI
AVULSION FRACTURES IN THE FRONTAL BONE AND THORACIC VERTEBRAE, NECK LIGAMENT DAMAGE.
UPPER ARM AND THIGH MUSCLE RUPTURES, FIRST-DEGREE BURNS ACROSS THE WHOLE BODY.
PI (BEEP)
...AND HE'S COMATOSE.
HE'S HAD QUITE A NUMBER DONE TO HIM, HASN'T HE?
THAT'S WHAT HE GETS FOR FAILING HIS MISSION.

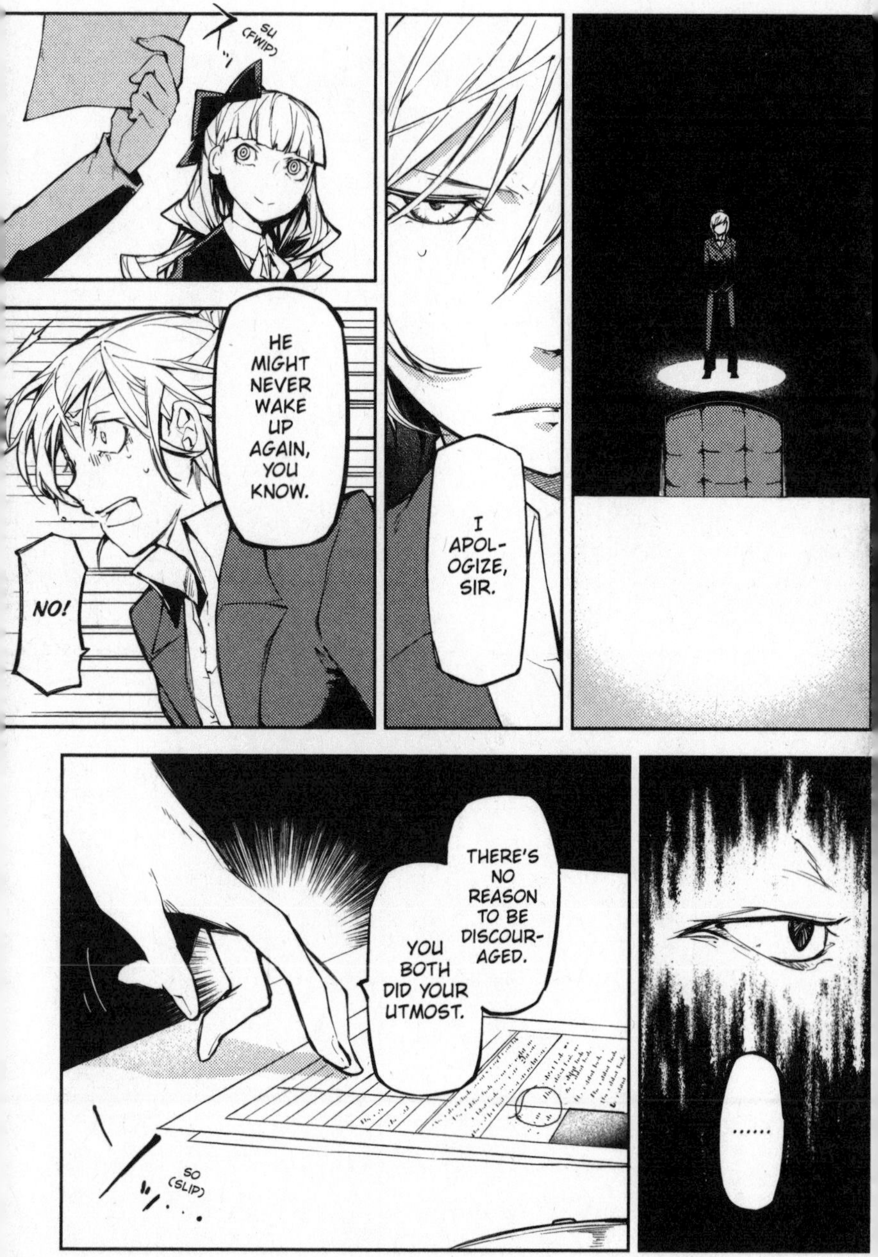
I APOLOGIZE, SIR.
SU (FWIP)
HE MIGHT NEVER WAKE UP AGAIN, YOU KNOW.
NO!
......
THERE'S NO REASON TO BE DISCOURAGED.
YOU BOTH DID YOUR UTMOST.
SO (SLIP)

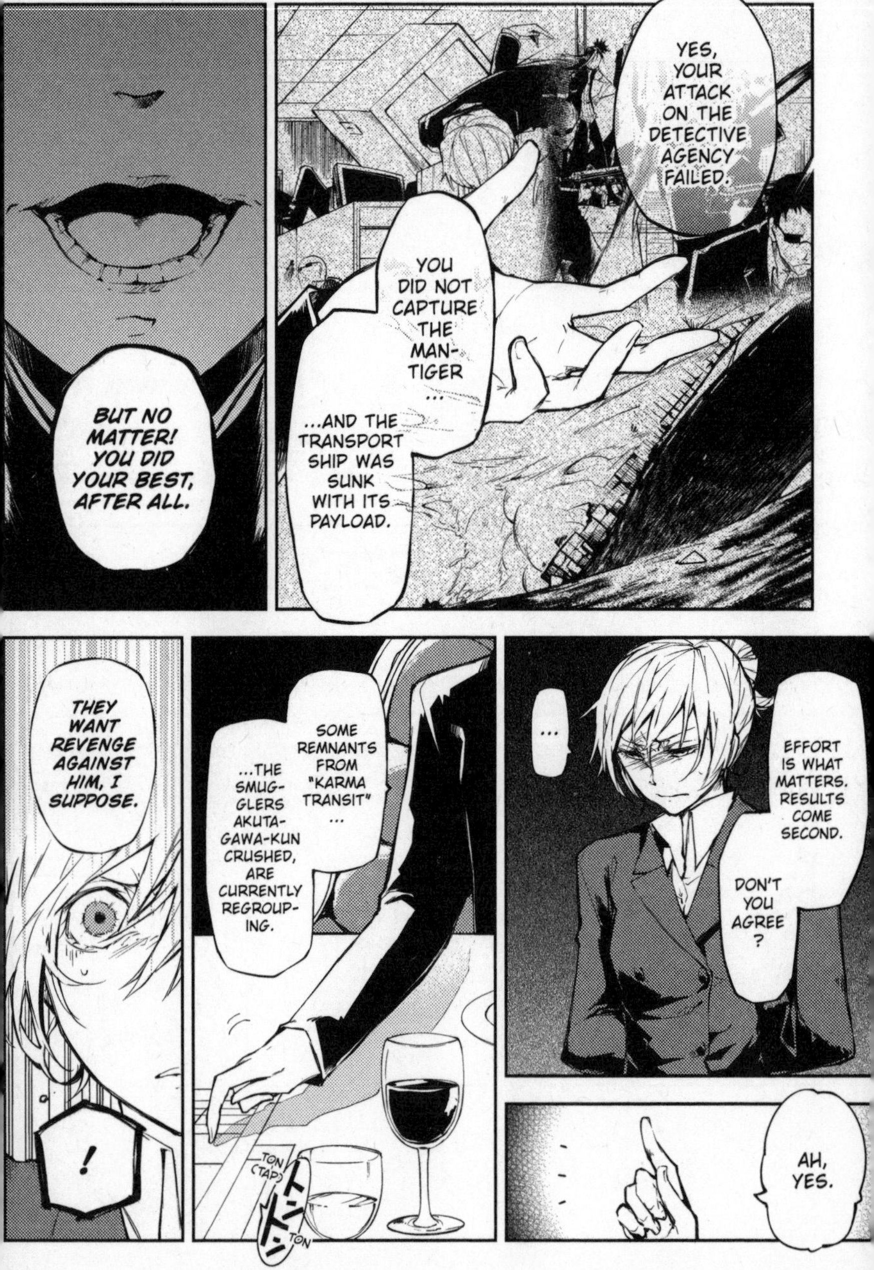
YES, YOUR ATTACK ON THE DETECTIVE AGENCY FAILED.
YOU DID NOT CAPTURE THE MAN-TIGER...
...AND THE TRANSPORT SHIP WAS SUNK WITH ITS PAYLOAD.
BUT NO MATTER! YOU DID YOUR BEST, AFTER ALL.
EFFORT IS WHAT MATTERS. RESULTS COME SECOND.
DON'T YOU AGREE?
...
AH, YES.
...
SOME REMNANTS FROM "KARMA TRANSIT"...
...THE SMUGGLERS AKUTAGAWA-KUN CRUSHED, ARE CURRENTLY REGROUPING.
TON (TAP)
TON
THEY WANT REVENGE AGAINST HIM, I SUPPOSE.
!

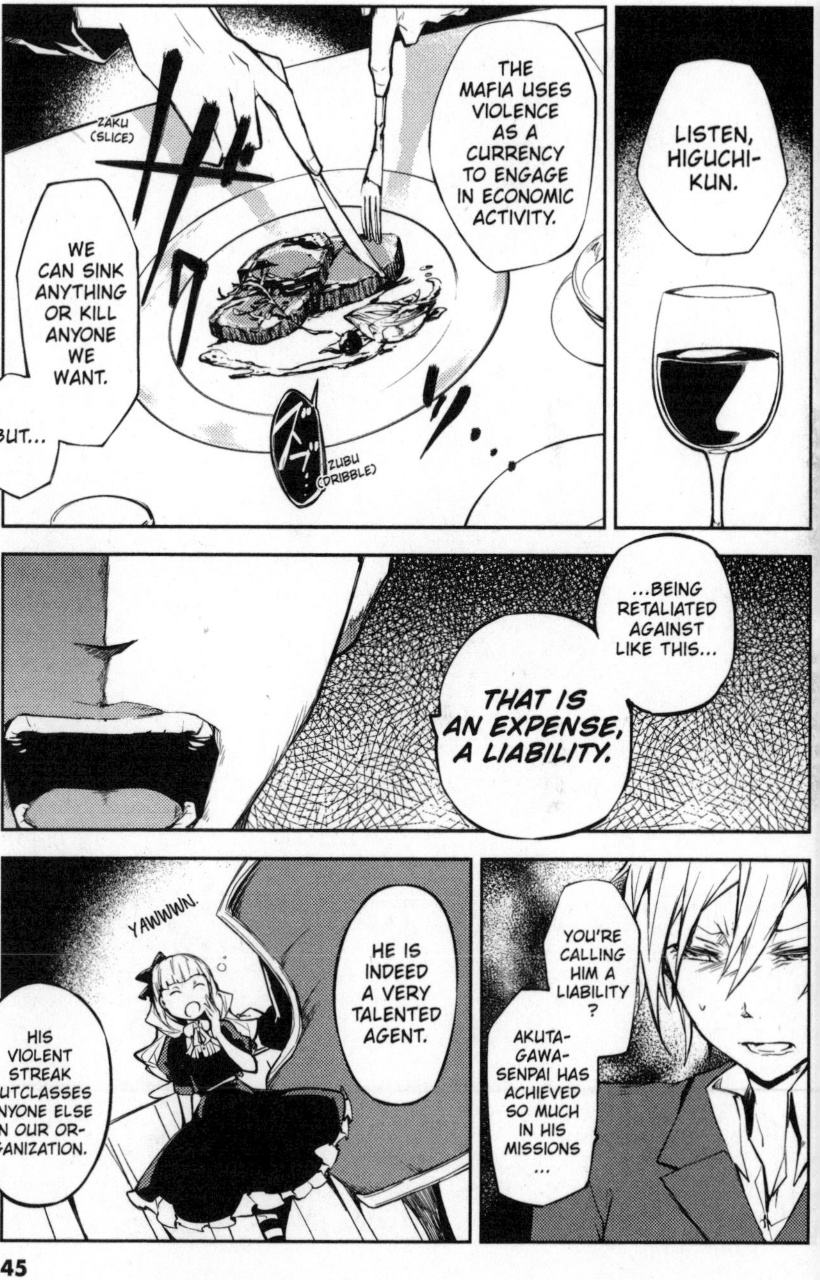
LISTEN, HIGUCHI-KUN.
THE MAFIA USES VIOLENCE AS A CURRENCY TO ENGAGE IN ECONOMIC ACTIVITY.
ZAKU (SLICE)
WE CAN SINK ANYTHING OR KILL ANYONE WE WANT.
BUT...
ZUBU (DRIBBLE)
...BEING RETALIATED AGAINST LIKE THIS...
THAT IS AN EXPENSE, A LIABILITY.
YOU'RE CALLING HIM A LIABILITY?
AKUTA-GAWA-SENPAI HAS ACHIEVED SO MUCH IN HIS MISSIONS...
HE IS INDEED A VERY TALENTED AGENT.
YAWWWN.
HIS VIOLENT STREAK OUTCLASSES ANYONE ELSE IN OUR OR-GANIZATION.

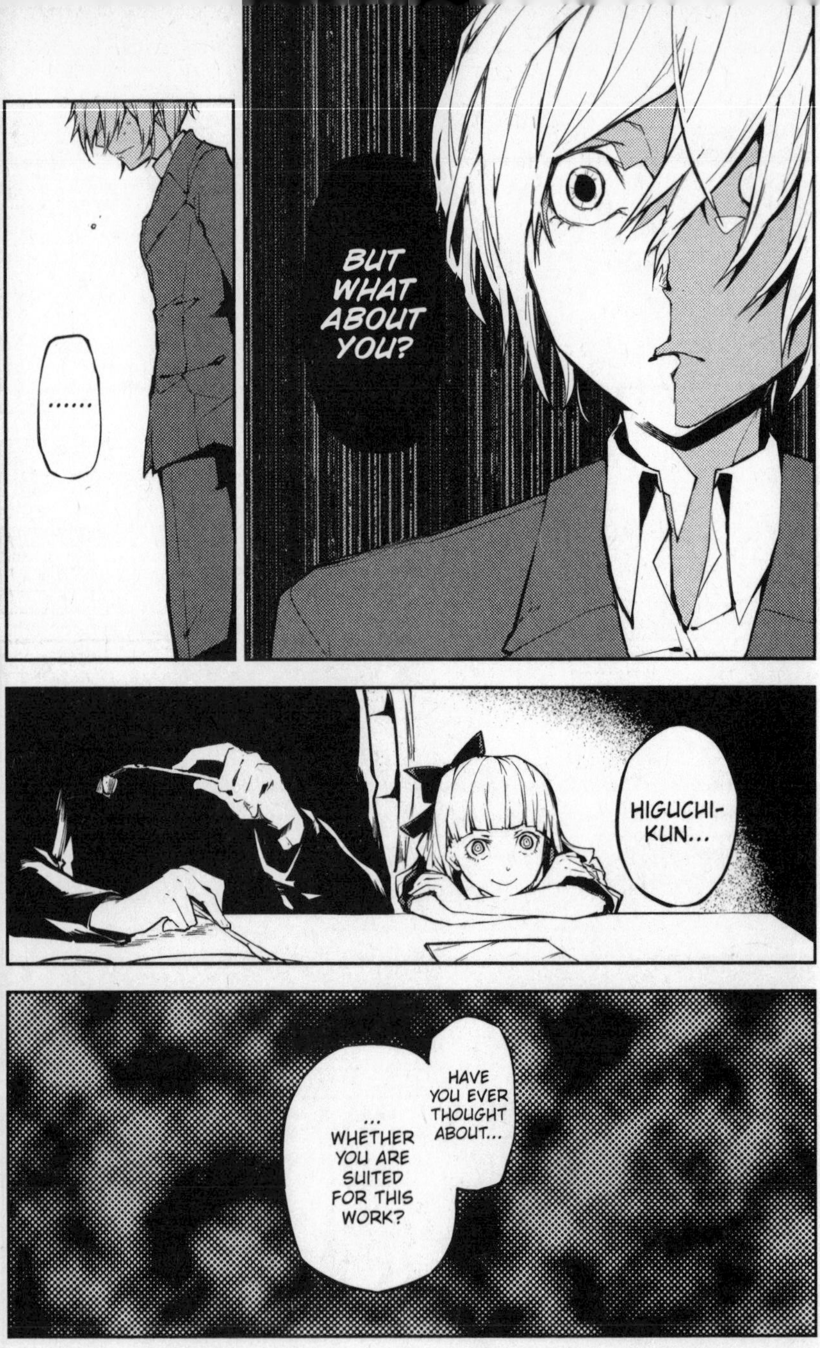
BUT WHAT ABOUT YOU?
......
HIGUCHI-KUN...
HAVE YOU EVER THOUGHT ABOUT...
...WHETHER YOU ARE SUITED FOR THIS WORK?

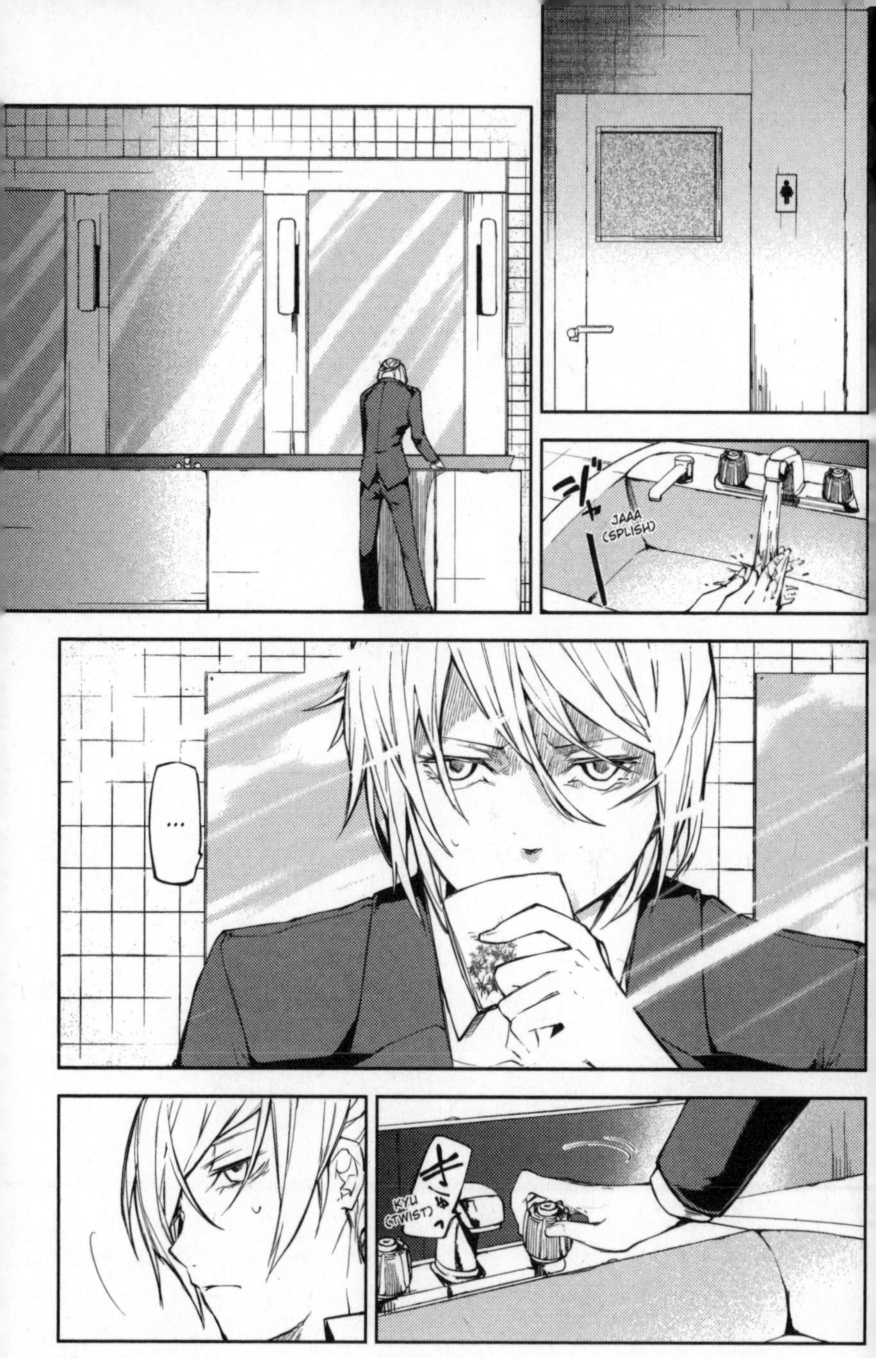

ジャー
JAAA (SPLISH)
...
キュッ
KYU (TWIST)

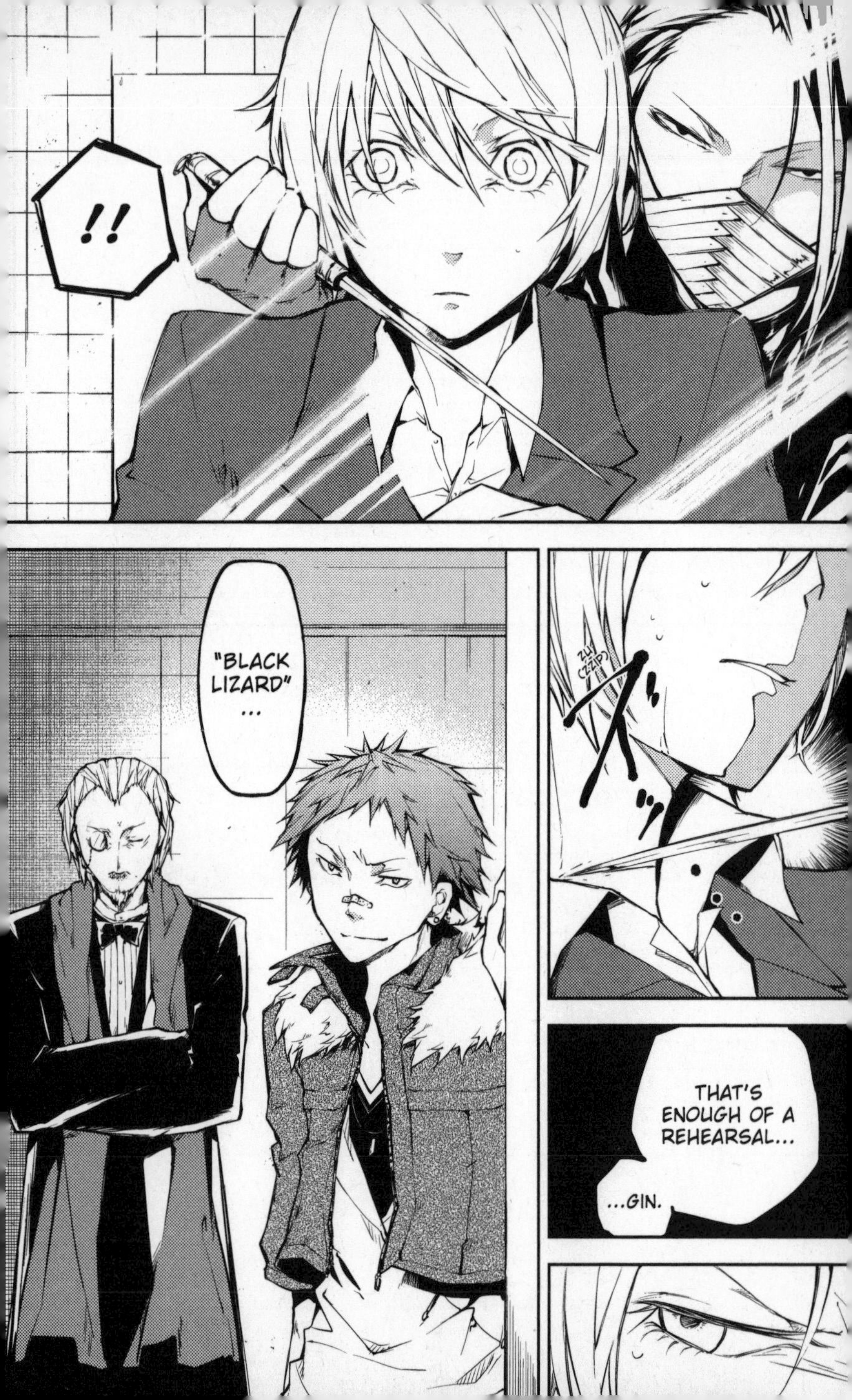
!!
ZU (ZZIP)
THAT'S ENOUGH OF A REHEARSAL...
...GIN.
"BLACK LIZARD" ...

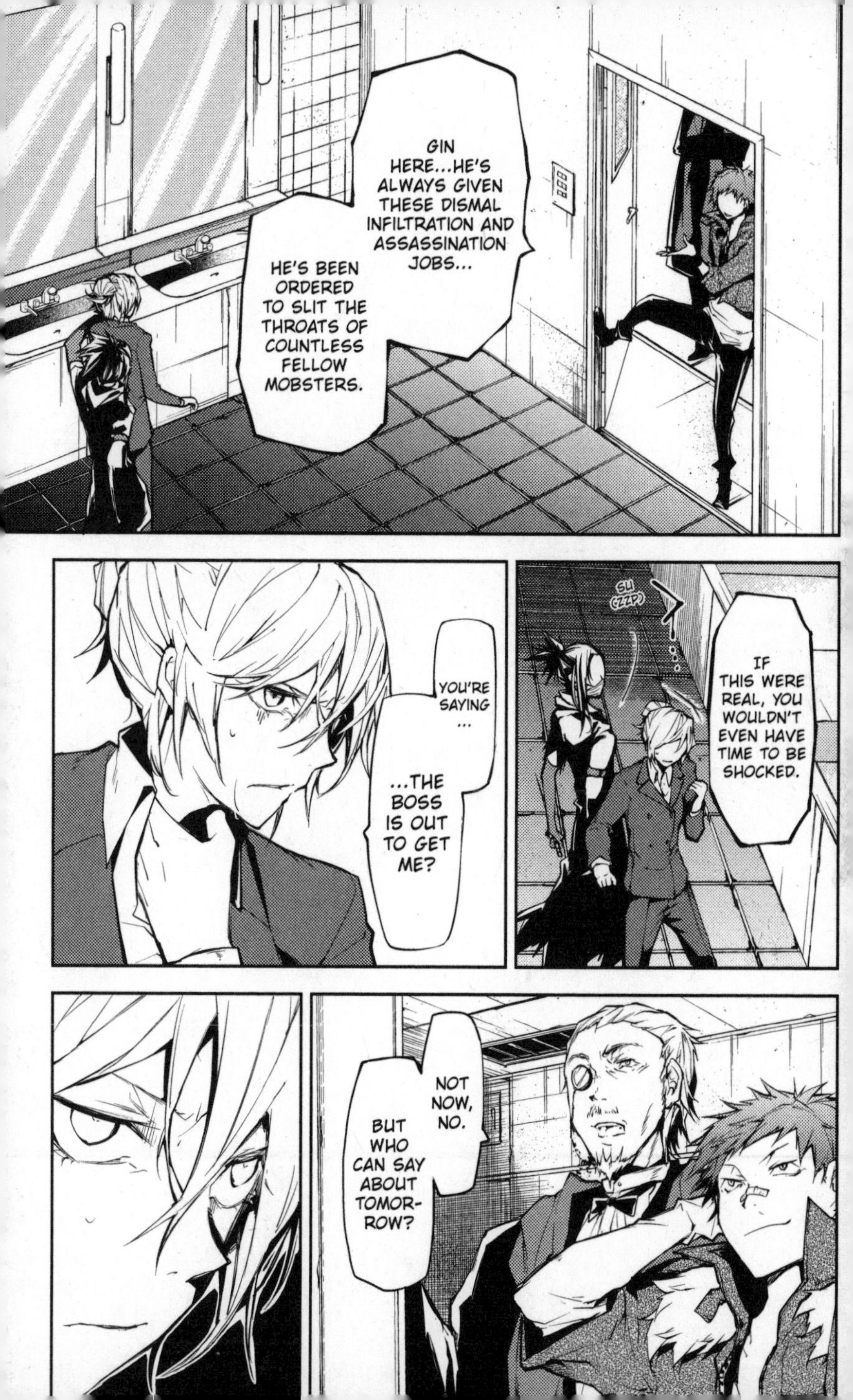
GIN HERE...HE'S ALWAYS GIVEN THESE DISMAL INFILTRATION AND ASSASSINATION JOBS...
HE'S BEEN ORDERED TO SLIT THE THROATS OF COUNTLESS FELLOW MOBSTERS.
SU (ZZIP)
IF THIS WERE REAL, YOU WOULDN'T EVEN HAVE TIME TO BE SHOCKED.
YOU'RE SAYING...
...THE BOSS IS OUT TO GET ME?
NOT NOW, NO.
BUT WHO CAN SAY ABOUT TOMORROW?

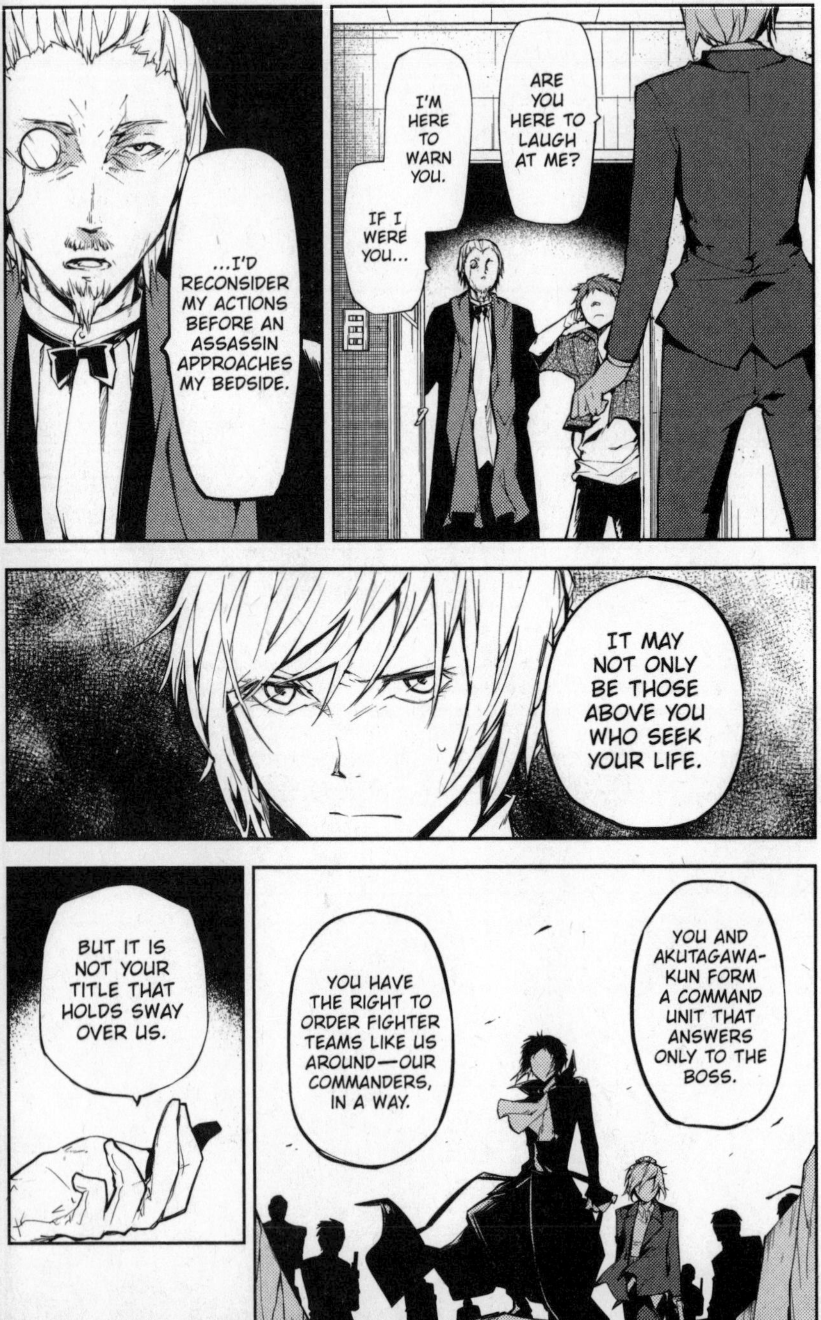
ARE YOU HERE TO LAUGH AT ME?
I'M HERE TO WARN YOU.
IF I WERE YOU...
...I'D RECONSIDER MY ACTIONS BEFORE AN ASSASSIN APPROACHES MY BEDSIDE.
IT MAY NOT ONLY BE THOSE ABOVE YOU WHO SEEK YOUR LIFE.
YOU AND AKUTAGAWA-KUN FORM A COMMAND UNIT THAT ANSWERS ONLY TO THE BOSS.
YOU HAVE THE RIGHT TO ORDER FIGHTER TEAMS LIKE US AROUND—OUR COMMANDERS, IN A WAY.
BUT IT IS NOT YOUR TITLE THAT HOLDS SWAY OVER US.

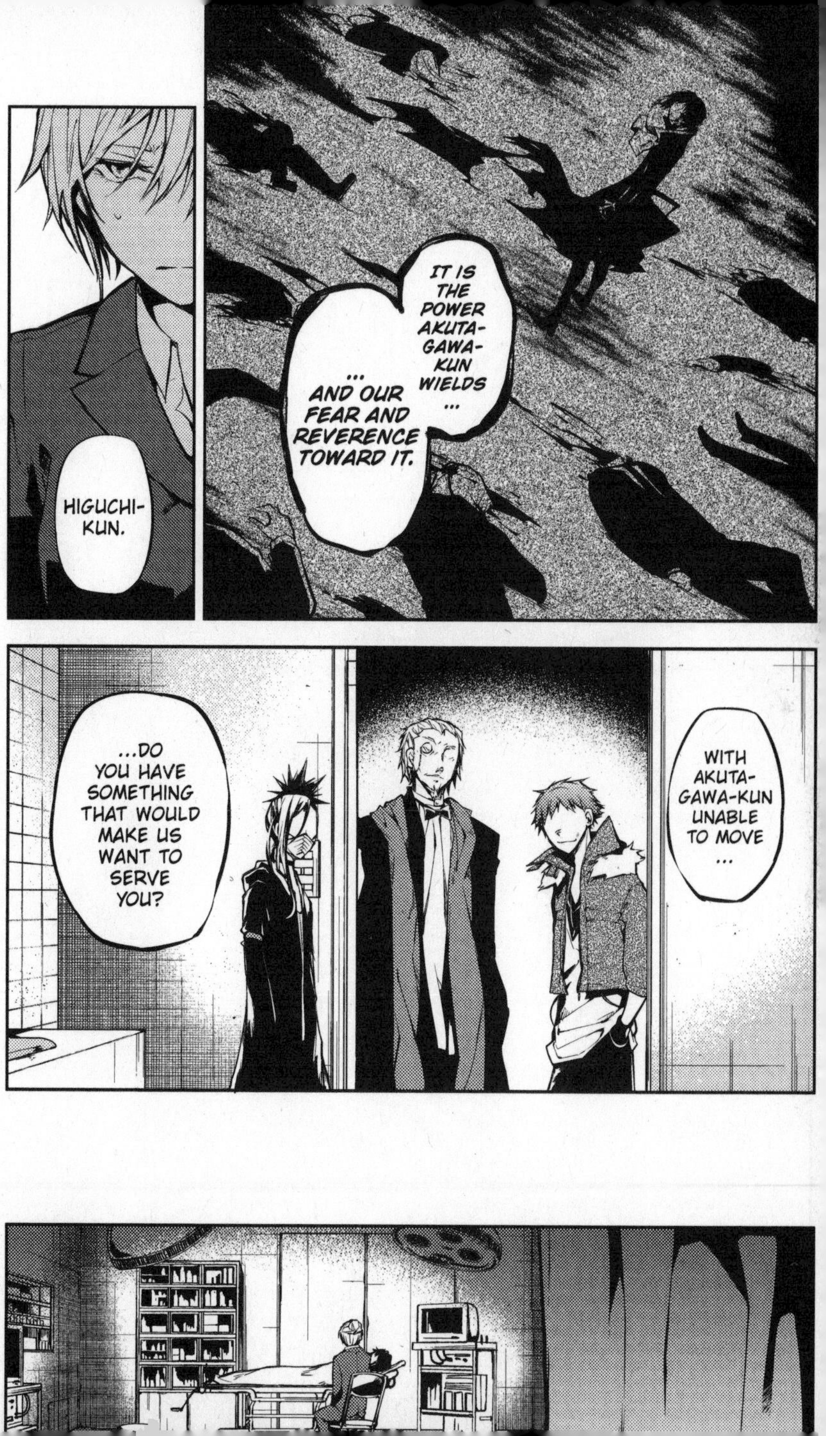
IT IS THE POWER AKUTAGAWA-KUN WIELDS ...
... AND OUR FEAR AND REVERENCE TOWARD IT.
HIGUCHI-KUN.
WITH AKUTAGAWA-KUN UNABLE TO MOVE ...
...DO YOU HAVE SOMETHING THAT WOULD MAKE US WANT TO SERVE YOU?

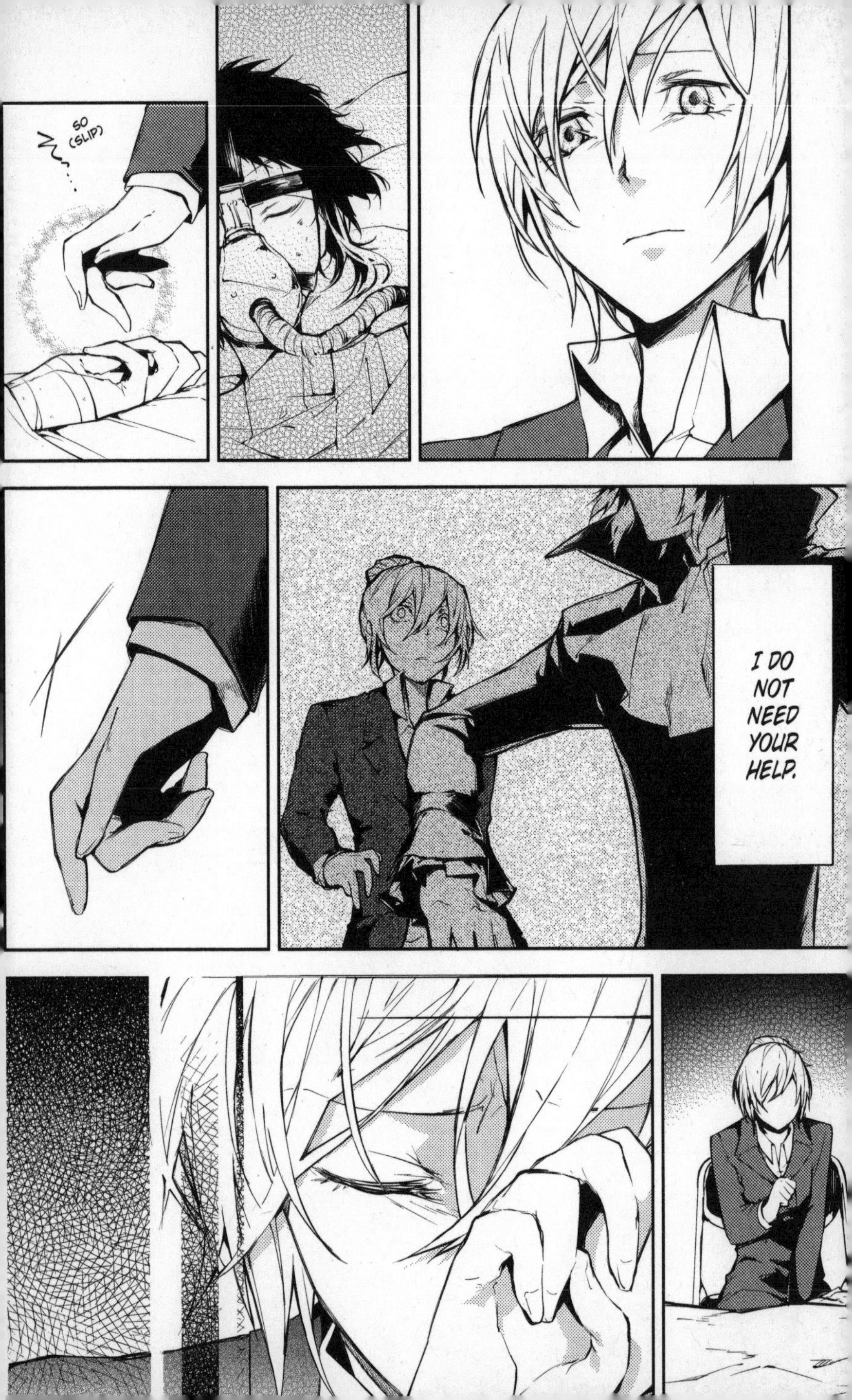
SO (SLIP)
I DO NOT NEED YOUR HELP.

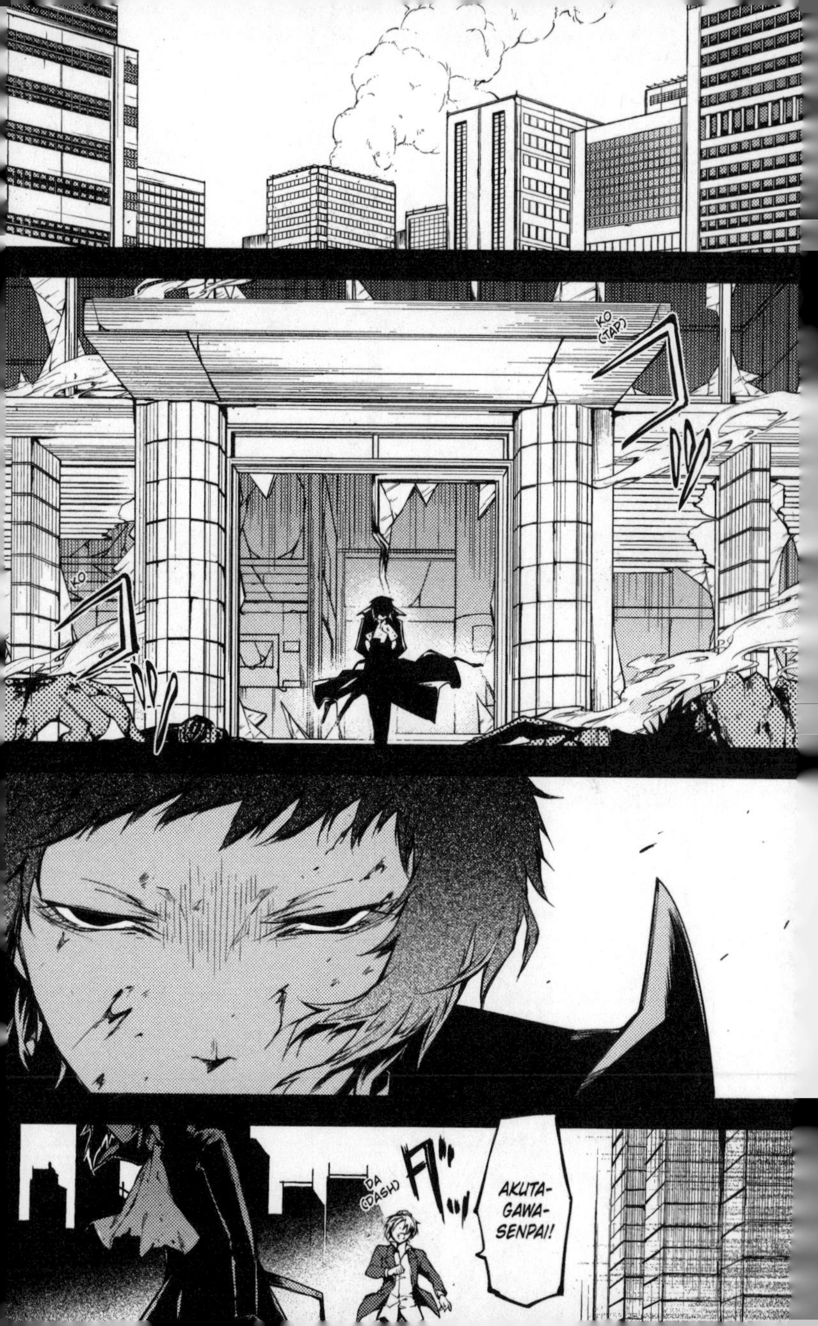
KO (TAP)
KO
AKUTA-GAWA-SENPAI!
DA (DASH)

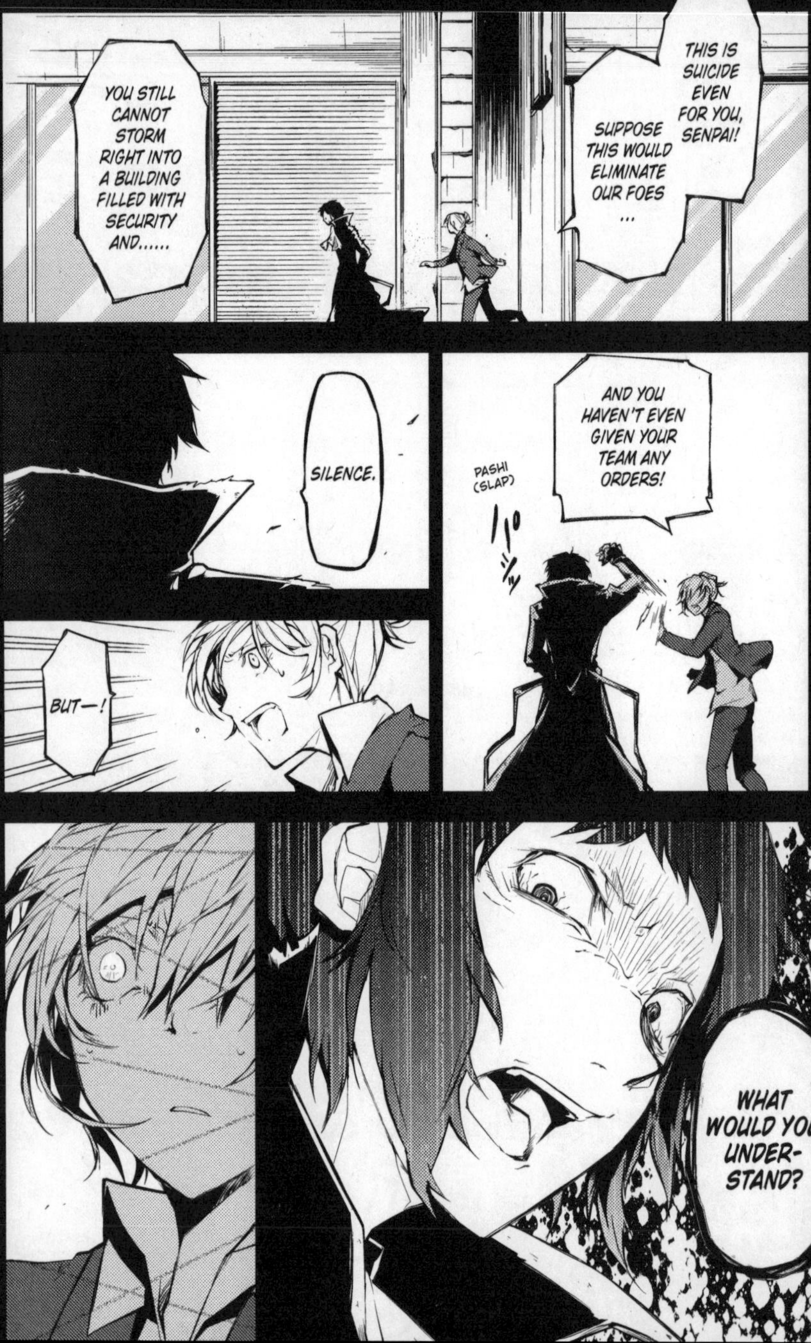
THIS IS SUICIDE EVEN FOR YOU, SENPAI!
SUPPOSE THIS WOULD ELIMINATE OUR FOES ...
YOU STILL CANNOT STORM RIGHT INTO A BUILDING FILLED WITH SECURITY AND......
AND YOU HAVEN'T EVEN GIVEN YOUR TEAM ANY ORDERS!
PASHI (SLAP)
SILENCE.
BUT—!
WHAT WOULD YOU UNDER-STAND?

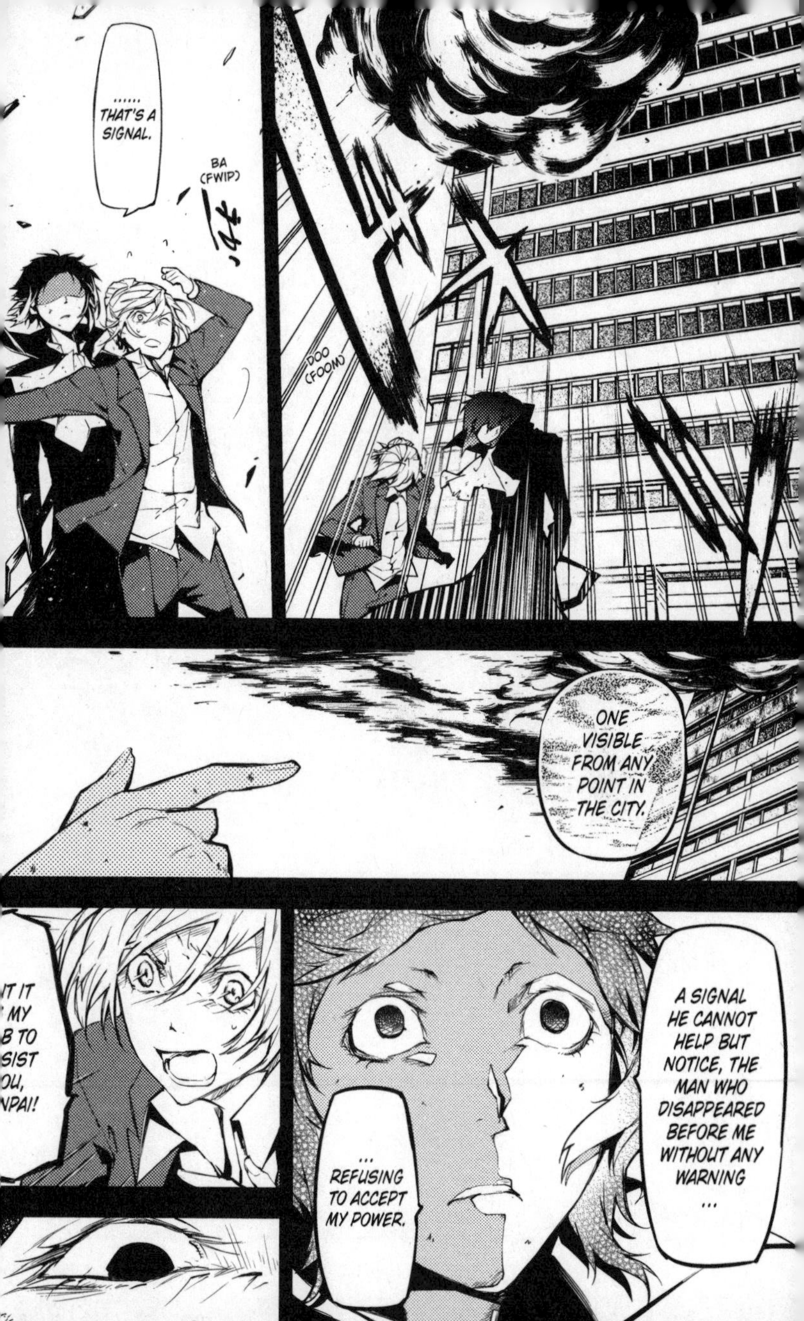
DOO
(FOOM)
...... THAT'S A SIGNAL.
BA
(FWIP)
ONE VISIBLE FROM ANY POINT IN THE CITY.
A SIGNAL HE CANNOT HELP BUT NOTICE, THE MAN WHO DISAPPEARED BEFORE ME WITHOUT ANY WARNING ...
... REFUSING TO ACCEPT MY POWER.

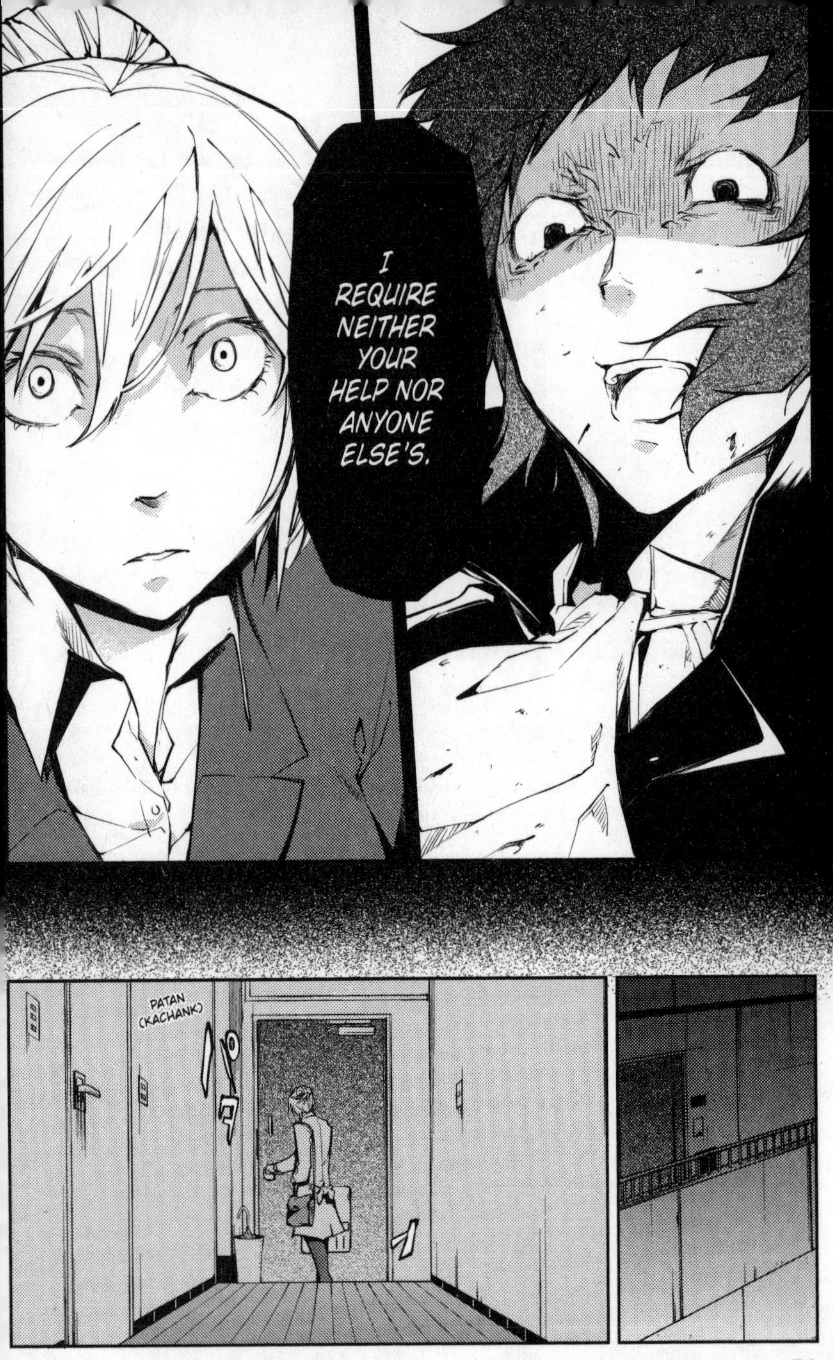
I REQUIRE NEITHER YOUR HELP NOR ANYONE ELSE'S.
PATAN (KACHANK)

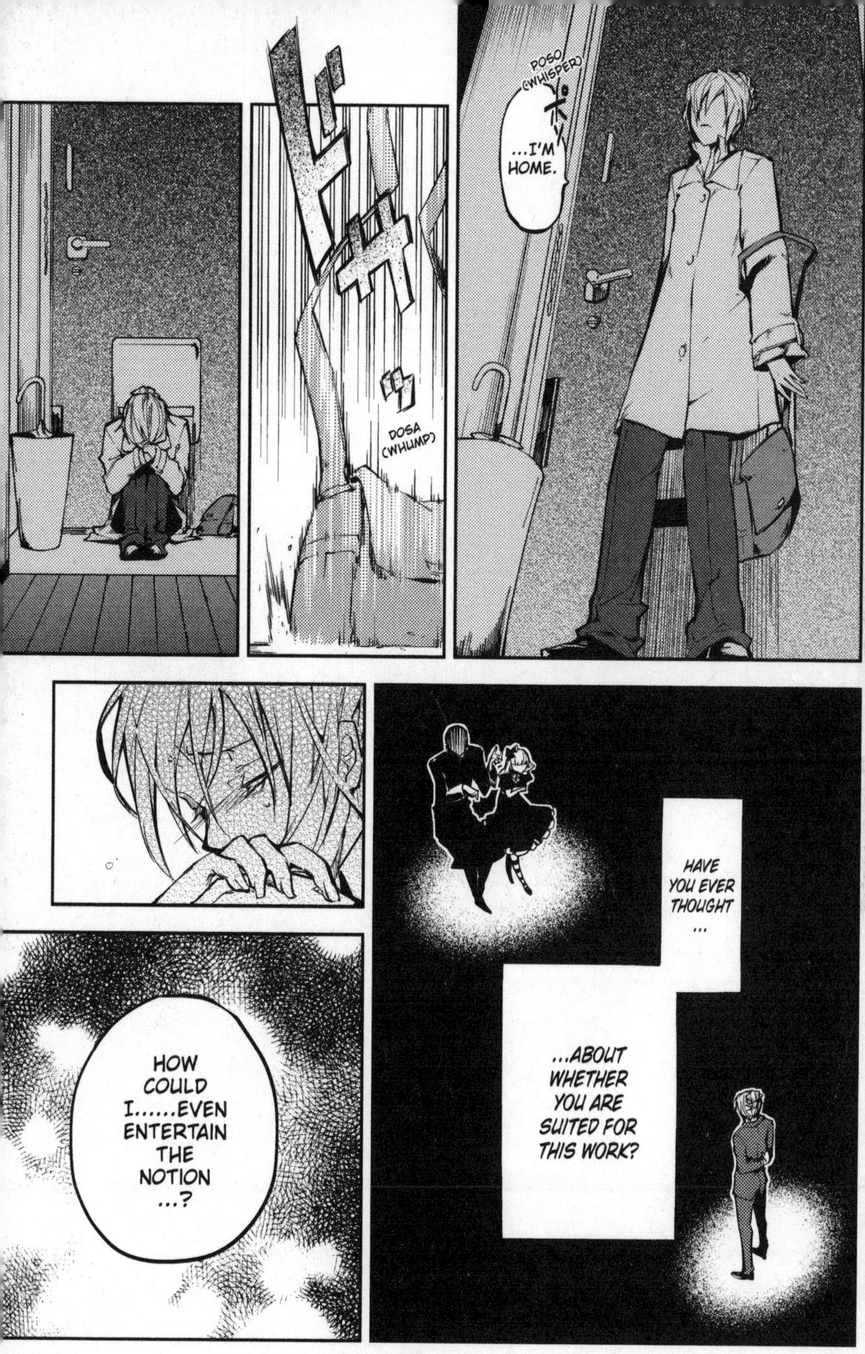
POSO (WHISPER)
...I'M HOME.
DOSA (WHUMP)
HAVE YOU EVER THOUGHT...
...ABOUT WHETHER YOU ARE SUITED FOR THIS WORK?
HOW COULD I......EVEN ENTERTAIN THE NOTION...?

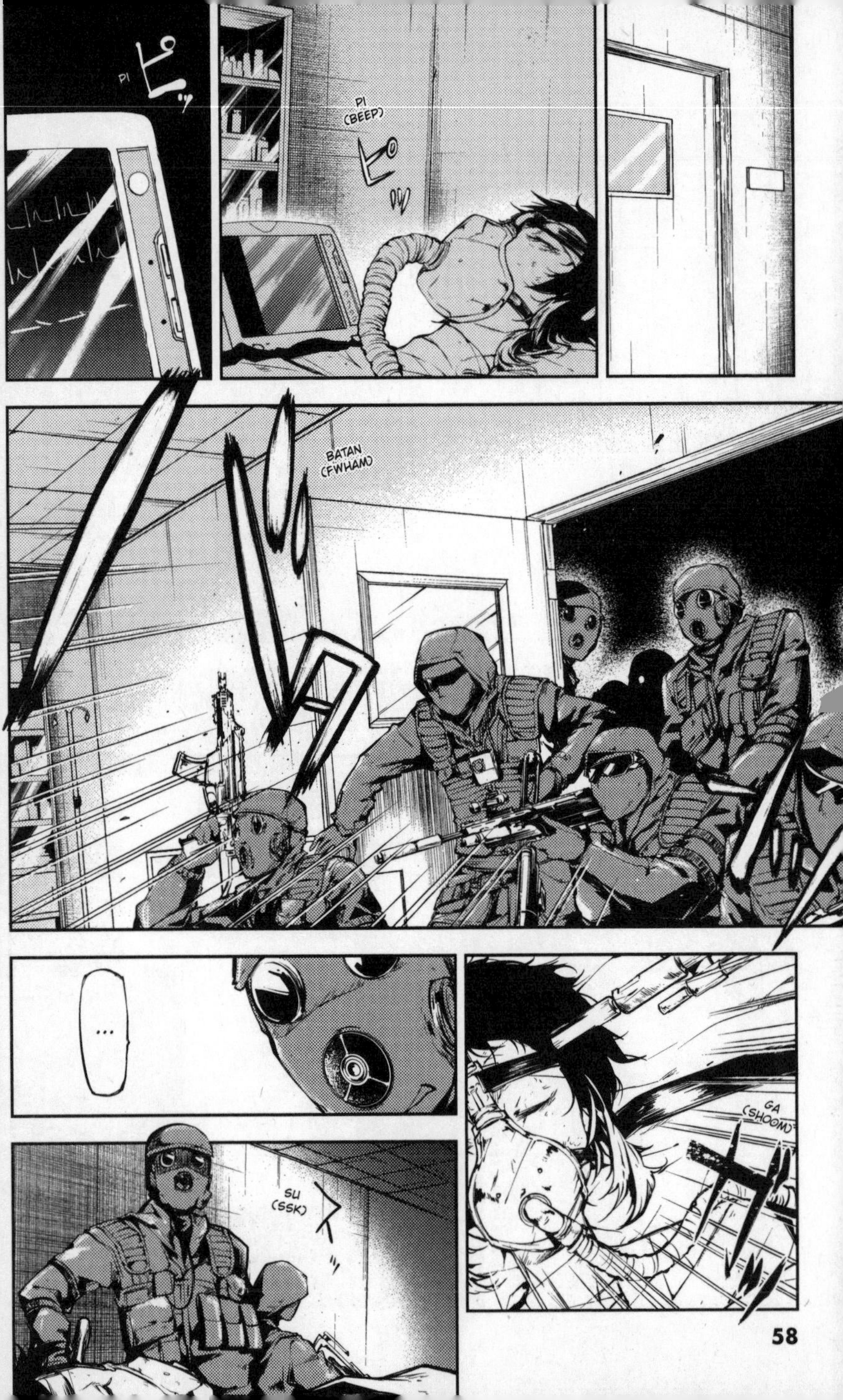
PI (BEEP)
PI
BATAN (FWHAM)
GA (SHOOM)
...
SU (SSK)

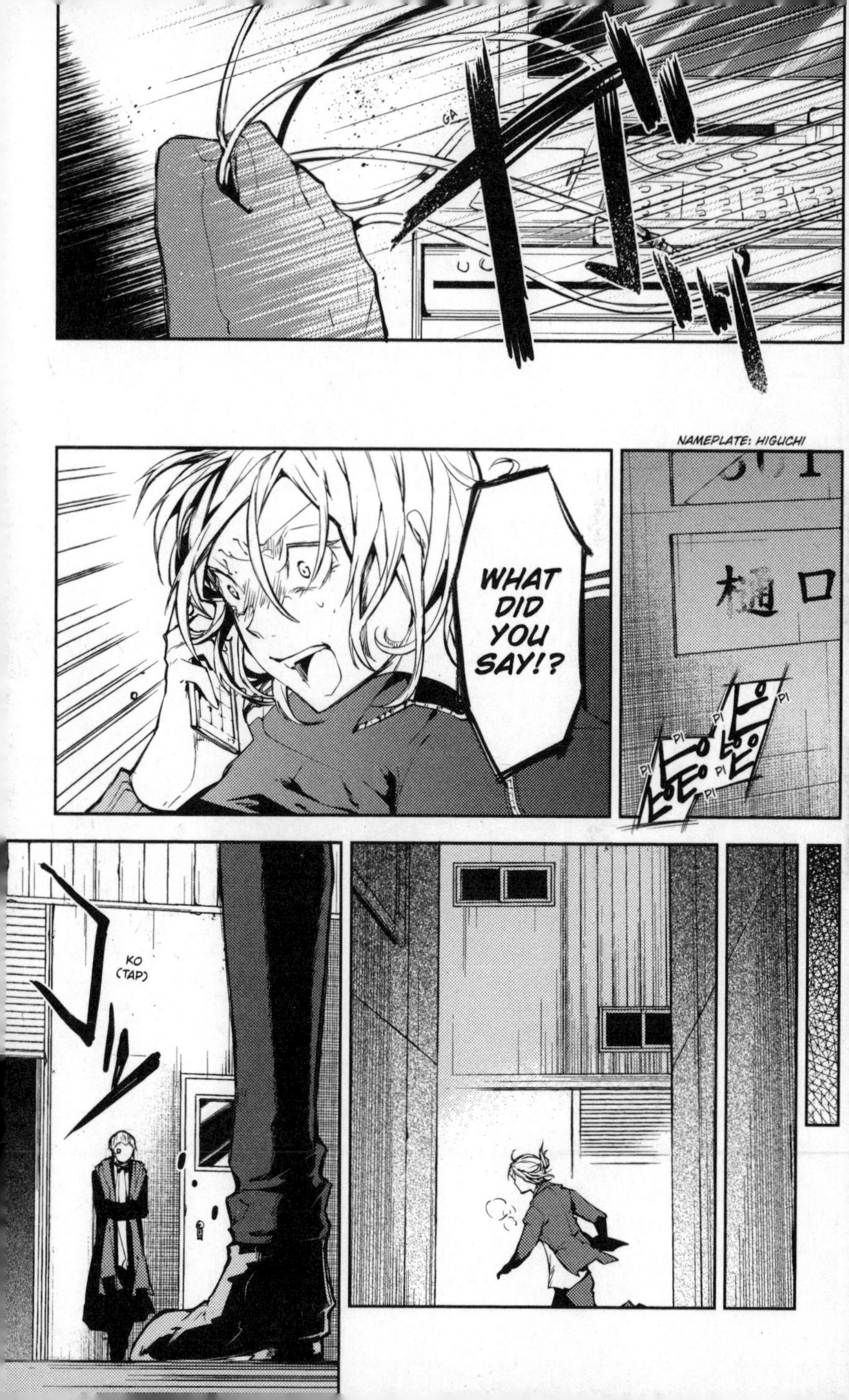
GA
NAMEPLATE: HIGUCHI
PI
PI
PI
PI
PI
WHAT DID YOU SAY!?
KO (TAP)

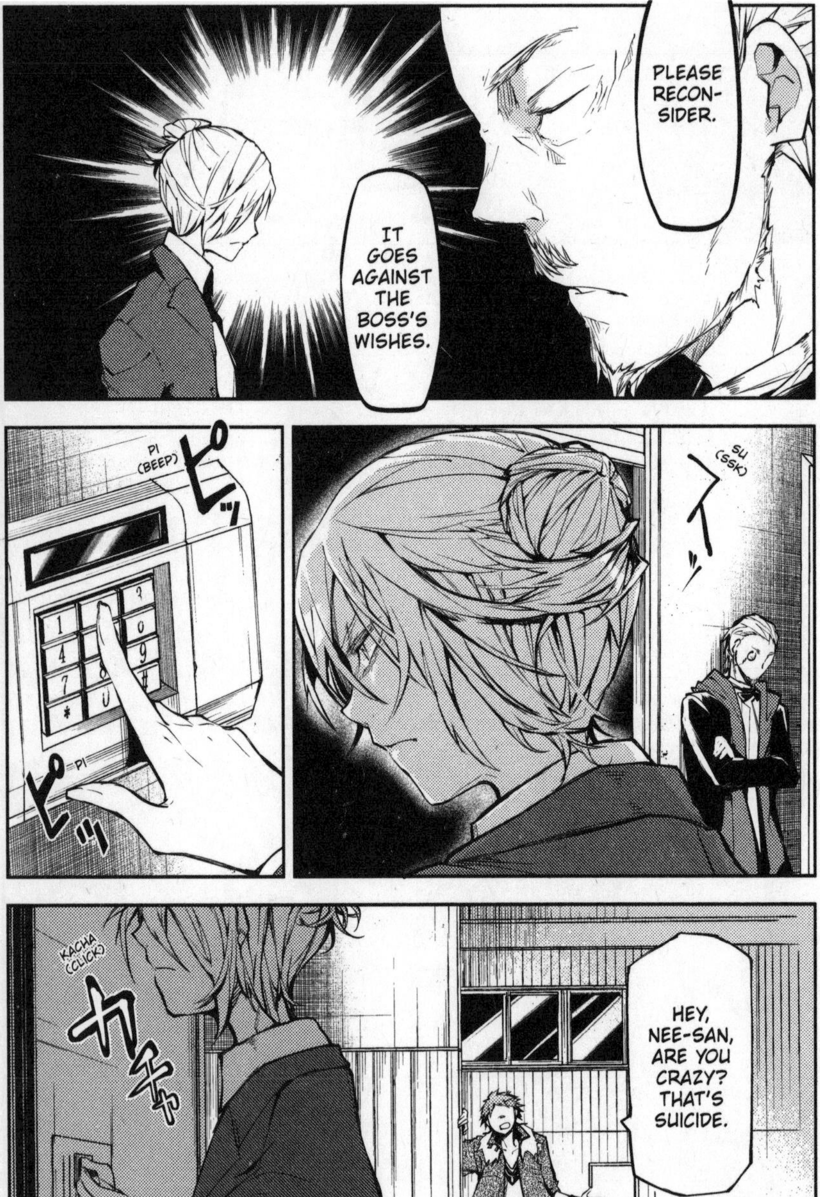
PLEASE RECONSIDER.
IT GOES AGAINST THE BOSS'S WISHES.
SU (SSK)
PI (BEEP)
PI
KACHA (CLICK)
HEY, NEE-SAN, ARE YOU CRAZY? THAT'S SUICIDE.

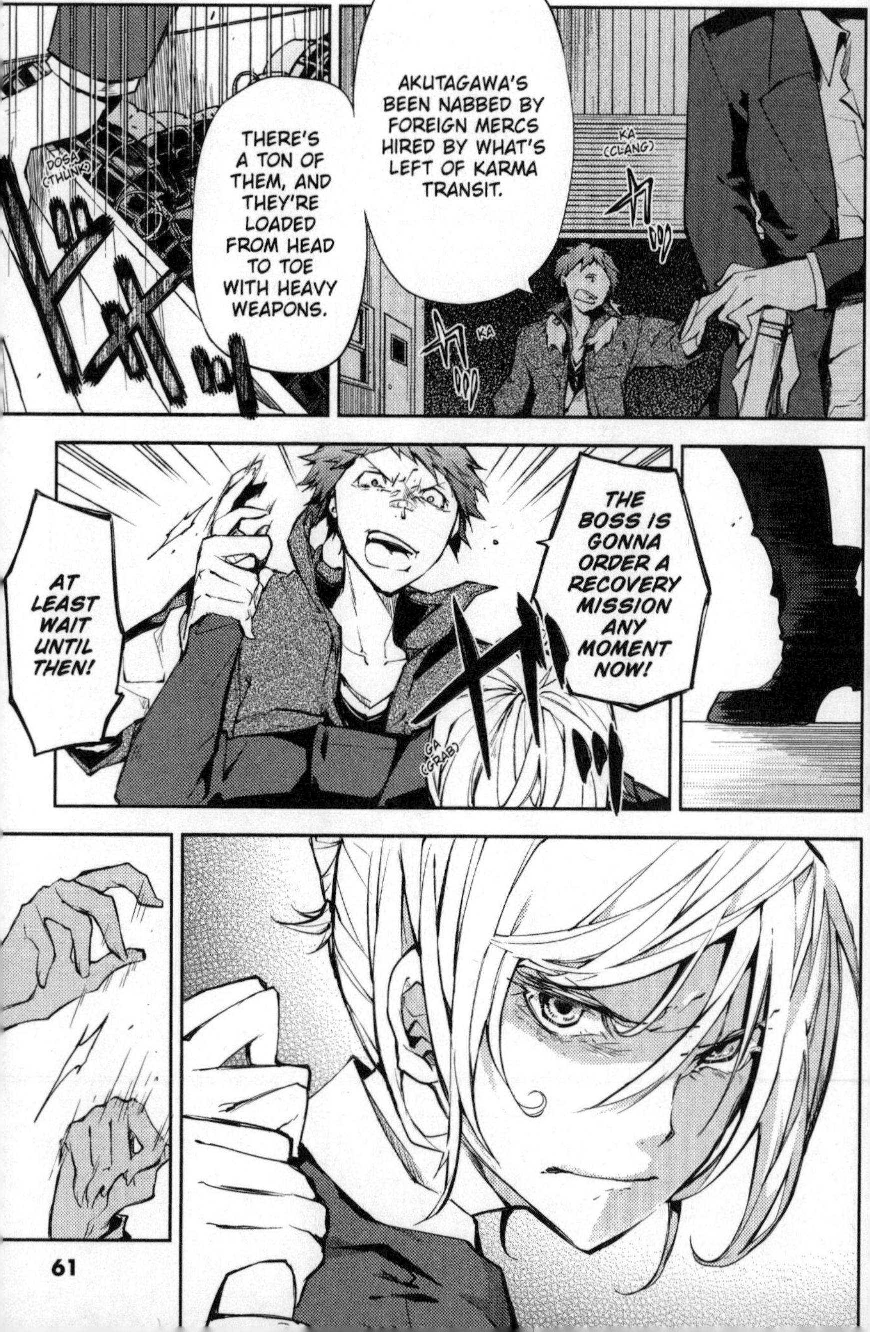
AKUTAGAWA'S BEEN NABBED BY FOREIGN MERCS HIRED BY WHAT'S LEFT OF KARMA TRANSIT.
KA (CLANG)
KA
THERE'S A TON OF THEM, AND THEY'RE LOADED FROM HEAD TO TOE WITH HEAVY WEAPONS.
DOSA (THUNK)
THE BOSS IS GONNA ORDER A RECOVERY MISSION ANY MOMENT NOW!
AT LEAST WAIT UNTIL THEN!
GA (GRAB)

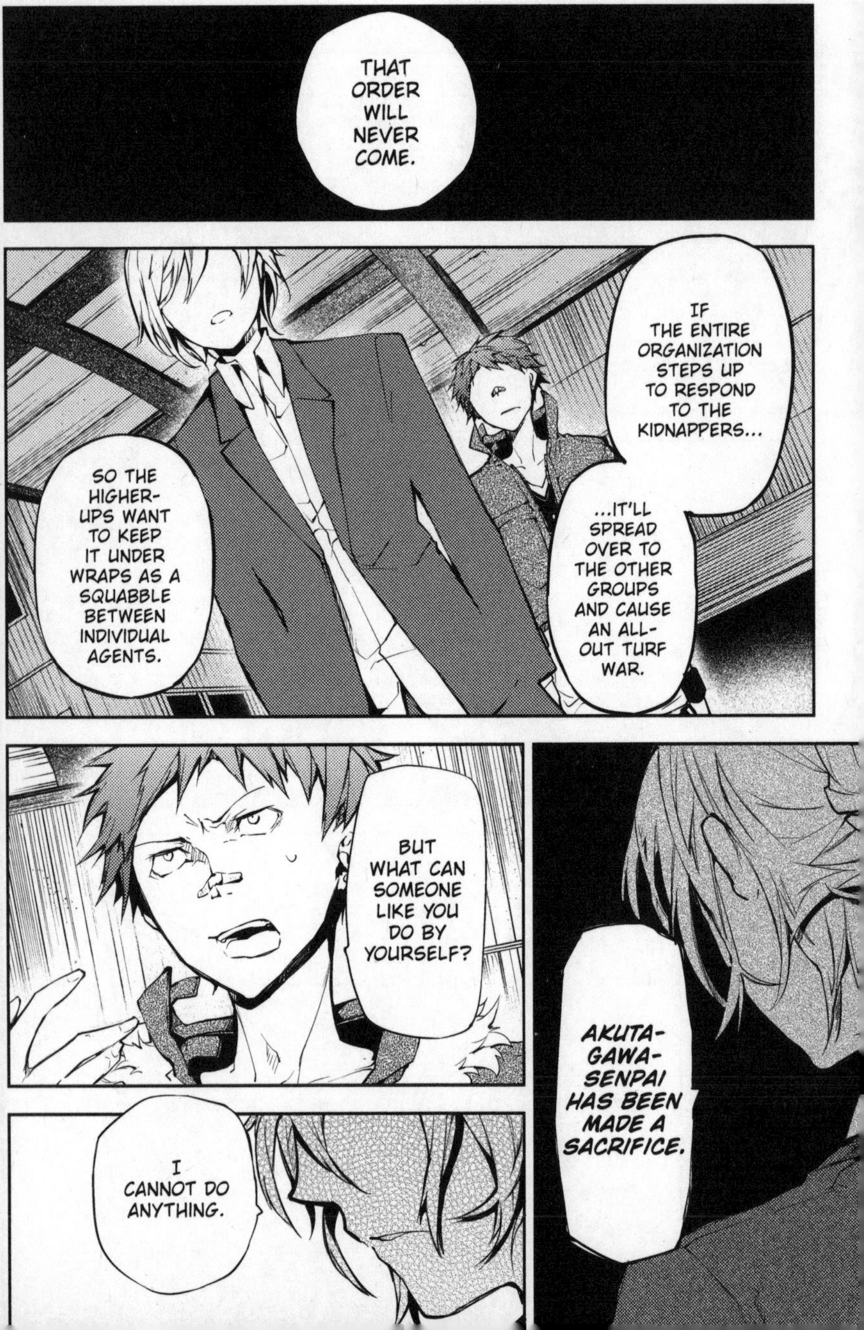
THAT ORDER WILL NEVER COME.
IF THE ENTIRE ORGANIZATION STEPS UP TO RESPOND TO THE KIDNAPPERS...
...IT'LL SPREAD OVER TO THE OTHER GROUPS AND CAUSE AN ALL-OUT TURF WAR.
SO THE HIGHER-UPS WANT TO KEEP IT UNDER WRAPS AS A SQUABBLE BETWEEN INDIVIDUAL AGENTS.
AKUTA-GAWA-SENPAI HAS BEEN MADE A SACRIFICE.
BUT WHAT CAN SOMEONE LIKE YOU DO BY YOURSELF?
I CANNOT DO ANYTHING.

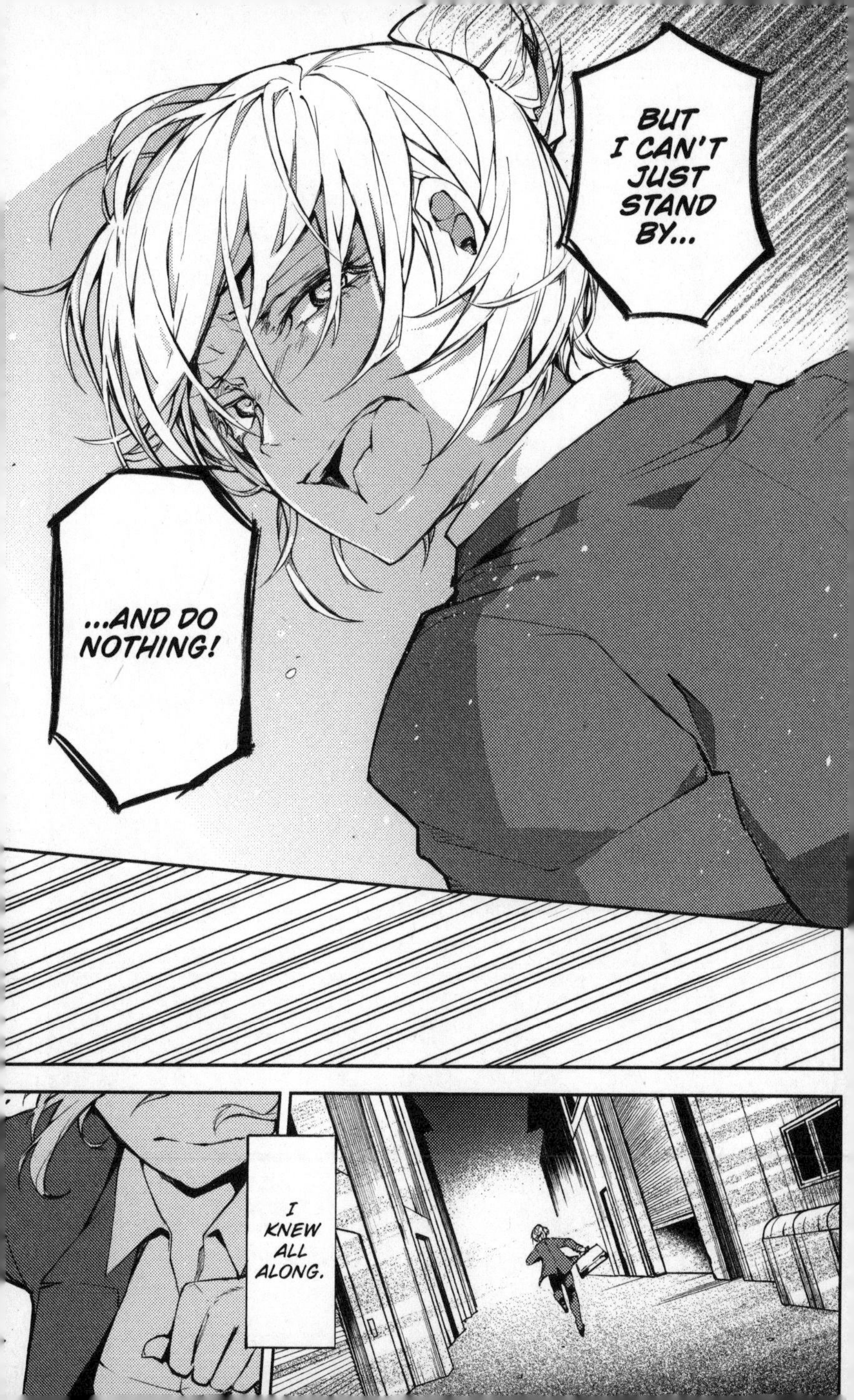
BUT I CAN'T JUST STAND BY...
...AND DO NOTHING!
I KNEW ALL ALONG.

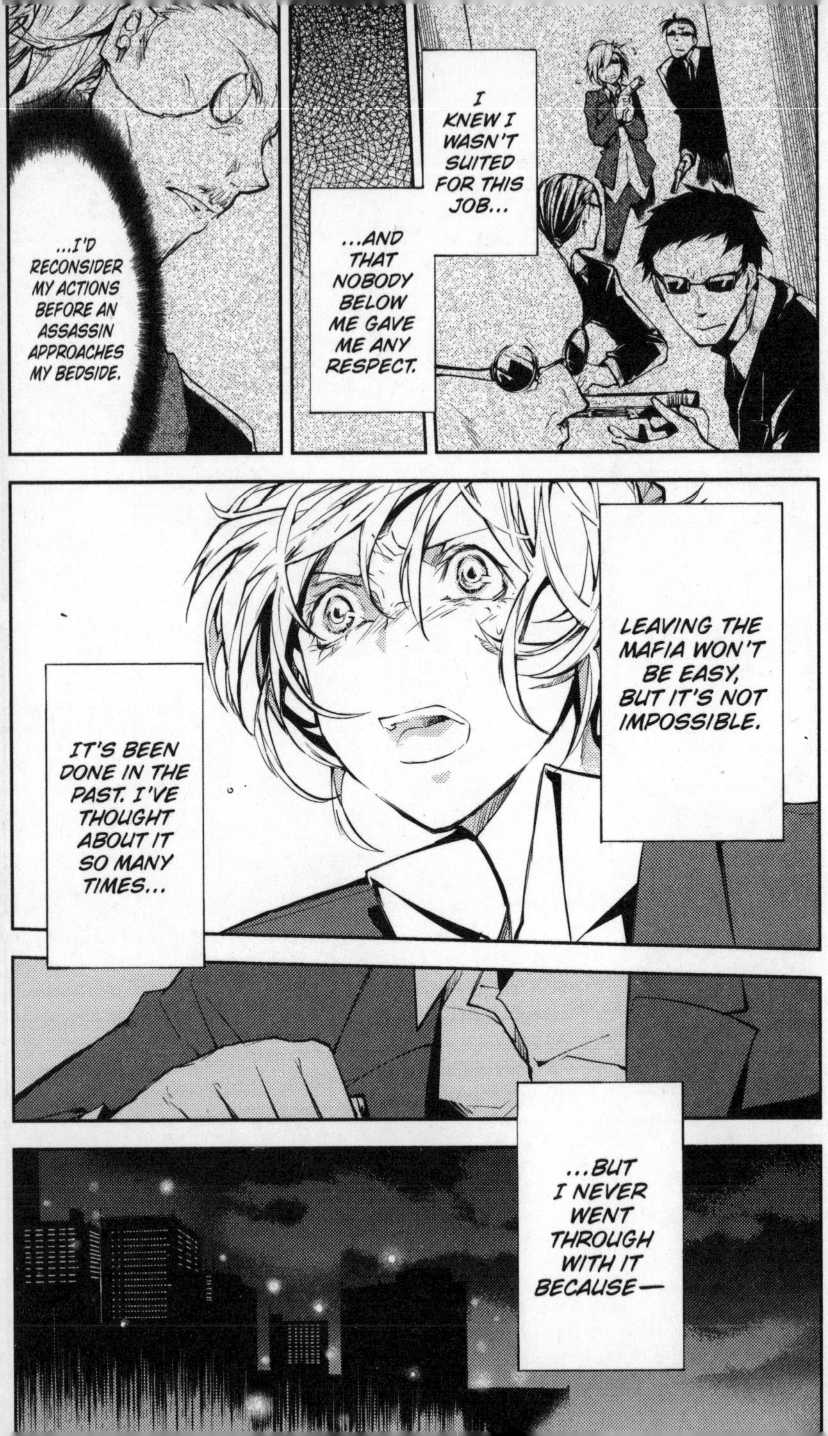
I KNEW I WASN'T SUITED FOR THIS JOB...
...AND THAT NOBODY BELOW ME GAVE ME ANY RESPECT.
...I'D RECONSIDER MY ACTIONS BEFORE AN ASSASSIN APPROACHES MY BEDSIDE.
LEAVING THE MAFIA WON'T BE EASY, BUT IT'S NOT IMPOSSIBLE.
IT'S BEEN DONE IN THE PAST. I'VE THOUGHT ABOUT IT SO MANY TIMES...
...BUT I NEVER WENT THROUGH WITH IT BECAUSE—

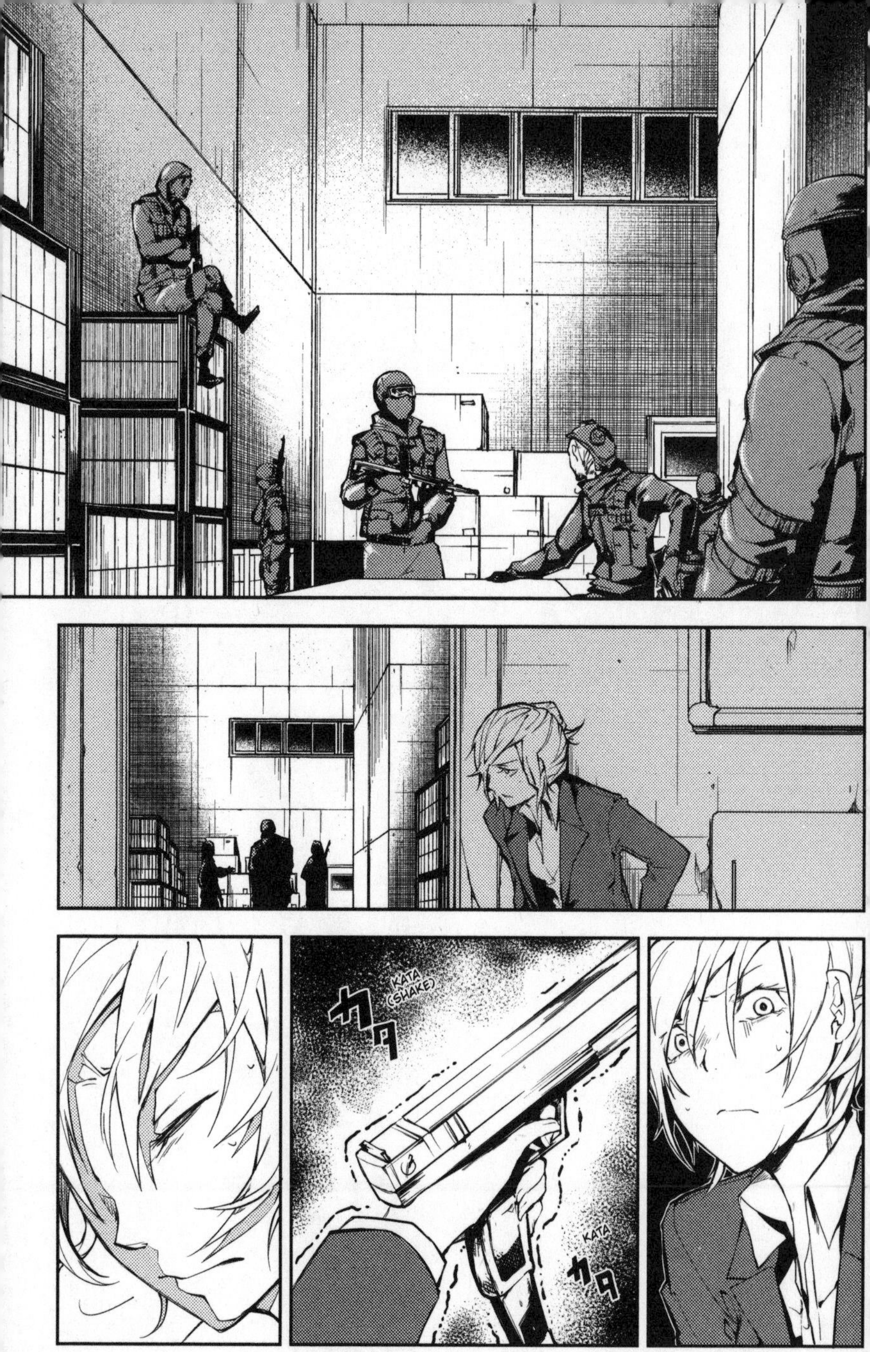
カタ
KATA (SHAKE)
カタ
KATA

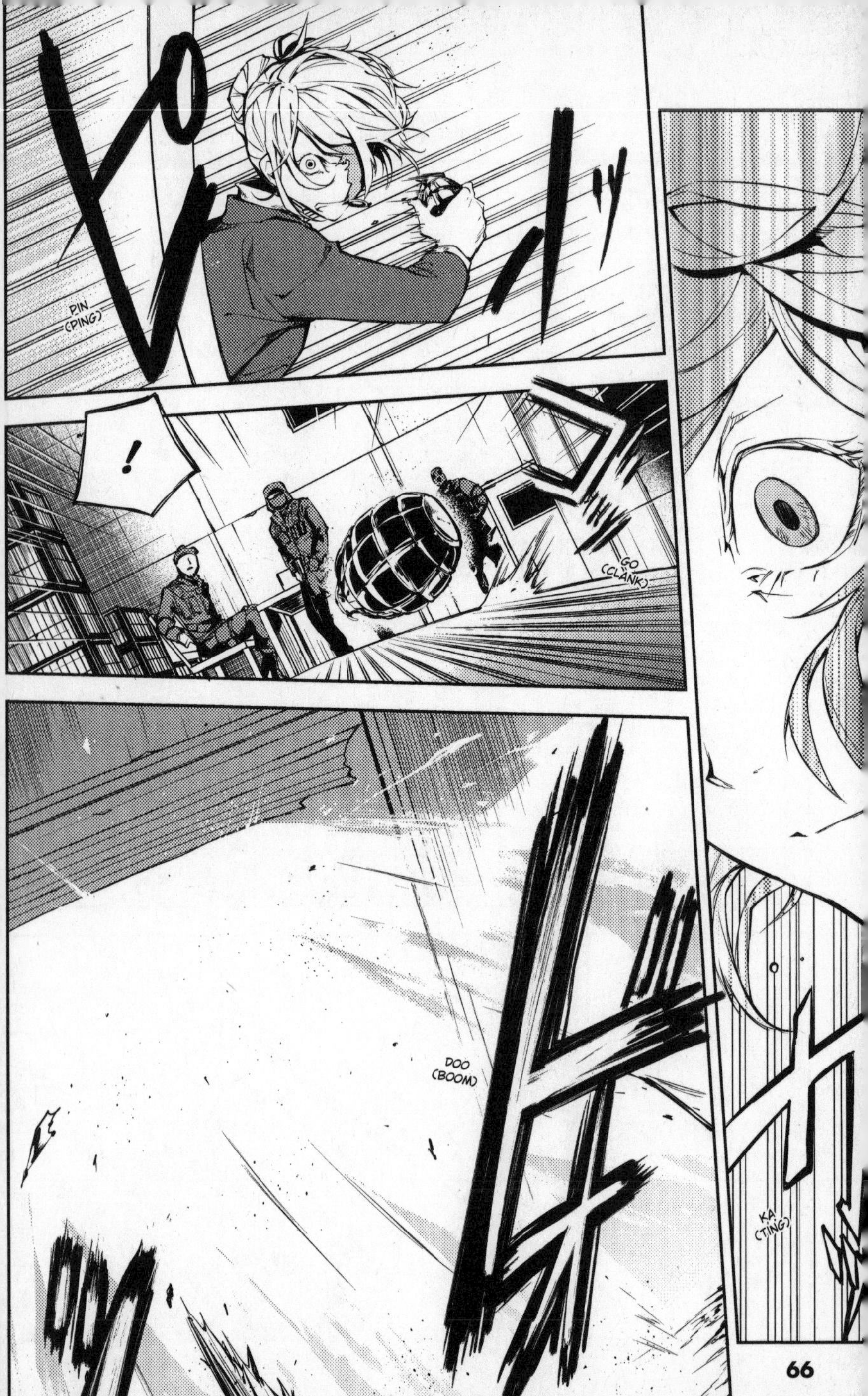
KA (TING)
PIN (PING)
!
GO (CLANK)
DOO (BOOM)

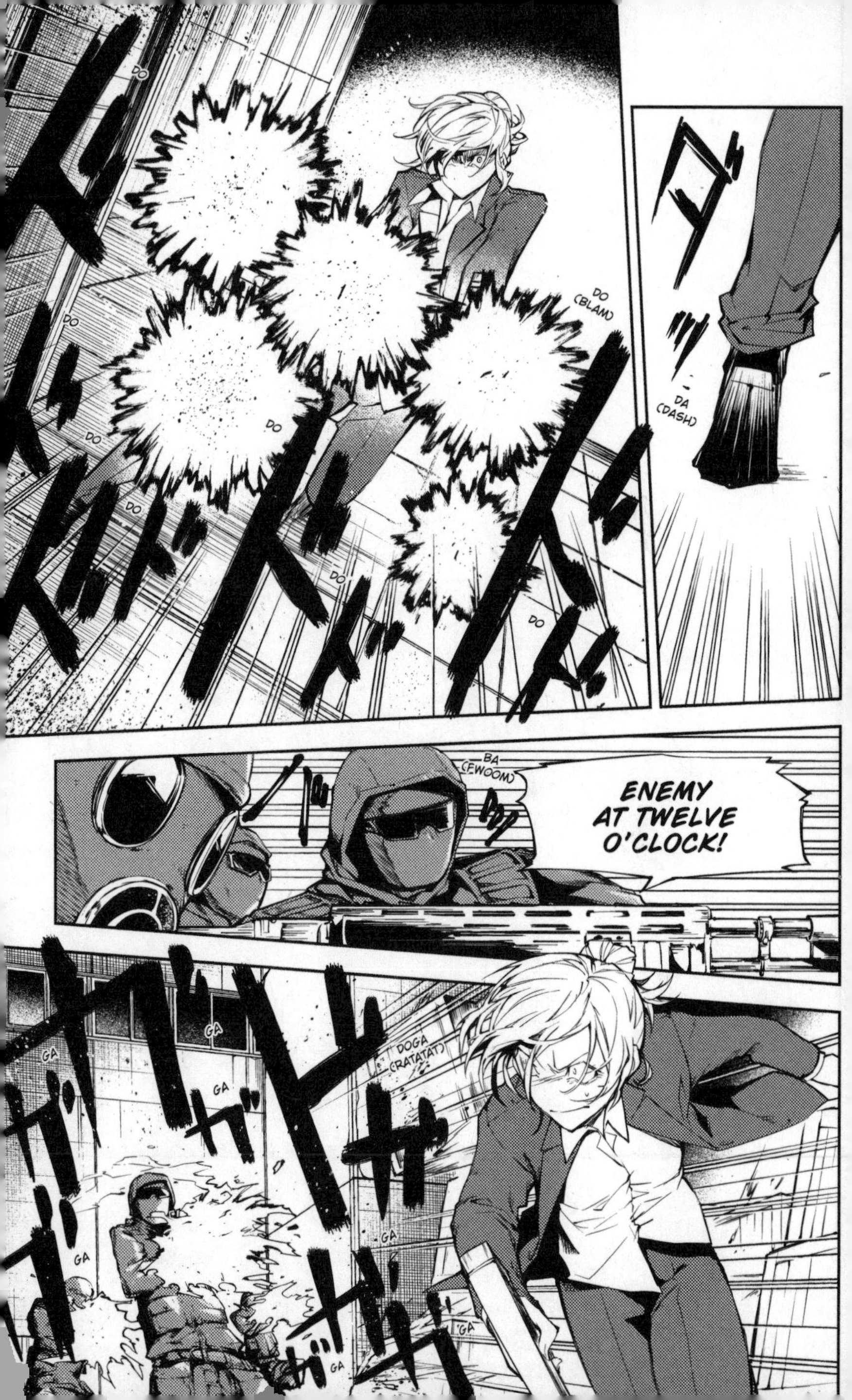
DA (DASH)
DO
DO (BLAM)
DO
DO
DO
DO
DO
DO
BA (FWOOM)
ENEMY AT TWELVE O'CLOCK!
DOGA (RATATAT)
GA
GA
GA
GA
GA
GA
GA

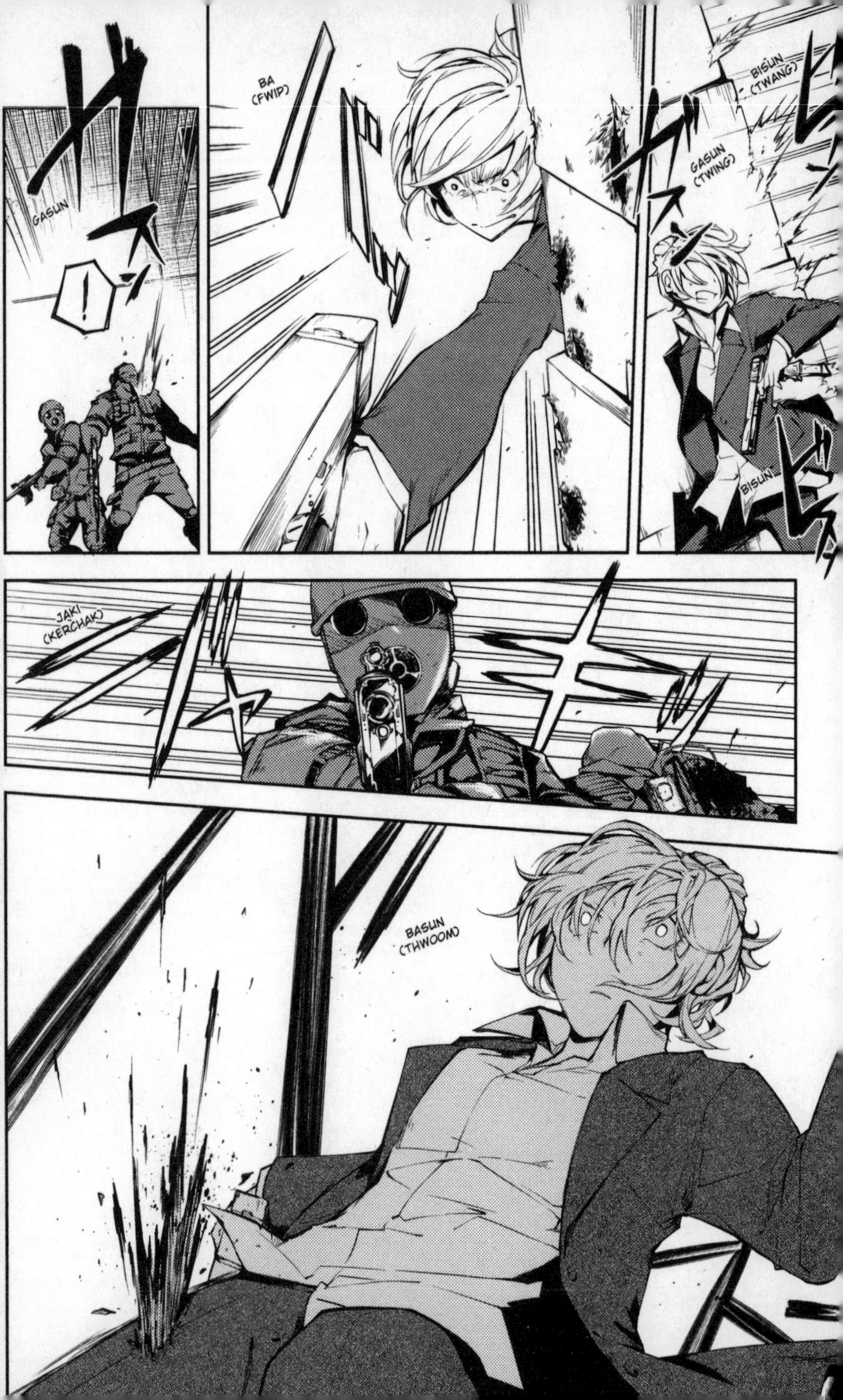
BISUN (TWANG)
GASUN (TWING)
BISUN
BA (FWIP)
GASUN
!
JAKI (KERCHAK)
BASUN (THWOOM)

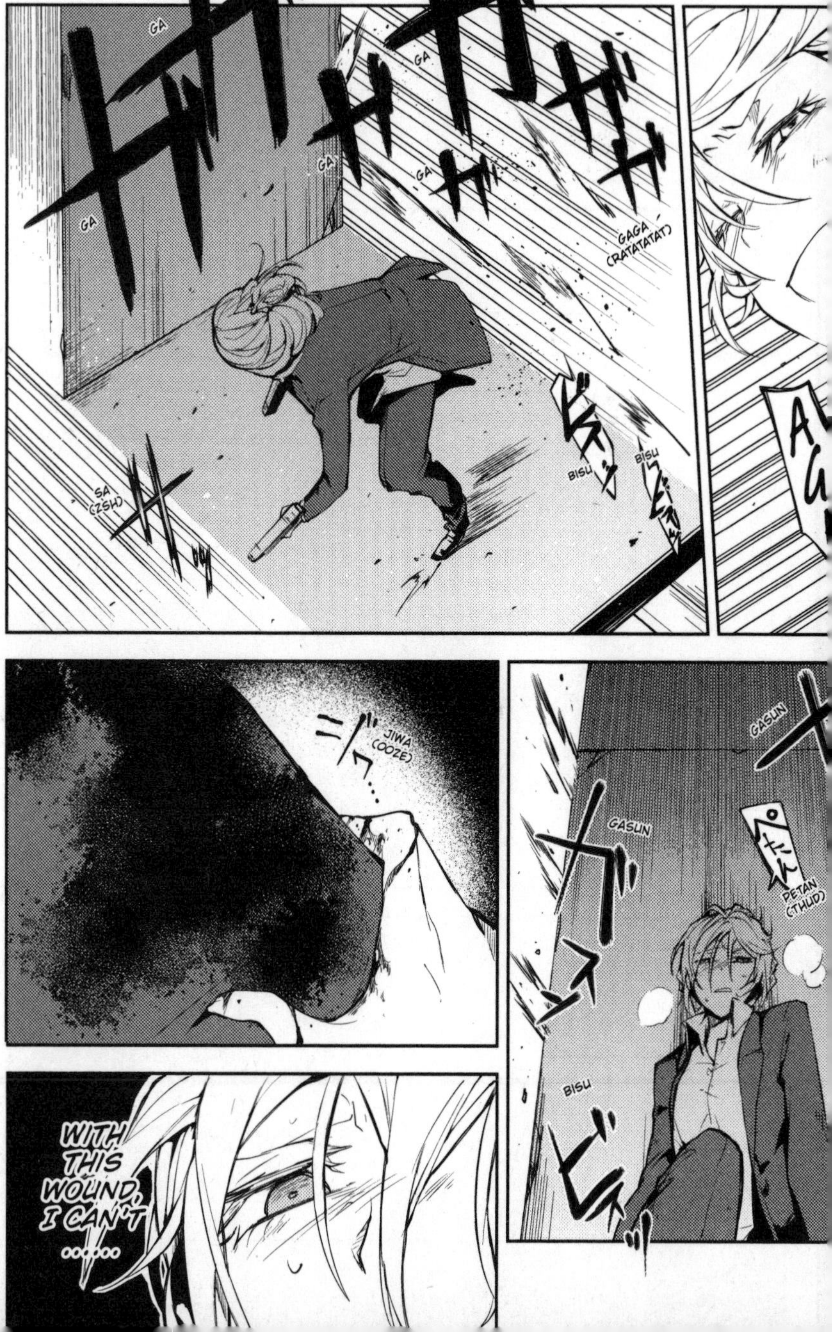
GA
GA
GA
GA
GA
GAGA (RATATATAT)
BISU
BISU
SA (ZSH)
GASUN
GASUN
PETAN (THUD)
BISU
JIWA (OOZE)
WITH THIS WOUND, I CAN'T ......

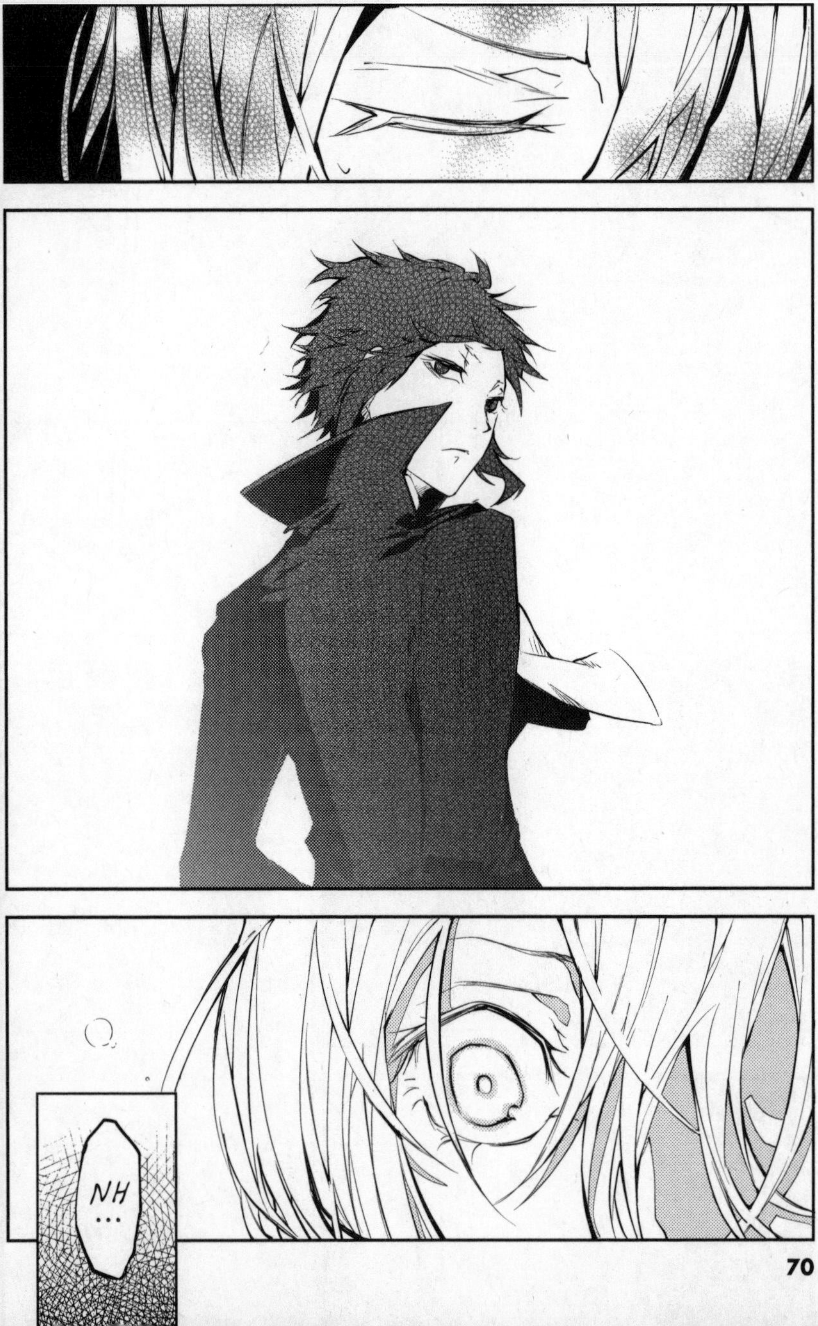
NH...

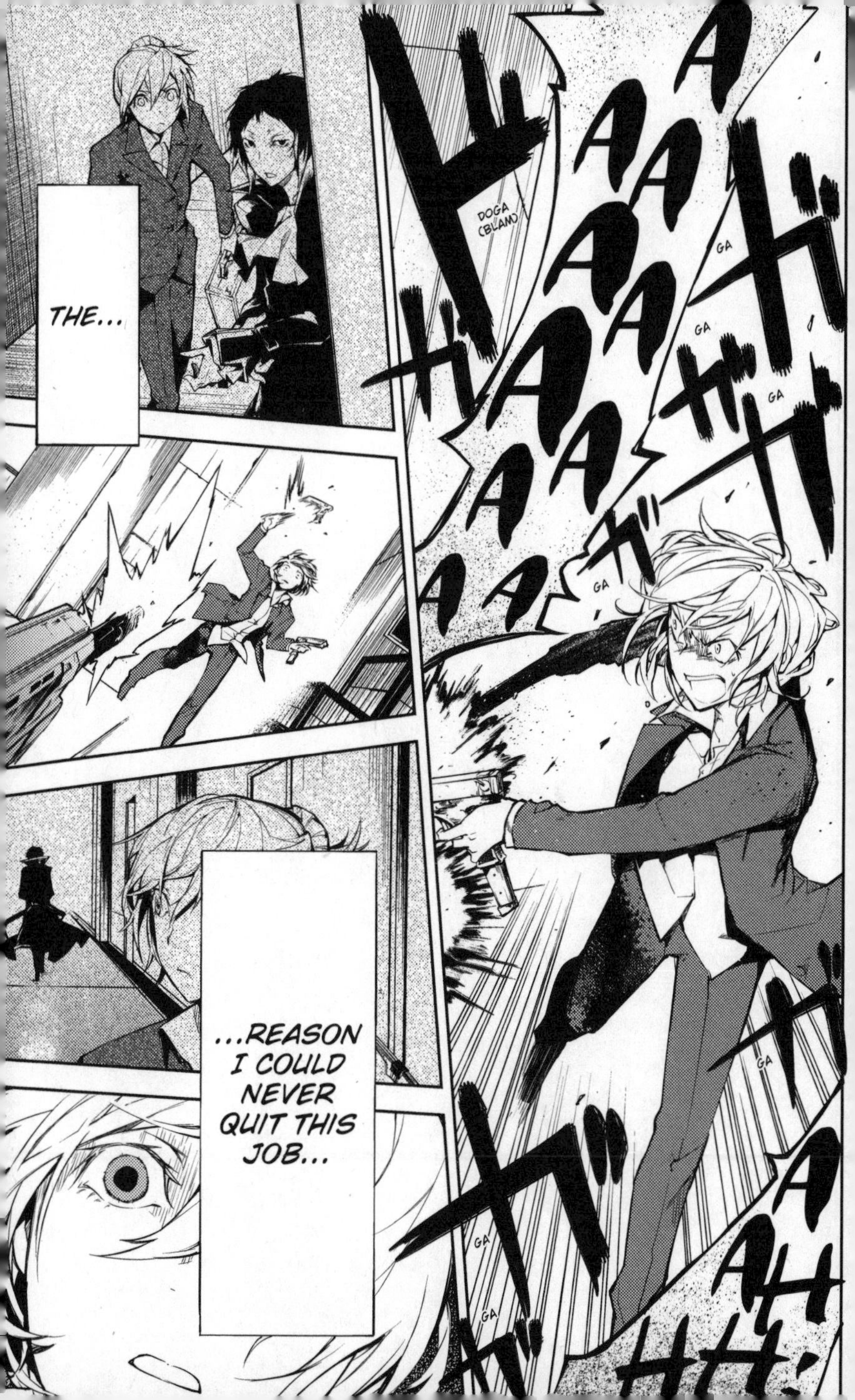
HAAAAAAAAAAAAAA
DOGA (BLAM)
GA
GA
GA
GA
GA
GA
GA
AAAHHH!
THE...
...REASON I COULD NEVER QUIT THIS JOB...

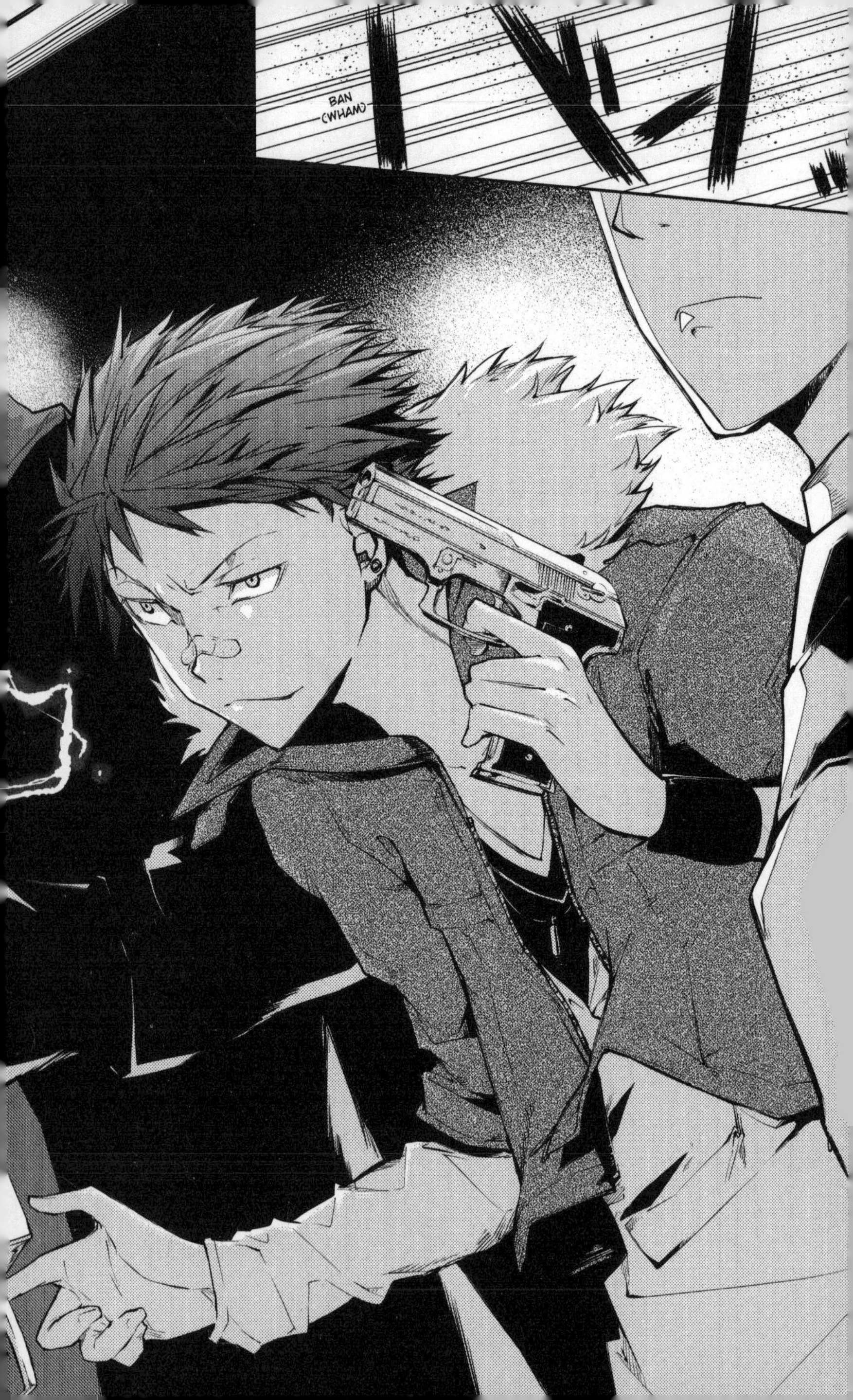
BAN
(WHAM)

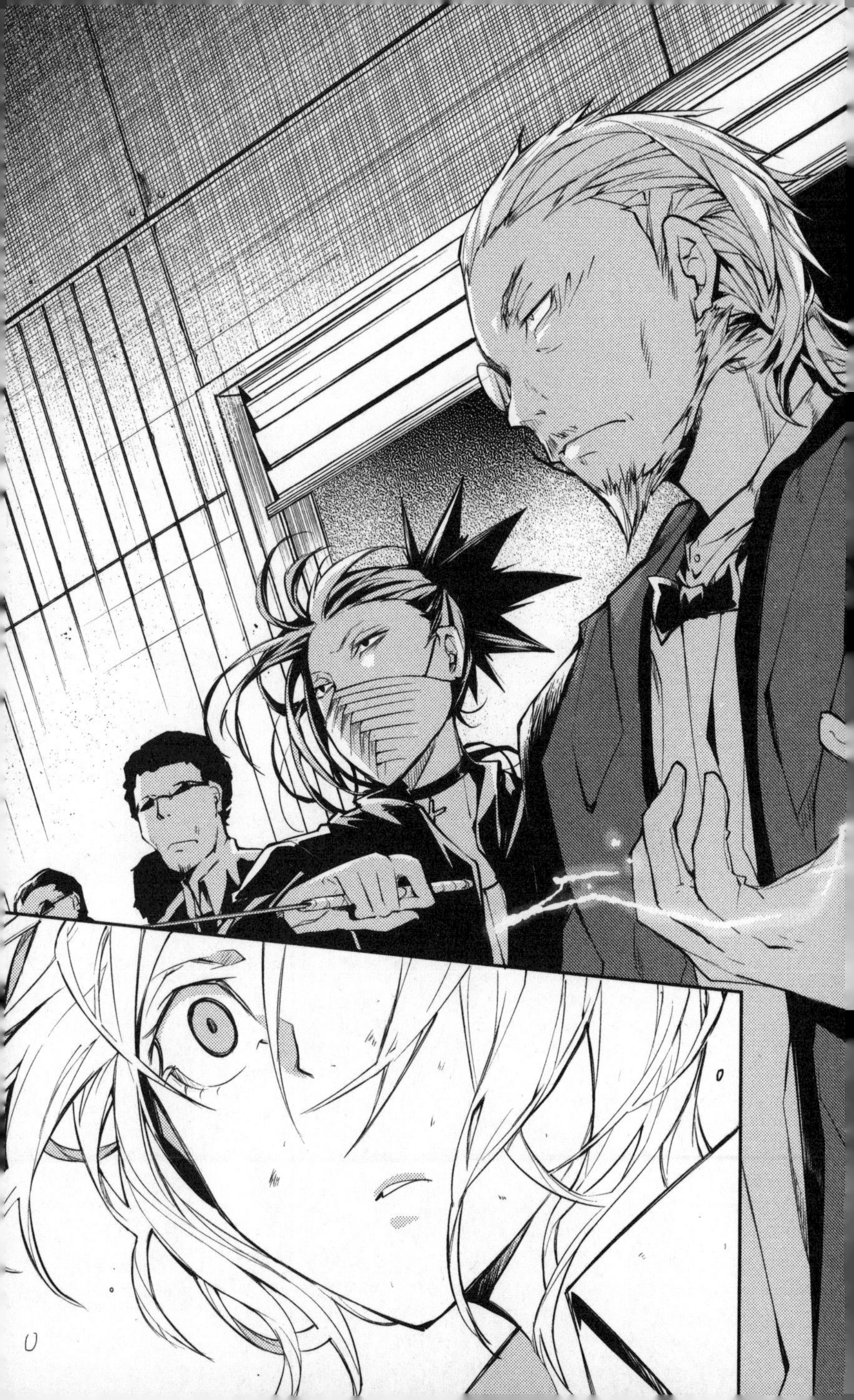

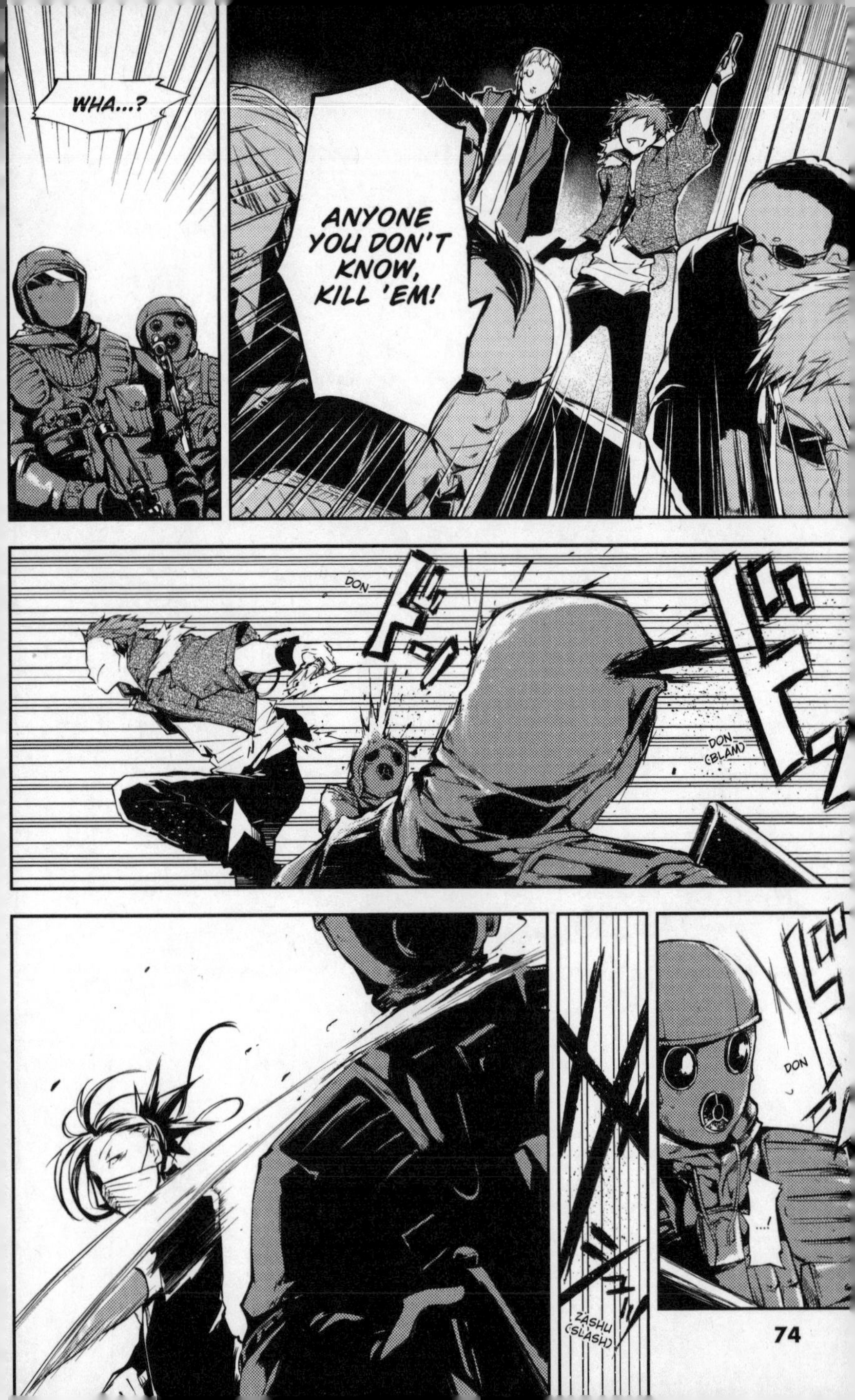
ANYONE YOU DON'T KNOW, KILL 'EM!
WHA...?
DON
DON (BLAM)
DON
...!
ZASHU (SLASH)

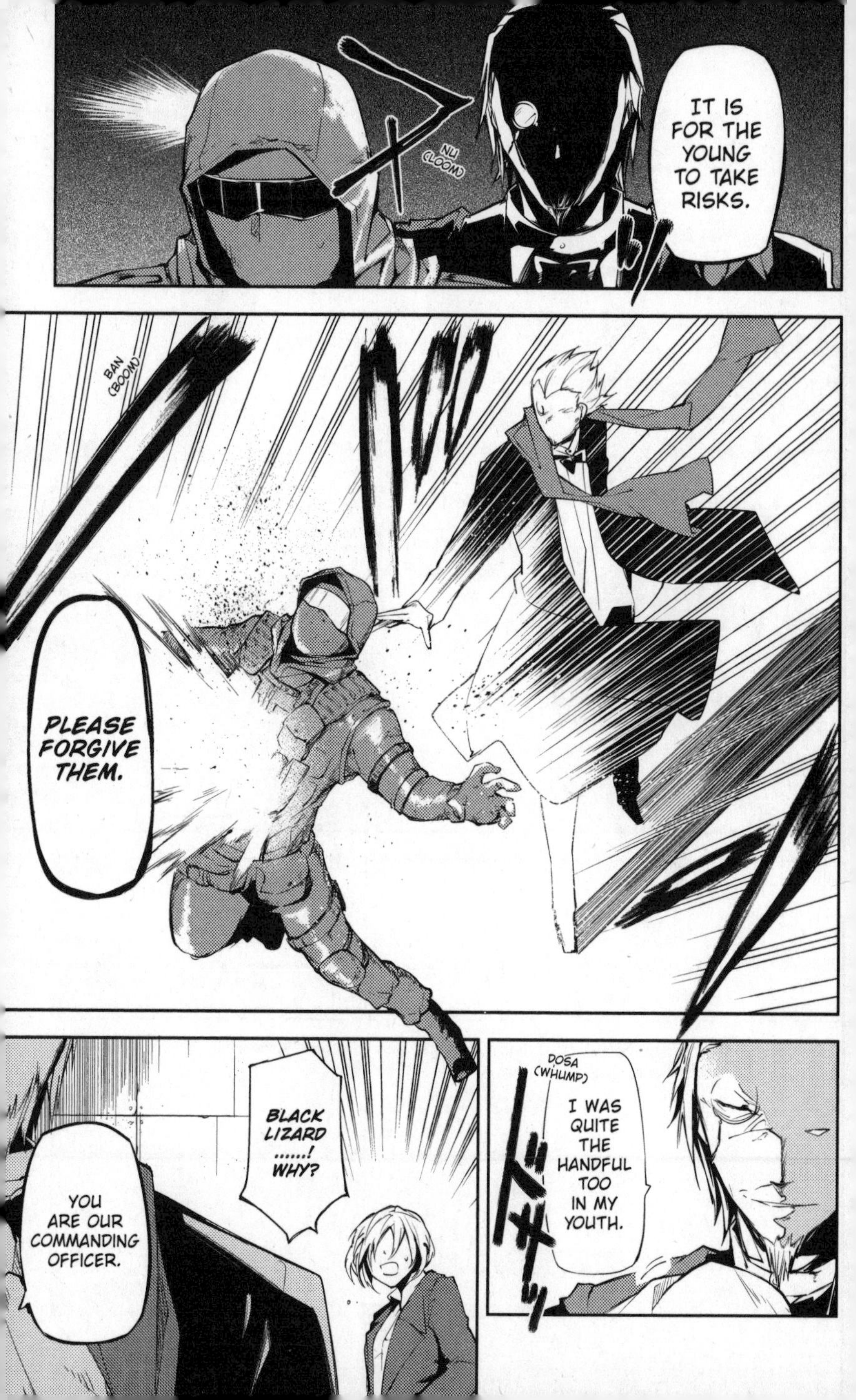
IT IS FOR THE YOUNG TO TAKE RISKS.
NU (LOOM)
BAN (BOOM)
PLEASE FORGIVE THEM.
DOSA (WHUMP)
I WAS QUITE THE HANDFUL TOO IN MY YOUTH.
BLACK LIZARD ......! WHY?
YOU ARE OUR COMMANDING OFFICER.

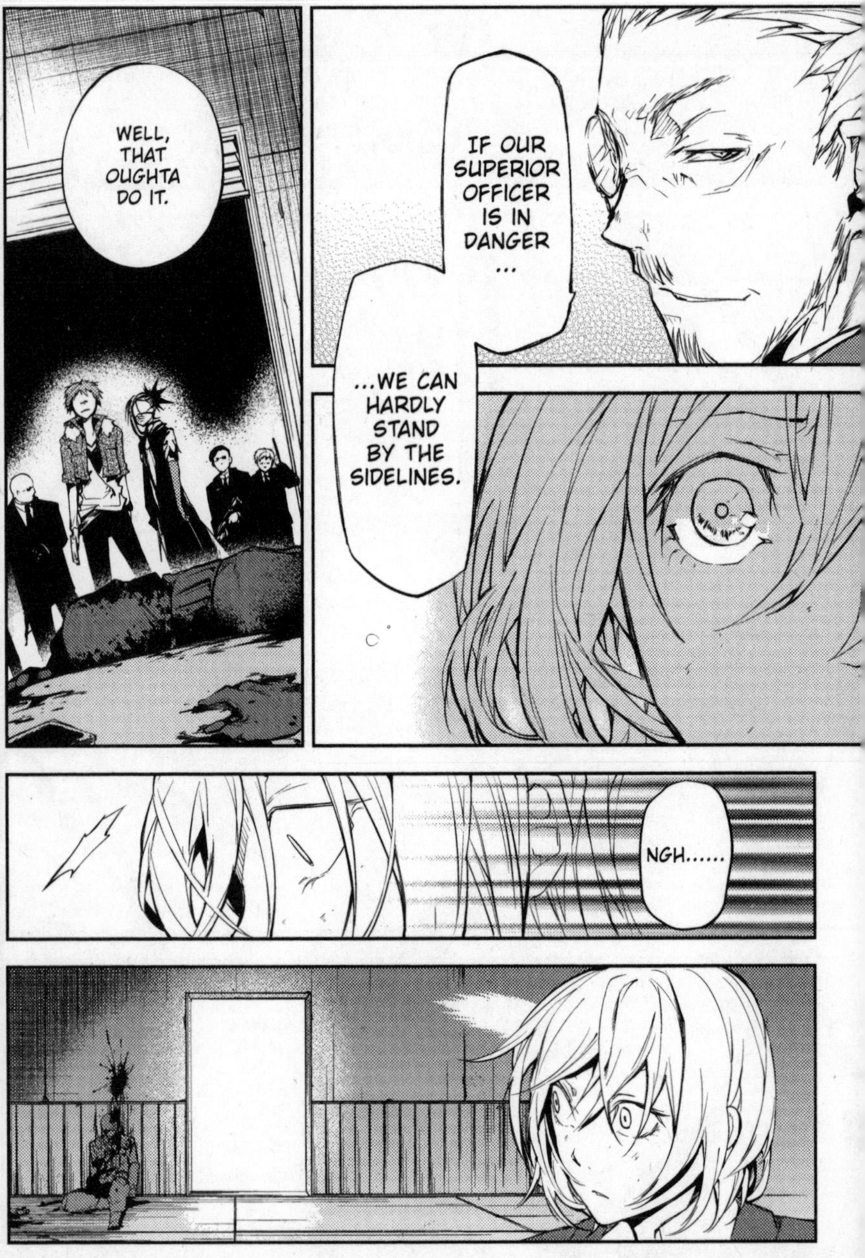
IF OUR SUPERIOR OFFICER IS IN DANGER...
...WE CAN HARDLY STAND BY THE SIDELINES.
WELL, THAT OUGHTA DO IT.
NGH......

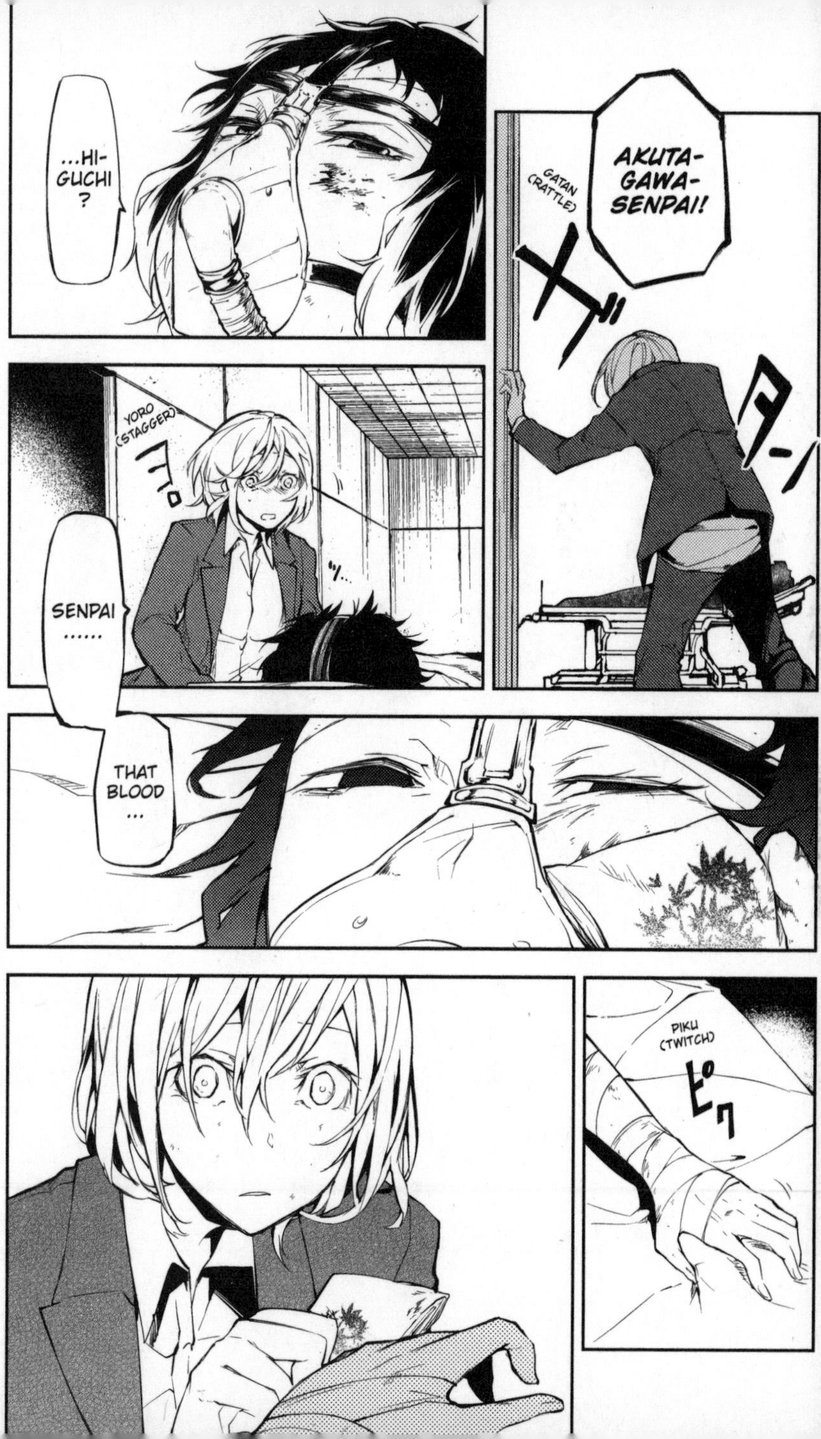

GATAN (RATTLE)
AKUTA-GAWA-SENPAI!
...HI-GUCHI?
YORO (STAGGER)
SENPAI......
THAT BLOOD...
PIKU (TWITCH)

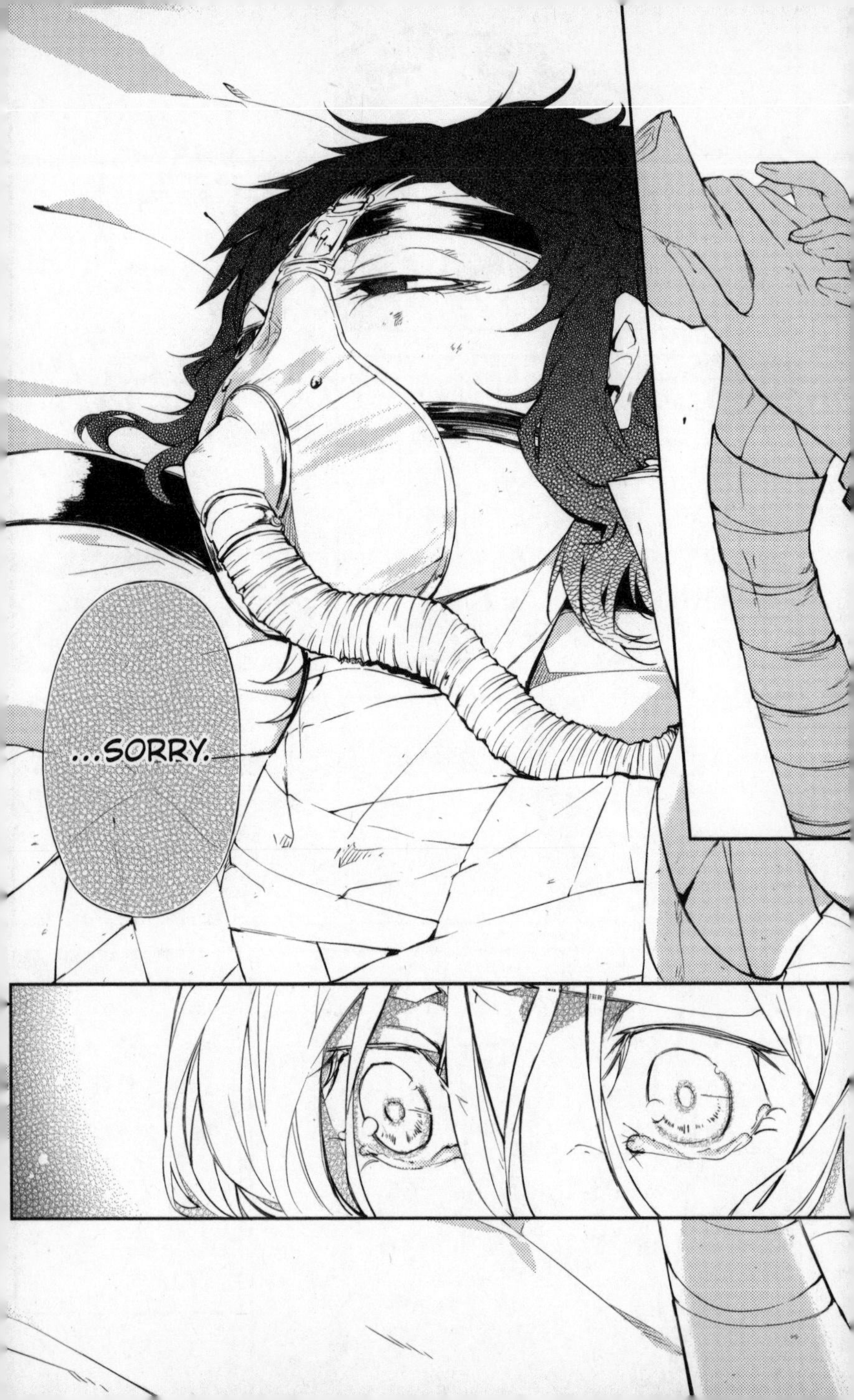
...SORRY.

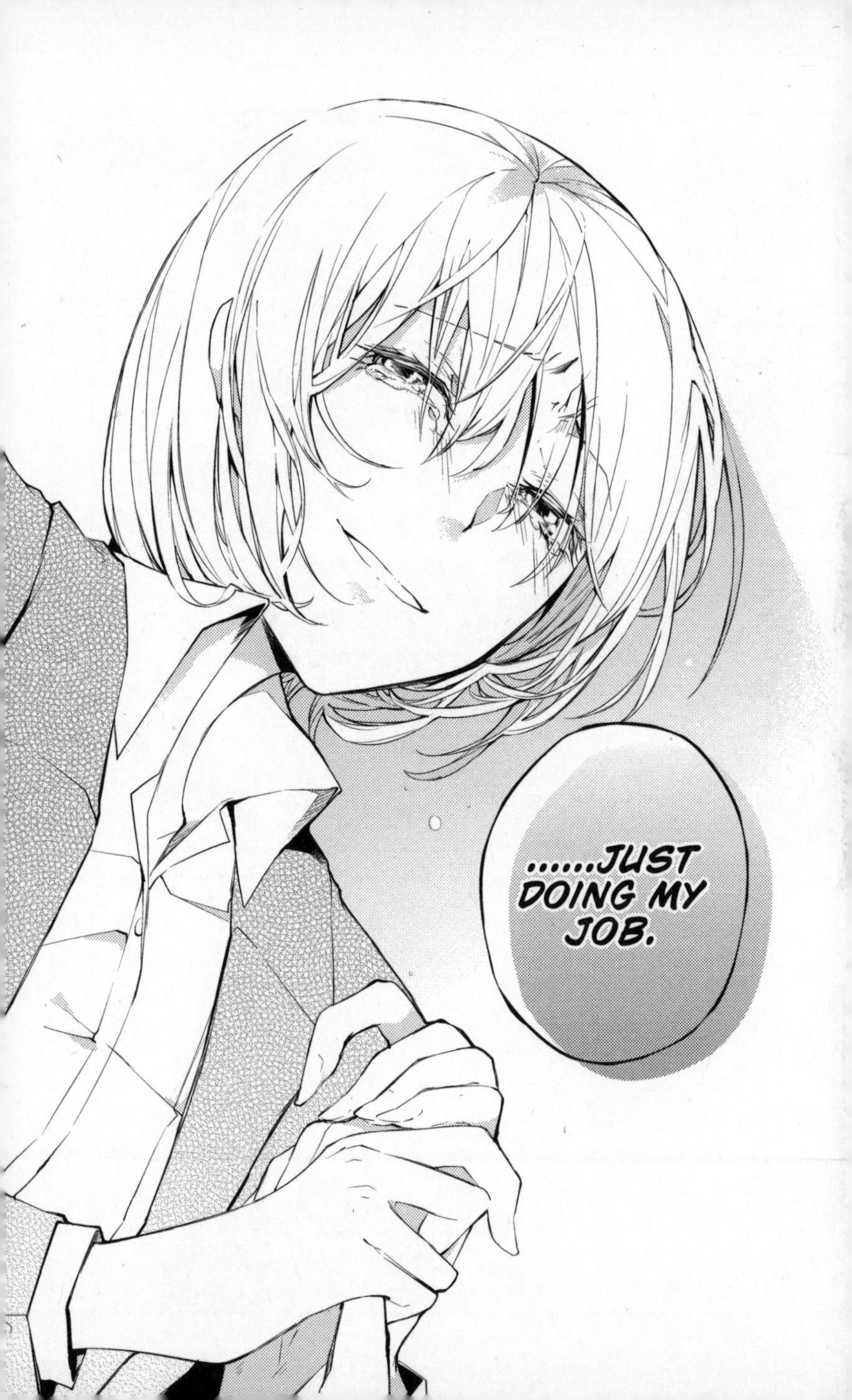
......JUST DOING MY JOB.

IT'S NOT IMPOSSIBLE TO GET OUT OF THE MAFIA...

...BUT I NEVER DID BECAUSE—

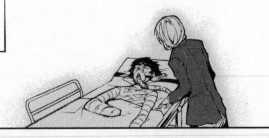

RYUUROU HIROTSU

SKILL: Falling Camellia
Able to send anything he touches flying backward.

AGE: *50*

BIRTH DATE: *July 15*

HEIGHT: *178cm*

WEIGHT: *66kg*

BLOOD TYPE: *A*

LIKES: *Smoking*

DISLIKES: *Society at large*

BUNGO
STRAY DOGS

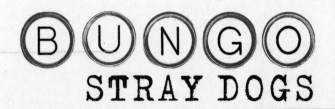

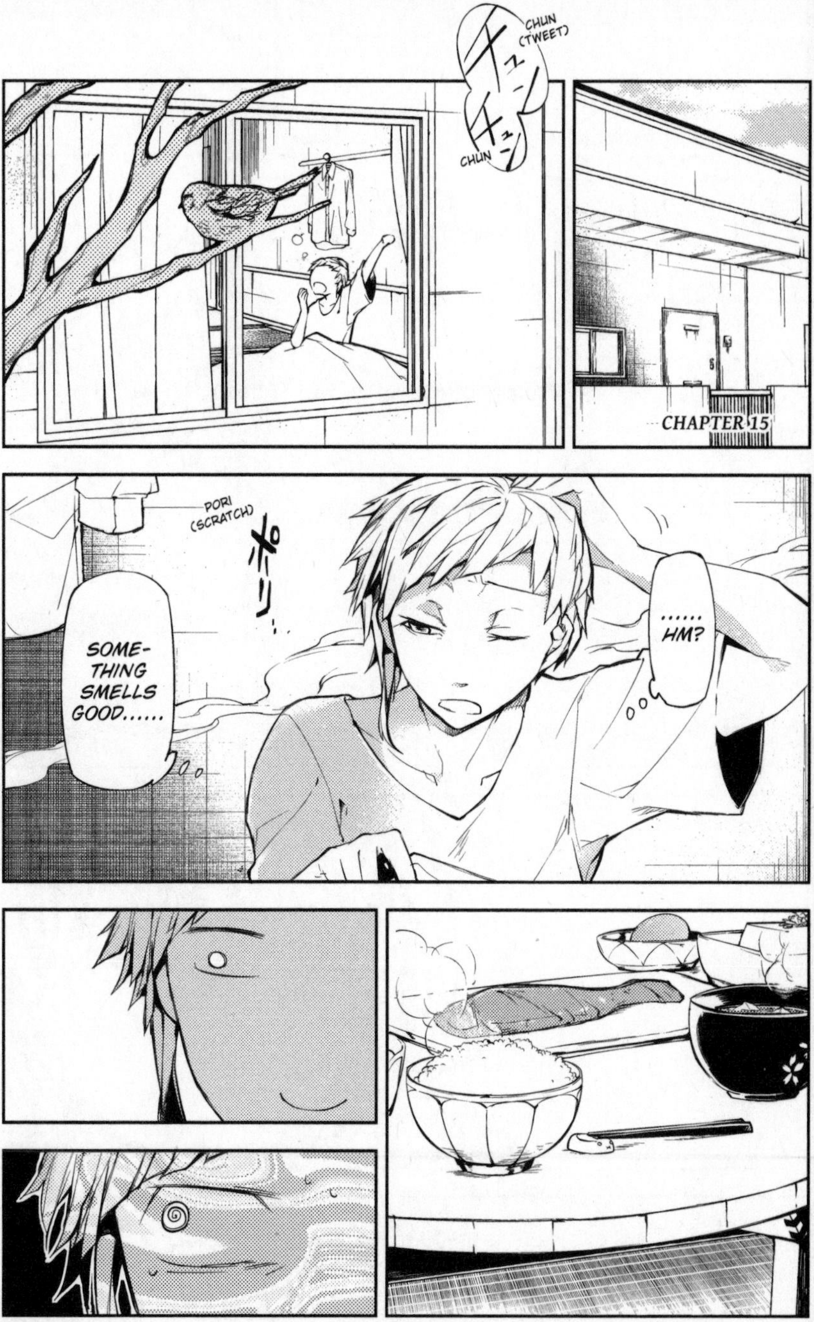
CHAPTER 15
CHUN (TWEET)
CHUN
...... HM?
PORI (SCRATCH)
SOME-THING SMELLS GOOD......

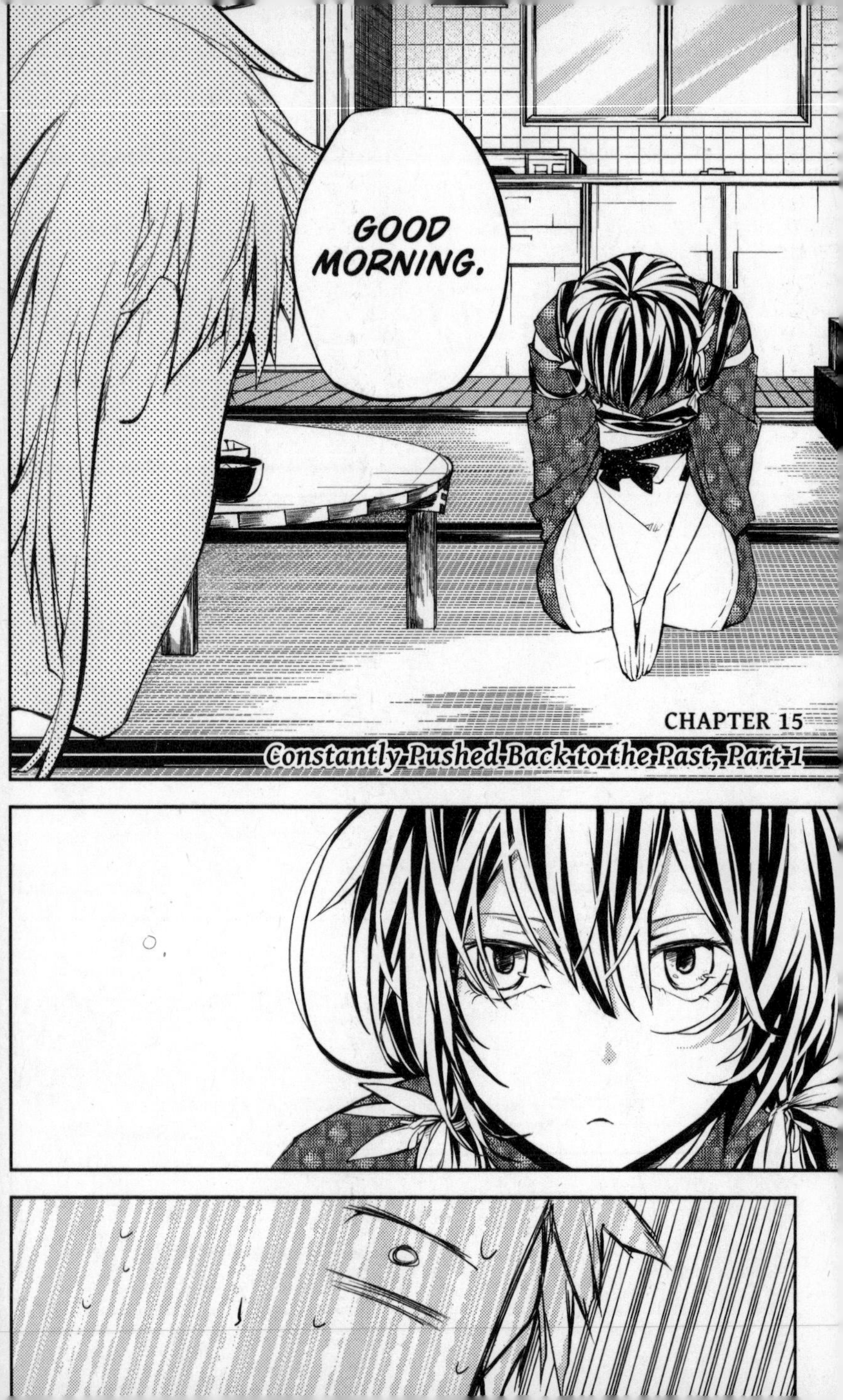
GOOD MORNING.
CHAPTER 15
Constantly Pushed Back to the Past, Part 1

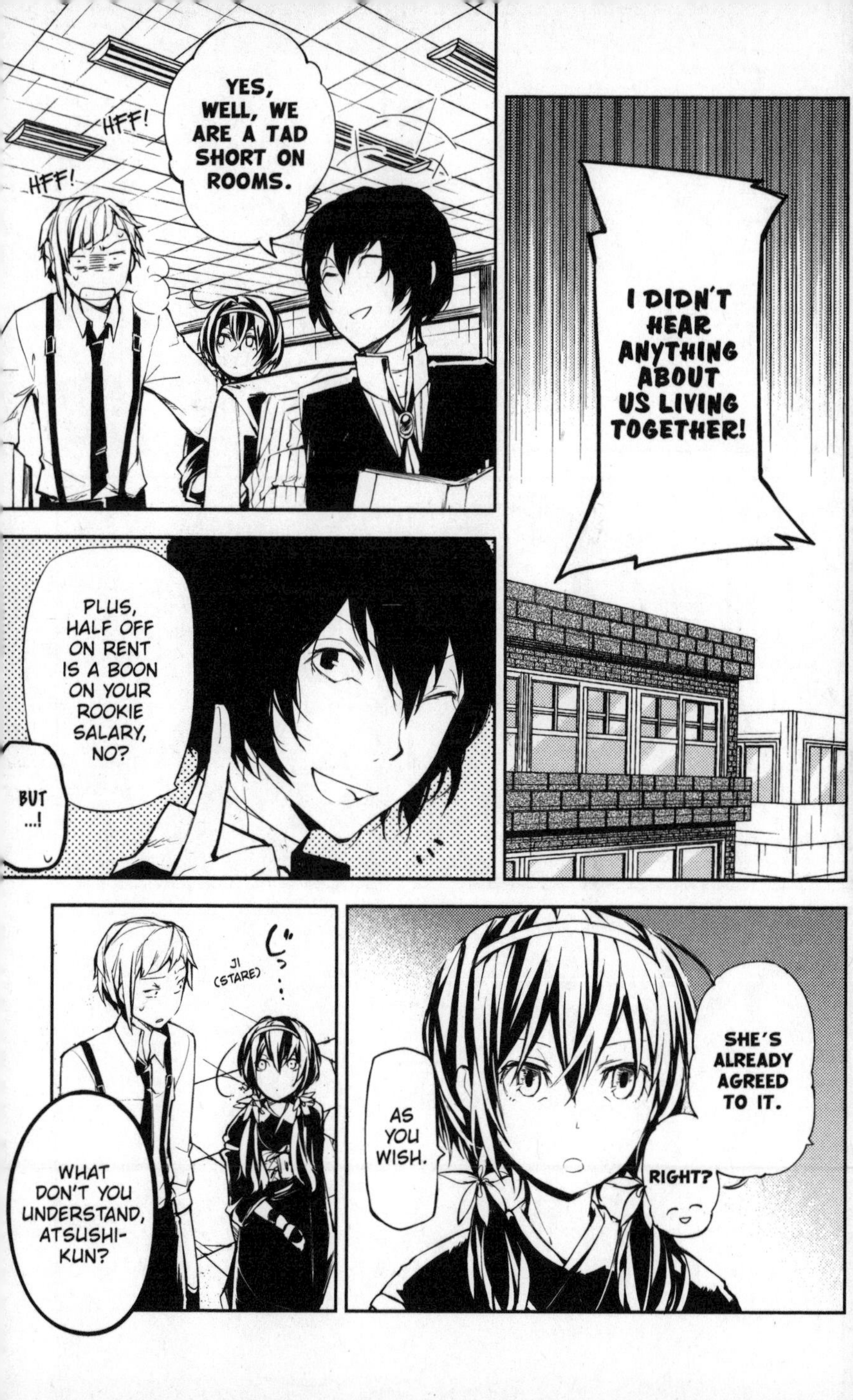
I DIDN'T HEAR ANYTHING ABOUT US LIVING TOGETHER!
YES, WELL, WE ARE A TAD SHORT ON ROOMS.
HFF!
HFF!
PLUS, HALF OFF ON RENT IS A BOON ON YOUR ROOKIE SALARY, NO?
BUT ...!
SHE'S ALREADY AGREED TO IT.
RIGHT?
AS YOU WISH.
じっ…
JI (STARE)
WHAT DON'T YOU UNDERSTAND, ATSUSHI-KUN?

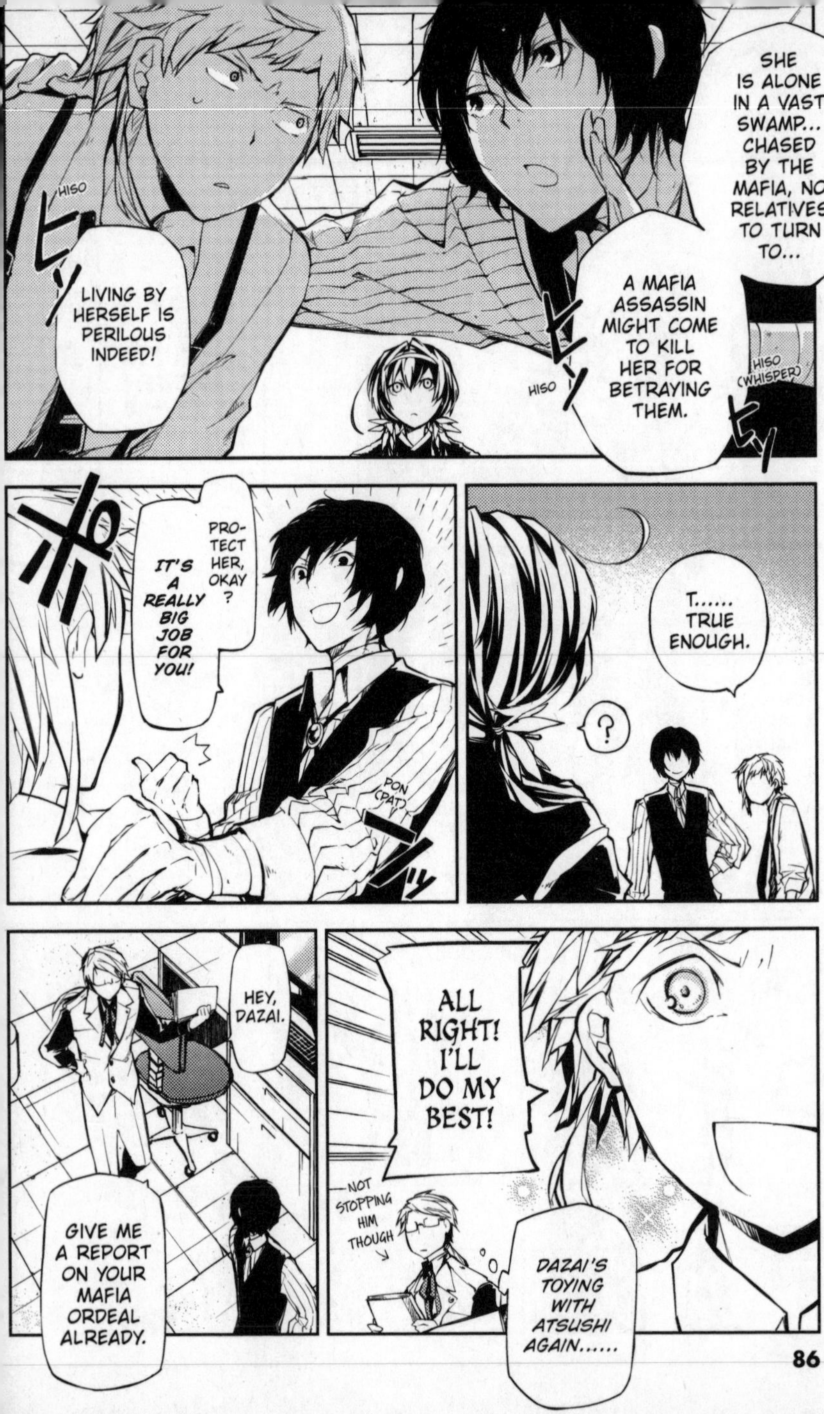
SHE IS ALONE IN A VAST SWAMP... CHASED BY THE MAFIA, NO RELATIVES TO TURN TO...
A MAFIA ASSASSIN MIGHT COME TO KILL HER FOR BETRAYING THEM.
HISO (WHISPER)
HISO
HISO
LIVING BY HERSELF IS PERILOUS INDEED!
T...... TRUE ENOUGH.
?
PRO-TECT HER, OKAY?
IT'S A REALLY BIG JOB FOR YOU!
PON (PAT)
ALL RIGHT! I'LL DO MY BEST!
DAZAI'S TOYING WITH ATSUSHI AGAIN......
NOT STOPPING HIM THOUGH
HEY, DAZAI.
GIVE ME A REPORT ON YOUR MAFIA ORDEAL ALREADY.

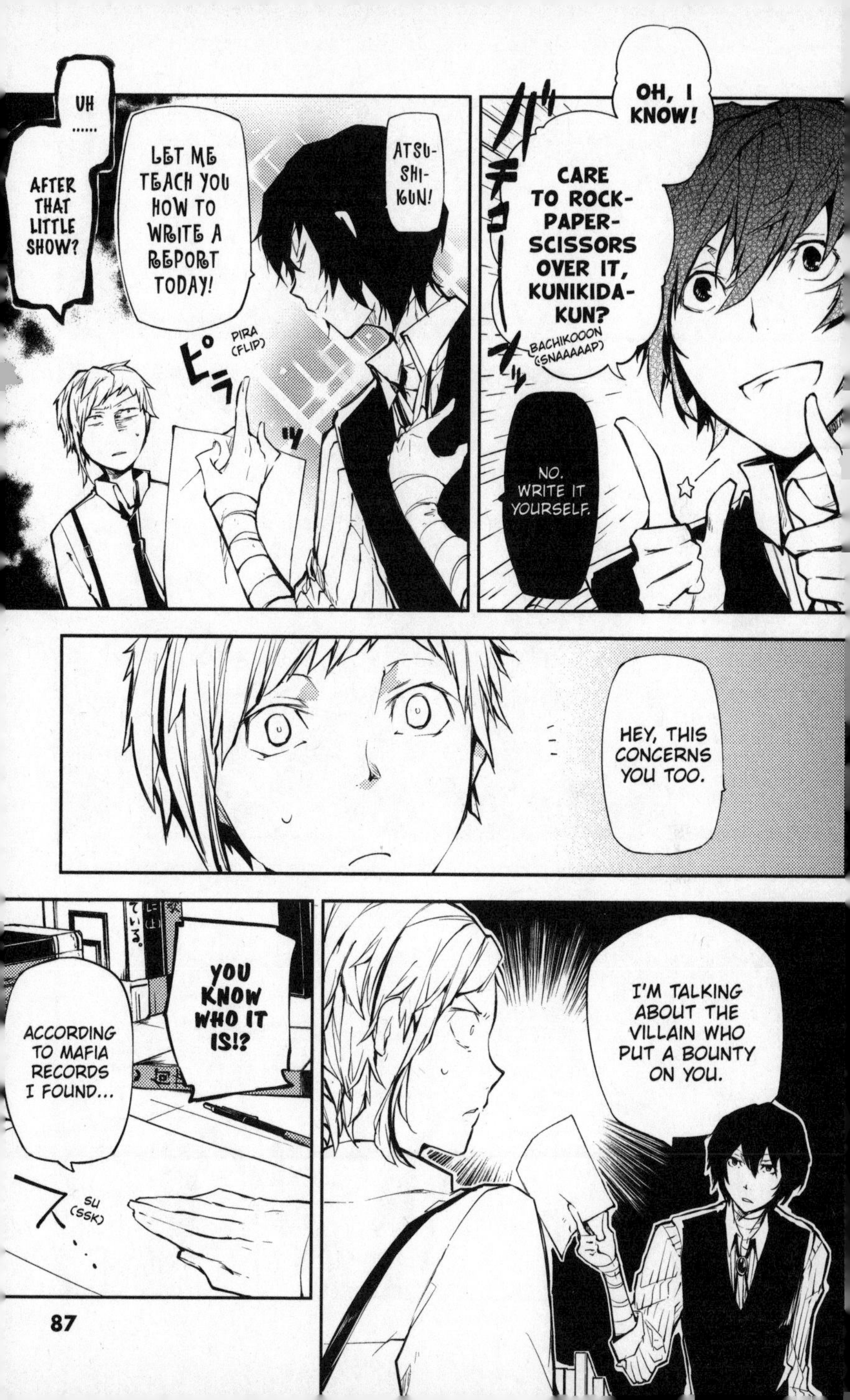
OH, I KNOW!
CARE TO ROCK-PAPER-SCISSORS OVER IT, KUNIKIDA-KUN?
BACHIKOOON (SNAAAAAP)
NO. WRITE IT YOURSELF.
ATSU-SHI-KUN!
LET ME TEACH YOU HOW TO WRITE A REPORT TODAY!
PIRA (FLIP)
UH ...... AFTER THAT LITTLE SHOW?
HEY, THIS CONCERNS YOU TOO.
I'M TALKING ABOUT THE VILLAIN WHO PUT A BOUNTY ON YOU.
YOU KNOW WHO IT IS!?
ACCORDING TO MAFIA RECORDS I FOUND...
SU (SSK)

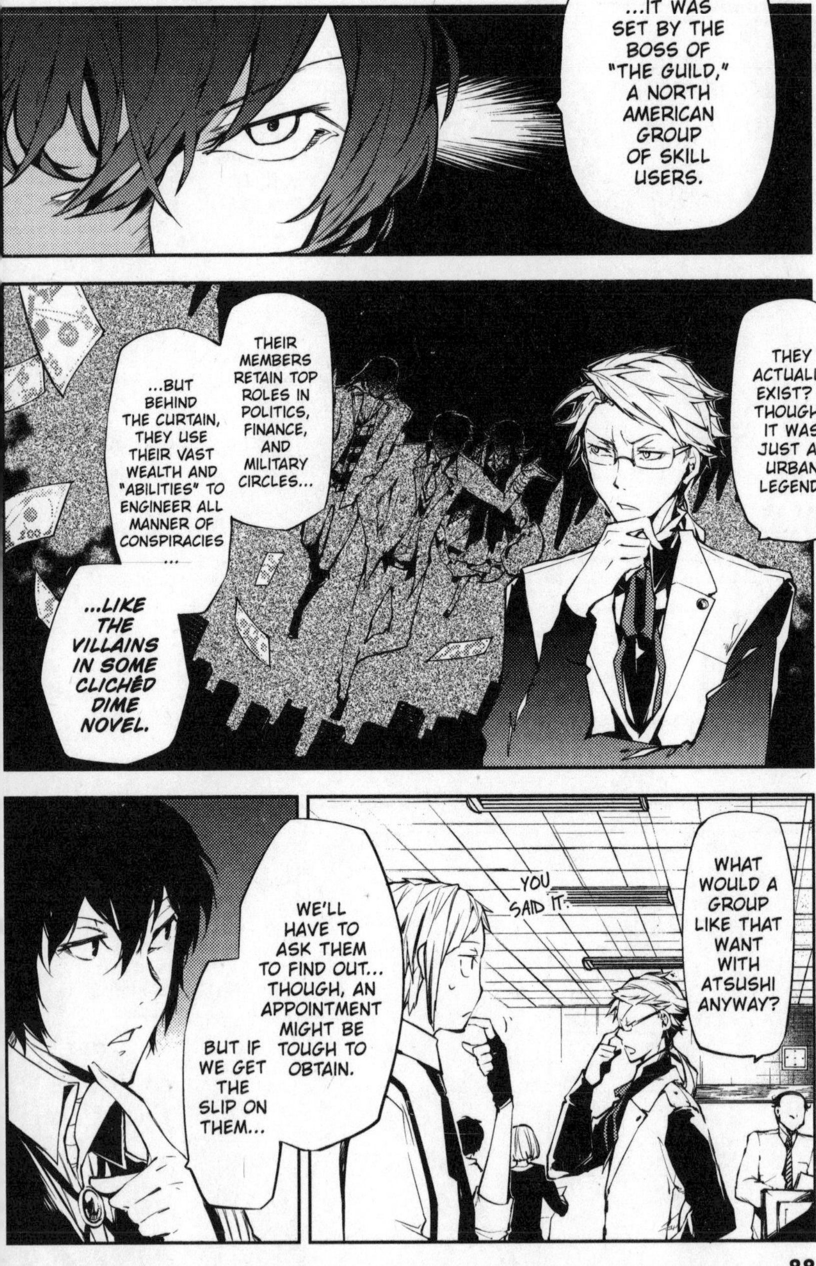
...IT WAS SET BY THE BOSS OF "THE GUILD," A NORTH AMERICAN GROUP OF SKILL USERS.
THEY ACTUALLY EXIST? I THOUGHT IT WAS JUST AN URBAN LEGEND.
THEIR MEMBERS RETAIN TOP ROLES IN POLITICS, FINANCE, AND MILITARY CIRCLES...
...BUT BEHIND THE CURTAIN, THEY USE THEIR VAST WEALTH AND "ABILITIES" TO ENGINEER ALL MANNER OF CONSPIRACIES...
...LIKE THE VILLAINS IN SOME CLICHÉD DIME NOVEL.
WHAT WOULD A GROUP LIKE THAT WANT WITH ATSUSHI ANYWAY?
YOU SAID IT.
WE'LL HAVE TO ASK THEM TO FIND OUT... THOUGH, AN APPOINTMENT MIGHT BE TOUGH TO OBTAIN.
BUT IF WE GET THE SLIP ON THEM...

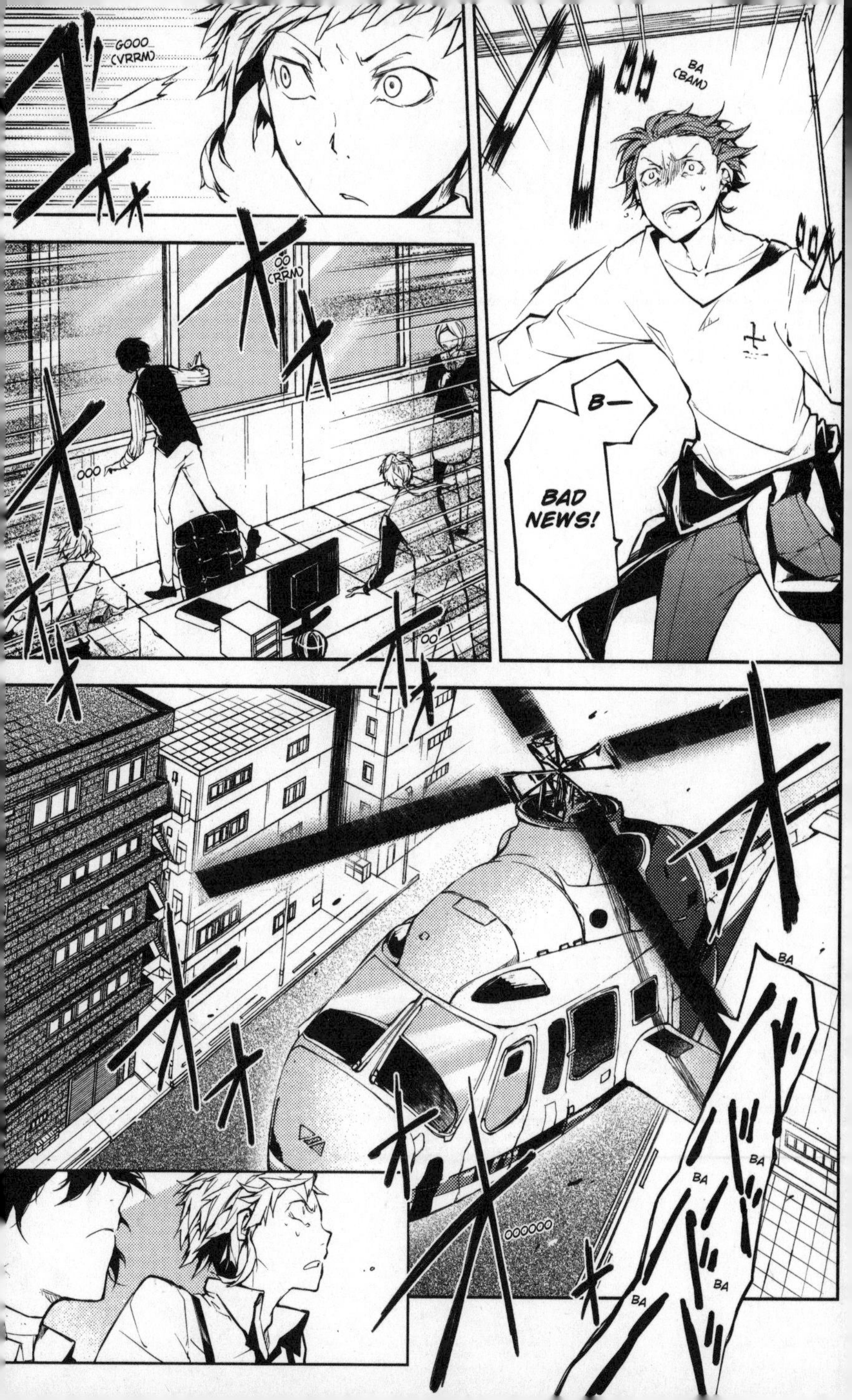
BA (BAM)
B—
BAD NEWS!
GOOO (VRRM)
OO (RRM)
OOO
BA
BA
BA
BA
BA
OOOOOO

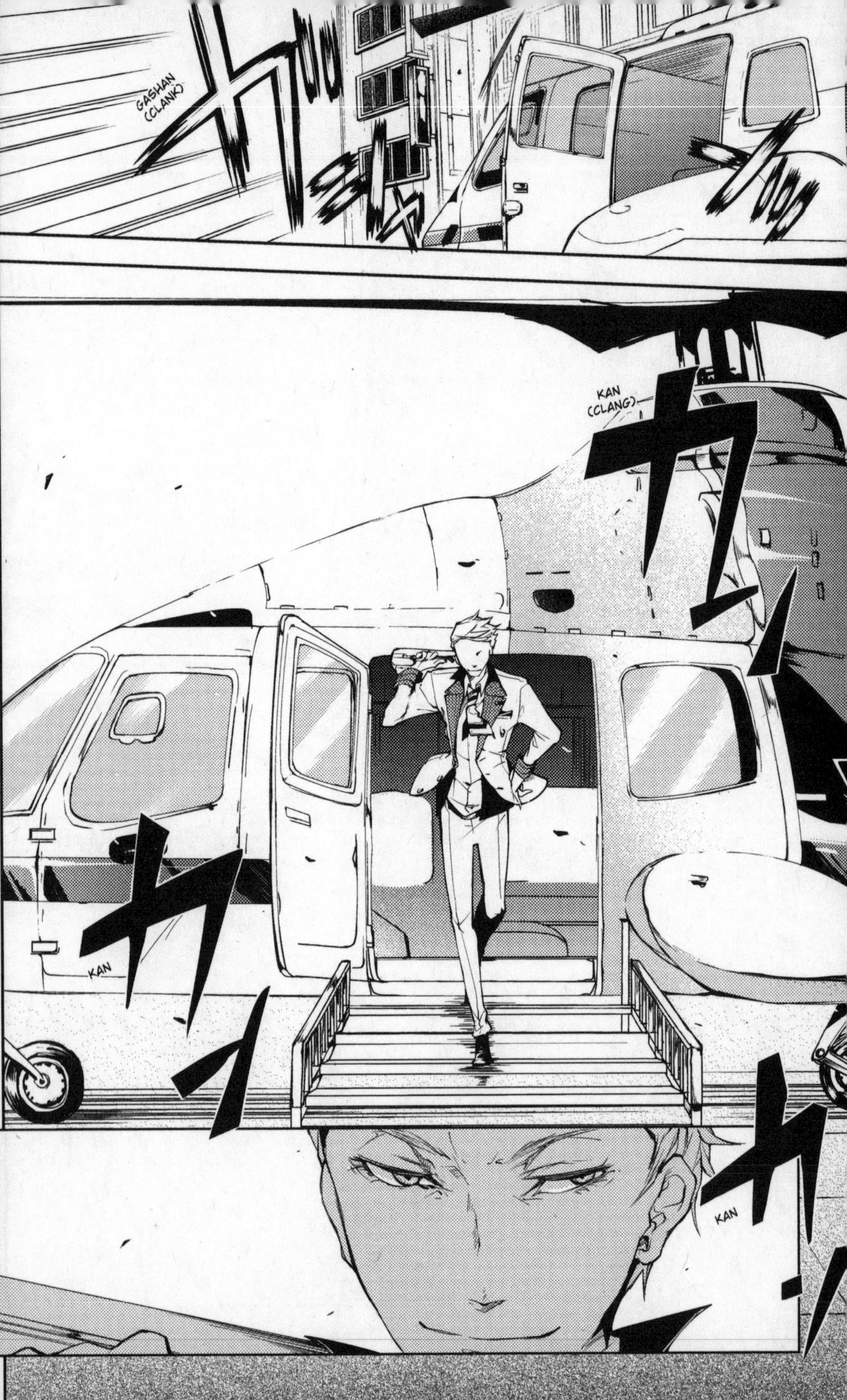
GASHAN (CLANK)
KAN (CLANG)
KAN
KAN

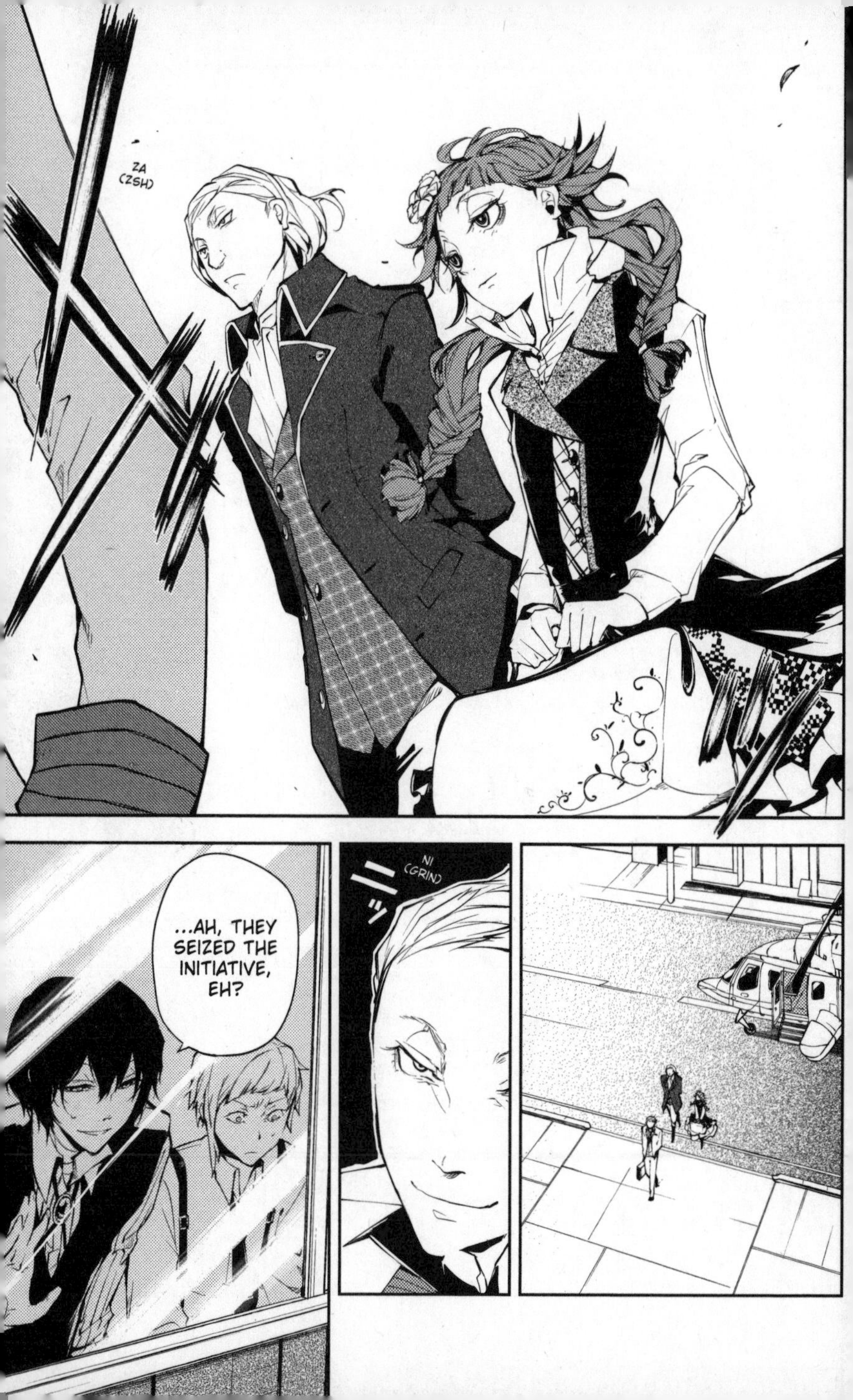
ZA
(ZSH)
NI
(GRIN)
...AH, THEY SEIZED THE INITIATIVE, EH?

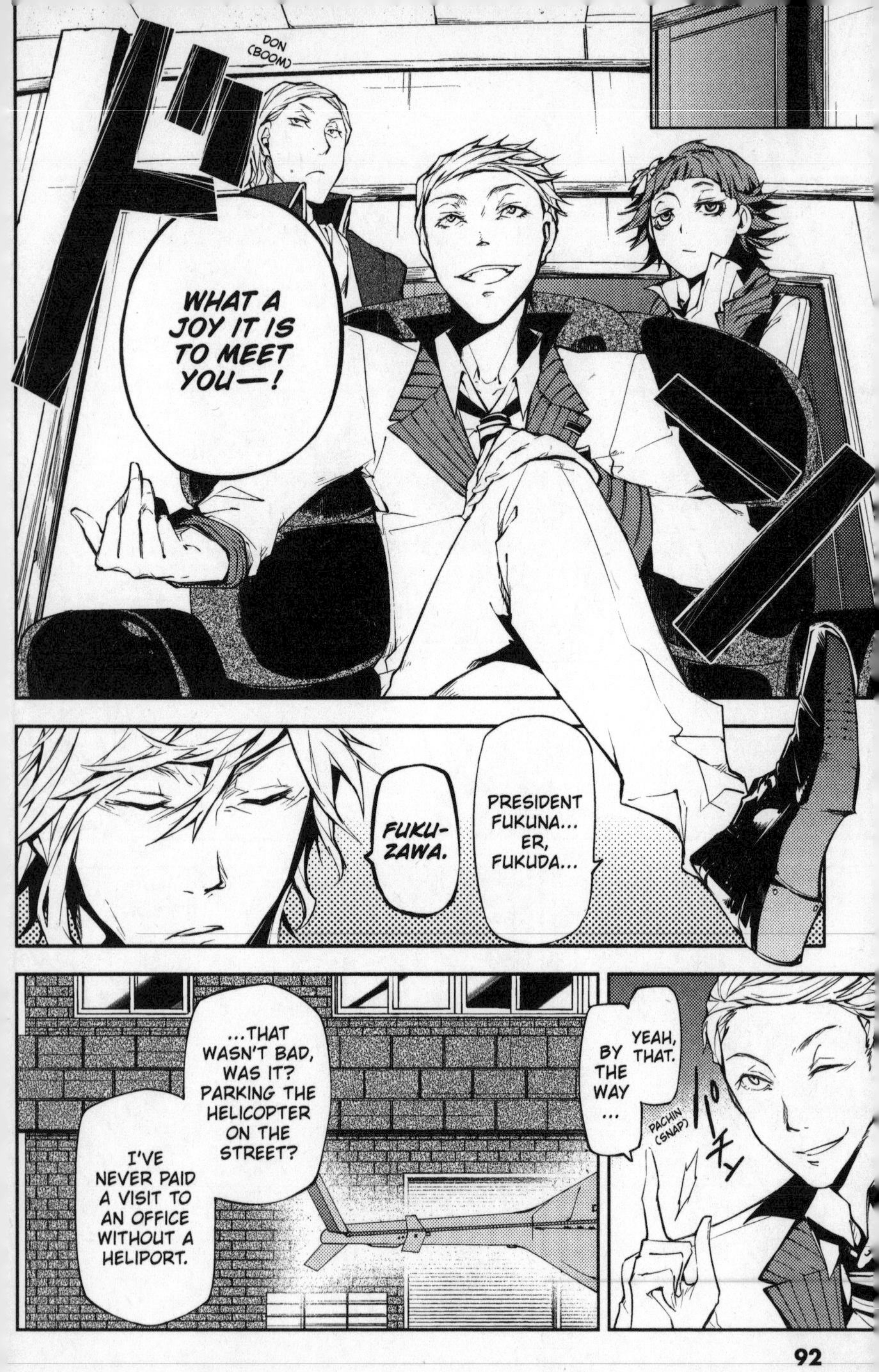
DON (BOOM)
WHAT A JOY IT IS TO MEET YOU—!
PRESIDENT FUKUNA... ER, FUKUDA...
FUKU-ZAWA.
YEAH, THAT.
BY THE WAY...
PACHIN (SNAP)
...THAT WASN'T BAD, WAS IT? PARKING THE HELICOPTER ON THE STREET?
I'VE NEVER PAID A VISIT TO AN OFFICE WITHOUT A HELIPORT.

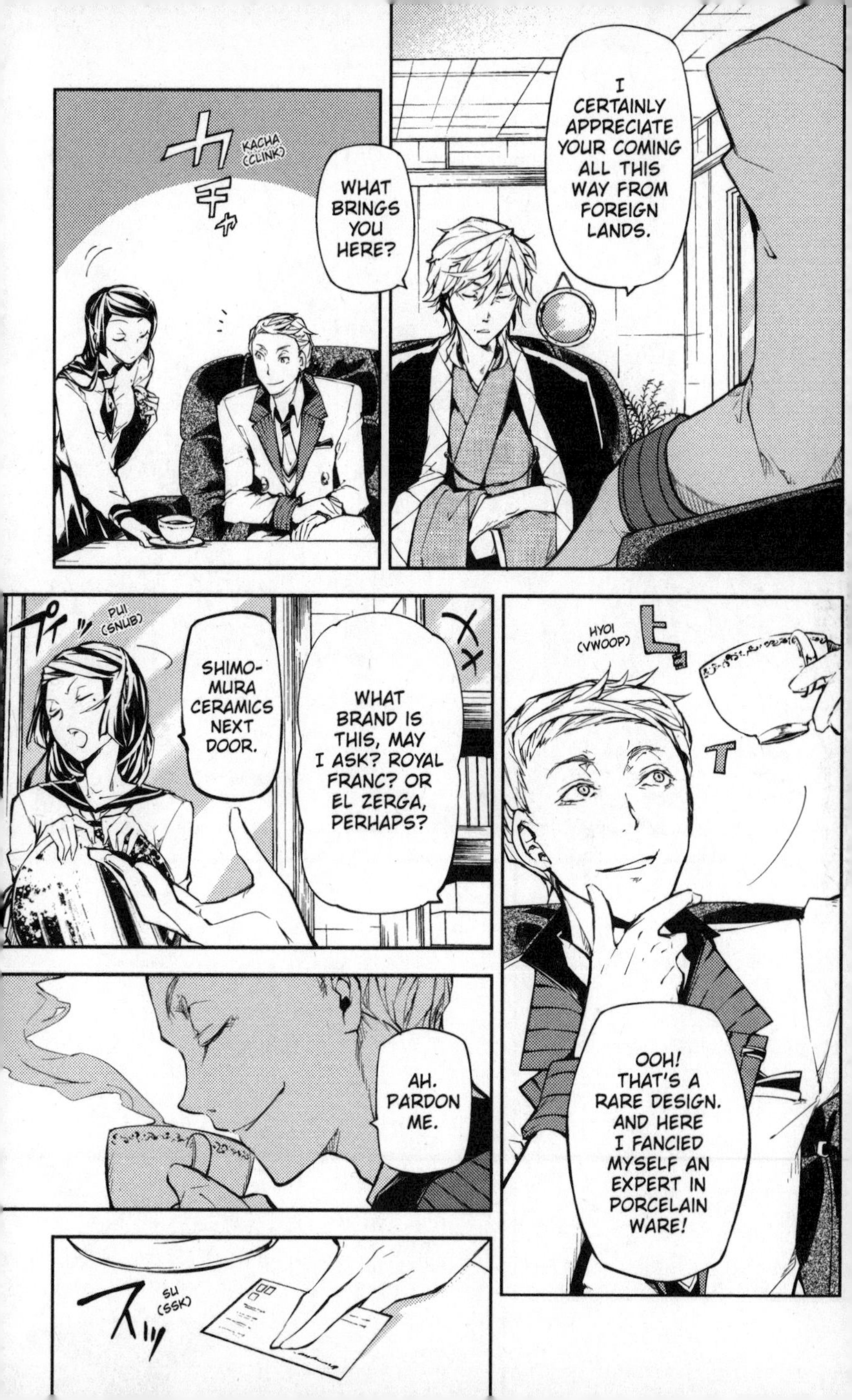
I CERTAINLY APPRECIATE YOUR COMING ALL THIS WAY FROM FOREIGN LANDS.
WHAT BRINGS YOU HERE?
KACHA (CLINK)
HYOI (VWOOP)
OOH! THAT'S A RARE DESIGN. AND HERE I FANCIED MYSELF AN EXPERT IN PORCELAIN WARE!
WHAT BRAND IS THIS, MAY I ASK? ROYAL FRANC? OR EL ZERGA, PERHAPS?
SHIMOMURA CERAMICS NEXT DOOR.
PUI (SNUB)
AH. PARDON ME.
SU (SSK)

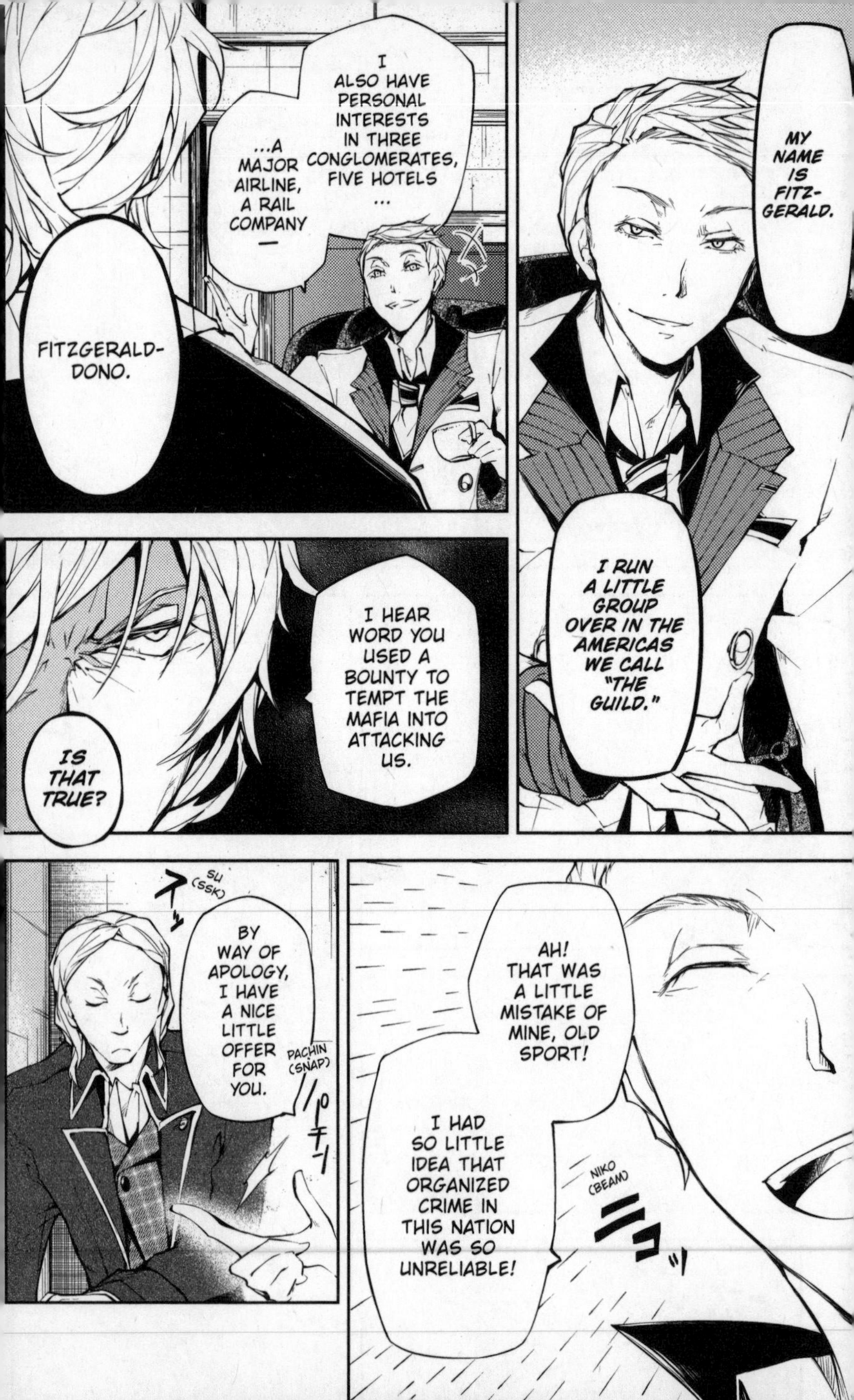
MY NAME IS FITZGERALD.
I RUN A LITTLE GROUP OVER IN THE AMERICAS WE CALL "THE GUILD."
I ALSO HAVE PERSONAL INTERESTS IN THREE CONGLOMERATES, FIVE HOTELS...
...A MAJOR AIRLINE, A RAIL COMPANY—
FITZGERALD-DONO.
I HEAR WORD YOU USED A BOUNTY TO TEMPT THE MAFIA INTO ATTACKING US.
IS THAT TRUE?
AH! THAT WAS A LITTLE MISTAKE OF MINE, OLD SPORT!
I HAD SO LITTLE IDEA THAT ORGANIZED CRIME IN THIS NATION WAS SO UNRELIABLE!
NIKO (BEAM)
SU (SSK)
BY WAY OF APOLOGY, I HAVE A NICE LITTLE OFFER FOR YOU.
PACHIN (SNAP)

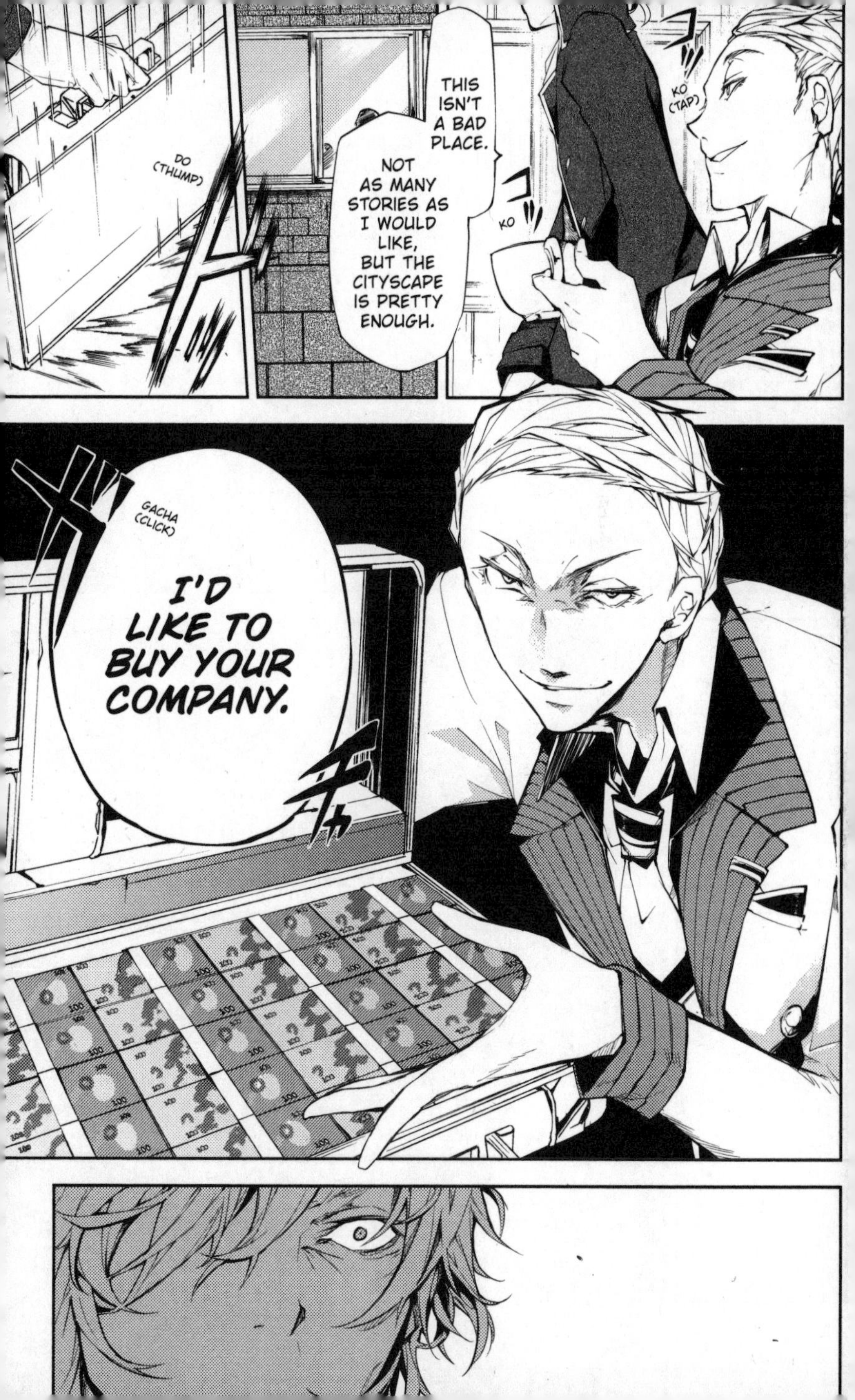
KO (TAP)
THIS ISN'T A BAD PLACE.
NOT AS MANY STORIES AS I WOULD LIKE, BUT THE CITYSCAPE IS PRETTY ENOUGH.
KO
DO (THUMP)
GACHA (CLICK)
I'D LIKE TO BUY YOUR COMPANY.

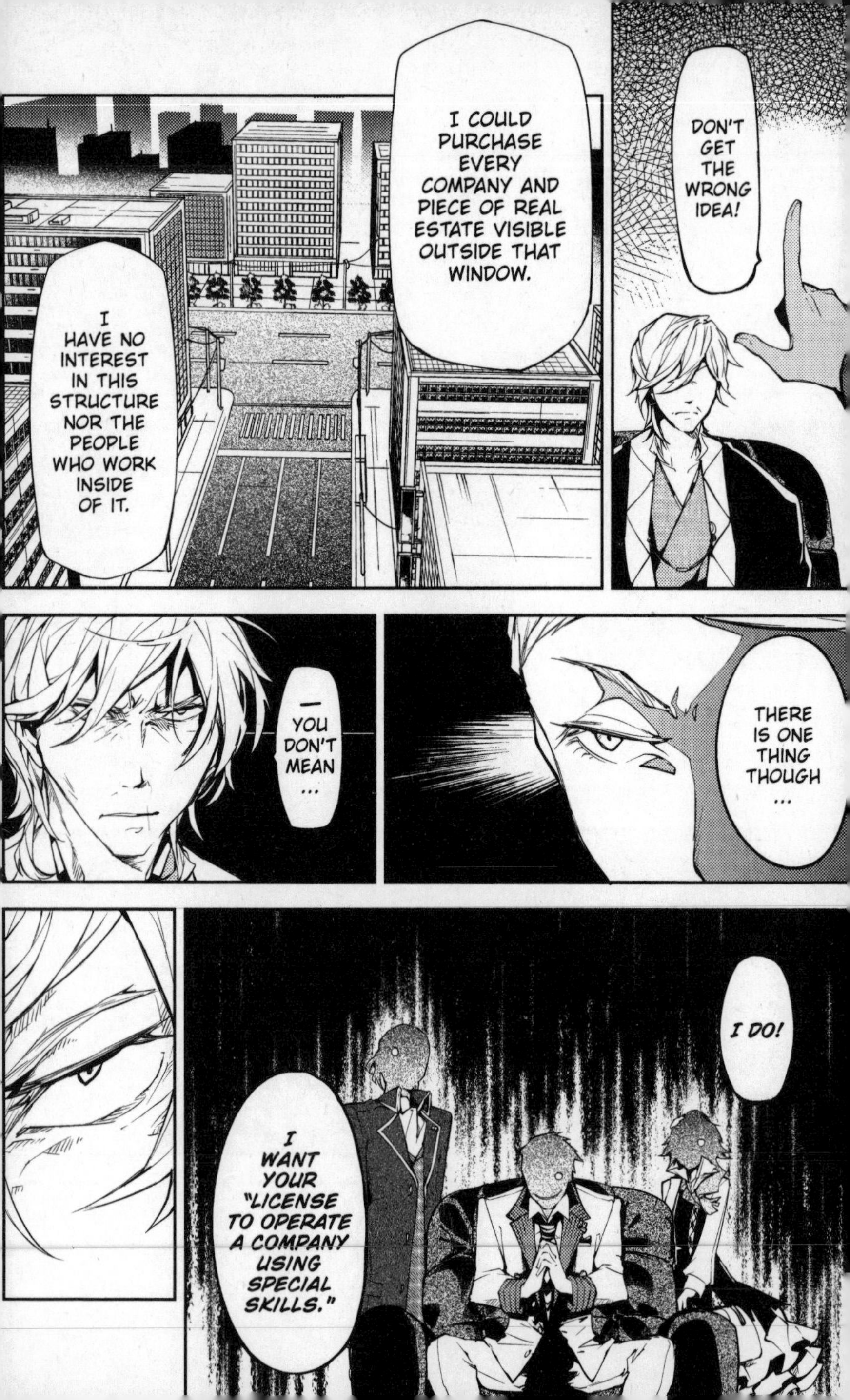
DON'T GET THE WRONG IDEA!
I COULD PURCHASE EVERY COMPANY AND PIECE OF REAL ESTATE VISIBLE OUTSIDE THAT WINDOW.
I HAVE NO INTEREST IN THIS STRUCTURE NOR THE PEOPLE WHO WORK INSIDE OF IT.
THERE IS ONE THING THOUGH...
—YOU DON'T MEAN...
I DO!
I WANT YOUR "LICENSE TO OPERATE A COMPANY USING SPECIAL SKILLS."

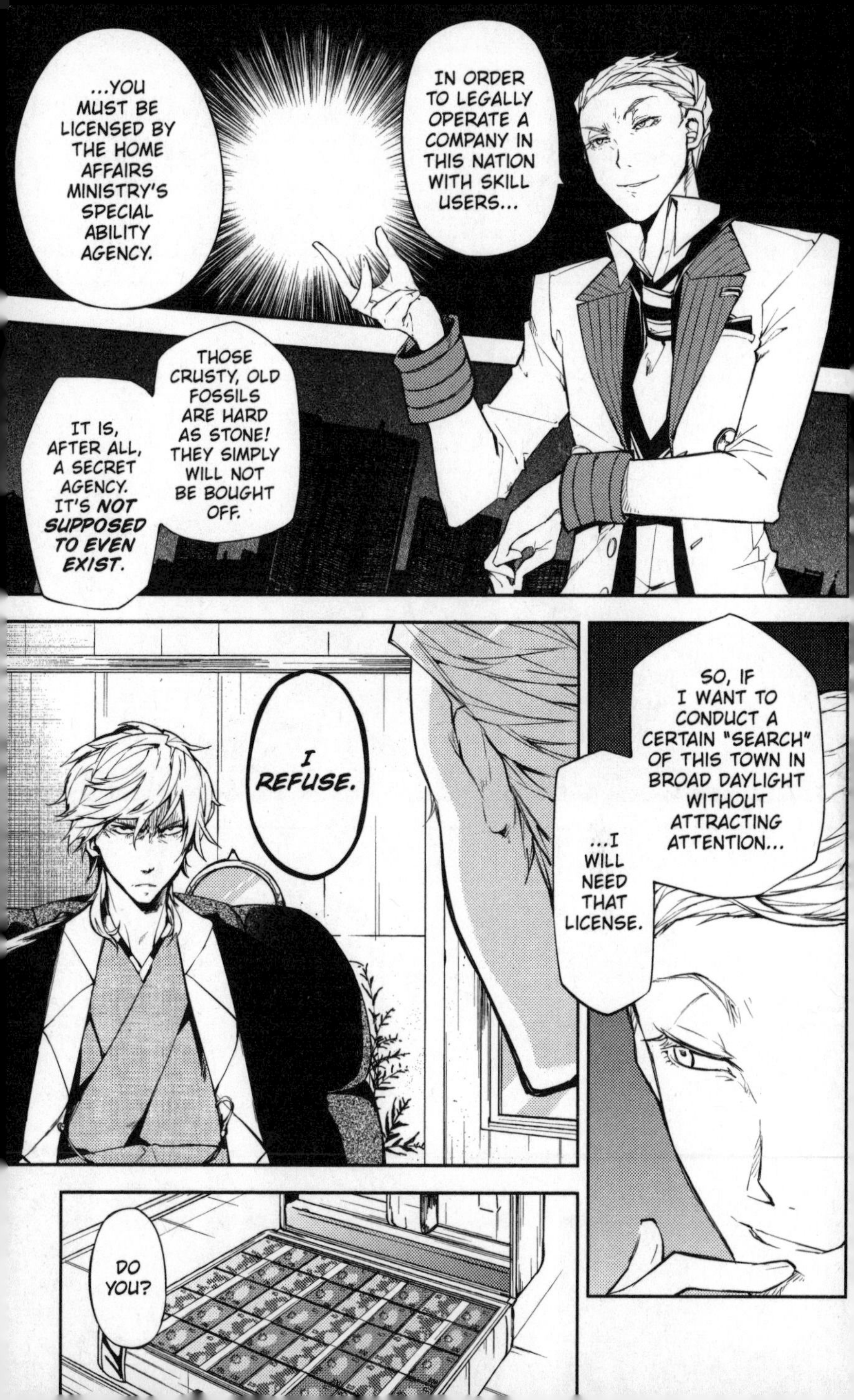
IN ORDER TO LEGALLY OPERATE A COMPANY IN THIS NATION WITH SKILL USERS...
...YOU MUST BE LICENSED BY THE HOME AFFAIRS MINISTRY'S SPECIAL ABILITY AGENCY.
THOSE CRUSTY, OLD FOSSILS ARE HARD AS STONE! THEY SIMPLY WILL NOT BE BOUGHT OFF.
IT IS, AFTER ALL, A SECRET AGENCY. IT'S *NOT SUPPOSED TO EVEN EXIST*.
SO, IF I WANT TO CONDUCT A CERTAIN "SEARCH" OF THIS TOWN IN BROAD DAYLIGHT WITHOUT ATTRACTING ATTENTION...
...I WILL NEED THAT LICENSE.
I REFUSE.
DO YOU?

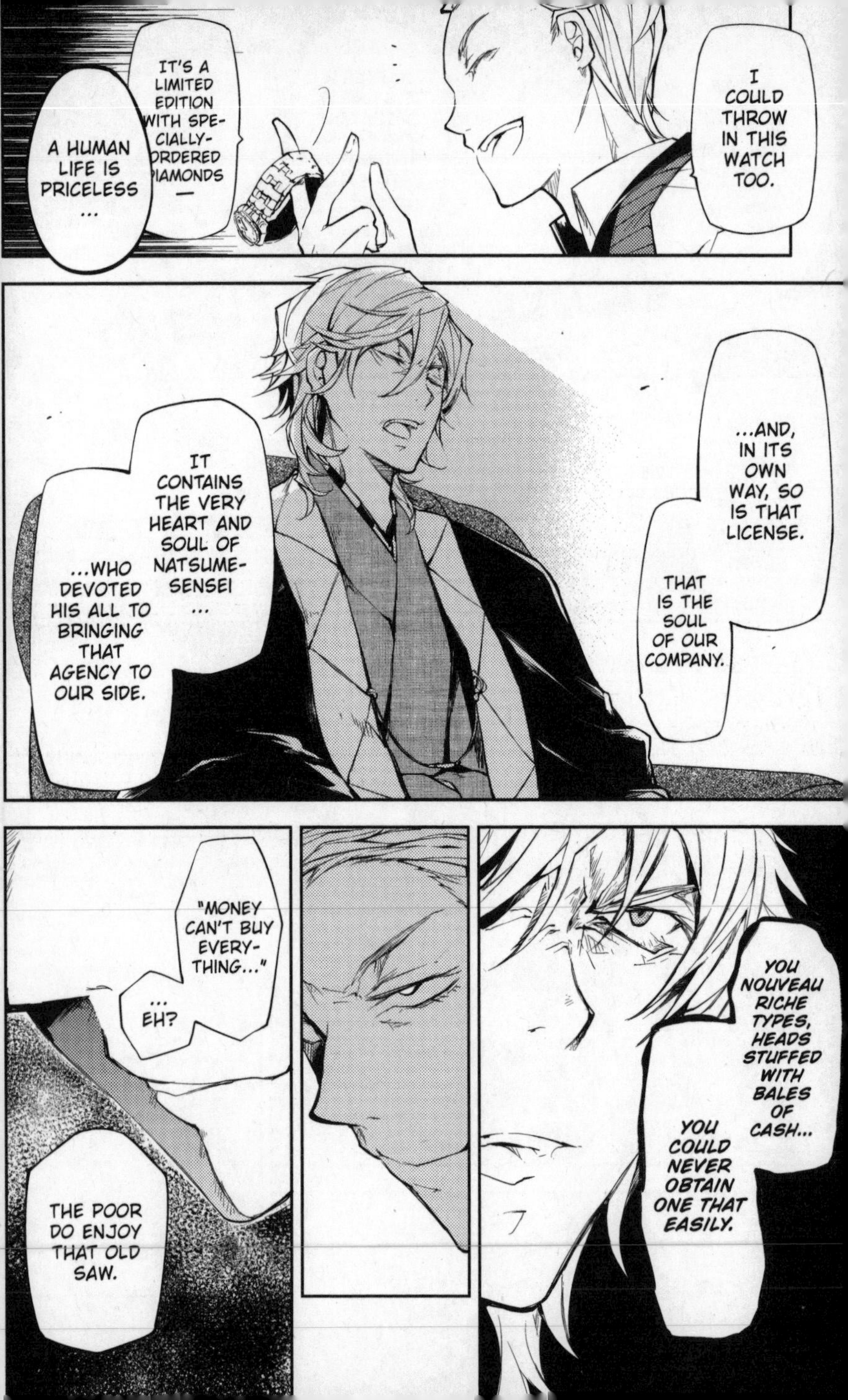
I COULD THROW IN THIS WATCH TOO.
IT'S A LIMITED EDITION WITH SPECIALLY-ORDERED DIAMONDS—
A HUMAN LIFE IS PRICELESS...
...AND, IN ITS OWN WAY, SO IS THAT LICENSE.
THAT IS THE SOUL OF OUR COMPANY.
IT CONTAINS THE VERY HEART AND SOUL OF NATSUME-SENSEI...
...WHO DEVOTED HIS ALL TO BRINGING THAT AGENCY TO OUR SIDE.
YOU NOUVEAU RICHE TYPES, HEADS STUFFED WITH BALES OF CASH...
YOU COULD NEVER OBTAIN ONE THAT EASILY.
"MONEY CAN'T BUY EVERYTHING..."
...EH?
THE POOR DO ENJOY THAT OLD SAW.

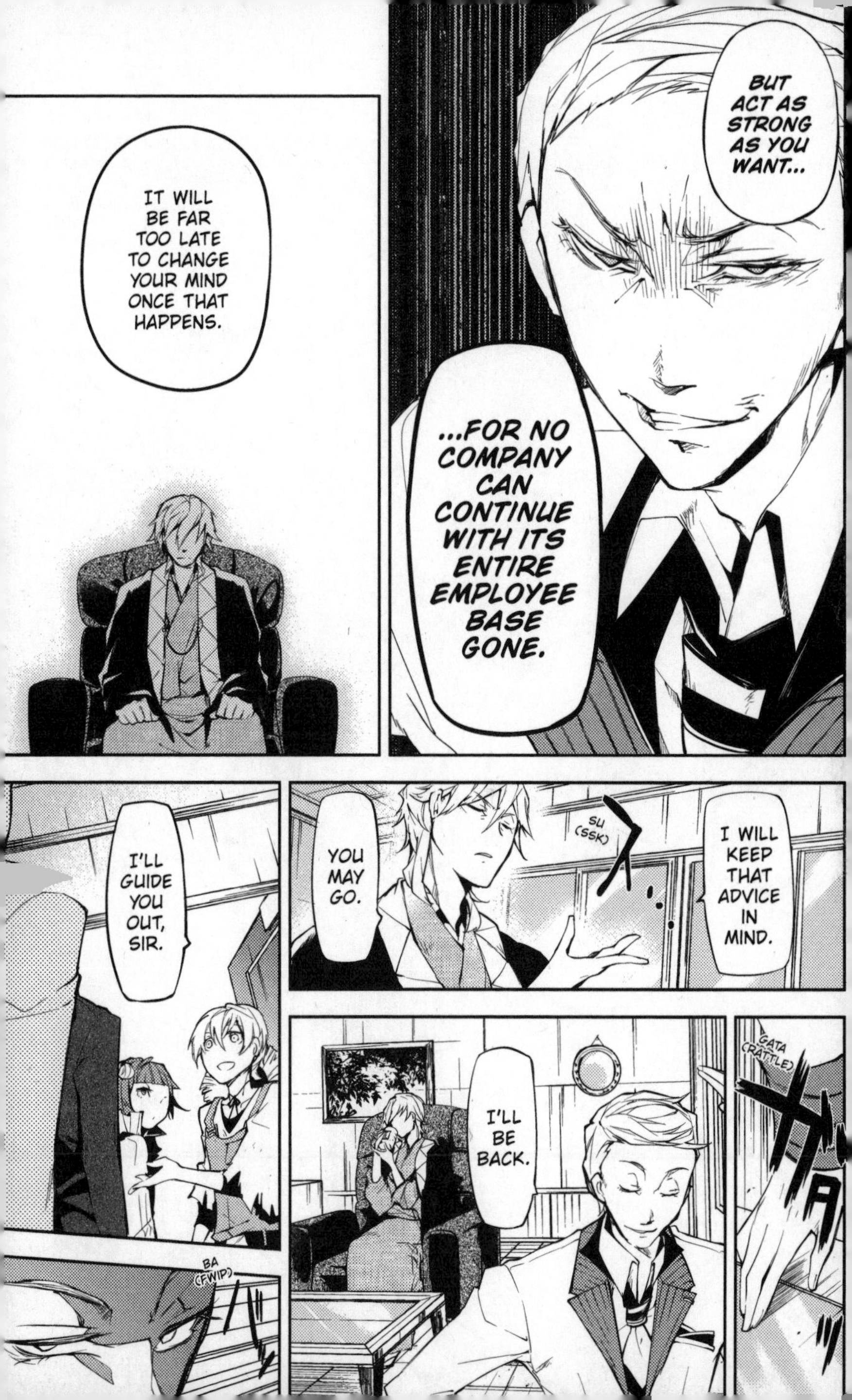
BUT ACT AS STRONG AS YOU WANT...
...FOR NO COMPANY CAN CONTINUE WITH ITS ENTIRE EMPLOYEE BASE GONE.
IT WILL BE FAR TOO LATE TO CHANGE YOUR MIND ONCE THAT HAPPENS.
I WILL KEEP THAT ADVICE IN MIND.
SU (SSK)
YOU MAY GO.
GATA (RATTLE)
I'LL BE BACK.
I'LL GUIDE YOU OUT, SIR.
BA (FWIP)

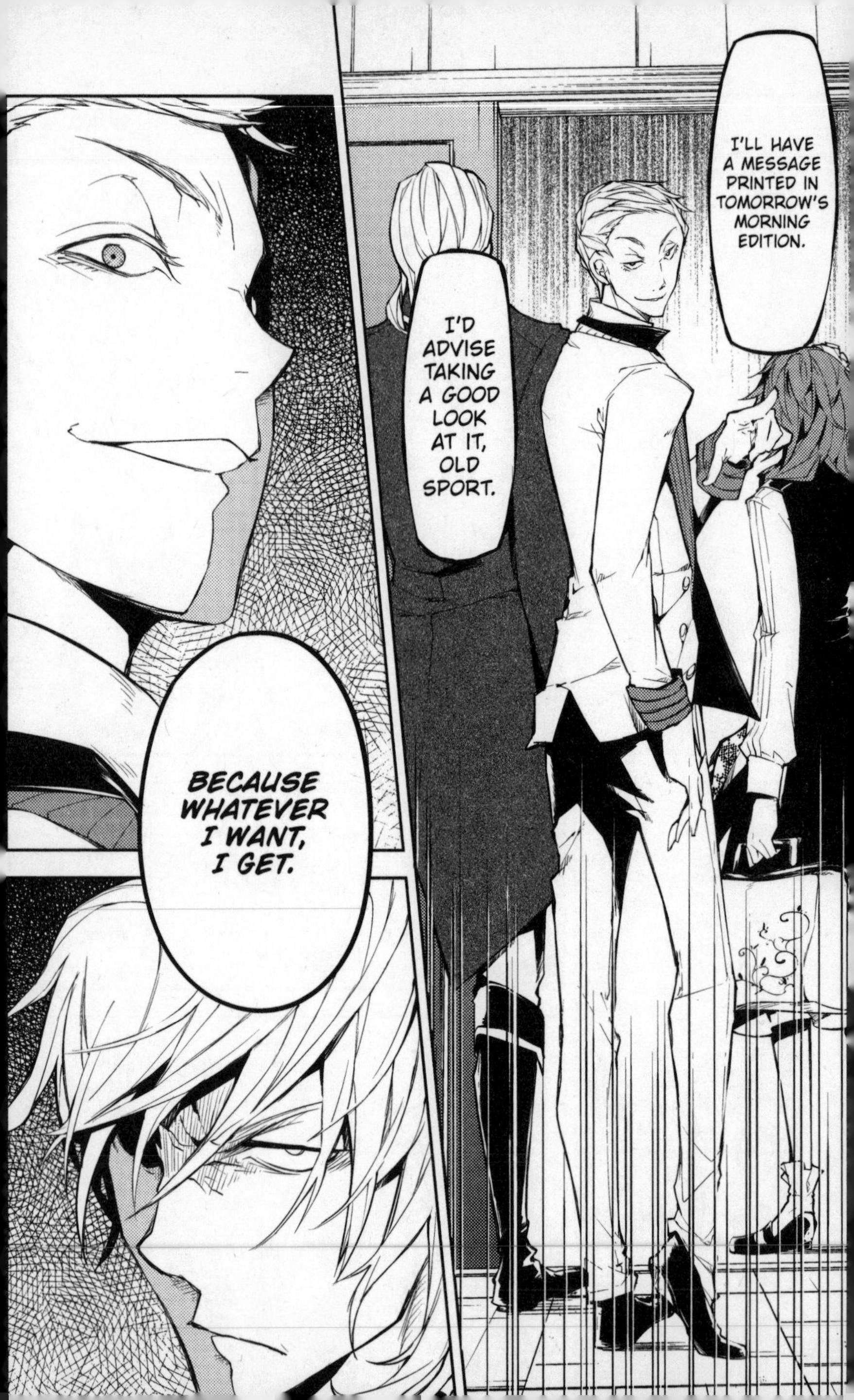
I'LL HAVE A MESSAGE PRINTED IN TOMORROW'S MORNING EDITION.
I'D ADVISE TAKING A GOOD LOOK AT IT, OLD SPORT.
BECAUSE WHATEVER I WANT, I GET.

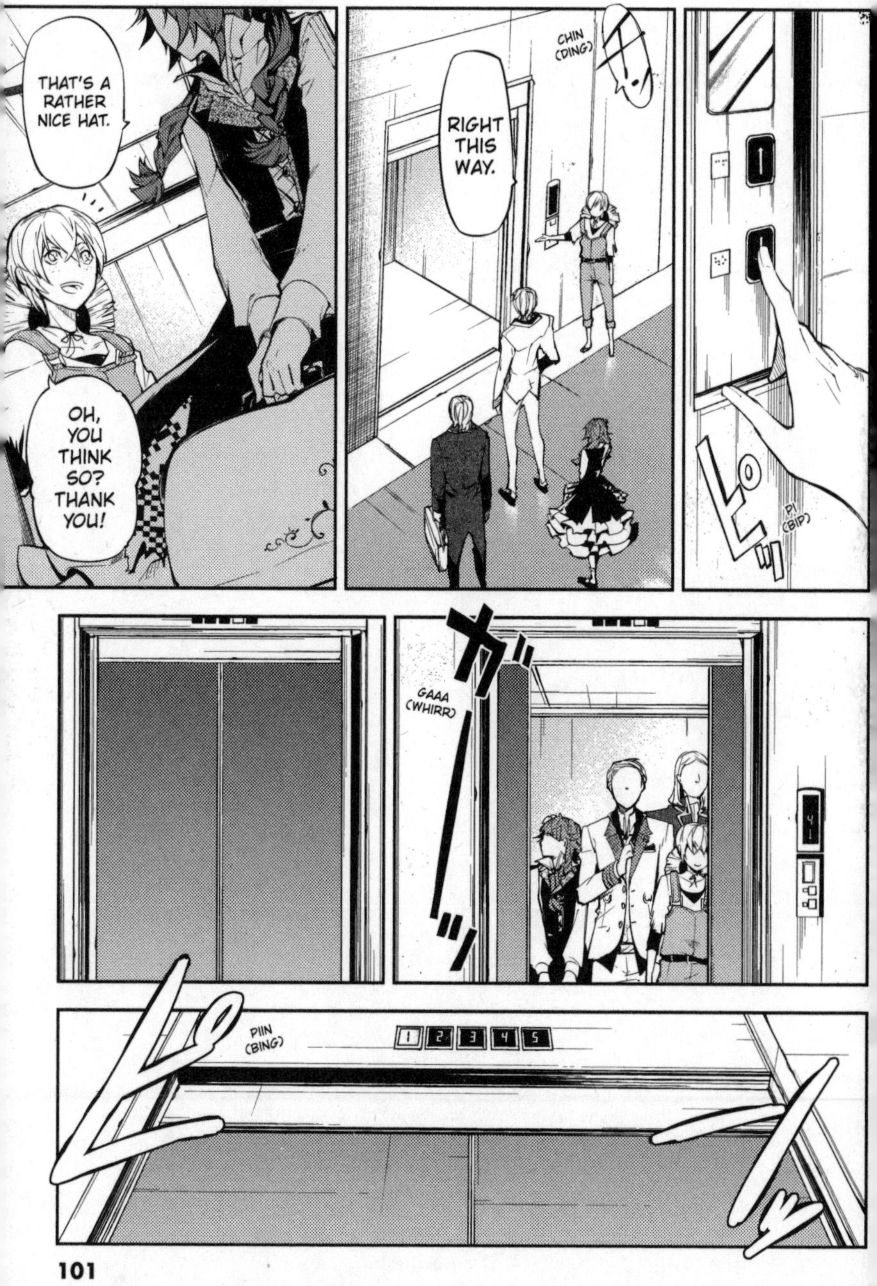
PI (BIP)
CHIN (DING)
RIGHT THIS WAY.
THAT'S A RATHER NICE HAT.
OH, YOU THINK SO? THANK YOU!
GAAA (WHIRR)
PIIN (BING)
1 2 3 4 5

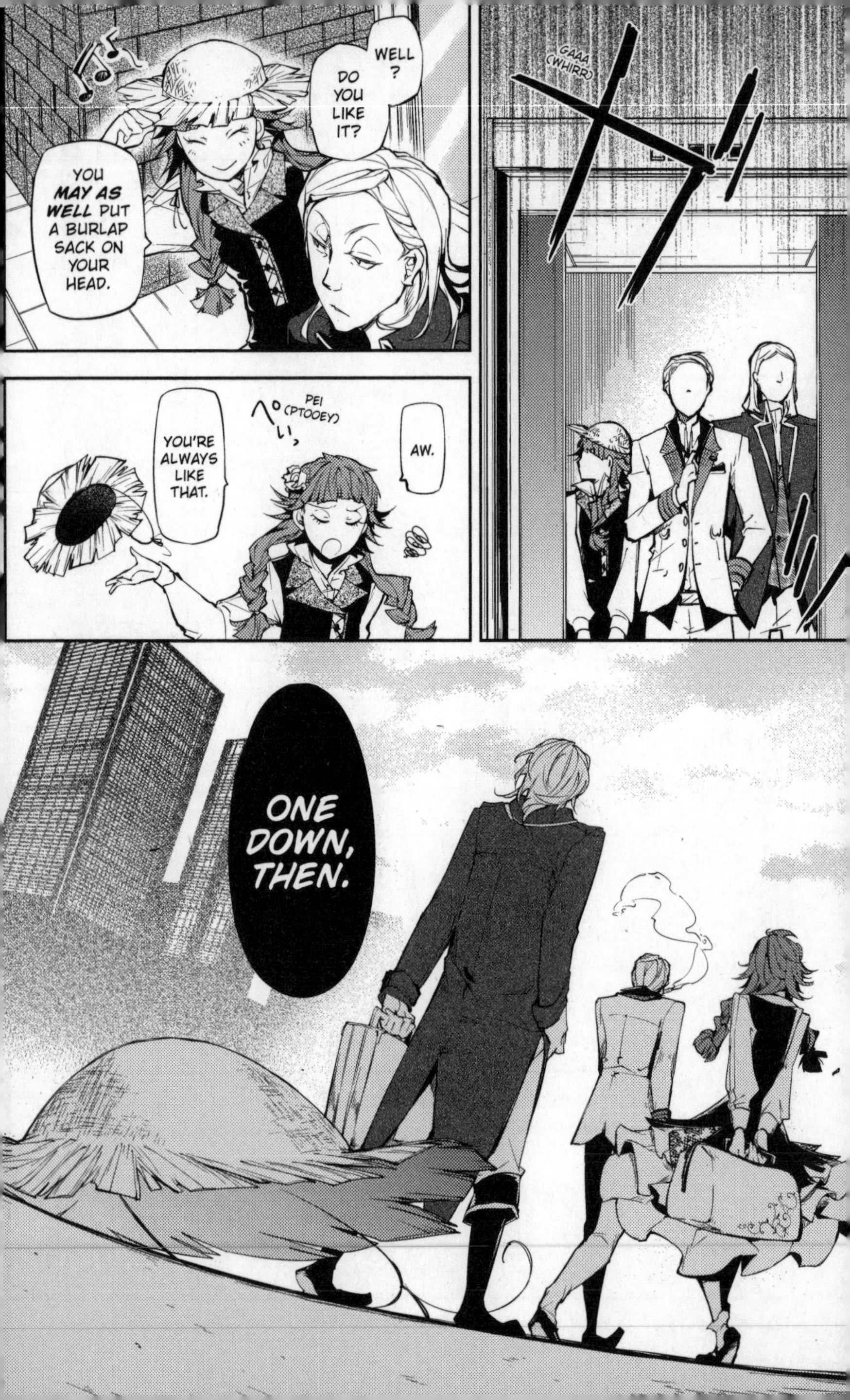
GAAA (WHIRR)
WELL? DO YOU LIKE IT?
YOU MAY AS WELL PUT A BURLAP SACK ON YOUR HEAD.
AW.
PEI (PTOOEY)
YOU'RE ALWAYS LIKE THAT.
ONE DOWN, THEN.

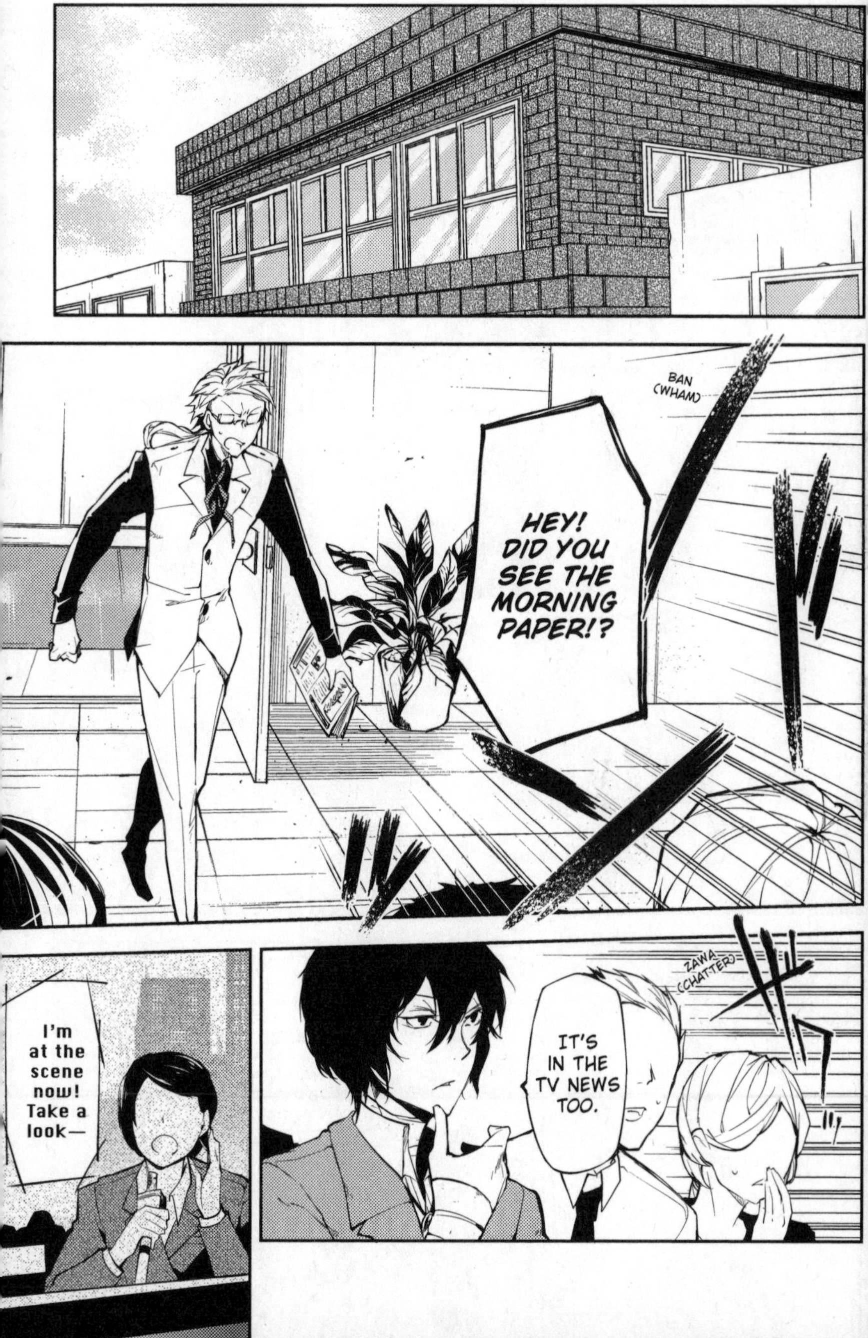
BAN (WHAM)
HEY! DID YOU SEE THE MORNING PAPER!?
ZAWA (CHATTER)
IT'S IN THE TV NEWS TOO.
I'm at the scene now! Take a look—

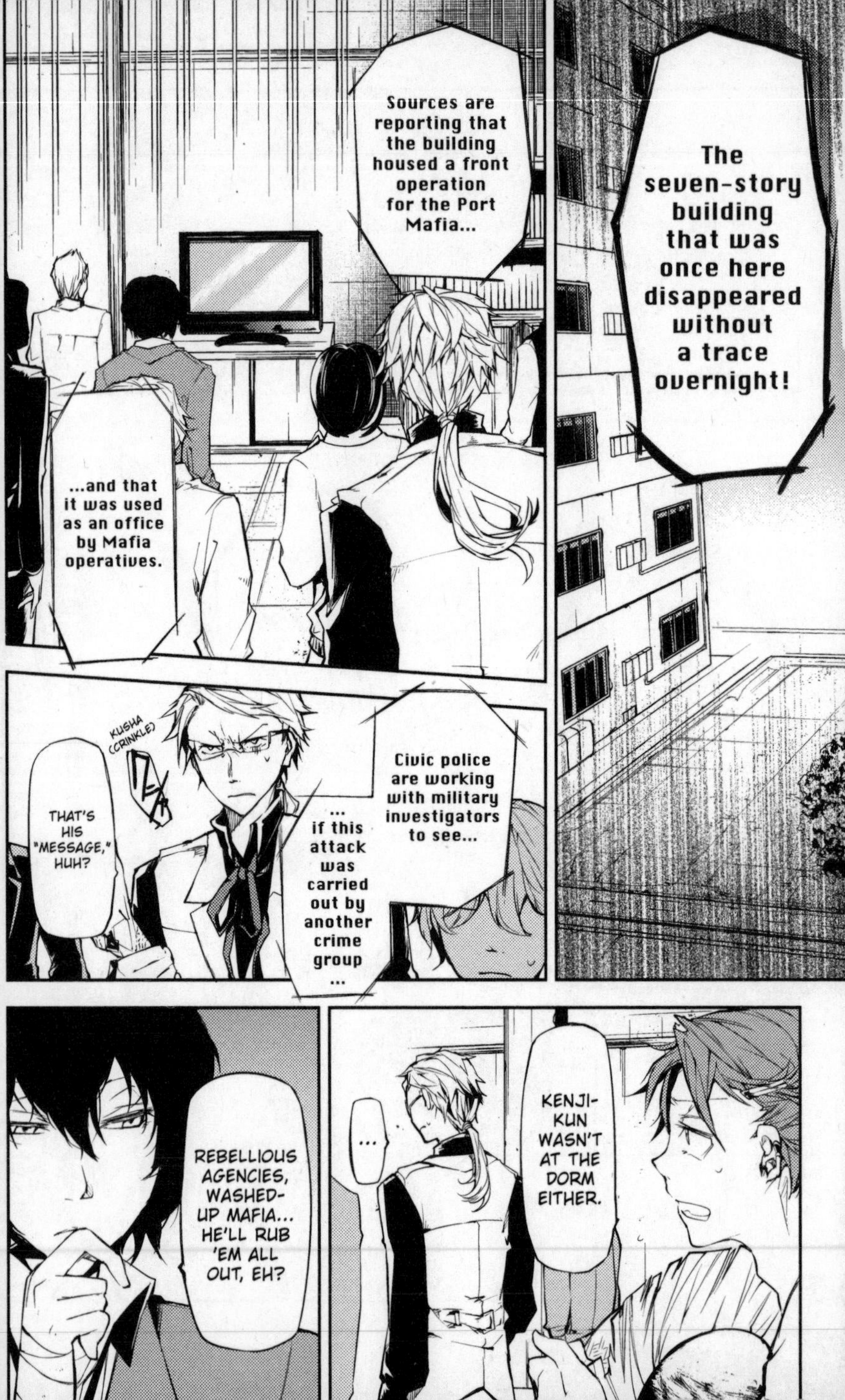
The seven-story building that was once here disappeared without a trace overnight!
Sources are reporting that the building housed a front operation for the Port Mafia...
...and that it was used as an office by Mafia operatives.
Civic police are working with military investigators to see...
...if this attack was carried out by another crime group...
KUSHA (CRINKLE)
THAT'S HIS "MESSAGE," HUH?
KENJI-KUN WASN'T AT THE DORM EITHER.
...
REBELLIOUS AGENCIES, WASHED-UP MAFIA... HE'LL RUB 'EM ALL OUT, EH?

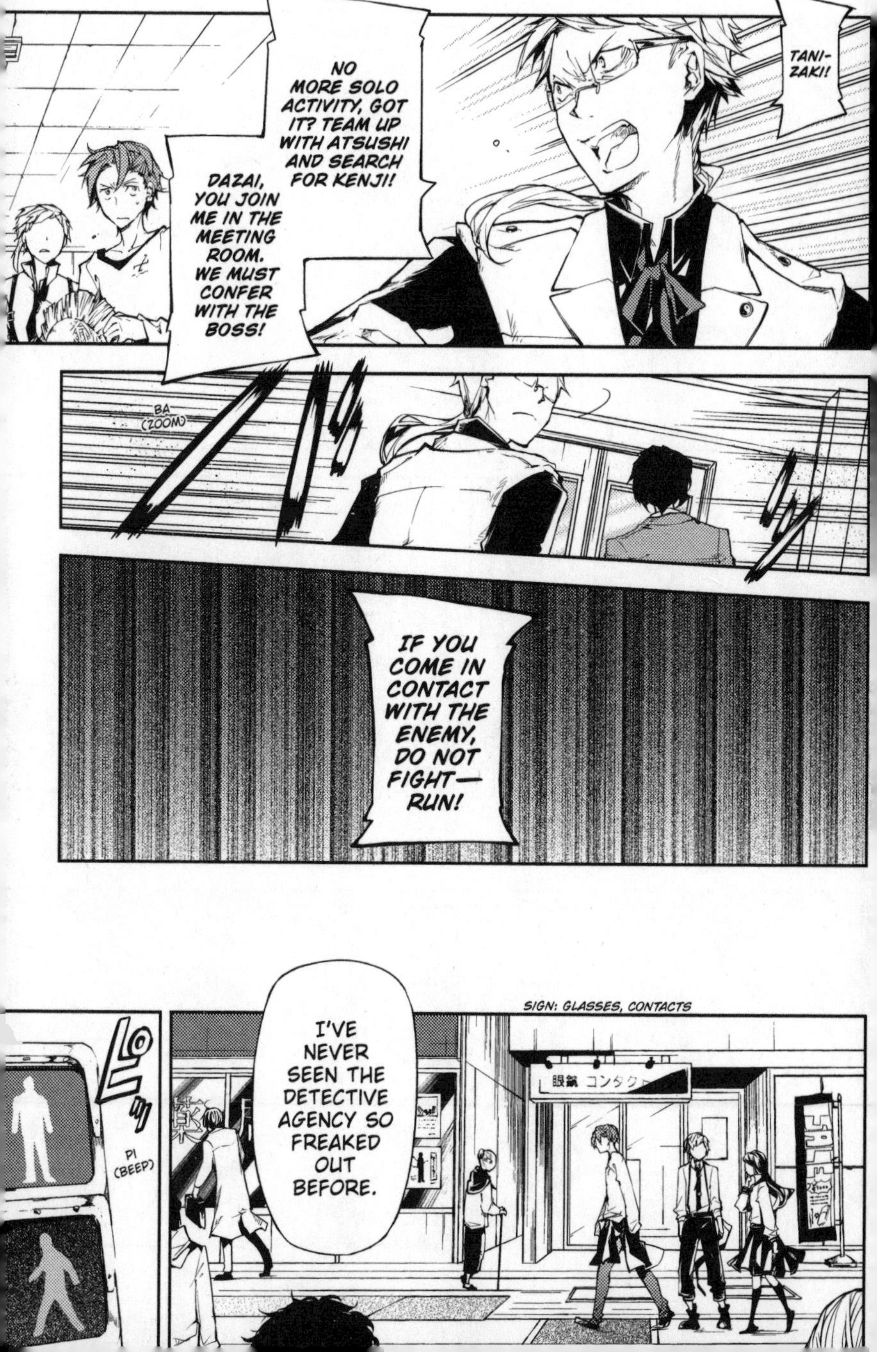
TANI-ZAKI!
NO MORE SOLO ACTIVITY, GOT IT? TEAM UP WITH ATSUSHI AND SEARCH FOR KENJI!
DAZAI, YOU JOIN ME IN THE MEETING ROOM. WE MUST CONFER WITH THE BOSS!
BA (ZOOM)
IF YOU COME IN CONTACT WITH THE ENEMY, DO NOT FIGHT—RUN!
SIGN: GLASSES, CONTACTS
眼鏡 コンタク
I'VE NEVER SEEN THE DETECTIVE AGENCY SO FREAKED OUT BEFORE.
PI (BEEP)

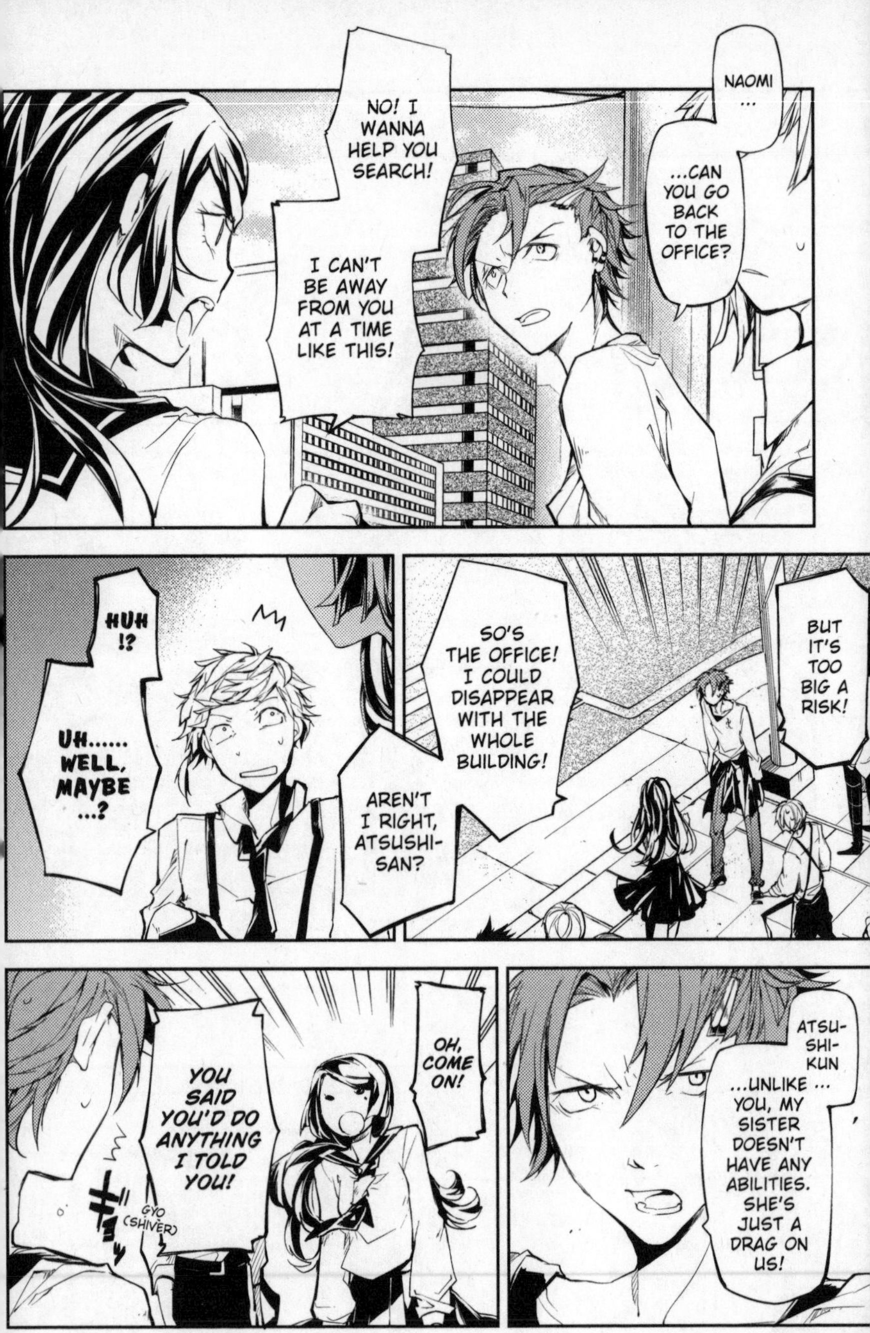
NAOMI ...
...CAN YOU GO BACK TO THE OFFICE?
NO! I WANNA HELP YOU SEARCH!
I CAN'T BE AWAY FROM YOU AT A TIME LIKE THIS!
BUT IT'S TOO BIG A RISK!
SO'S THE OFFICE! I COULD DISAPPEAR WITH THE WHOLE BUILDING!
AREN'T I RIGHT, ATSUSHI-SAN?
HUH!?
UH...... WELL, MAYBE ...?
ATSUSHI-KUN ...UNLIKE ... YOU, MY SISTER DOESN'T HAVE ANY ABILITIES. SHE'S JUST A DRAG ON US!
OH, COME ON!
YOU SAID YOU'D DO ANYTHING I TOLD YOU!
GYO (SHIVER)

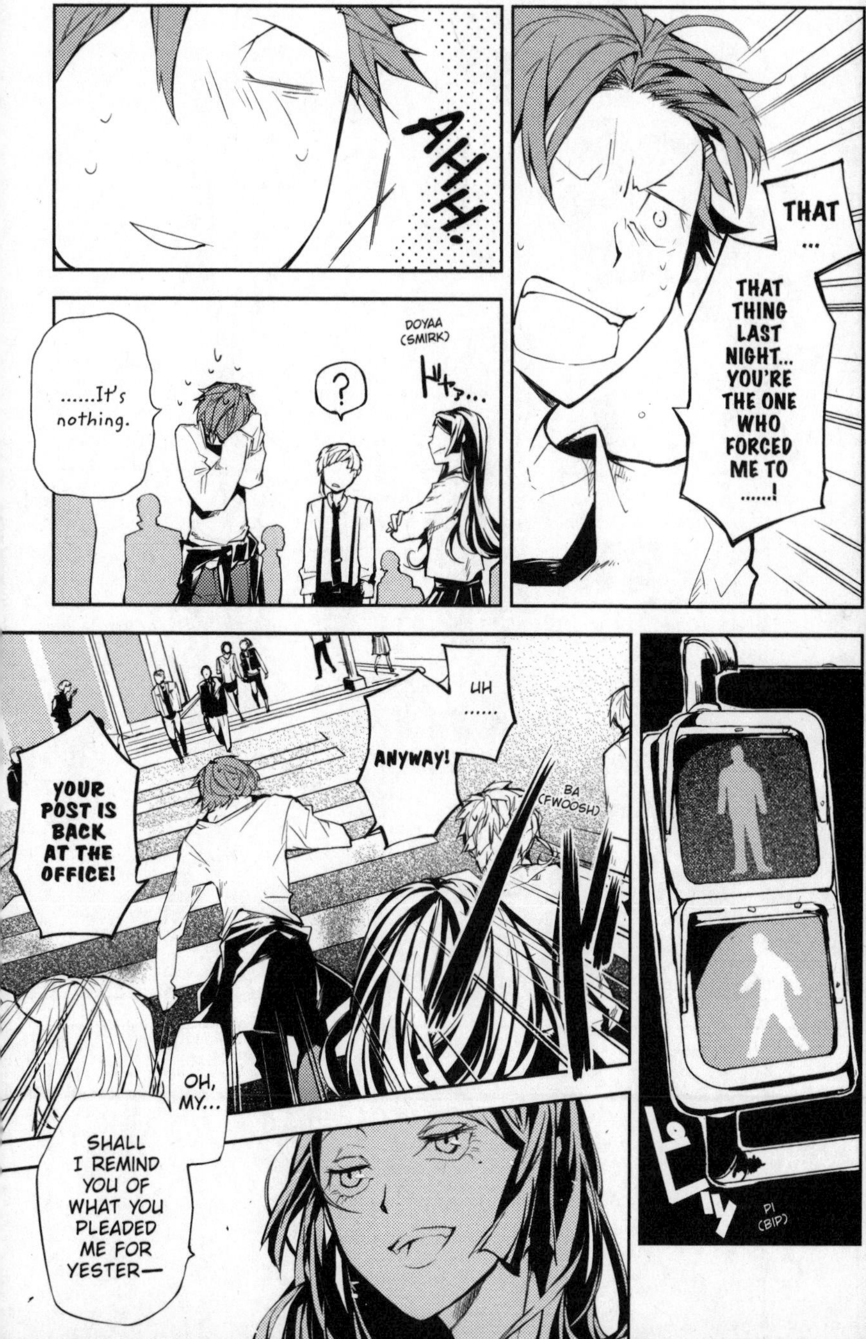
THAT ...
THAT THING LAST NIGHT... YOU'RE THE ONE WHO FORCED ME TO ......!
AHHH.
DOYAA (SMIRK)
?
......It's nothing.
PI (BIP)
UH ......
ANYWAY!
BA (FWOOSH)
YOUR POST IS BACK AT THE OFFICE!
OH, MY...
SHALL I REMIND YOU OF WHAT YOU PLEADED ME FOR YESTER—

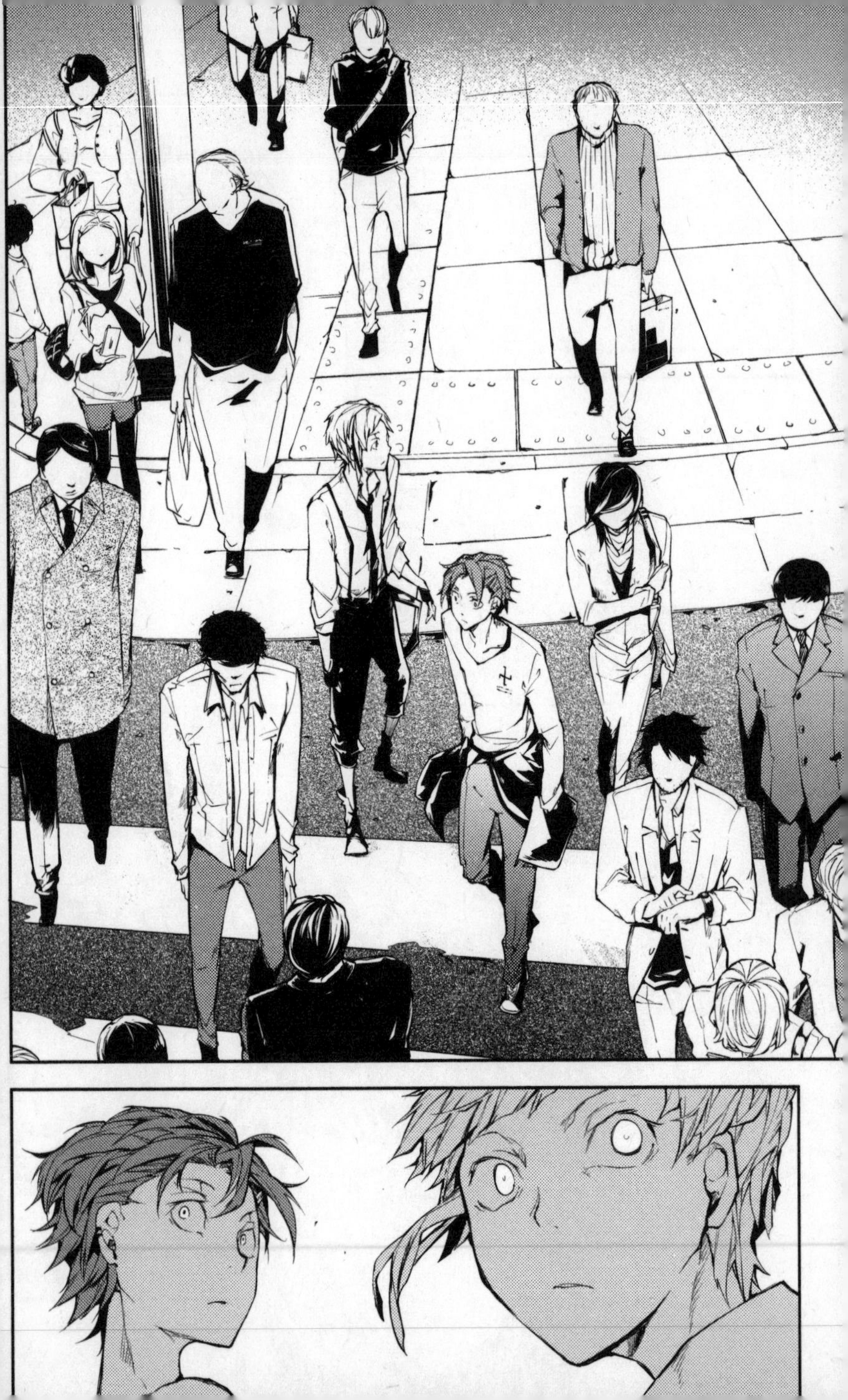

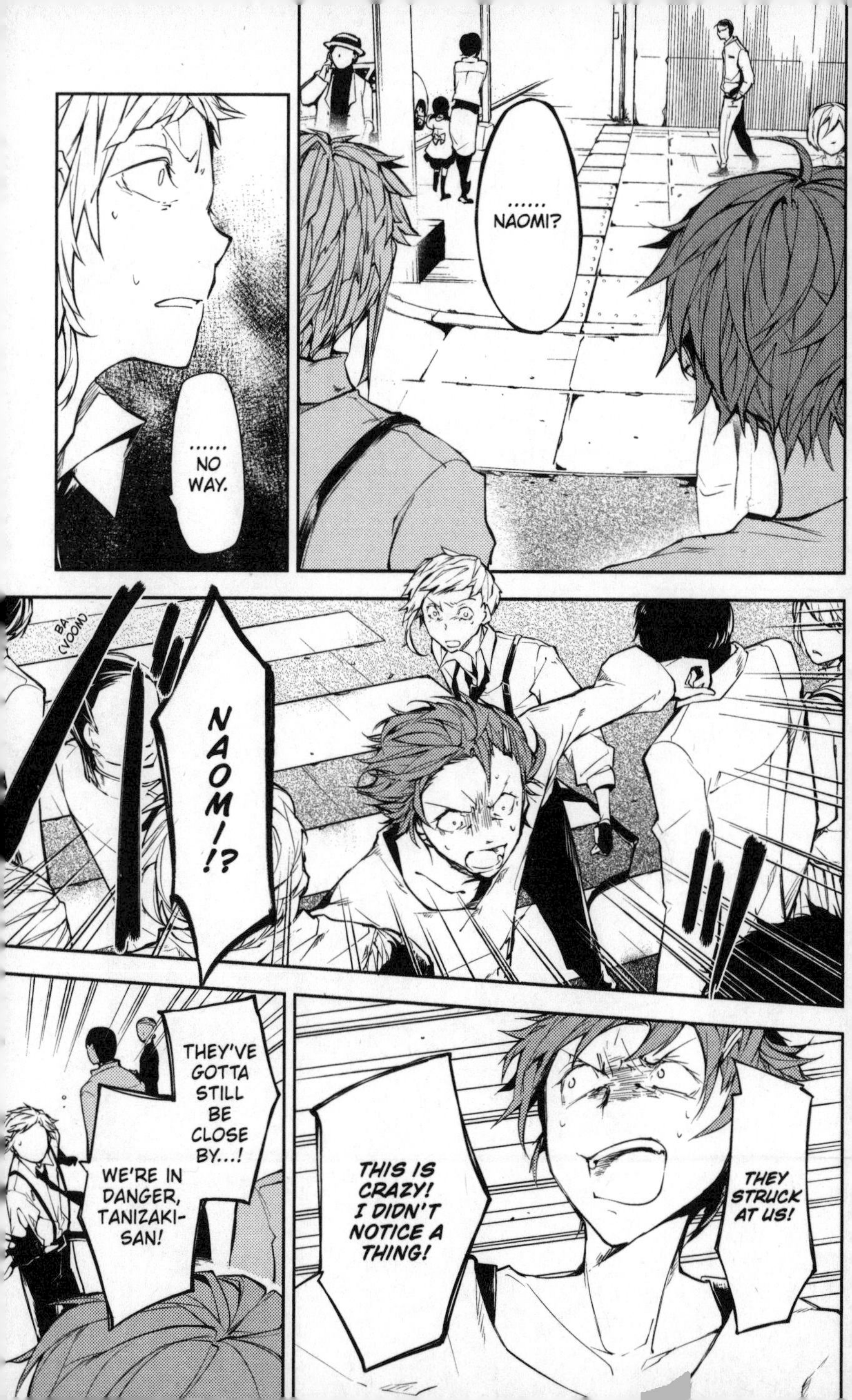

...... NAOMI?
...... NO WAY.
BA (VOOM)
NAOMI!?
THEY STRUCK AT US!
THIS IS CRAZY! I DIDN'T NOTICE A THING!
THEY'VE GOTTA STILL BE CLOSE BY...!
WE'RE IN DANGER, TANIZAKI-SAN!

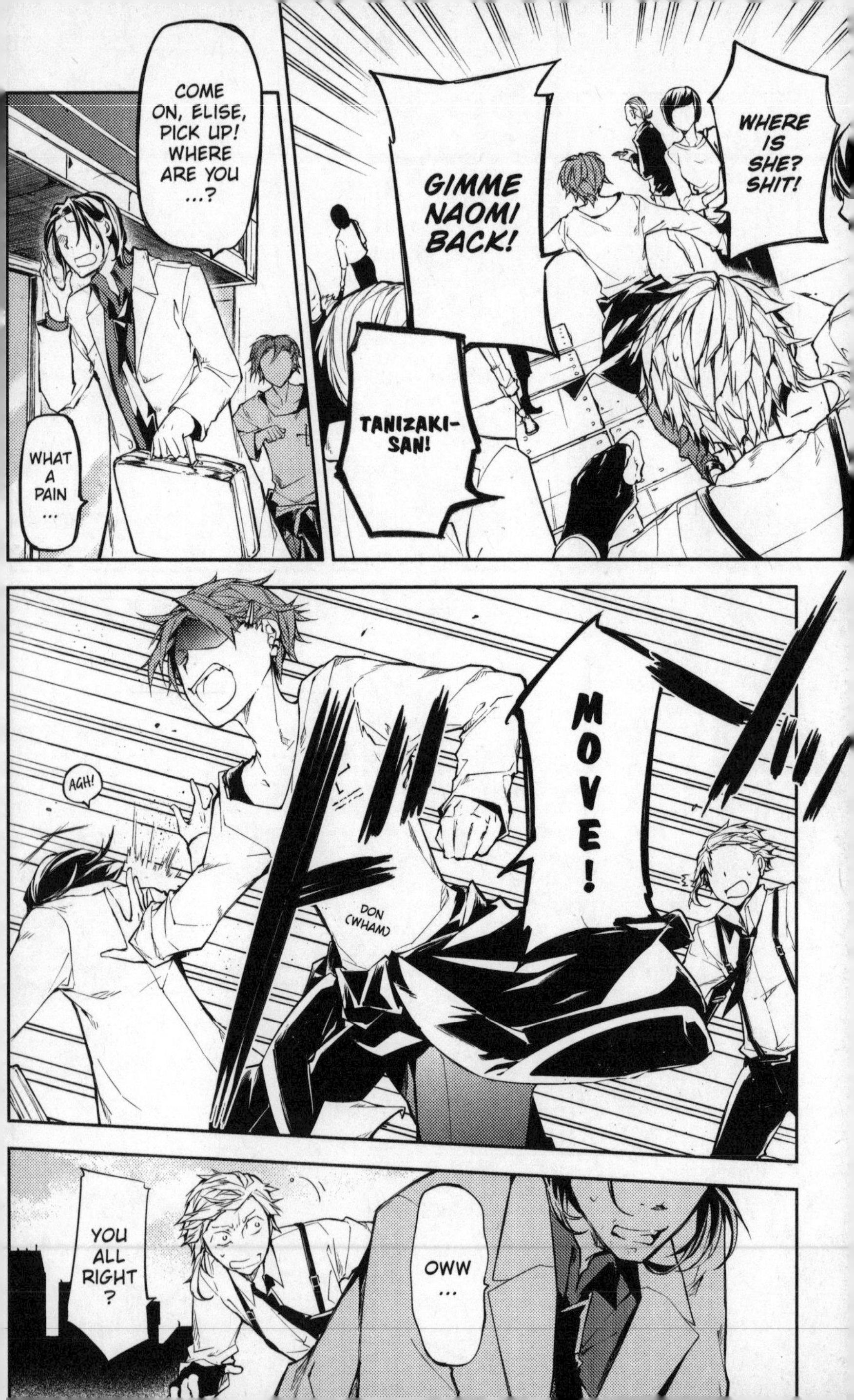
WHERE IS SHE? SHIT!
GIMME NAOMI BACK!
TANIZAKI-SAN!
COME ON, ELISE, PICK UP! WHERE ARE YOU ...?
WHAT A PAIN ...
MOVE!
DON (WHAM)
AGH!
OWW ...
YOU ALL RIGHT ?

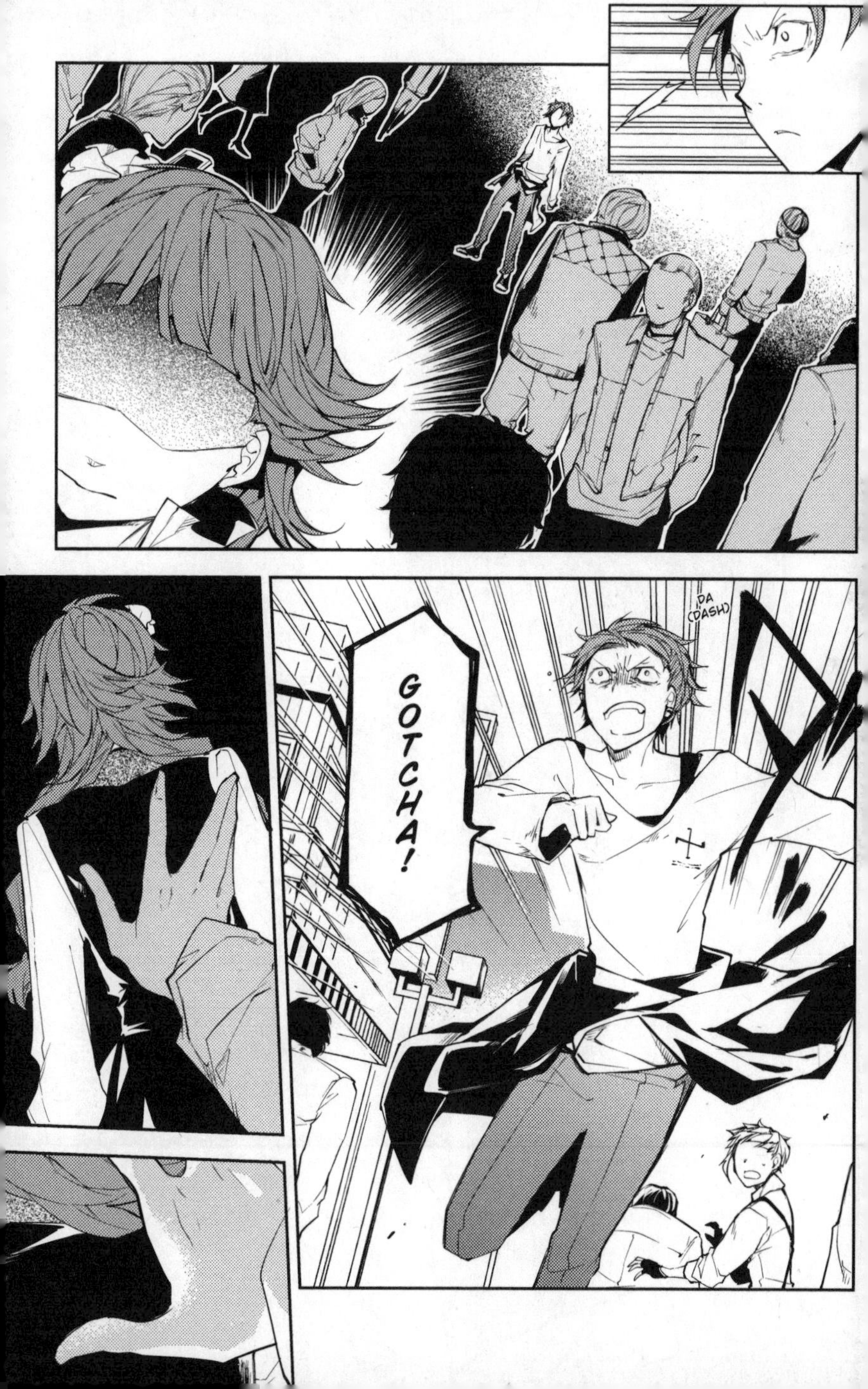
DA (DASH)
GOTCHA!

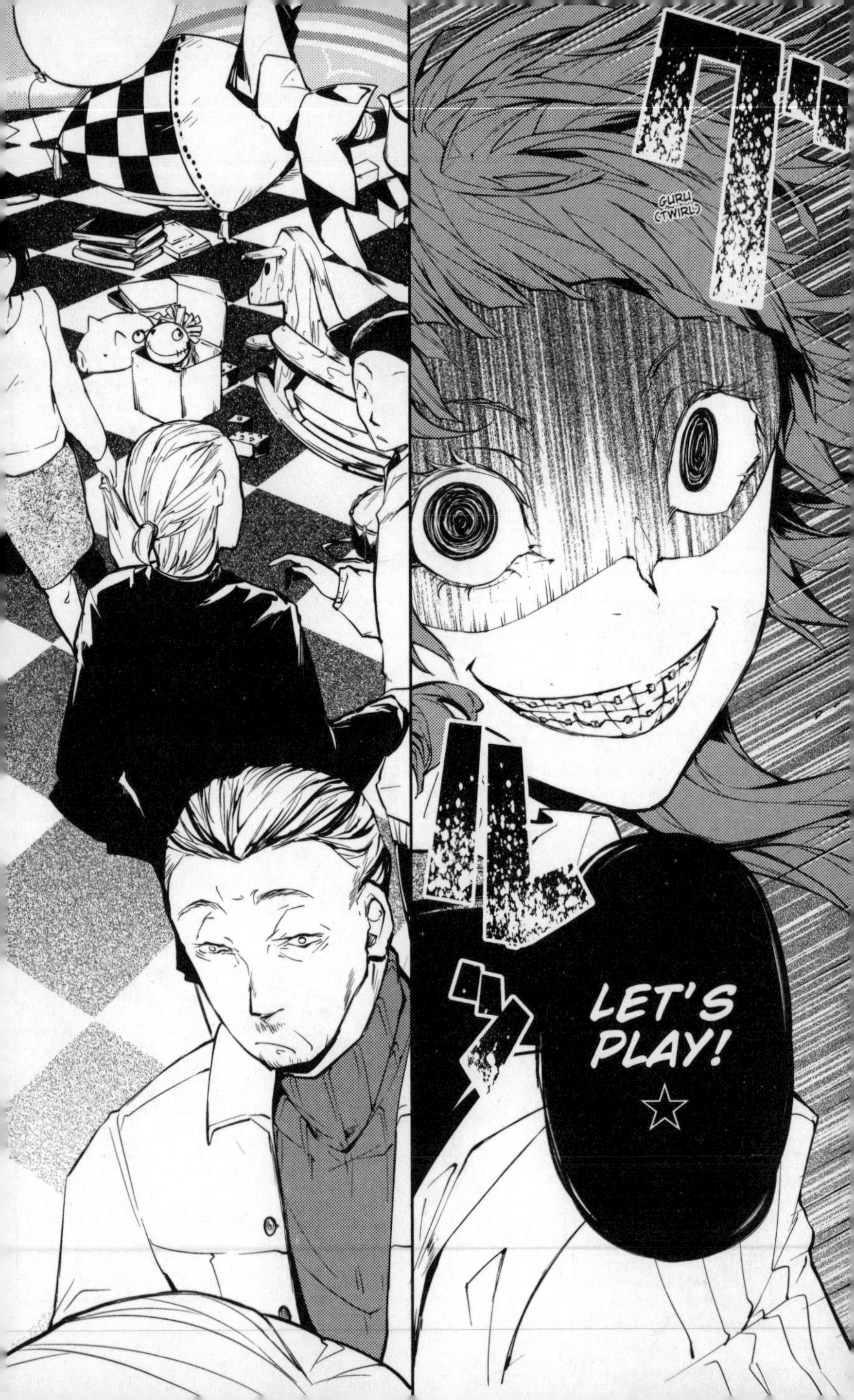
GURU (TWIRL)
LET'S PLAY! ☆

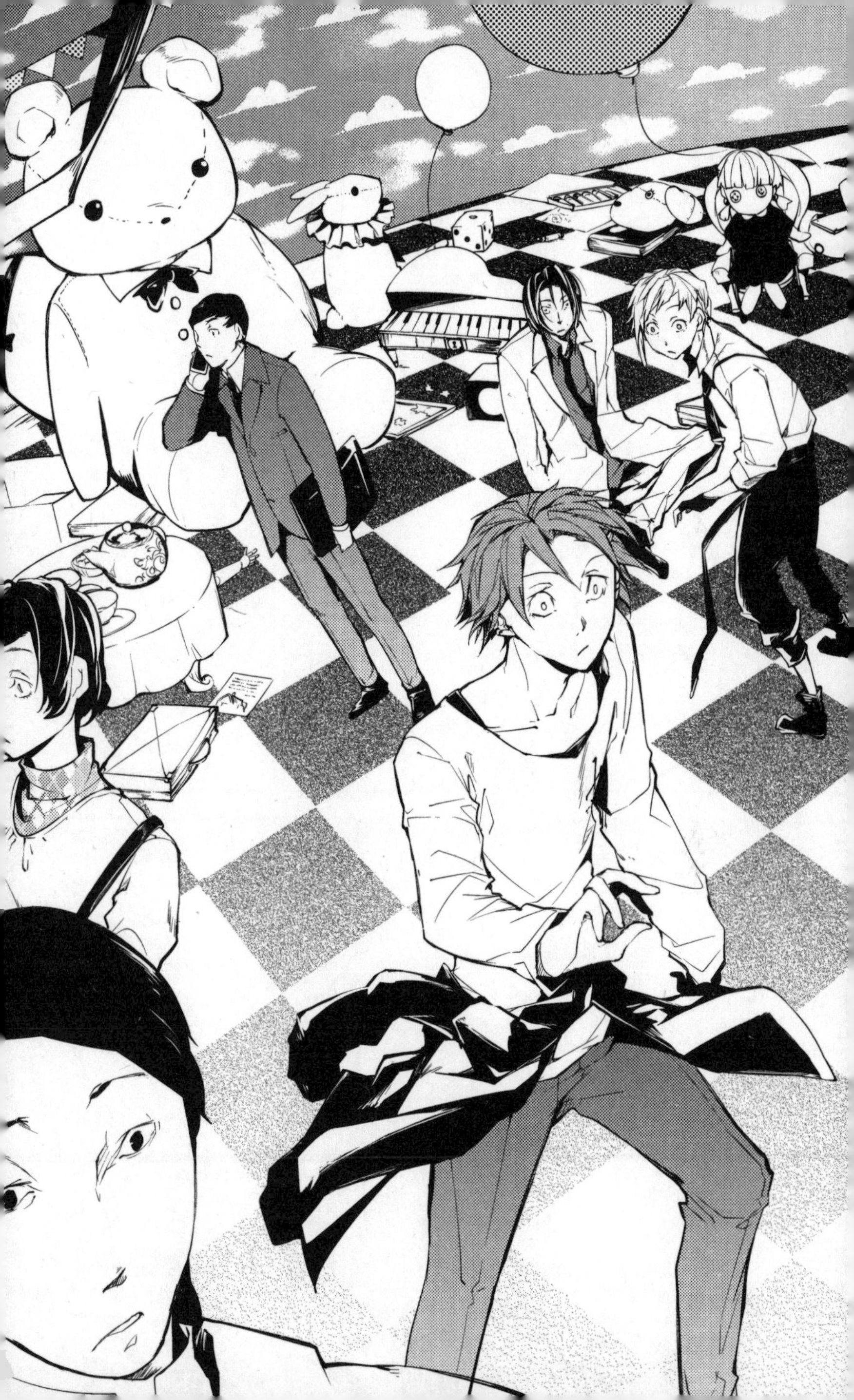

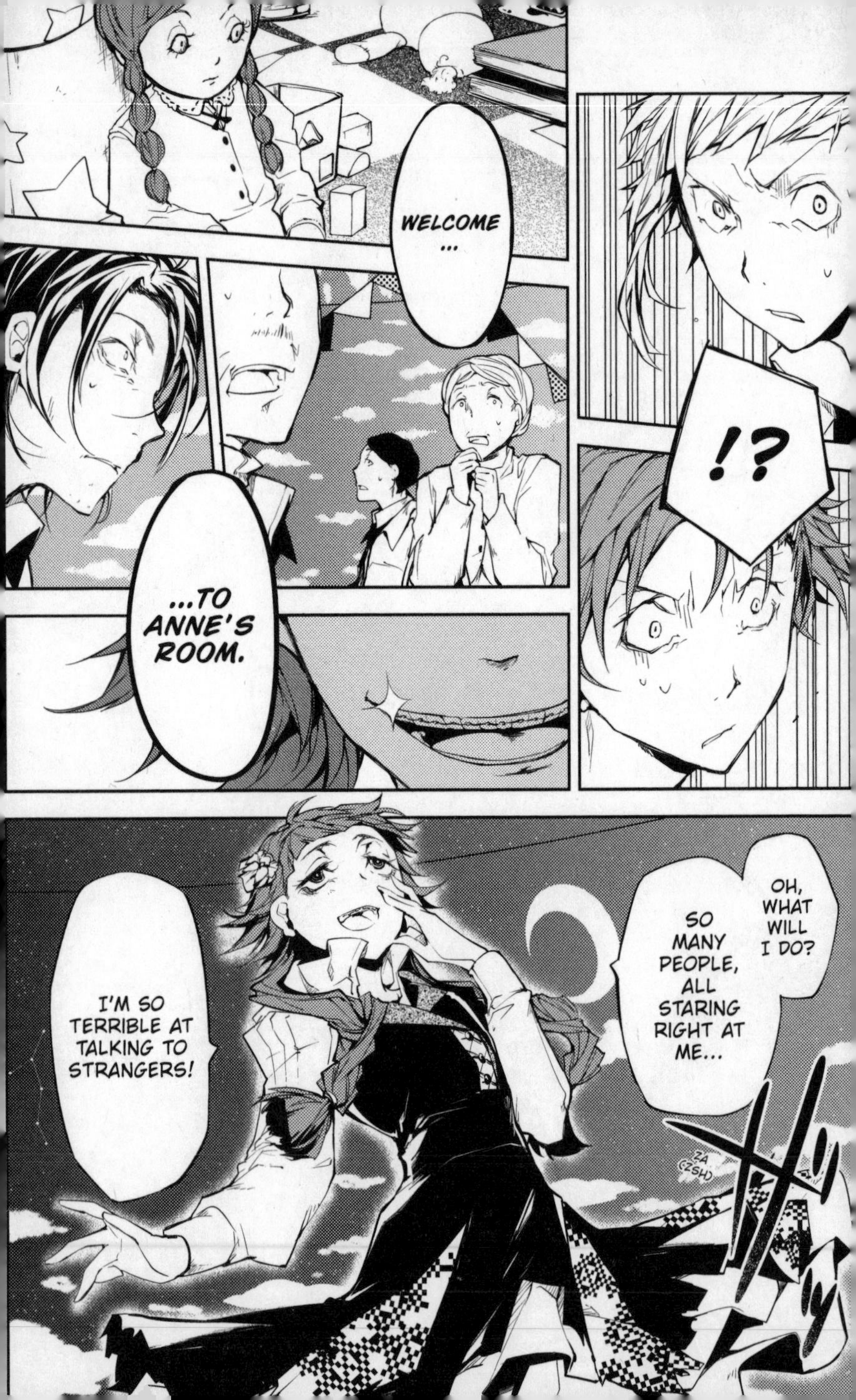
WELCOME...
...TO ANNE'S ROOM.
!?
OH, WHAT WILL I DO?
SO MANY PEOPLE, ALL STARING RIGHT AT ME...
ZA (ZSH)
I'M SO TERRIBLE AT TALKING TO STRANGERS!

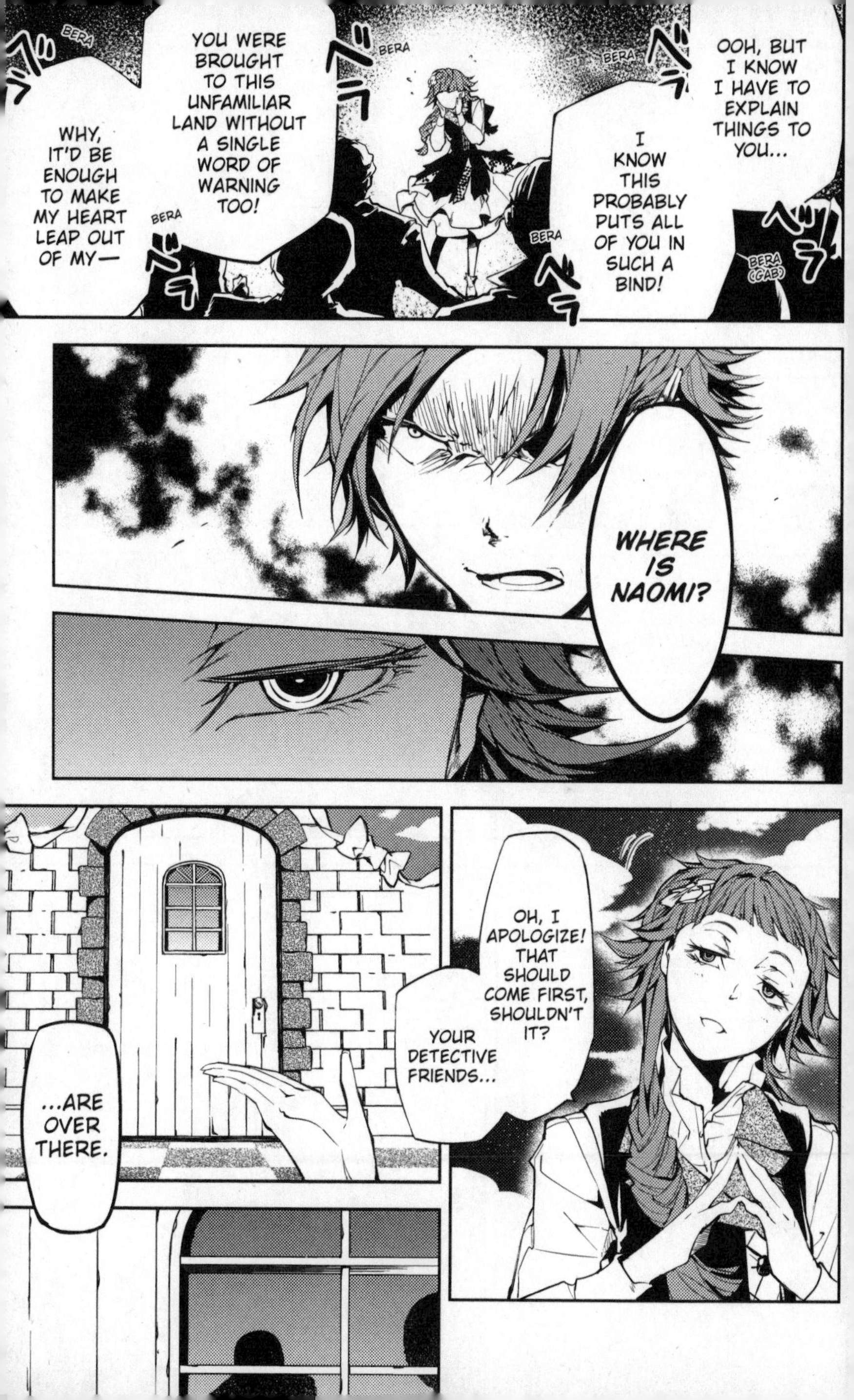
OOH, BUT I KNOW I HAVE TO EXPLAIN THINGS TO YOU...
BERA
BERA (GAB)
I KNOW THIS PROBABLY PUTS ALL OF YOU IN SUCH A BIND!
BERA
BERA
YOU WERE BROUGHT TO THIS UNFAMILIAR LAND WITHOUT A SINGLE WORD OF WARNING TOO!
BERA
BERA
WHY, IT'D BE ENOUGH TO MAKE MY HEART LEAP OUT OF MY—
WHERE IS NAOMI?
OH, I APOLOGIZE! THAT SHOULD COME FIRST, SHOULDN'T IT?
YOUR DETECTIVE FRIENDS...
...ARE OVER THERE.

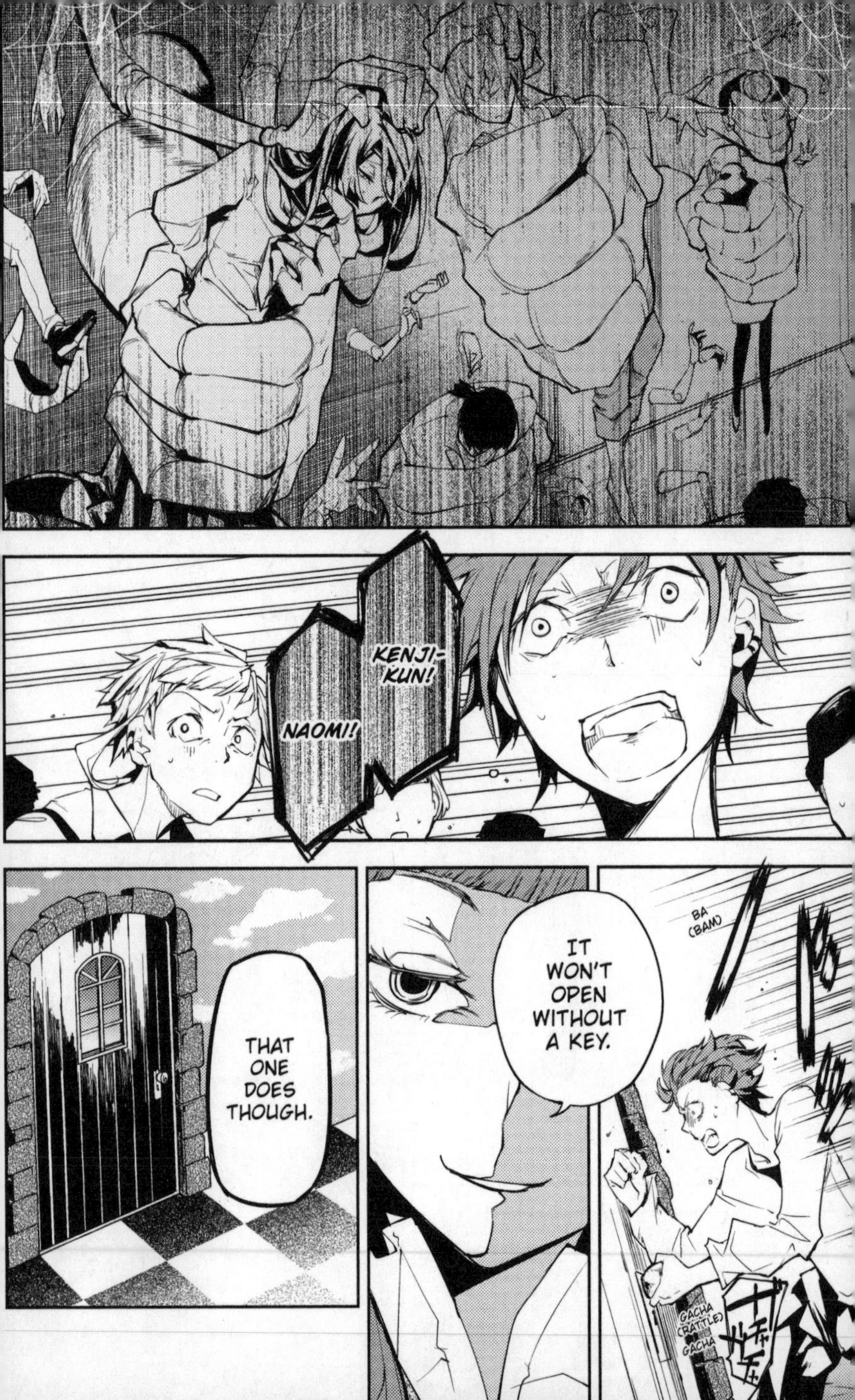
KENJI-KUN!
NAOMI!
BA (BAM)
GACHA (RATTLE) GACHA
IT WON'T OPEN WITHOUT A KEY.
THAT ONE DOES THOUGH.

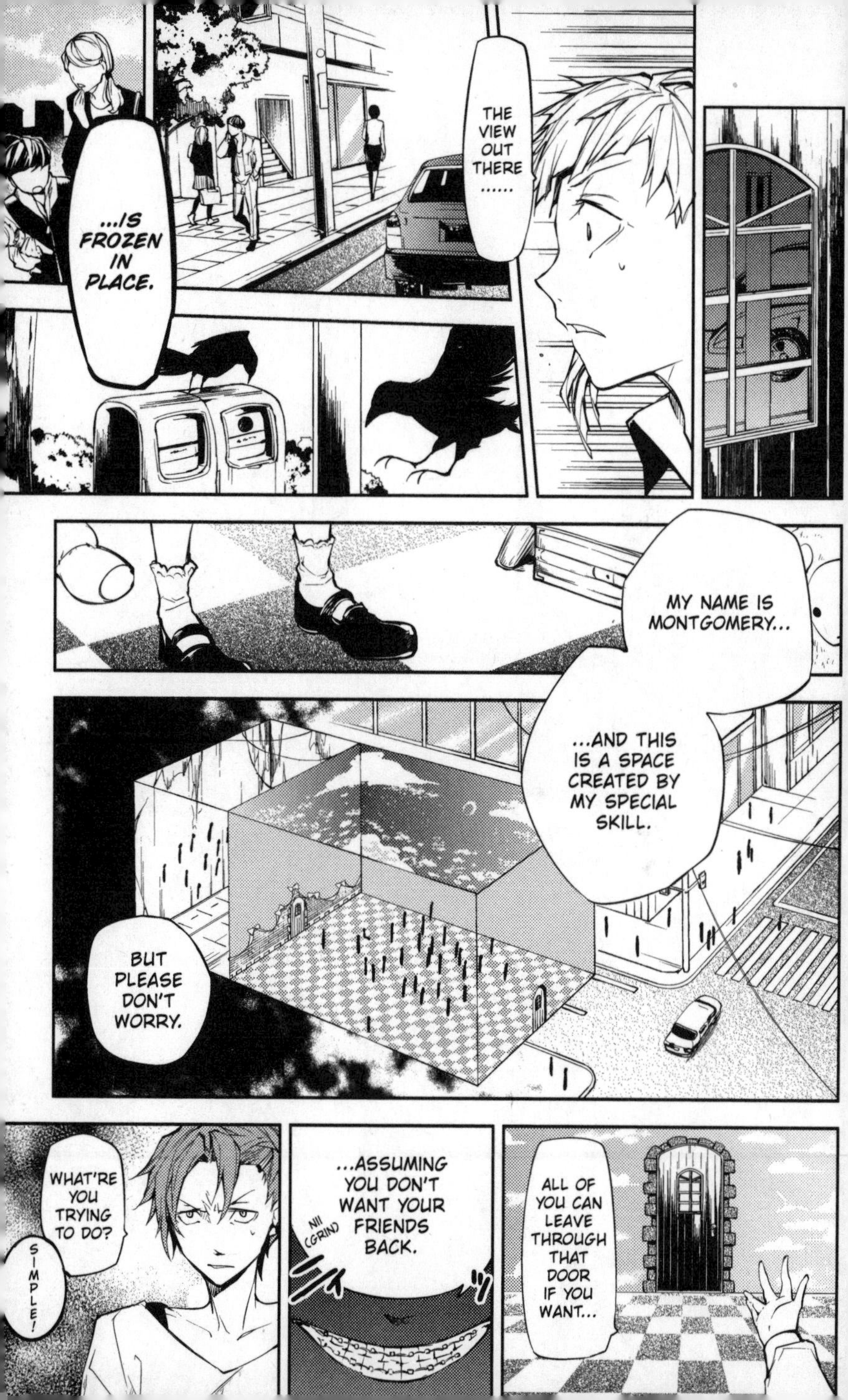
THE VIEW OUT THERE......
...IS FROZEN IN PLACE.
MY NAME IS MONTGOMERY...
...AND THIS IS A SPACE CREATED BY MY SPECIAL SKILL.
BUT PLEASE DON'T WORRY.
ALL OF YOU CAN LEAVE THROUGH THAT DOOR IF YOU WANT...
...ASSUMING YOU DON'T WANT YOUR FRIENDS BACK.
NII (GRIN)
WHAT'RE YOU TRYING TO DO?
SIMPLE!

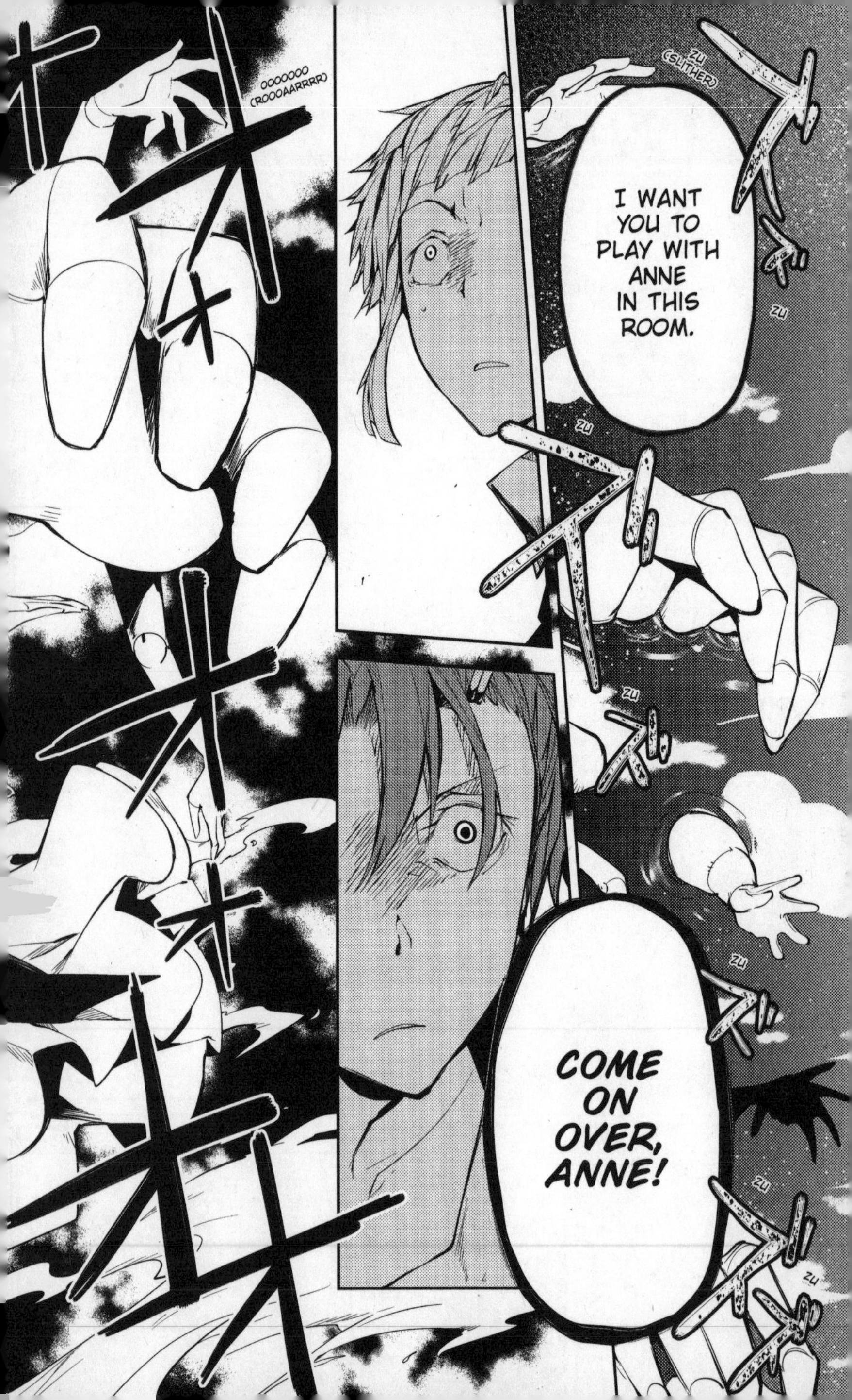
ZU
(SLITHER)
I WANT YOU TO PLAY WITH ANNE IN THIS ROOM.
ZU
ZU
ZU
ZU
COME ON OVER, ANNE!
ZU
ZU
OOOOOOO
(ROOOAARRRR)

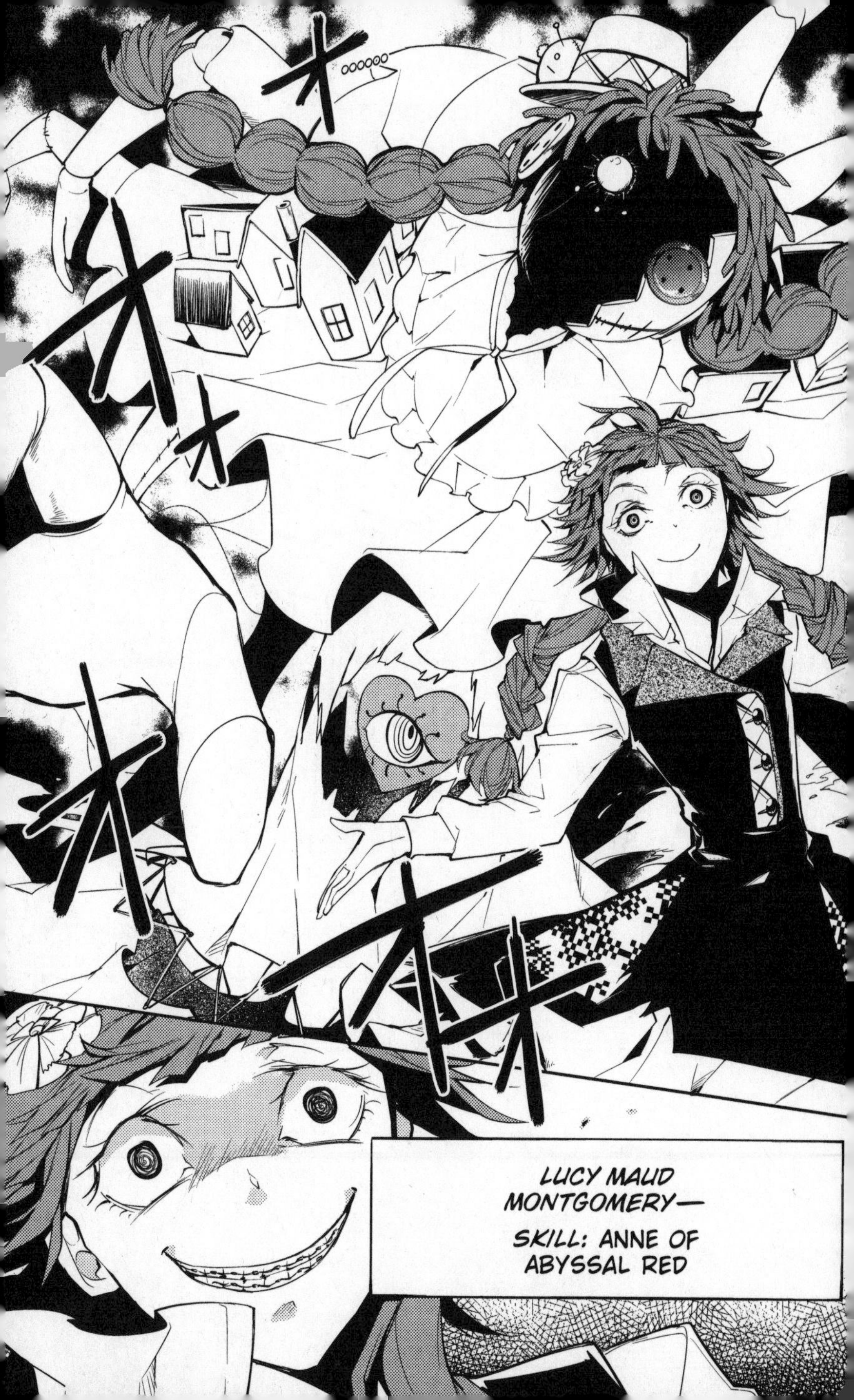
oooooo
LUCY MAUD MONTGOMERY—
SKILL: ANNE OF ABYSSAL RED

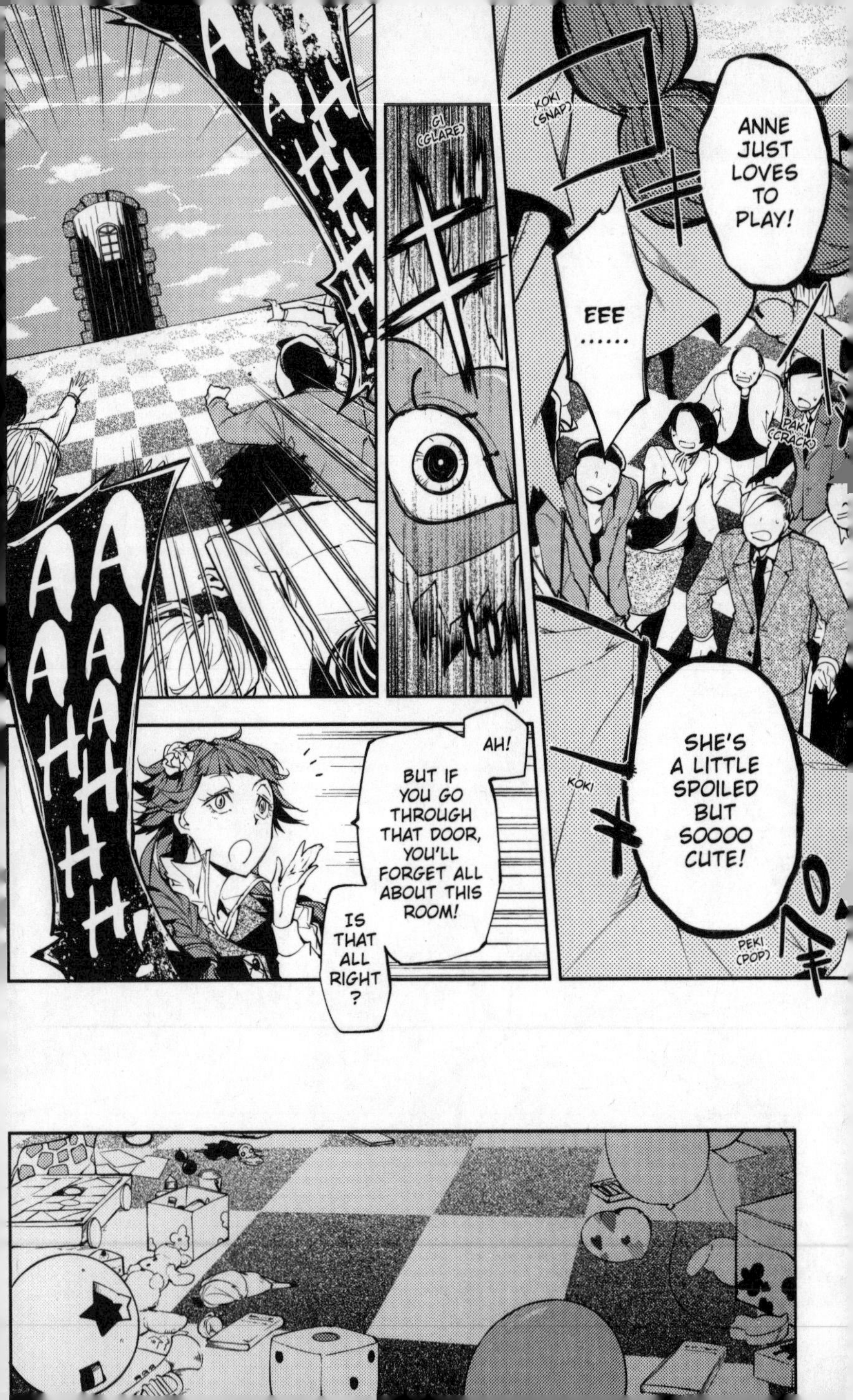
KOKI (SNAP)
ANNE JUST LOVES TO PLAY!
EEE......
PAKI (CRACK)
KOKI
SHE'S A LITTLE SPOILED BUT SOOOO CUTE!
PEKI (POP)
GI (GLARE)
AAAAHHHHHHH
AAAAAAHHHHHH!
AH!
BUT IF YOU GO THROUGH THAT DOOR, YOU'LL FORGET ALL ABOUT THIS ROOM!
IS THAT ALL RIGHT?

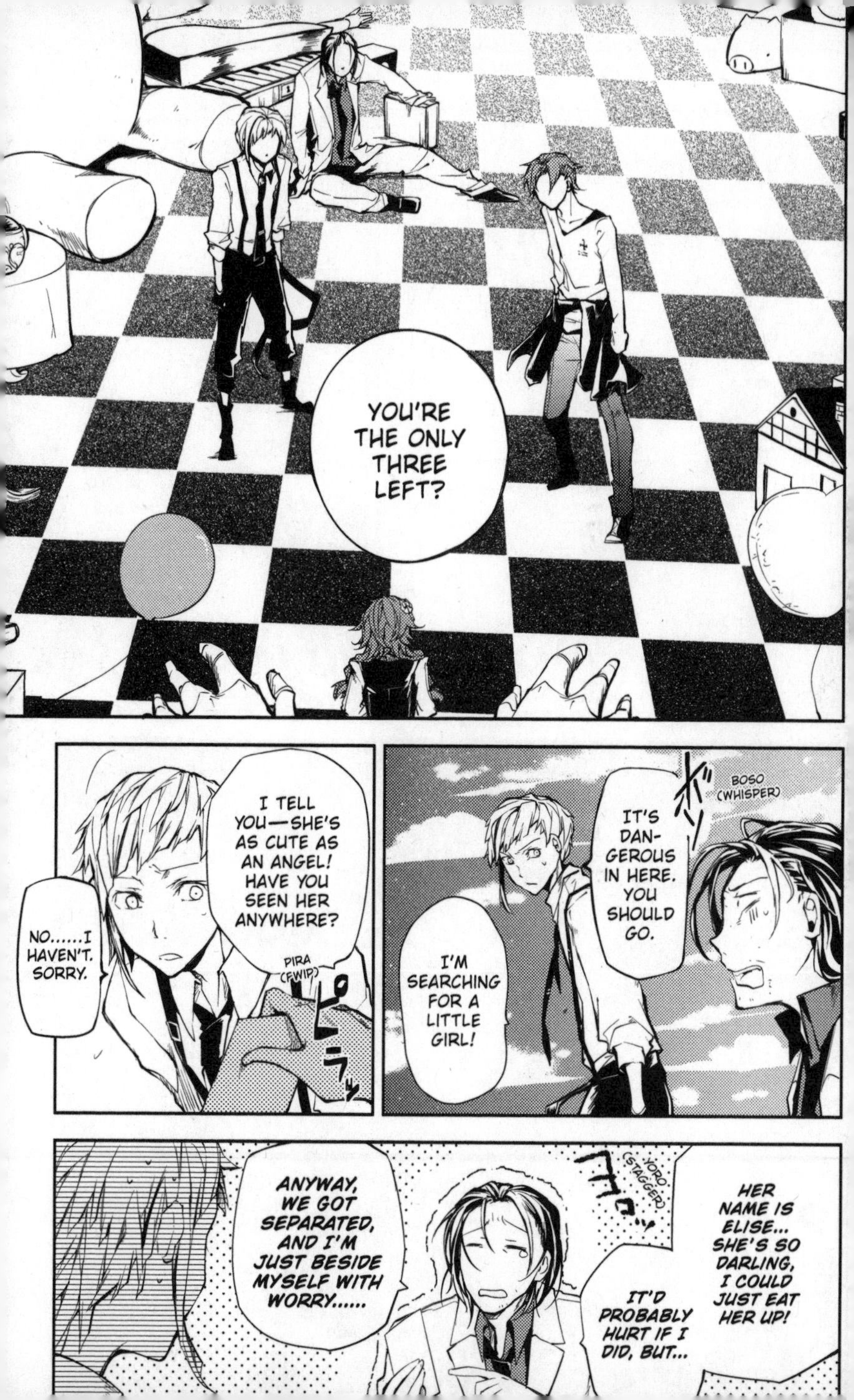
YOU'RE THE ONLY THREE LEFT?
BOSO (WHISPER)
IT'S DAN-GEROUS IN HERE. YOU SHOULD GO.
I'M SEARCHING FOR A LITTLE GIRL!
I TELL YOU—SHE'S AS CUTE AS AN ANGEL! HAVE YOU SEEN HER ANYWHERE?
PIRA (FWIP)
NO......I HAVEN'T. SORRY.
HER NAME IS ELISE... SHE'S SO DARLING, I COULD JUST EAT HER UP!
IT'D PROBABLY HURT IF I DID, BUT...
YORO (STAGGER)
ANYWAY, WE GOT SEPARATED, AND I'M JUST BESIDE MYSELF WITH WORRY......

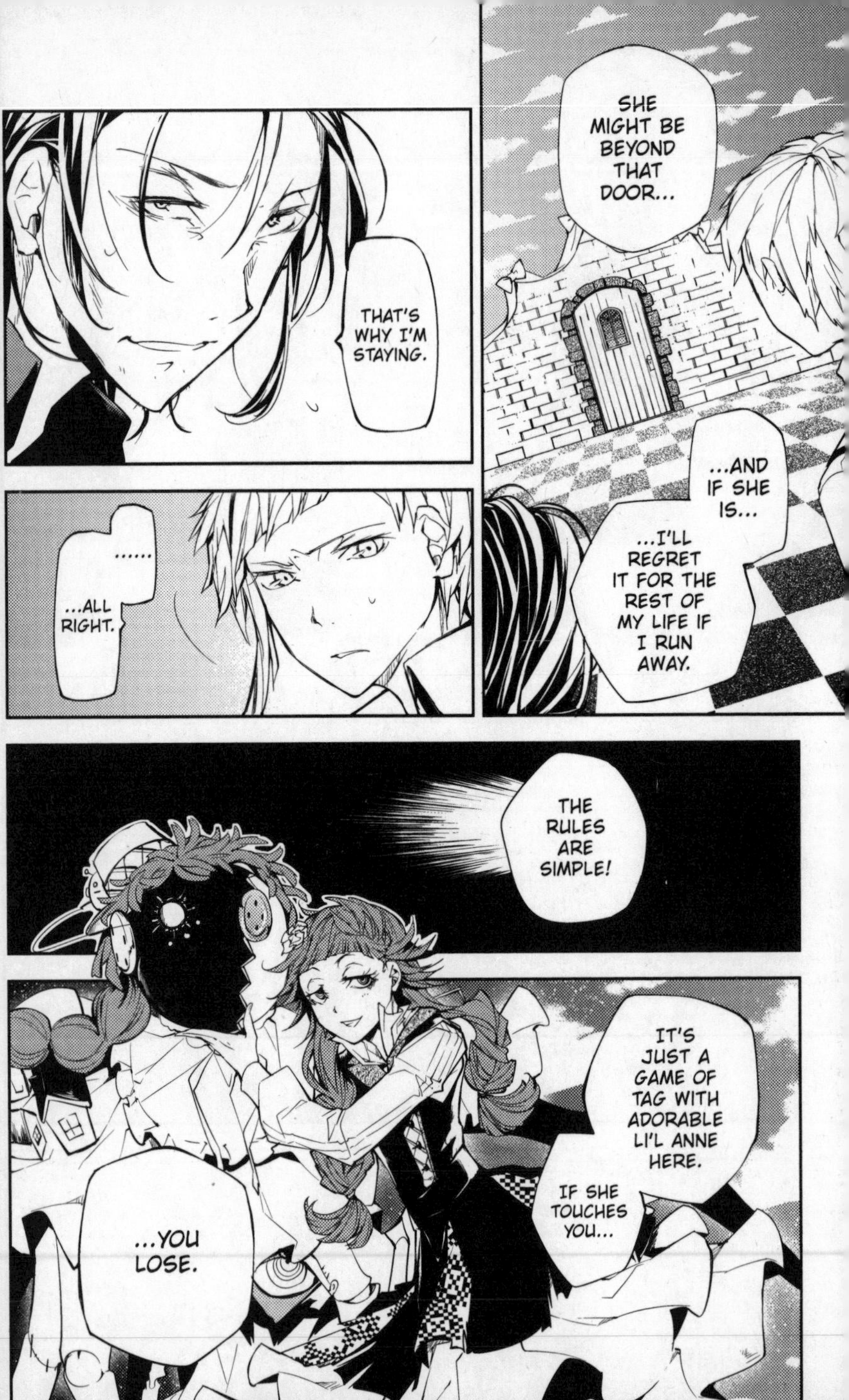
SHE MIGHT BE BEYOND THAT DOOR...
...AND IF SHE IS...
...I'LL REGRET IT FOR THE REST OF MY LIFE IF I RUN AWAY.
THAT'S WHY I'M STAYING.
......
...ALL RIGHT.
THE RULES ARE SIMPLE!
IT'S JUST A GAME OF TAG WITH ADORABLE LI'L ANNE HERE.
IF SHE TOUCHES YOU...
...YOU LOSE.

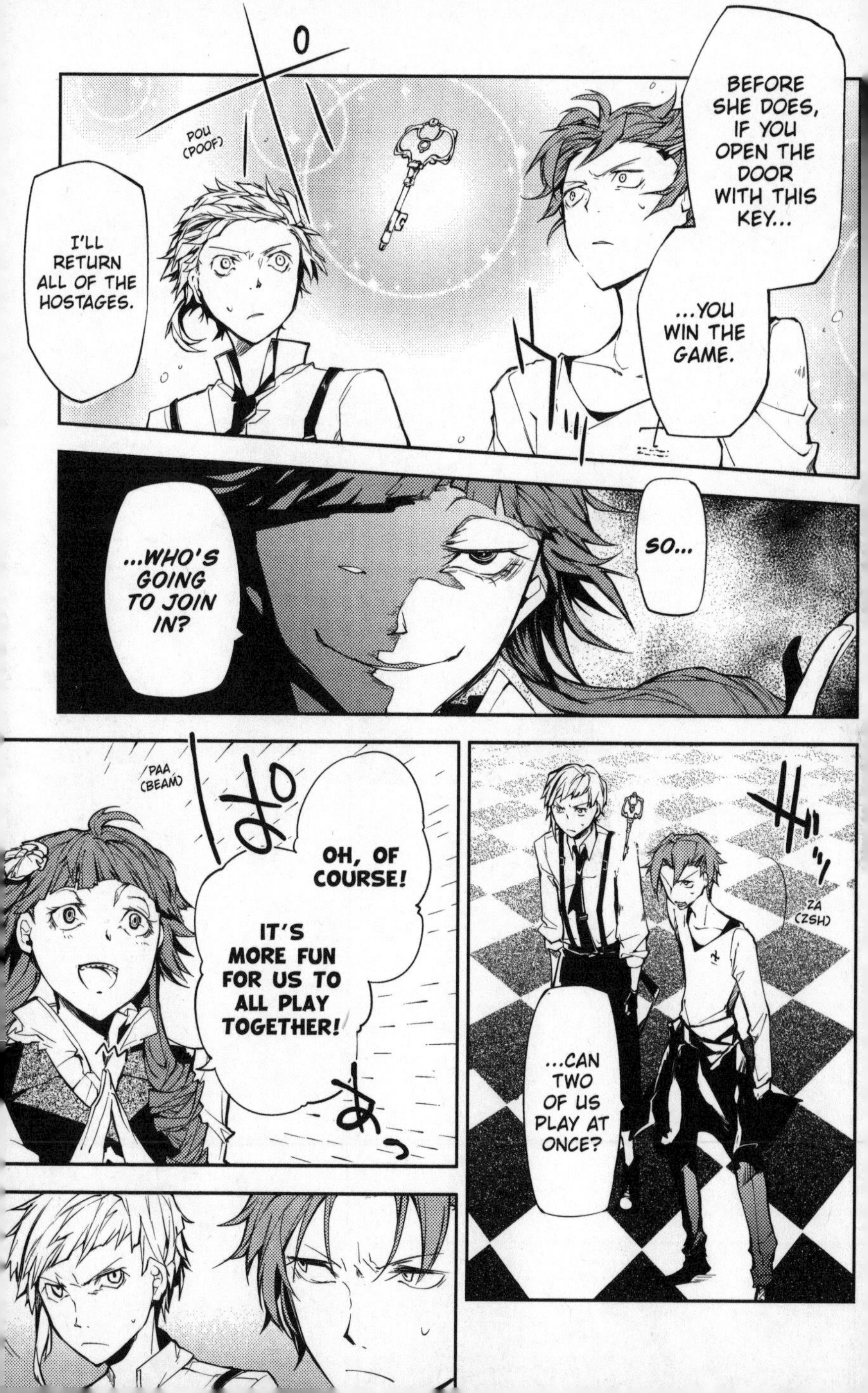
POU (POOF)
BEFORE SHE DOES, IF YOU OPEN THE DOOR WITH THIS KEY...
...YOU WIN THE GAME.
I'LL RETURN ALL OF THE HOSTAGES.
SO...
...WHO'S GOING TO JOIN IN?
ZA (ZSH)
...CAN TWO OF US PLAY AT ONCE?
PAA (BEAM)
OH, OF COURSE!
IT'S MORE FUN FOR US TO ALL PLAY TOGETHER!

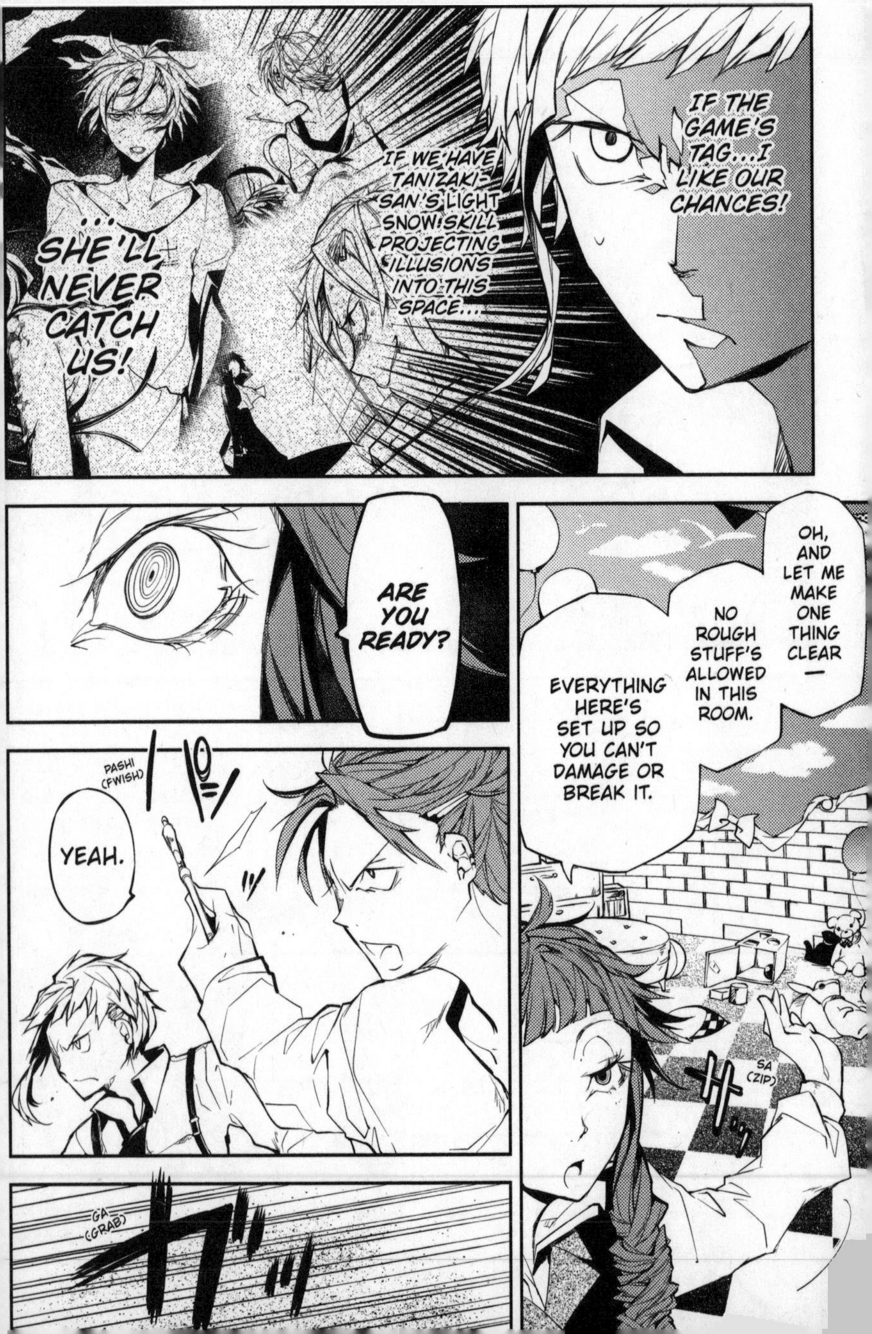
IF THE GAME'S TAG...I LIKE OUR CHANCES!
IF WE HAVE TANIZAKI-SAN'S LIGHT SNOW SKILL PROJECTING ILLUSIONS INTO THIS SPACE...
...SHE'LL NEVER CATCH US!
OH, AND LET ME MAKE ONE THING CLEAR —
NO ROUGH STUFF'S ALLOWED IN THIS ROOM.
EVERYTHING HERE'S SET UP SO YOU CAN'T DAMAGE OR BREAK IT.
SA (ZIP)
ARE YOU READY?
PASHI (FWISH)
YEAH.
GA (GRAB)

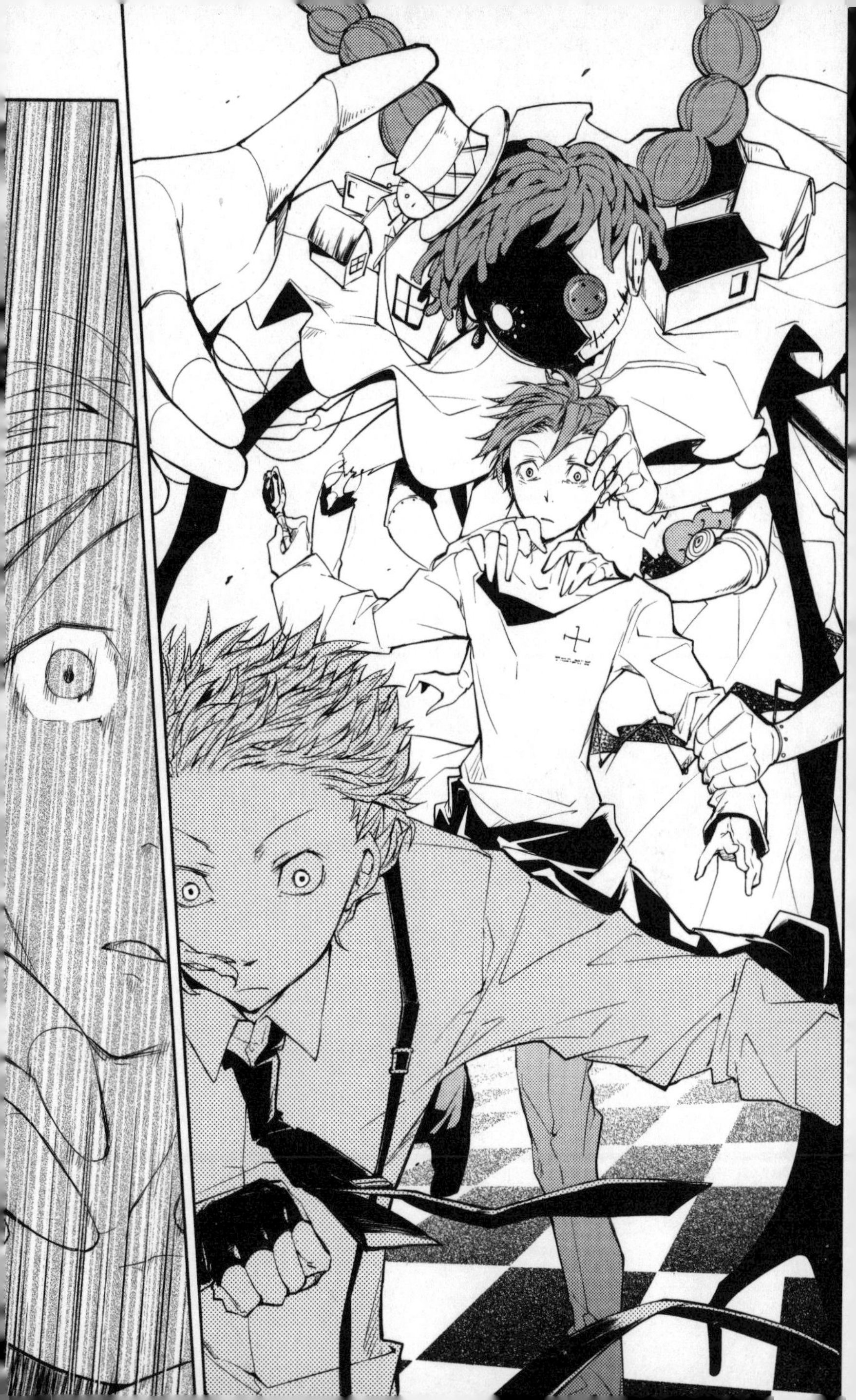

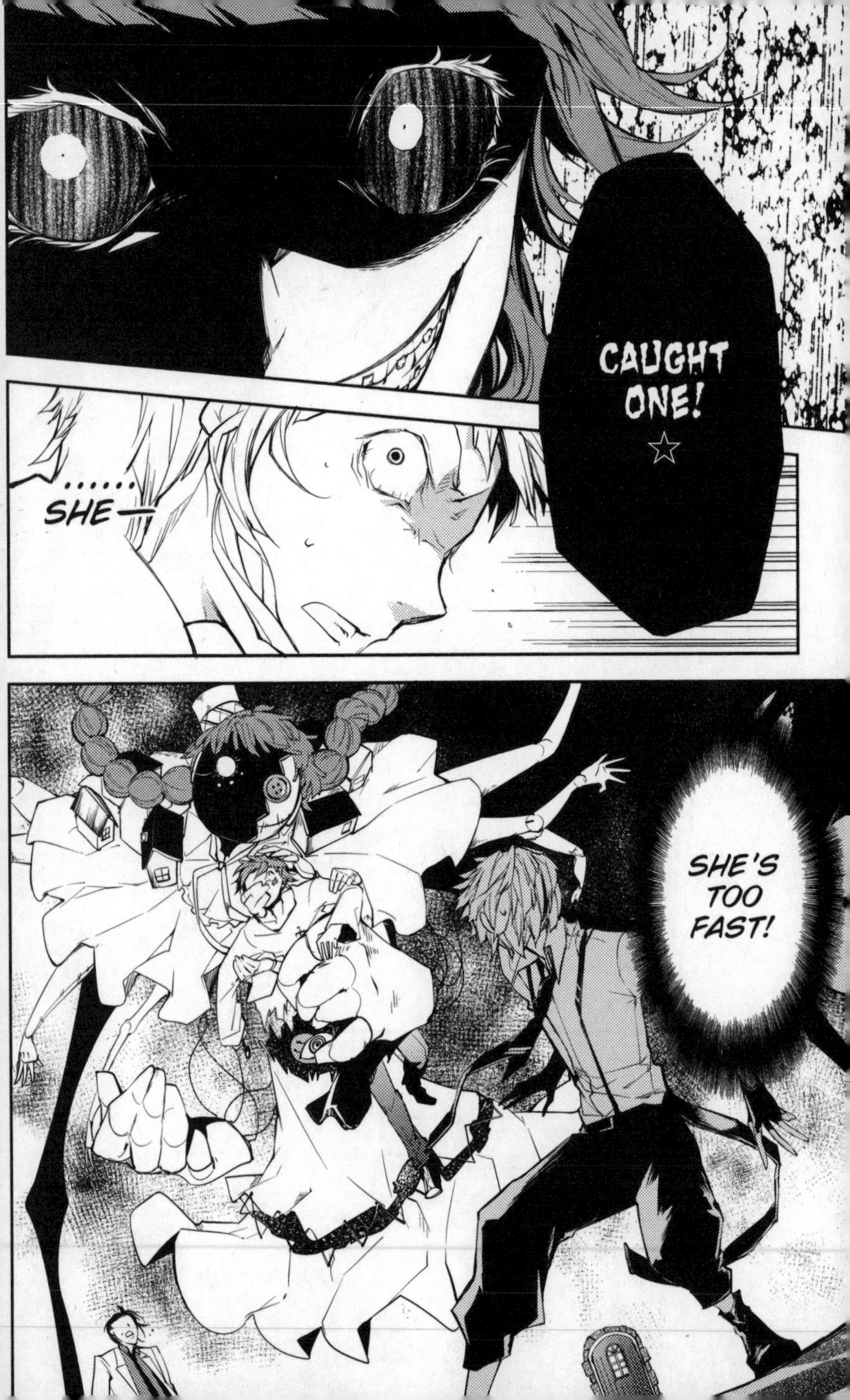
CAUGHT ONE! ☆
......SHE—
SHE'S TOO FAST!

KENJI MIYAZAWA

SKILL: Undefeated by the Rain
Unleashes untold strength and stoutness but only when hungry.

AGE: *14*

BIRTH DATE: *August 27*

HEIGHT: *158cm*

WEIGHT: *53kg*

BLOOD TYPE: *O*

LIKES: *Music, tempura soba, Mitsuya Cider*

DISLIKES: *Poverty*

BUNGO
STRAY DOGS

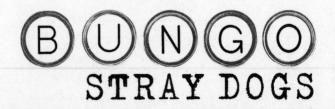

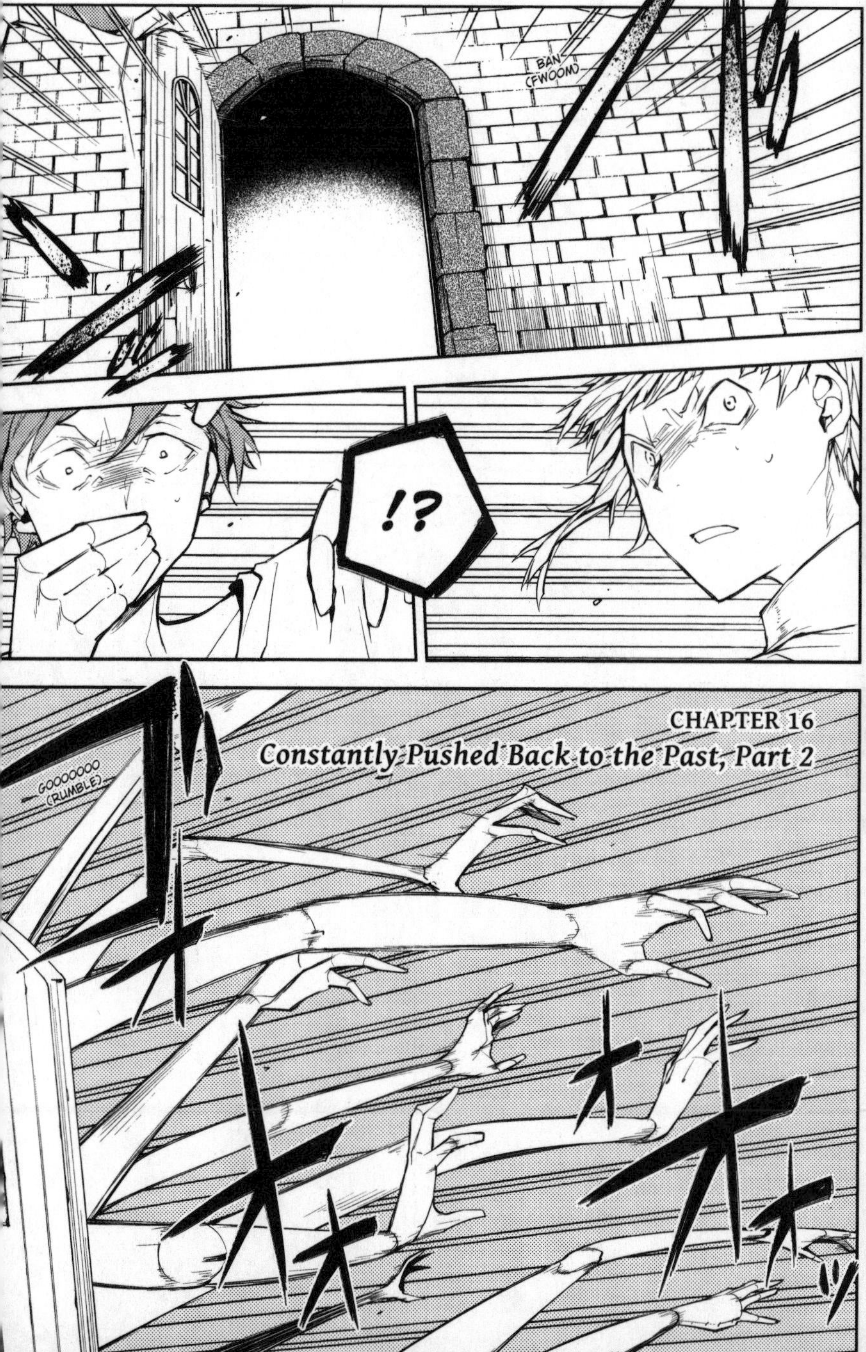
BAN
(FWOOM)
!?
CHAPTER 16
Constantly Pushed Back to the Past, Part 2
GOOOOOOO
(RUMBLE)

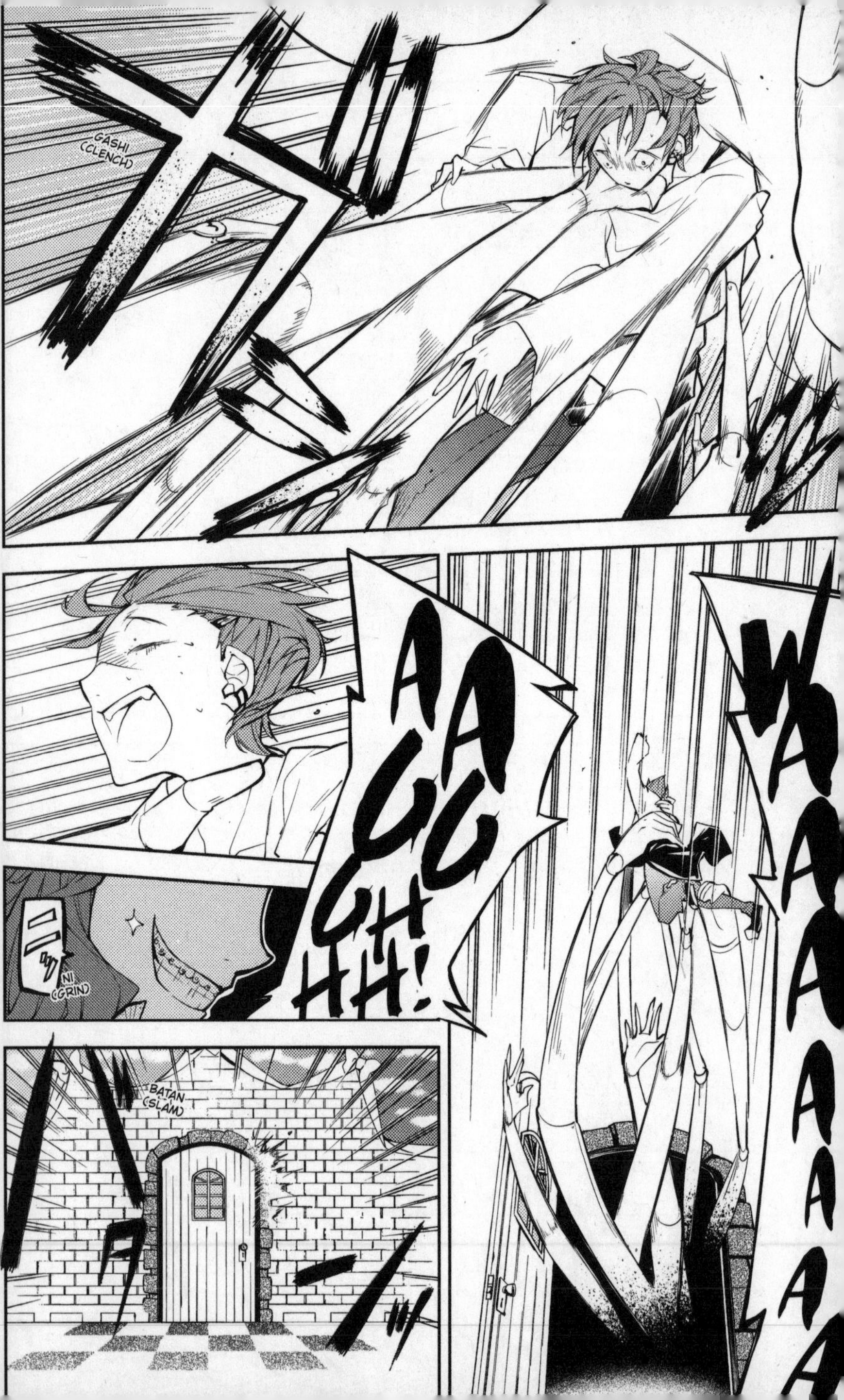
GASHI
(CLENCH)
WAAAAAAAA
AAUGHHH!
NI
(GRIN)
BATAN
(SLAM)

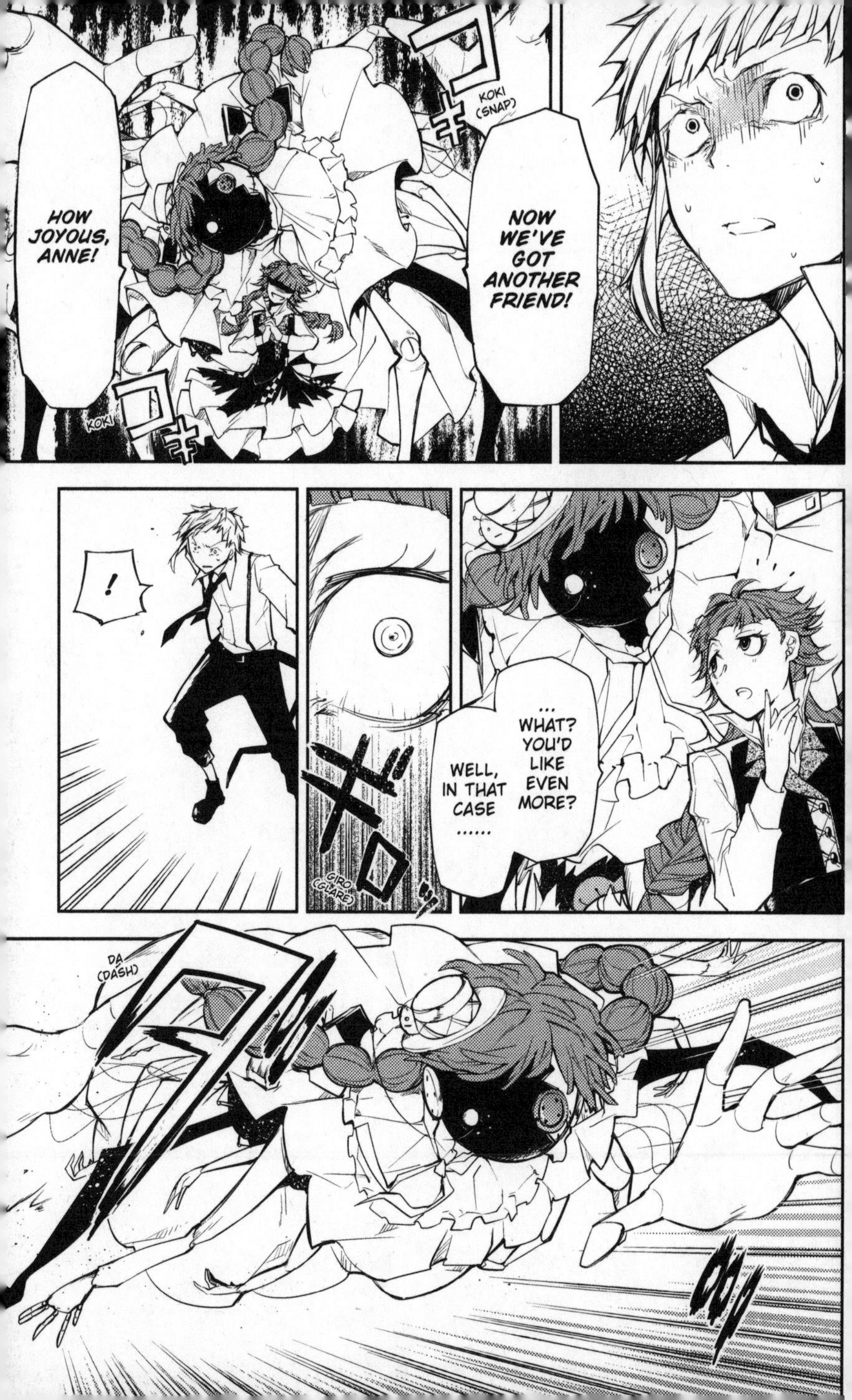
KOKI (SNAP)
NOW WE'VE GOT ANOTHER FRIEND!
HOW JOYOUS, ANNE!
KOKI
... WHAT? YOU'D LIKE EVEN MORE?
WELL, IN THAT CASE ......
GIRO (GLARE)
!
DA (DASH)

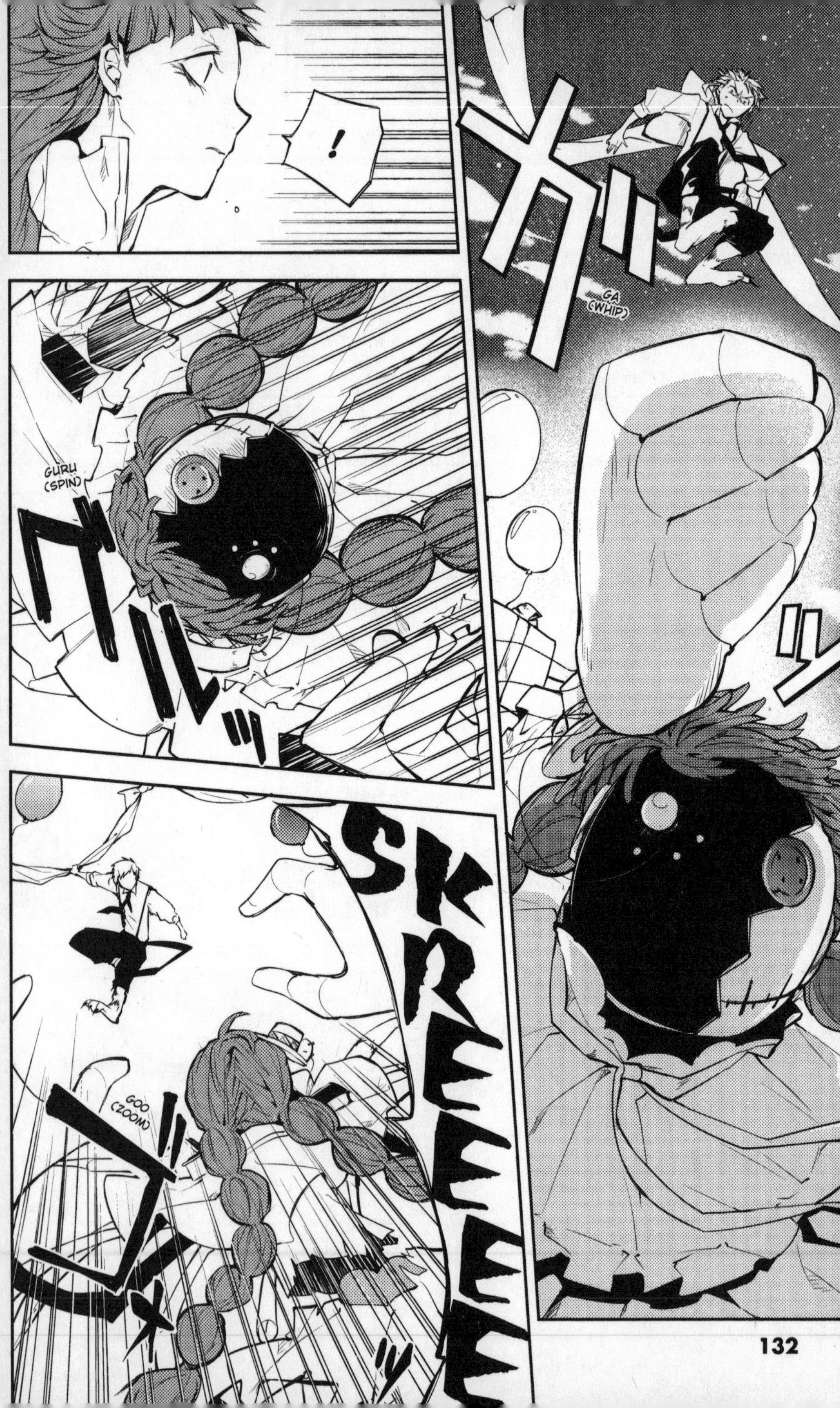
GA
(WHIP)
!
GURU
(SPIN)
SKREEE
GOO
(ZOOM)

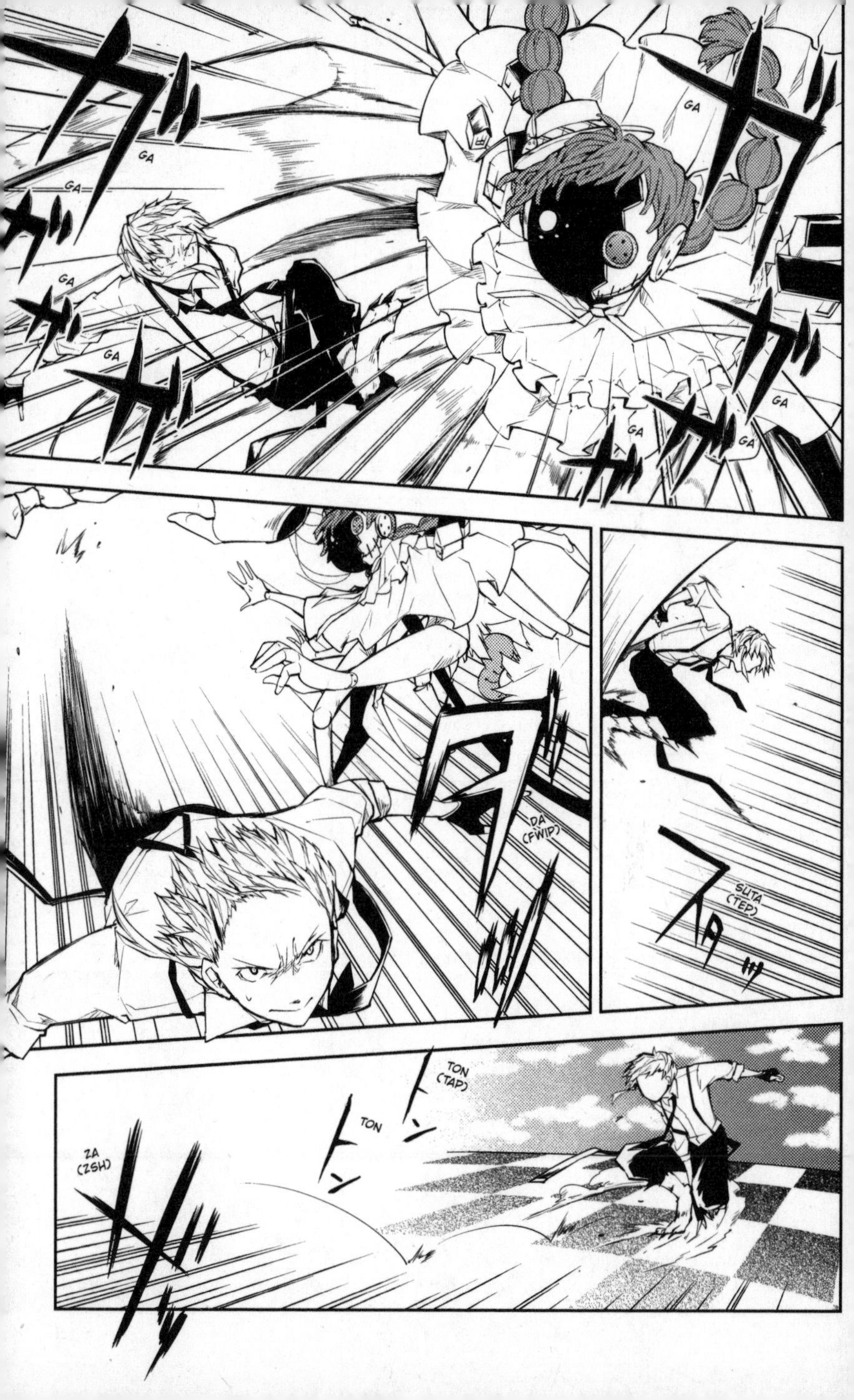
GA
GA
GA
GA
GA
GA
GA
GA
SUTA (TEP)
DA (FWIP)
TON (TAP)
TON
ZA (ZSH)

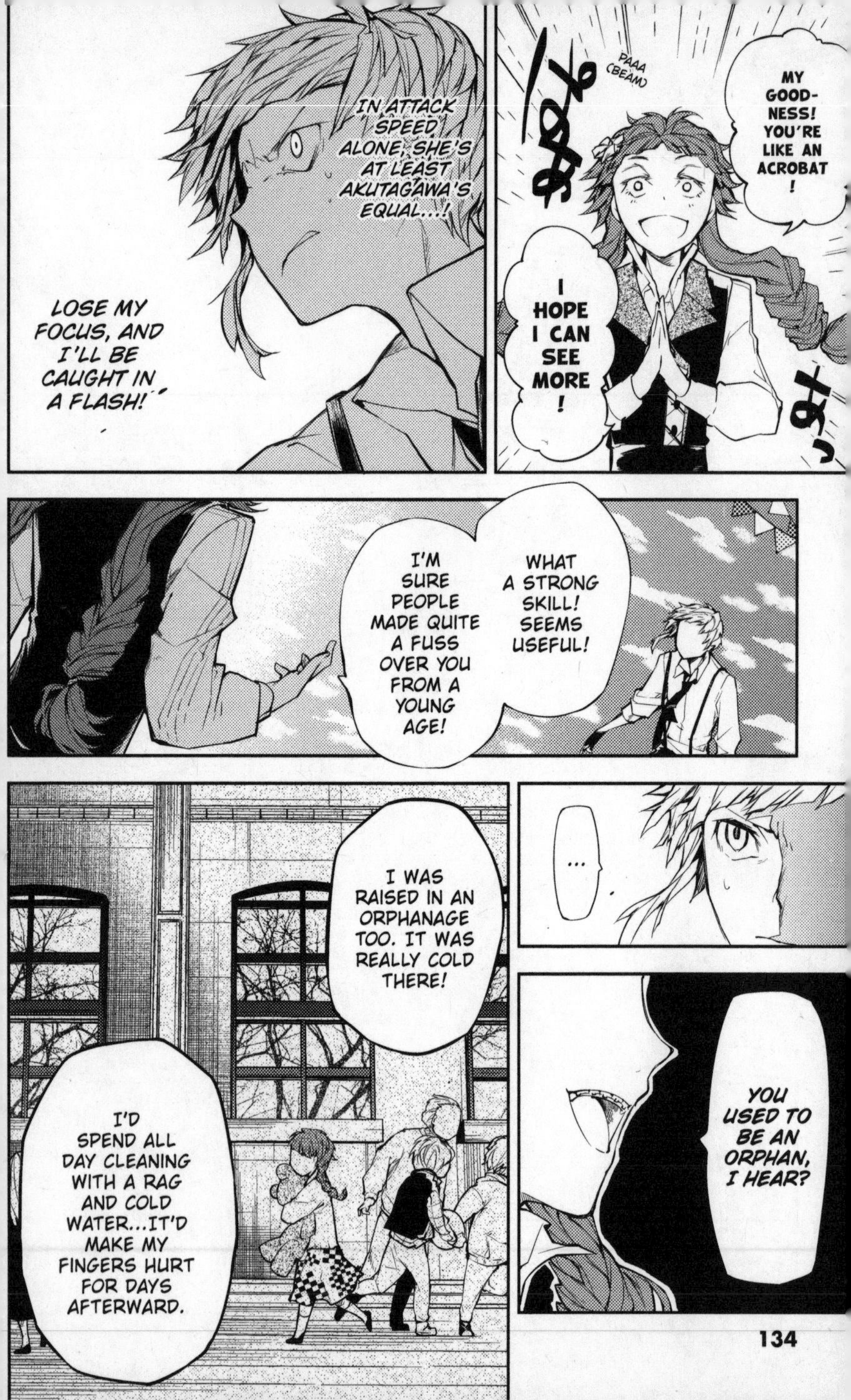
PAAA (BEAM)
MY GOODNESS! YOU'RE LIKE AN ACROBAT!
I HOPE I CAN SEE MORE!
IN ATTACK SPEED ALONE, SHE'S AT LEAST AKUTAGAWA'S EQUAL...!
LOSE MY FOCUS, AND I'LL BE CAUGHT IN A FLASH!
WHAT A STRONG SKILL! SEEMS USEFUL!
I'M SURE PEOPLE MADE QUITE A FUSS OVER YOU FROM A YOUNG AGE!
...
YOU USED TO BE AN ORPHAN, I HEAR?
I WAS RAISED IN AN ORPHANAGE TOO. IT WAS REALLY COLD THERE!
I'D SPEND ALL DAY CLEANING WITH A RAG AND COLD WATER...IT'D MAKE MY FINGERS HURT FOR DAYS AFTERWARD.

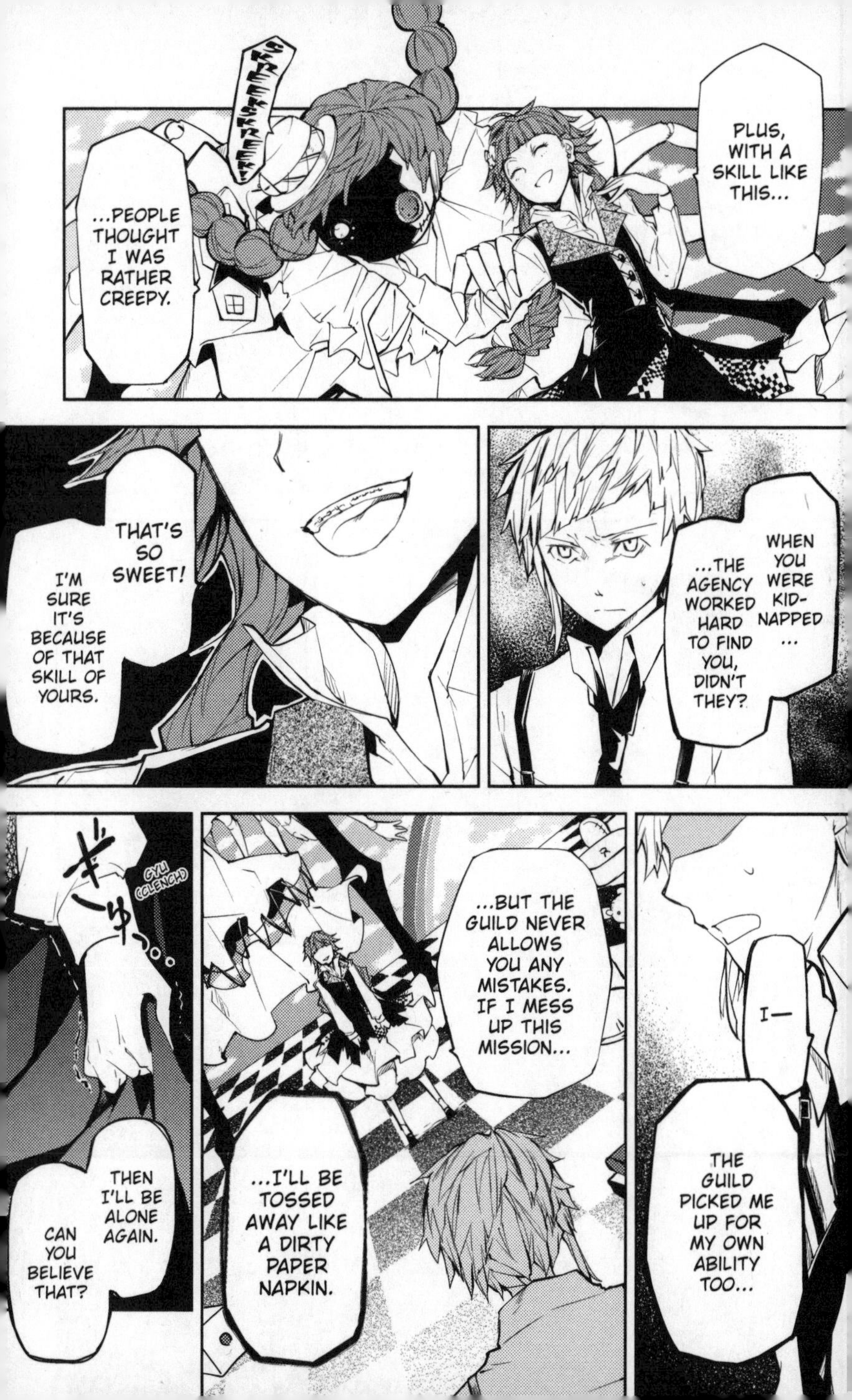
PLUS, WITH A SKILL LIKE THIS...
SKREEKSKREEK!
...PEOPLE THOUGHT I WAS RATHER CREEPY.
WHEN YOU WERE KID-NAPPED...
...THE AGENCY WORKED HARD TO FIND YOU, DIDN'T THEY?
THAT'S SO SWEET!
I'M SURE IT'S BECAUSE OF THAT SKILL OF YOURS.
I—
THE GUILD PICKED ME UP FOR MY OWN ABILITY TOO...
...BUT THE GUILD NEVER ALLOWS YOU ANY MISTAKES. IF I MESS UP THIS MISSION...
...I'LL BE TOSSED AWAY LIKE A DIRTY PAPER NAPKIN.
GYU (CLENCH)
THEN I'LL BE ALONE AGAIN.
CAN YOU BELIEVE THAT?

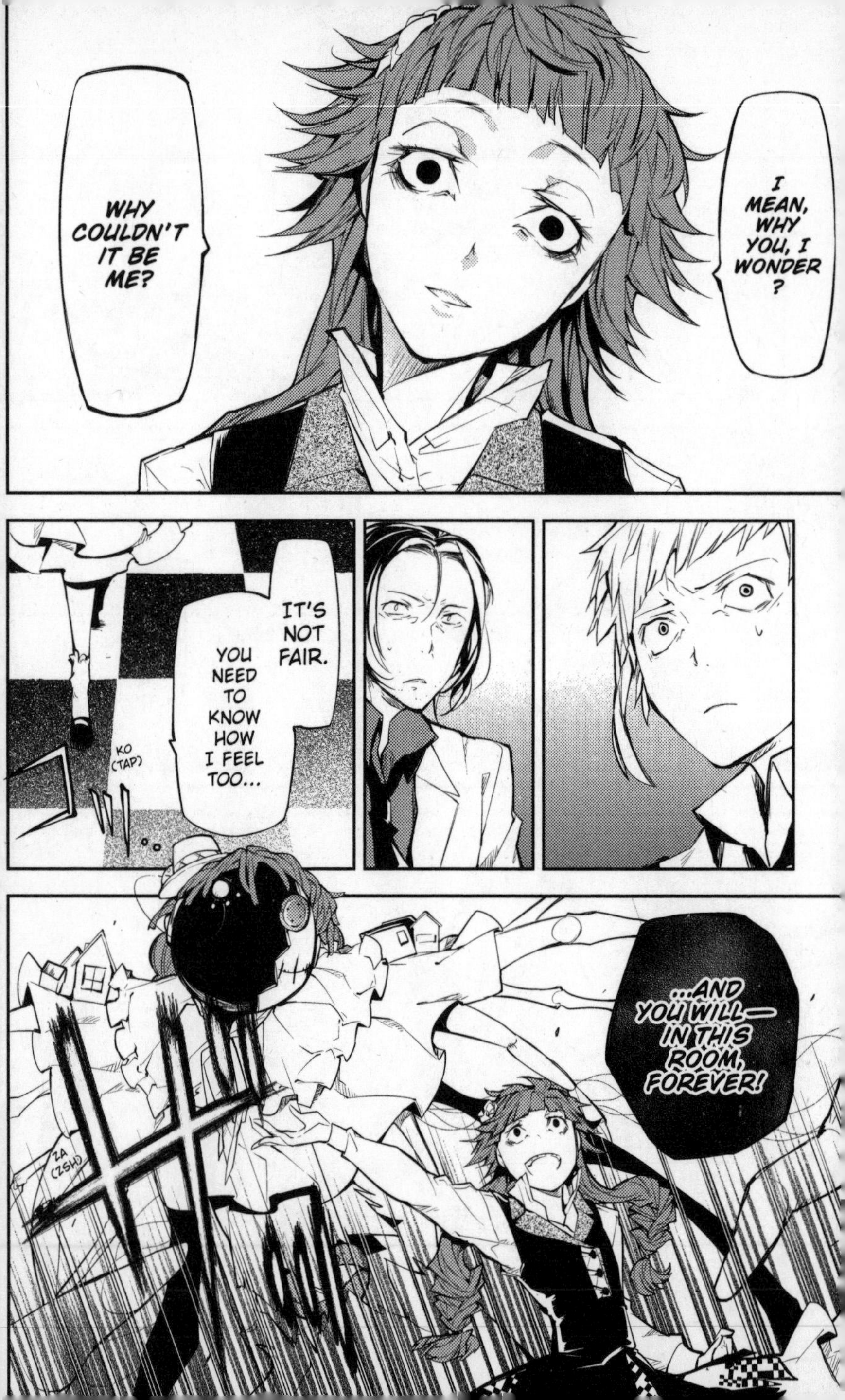
I MEAN, WHY YOU, I WONDER?
WHY COULDN'T IT BE ME?
IT'S NOT FAIR.
YOU NEED TO KNOW HOW I FEEL TOO...
KO (TAP)
...AND YOU WILL— IN THIS ROOM, FOREVER!
ZA (ZSH)

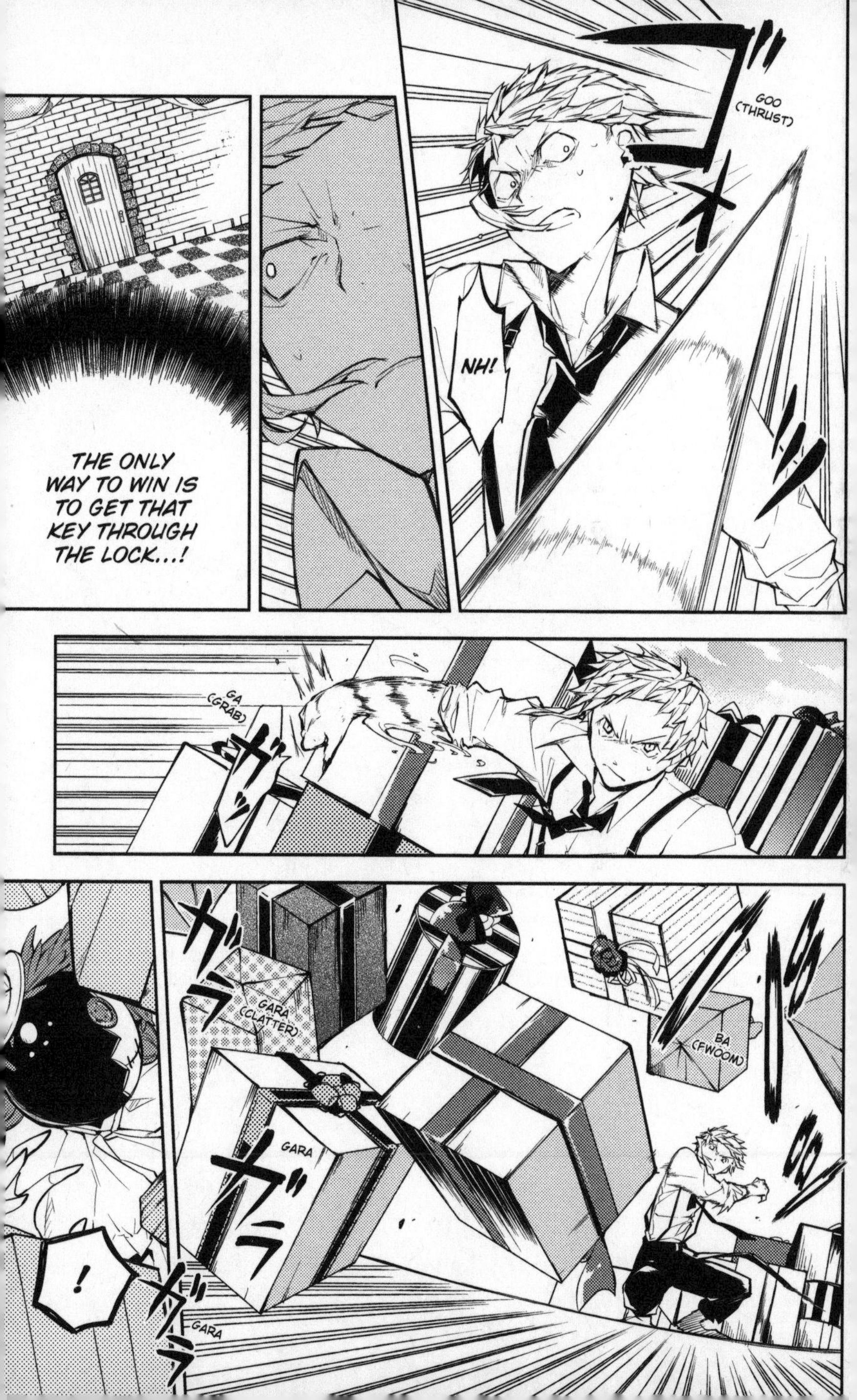
GOO (THRUST)
NH!
THE ONLY WAY TO WIN IS TO GET THAT KEY THROUGH THE LOCK...!
GA (GRAB)
BA (FWOOM)
GARA (CLATTER)
GARA
GARA
!

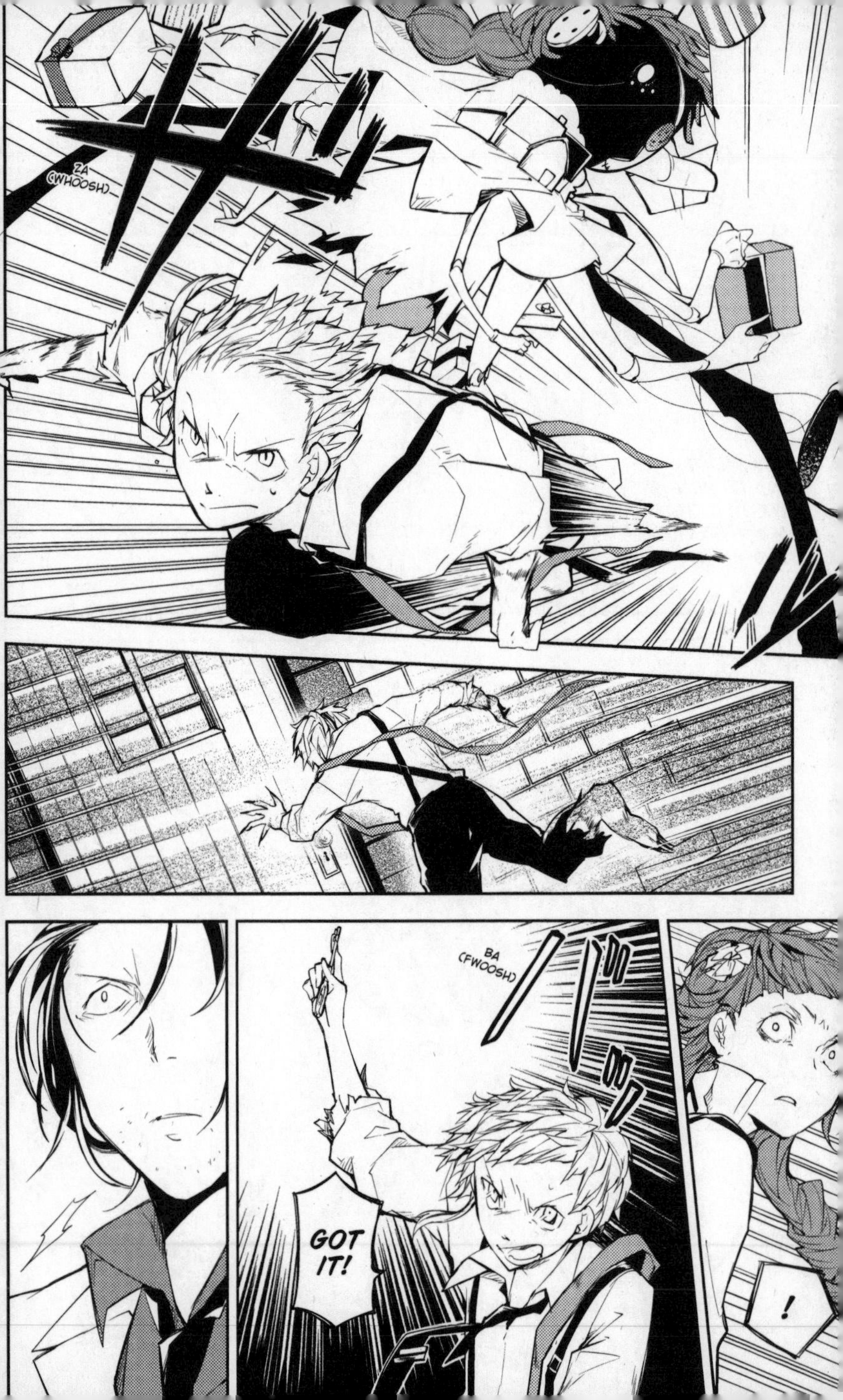
ZA
(WHOOSH)
!
BA
(FWOOSH)
GOT IT!

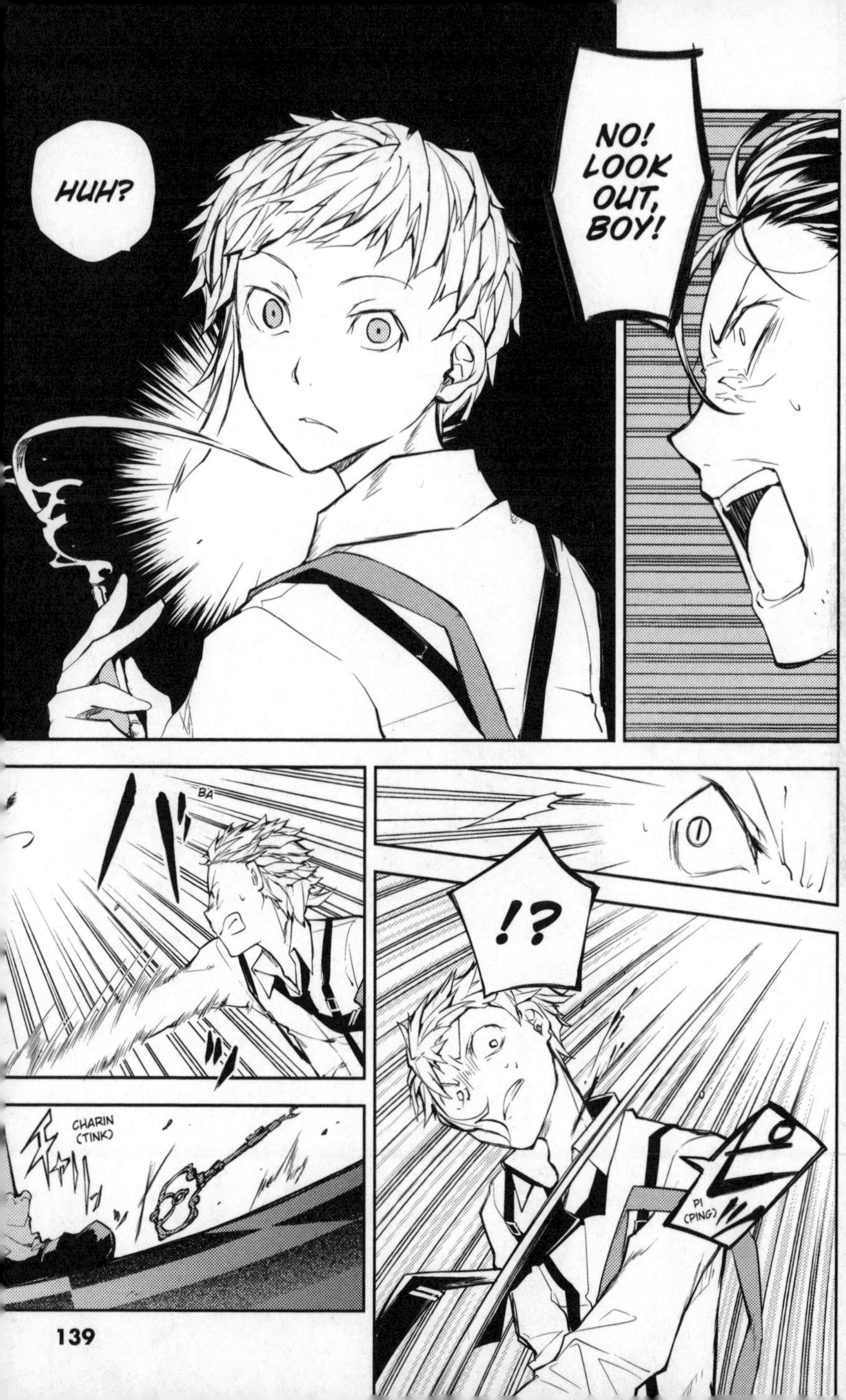
NO! LOOK OUT, BOY!
HUH?
!?
PI (PING)
BA
CHARIN (TINK)

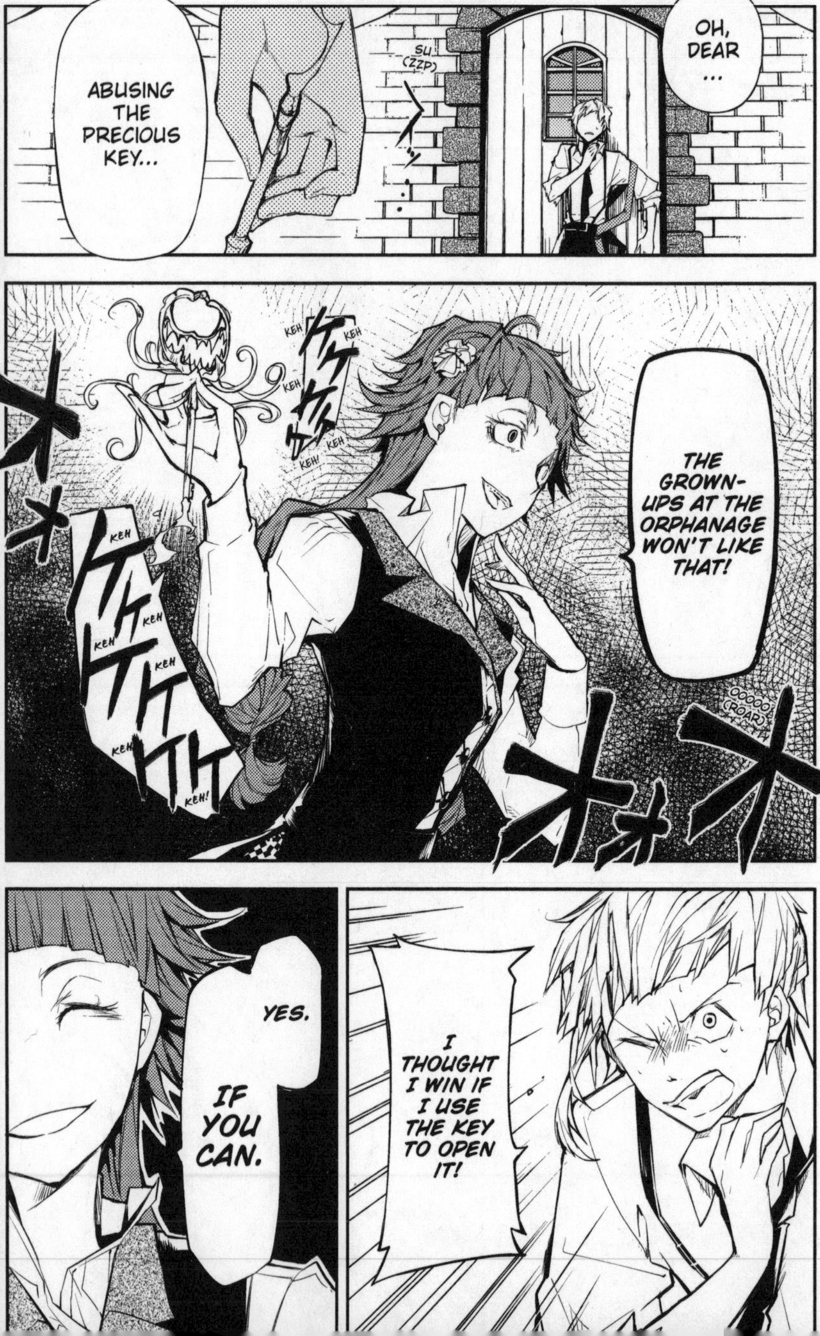
OH, DEAR ...
SU (ZZP)
ABUSING THE PRECIOUS KEY...
THE GROWN-UPS AT THE ORPHANAGE WON'T LIKE THAT!
OOOOO (ROAR)
KEH KEH KEH KEH KEH!
KEH KEH KEH KEH KEH KEH!
I THOUGHT I WIN IF I USE THE KEY TO OPEN IT!
YES.
IF YOU CAN.

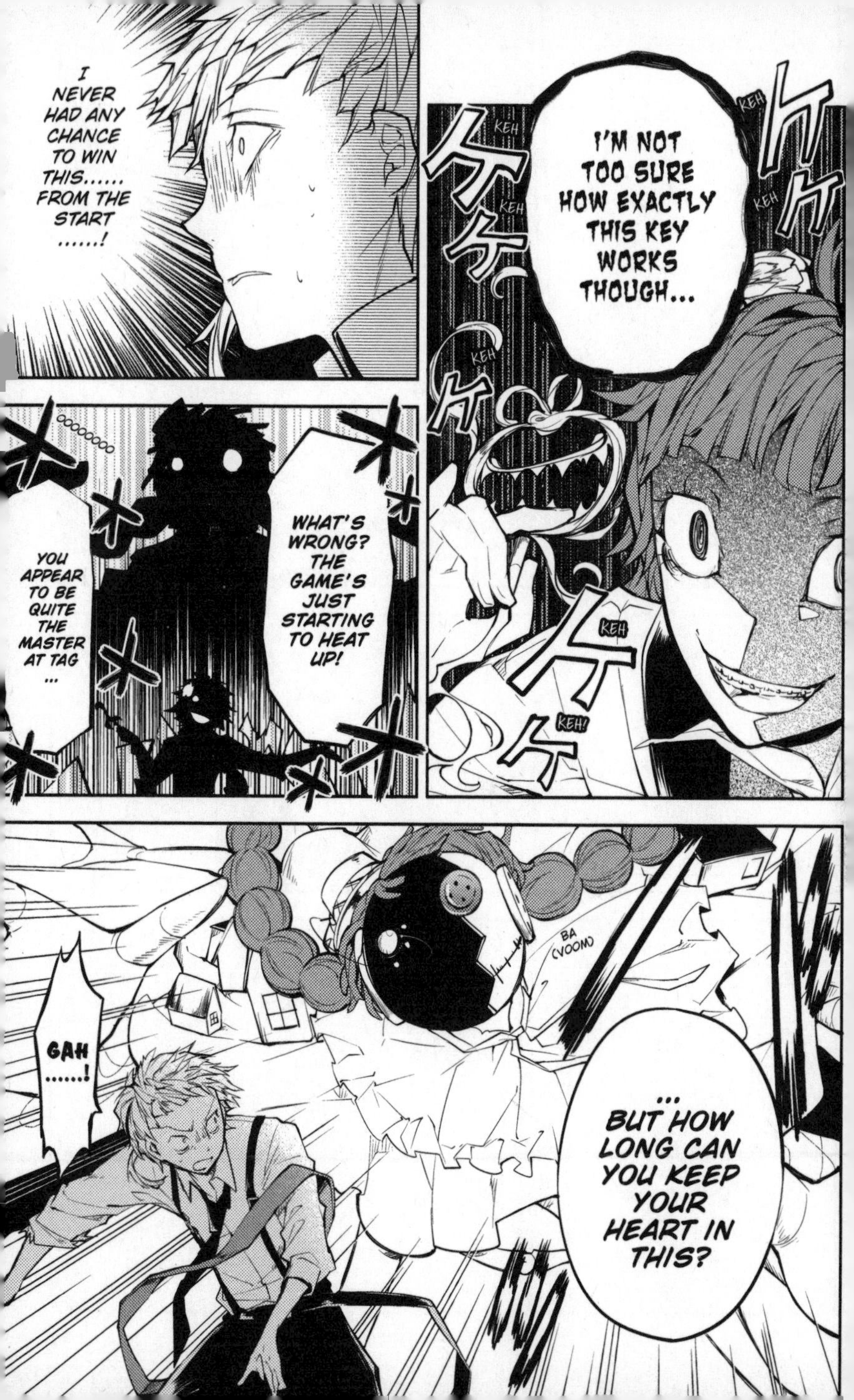
KEH
KEH
I'M NOT TOO SURE HOW EXACTLY THIS KEY WORKS THOUGH...
KEH
KEH
KEH
KEH
KEH!
I NEVER HAD ANY CHANCE TO WIN THIS...... FROM THE START ......!
WHAT'S WRONG? THE GAME'S JUST STARTING TO HEAT UP!
OOOOOOOO
YOU APPEAR TO BE QUITE THE MASTER AT TAG ...
... BUT HOW LONG CAN YOU KEEP YOUR HEART IN THIS?
BA (VOOM)
GAH ......!

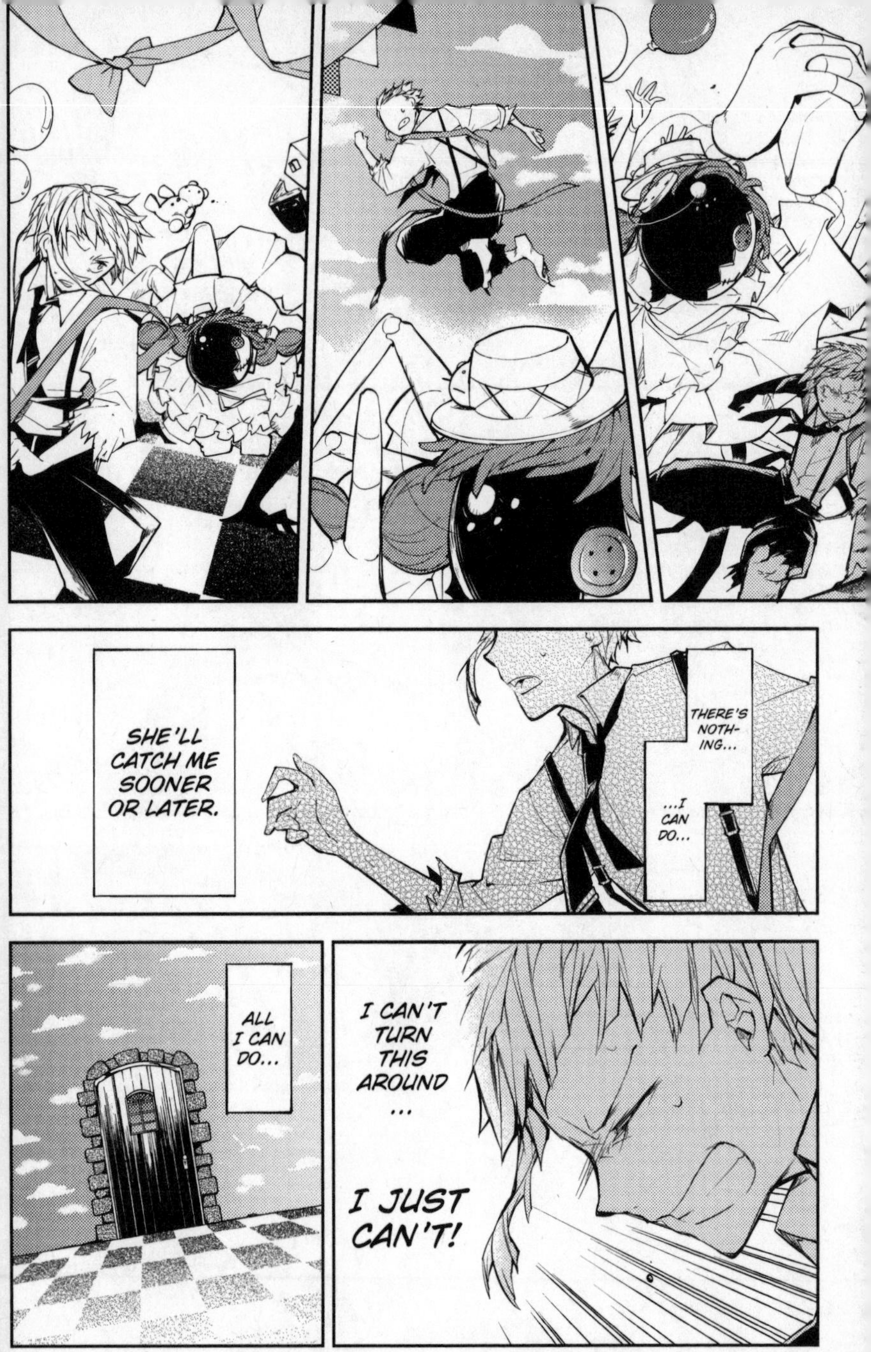
THERE'S NOTHING...
...I CAN DO...
SHE'LL CATCH ME SOONER OR LATER.
I CAN'T TURN THIS AROUND...
I JUST CAN'T!
ALL I CAN DO...

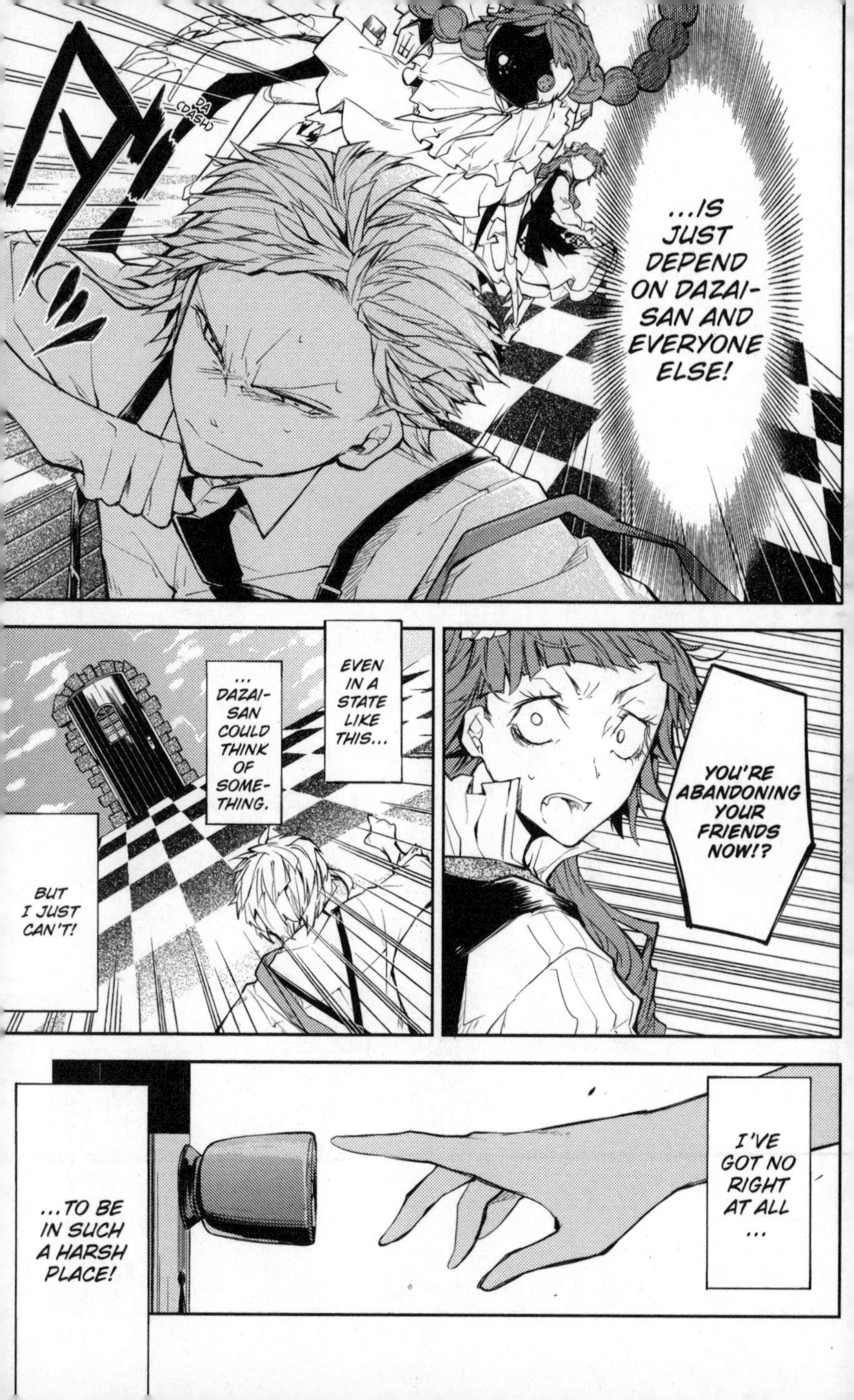
...IS JUST DEPEND ON DAZAI-SAN AND EVERYONE ELSE!
DA (DASH)
YOU'RE ABANDONING YOUR FRIENDS NOW!?
EVEN IN A STATE LIKE THIS...
...DAZAI-SAN COULD THINK OF SOME-THING.
BUT I JUST CAN'T!
I'VE GOT NO RIGHT AT ALL...
...TO BE IN SUCH A HARSH PLACE!

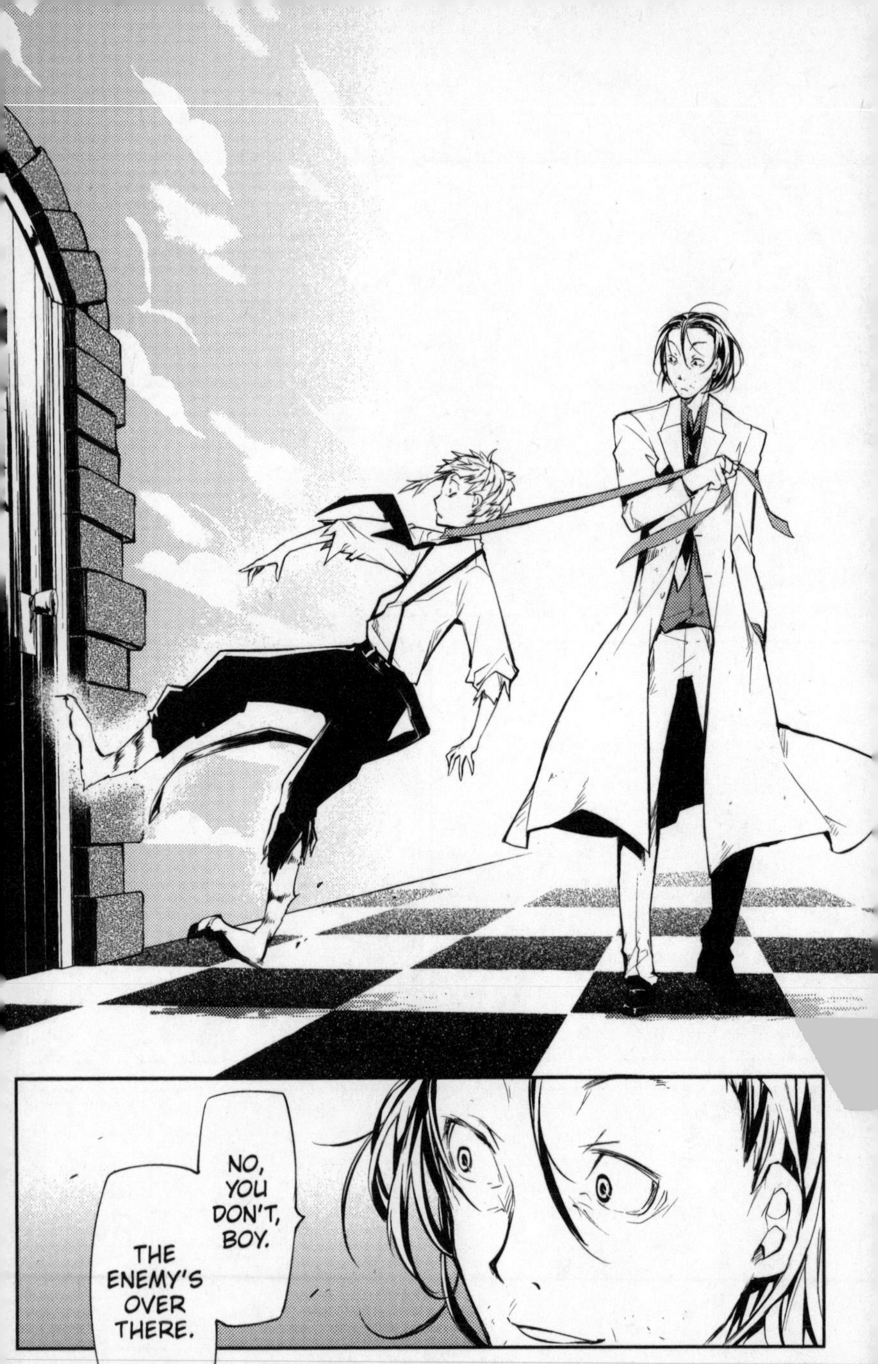
NO, YOU DON'T, BOY.
THE ENEMY'S OVER THERE.

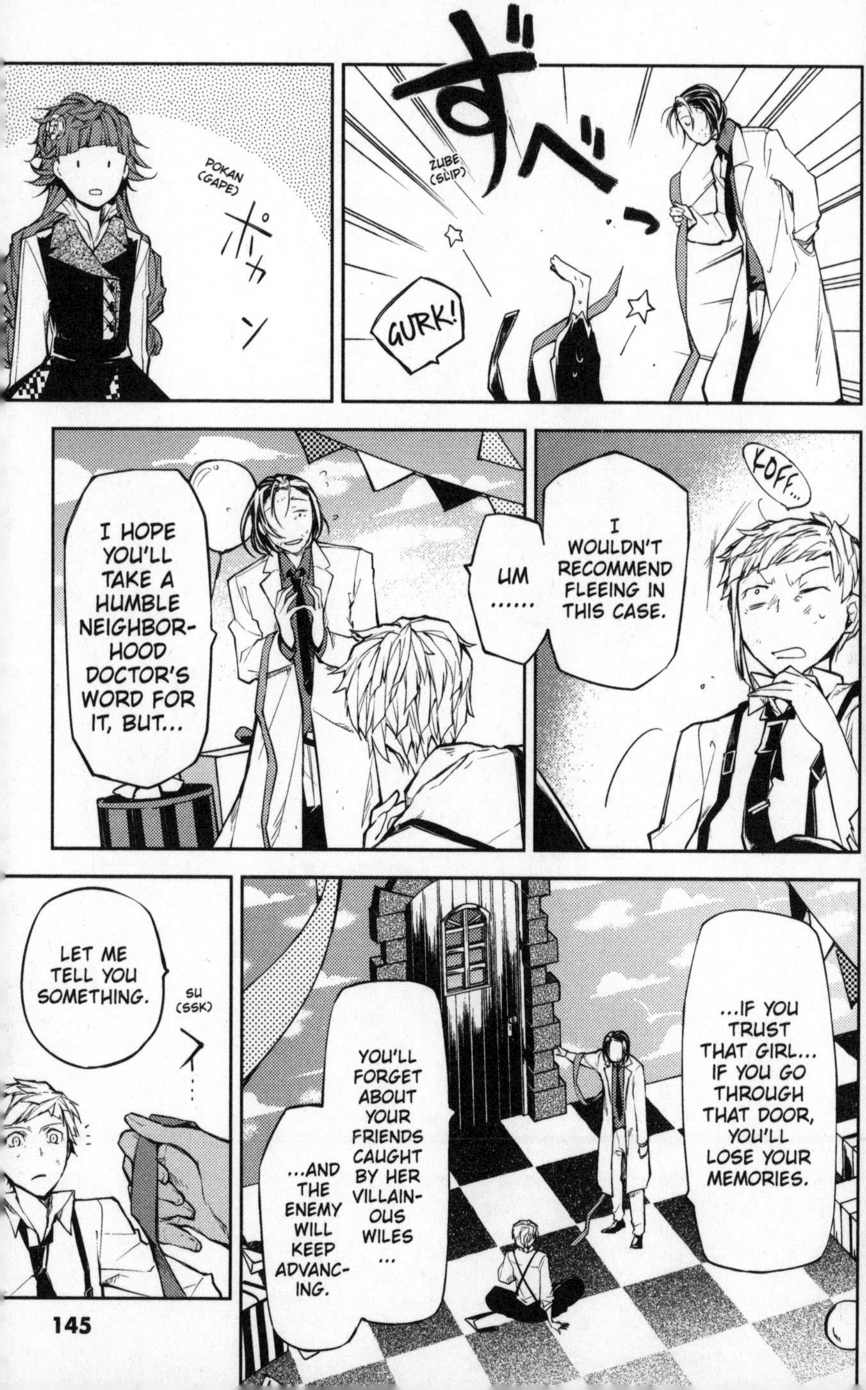
ずべっ
ZUBE (SLIP)
GURK!
ポカン
POKAN (GAPE)
KOFF...
I WOULDN'T RECOMMEND FLEEING IN THIS CASE.
UM ......
I HOPE YOU'LL TAKE A HUMBLE NEIGHBOR-HOOD DOCTOR'S WORD FOR IT, BUT...
...IF YOU TRUST THAT GIRL... IF YOU GO THROUGH THAT DOOR, YOU'LL LOSE YOUR MEMORIES.
YOU'LL FORGET ABOUT YOUR FRIENDS CAUGHT BY HER VILLAIN-OUS WILES ...
...AND THE ENEMY WILL KEEP ADVANC-ING.
LET ME TELL YOU SOMETHING.
SU (SSK)

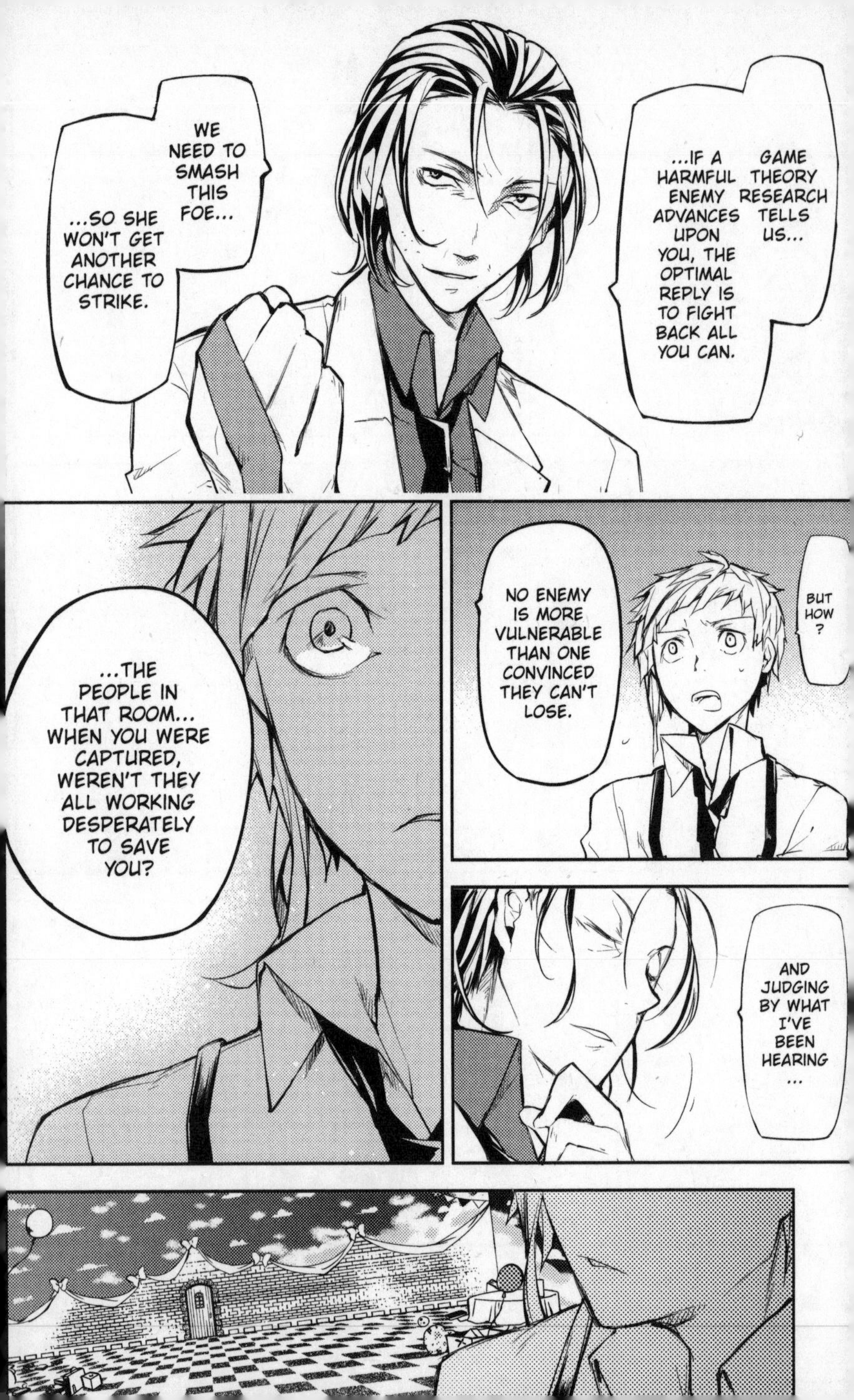
GAME THEORY RESEARCH TELLS US...
...IF A HARMFUL ENEMY ADVANCES UPON YOU, THE OPTIMAL REPLY IS TO FIGHT BACK ALL YOU CAN.
WE NEED TO SMASH THIS FOE...
...SO SHE WON'T GET ANOTHER CHANCE TO STRIKE.
BUT HOW?
NO ENEMY IS MORE VULNERABLE THAN ONE CONVINCED THEY CAN'T LOSE.
AND JUDGING BY WHAT I'VE BEEN HEARING...
...THE PEOPLE IN THAT ROOM... WHEN YOU WERE CAPTURED, WEREN'T THEY ALL WORKING DESPERATELY TO SAVE YOU?

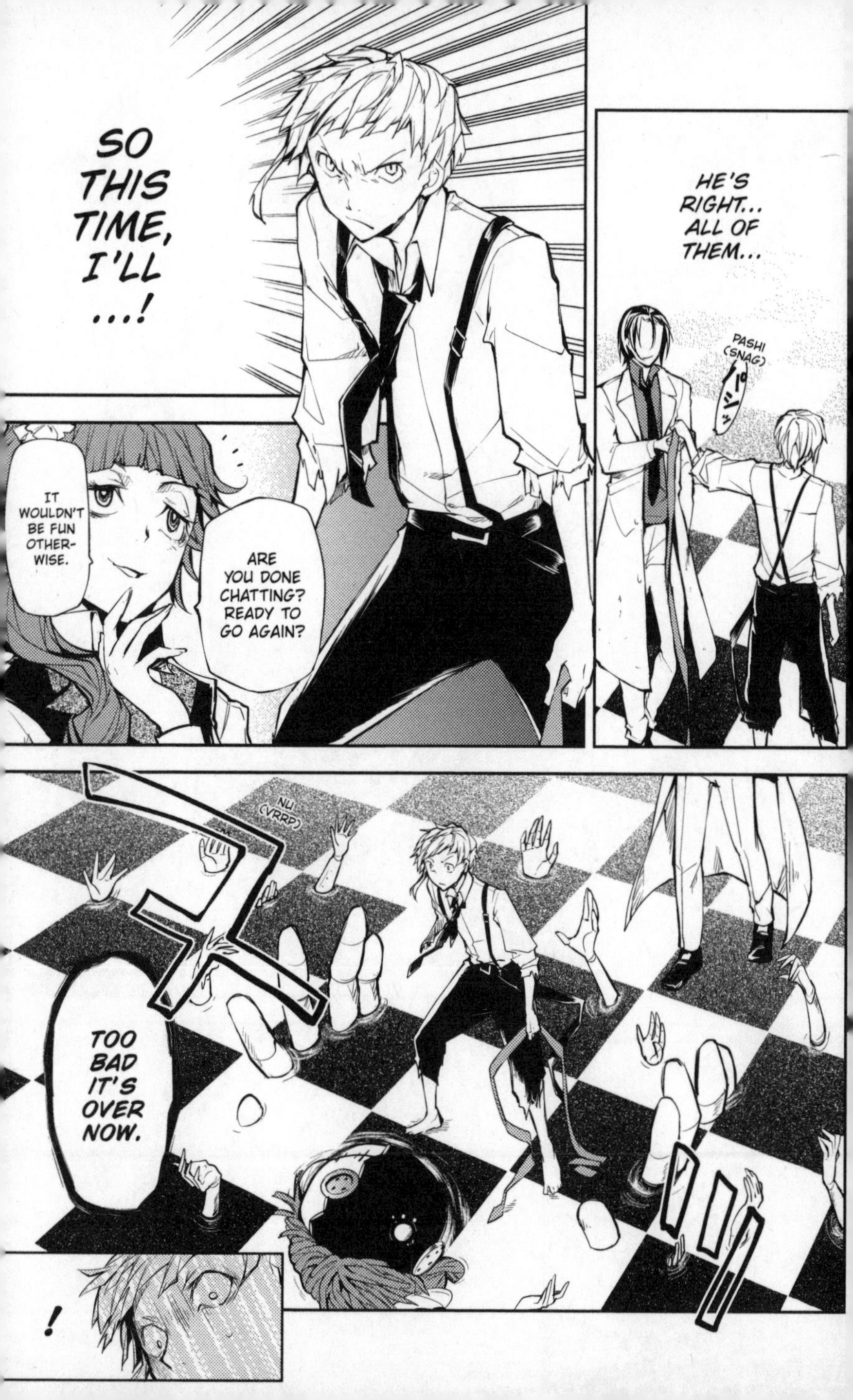
HE'S RIGHT... ALL OF THEM...
PASHI (SNAG)
SO THIS TIME, I'LL ...!
ARE YOU DONE CHATTING? READY TO GO AGAIN?
IT WOULDN'T BE FUN OTHERWISE.
NU (VRRP)
TOO BAD IT'S OVER NOW.
!

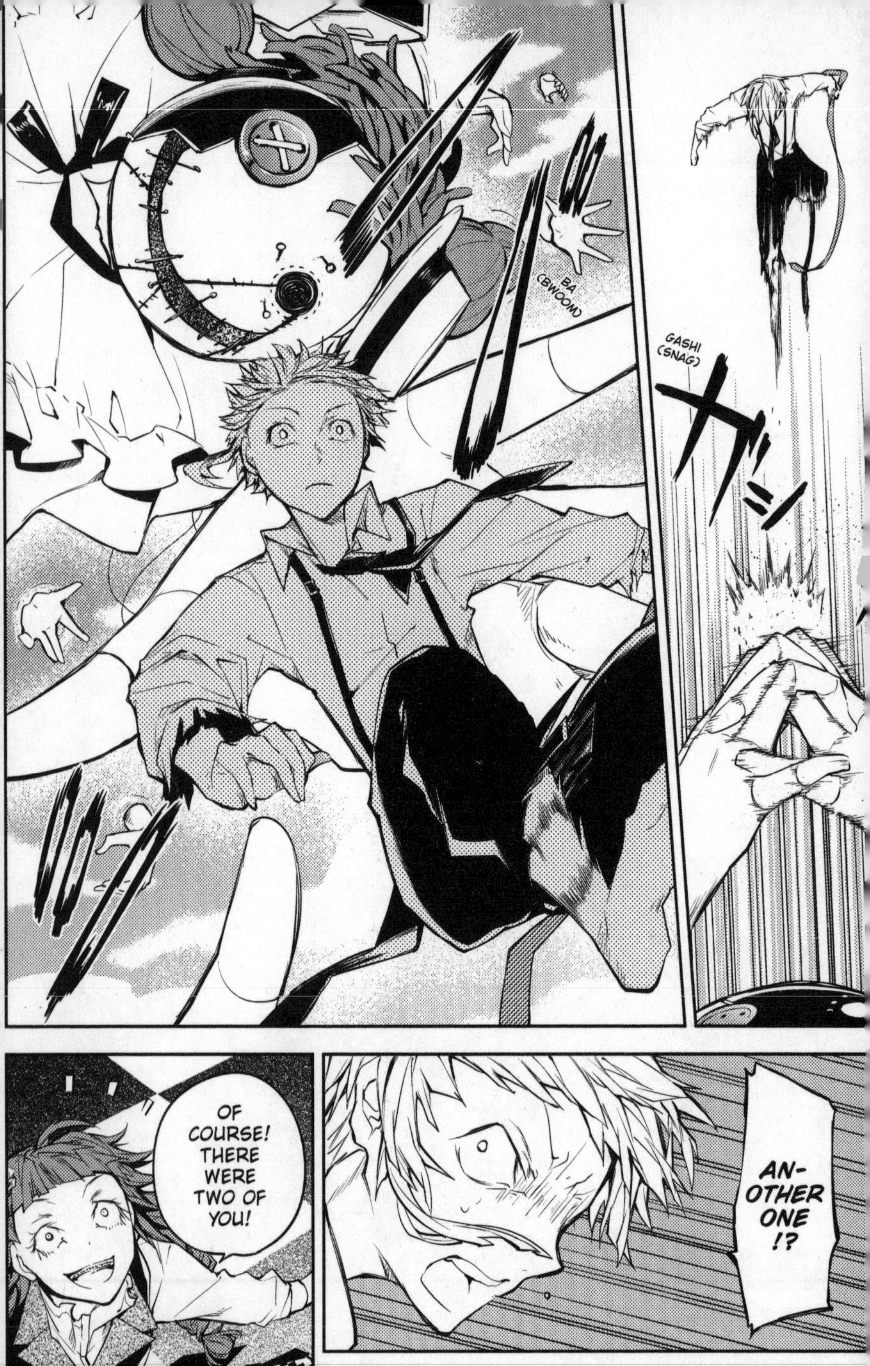
GASHI (SNAG)
BA (BWOOM)
AN-OTHER ONE !?
OF COURSE! THERE WERE TWO OF YOU!

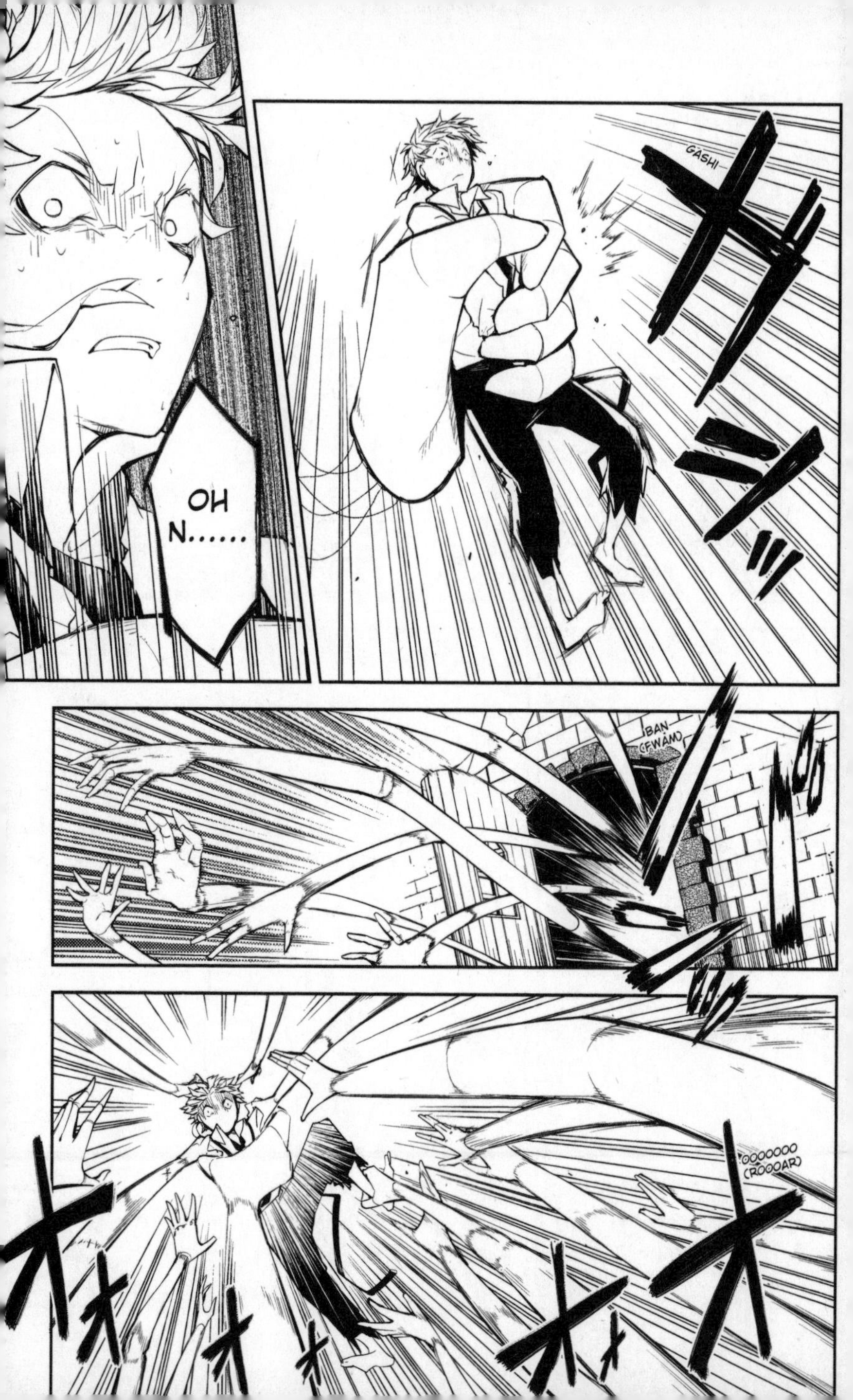
GASHI
OH
N......
BAN
(FWAM)
OOOOOOO
(ROOOAR)

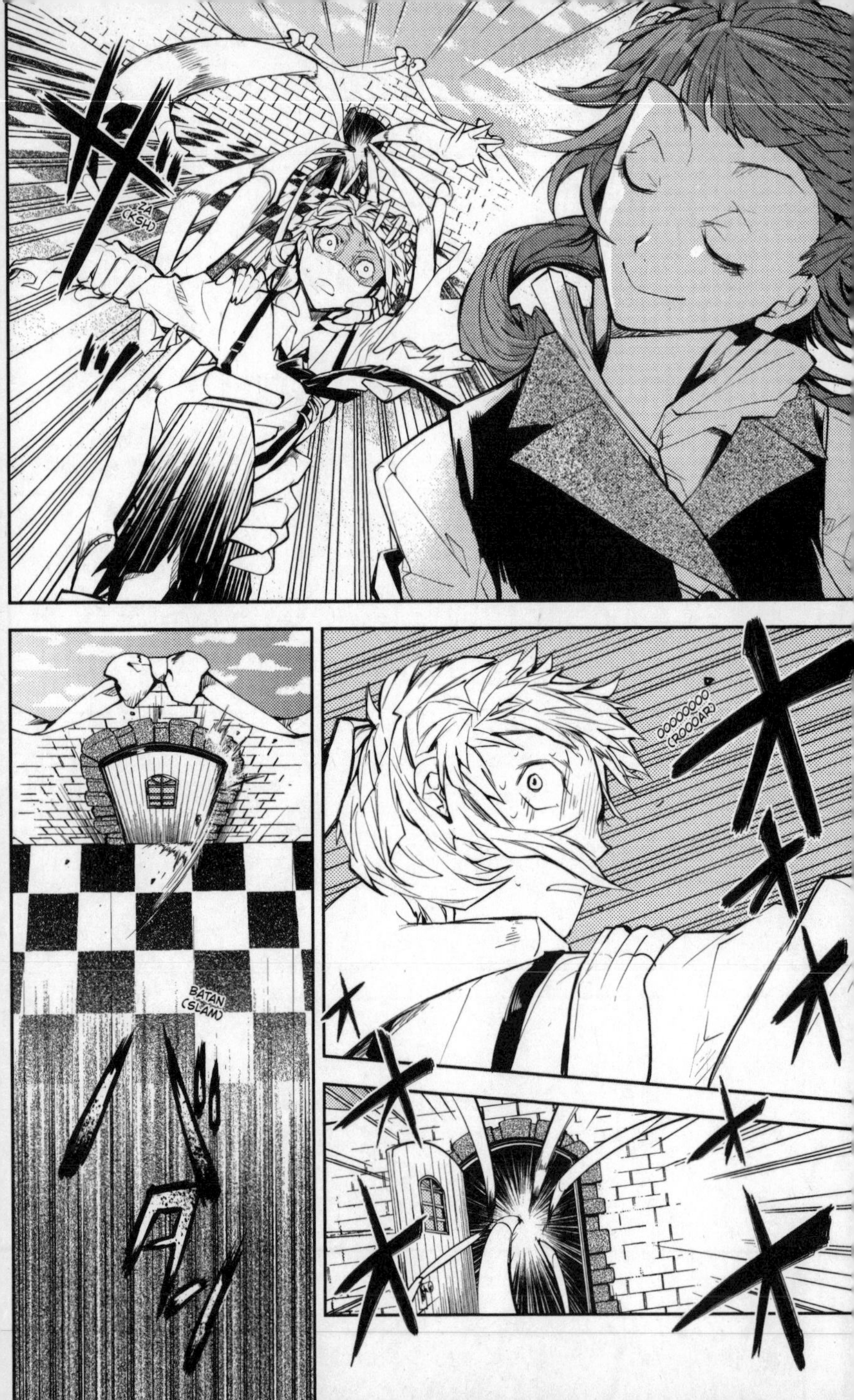
ZA
(KSH)
OOOOOOOO
(ROOOAR)
BATAN
(SLAM)

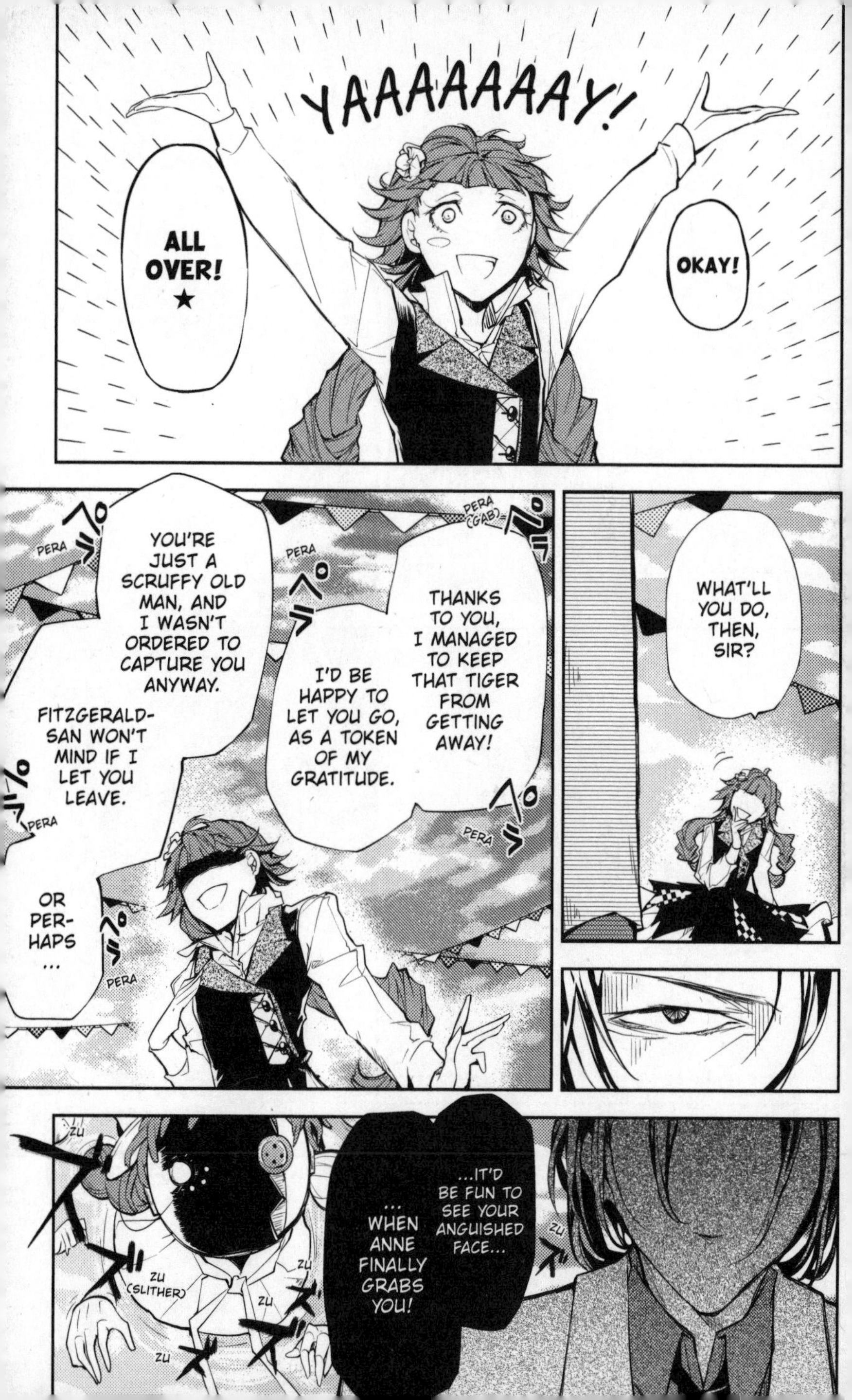

YAAAAAAAY!
OKAY!
ALL OVER! ★
WHAT'LL YOU DO, THEN, SIR?
PERA (GAB)
THANKS TO YOU, I MANAGED TO KEEP THAT TIGER FROM GETTING AWAY!
PERA
I'D BE HAPPY TO LET YOU GO, AS A TOKEN OF MY GRATITUDE.
PERA
YOU'RE JUST A SCRUFFY OLD MAN, AND I WASN'T ORDERED TO CAPTURE YOU ANYWAY.
PERA
FITZGERALD-SAN WON'T MIND IF I LET YOU LEAVE.
PERA
OR PER-HAPS ...
PERA
ZU
...IT'D BE FUN TO SEE YOUR ANGUISHED FACE...
... WHEN ANNE FINALLY GRABS YOU!
ZU
ZU (SLITHER)
ZU
ZU
ZU

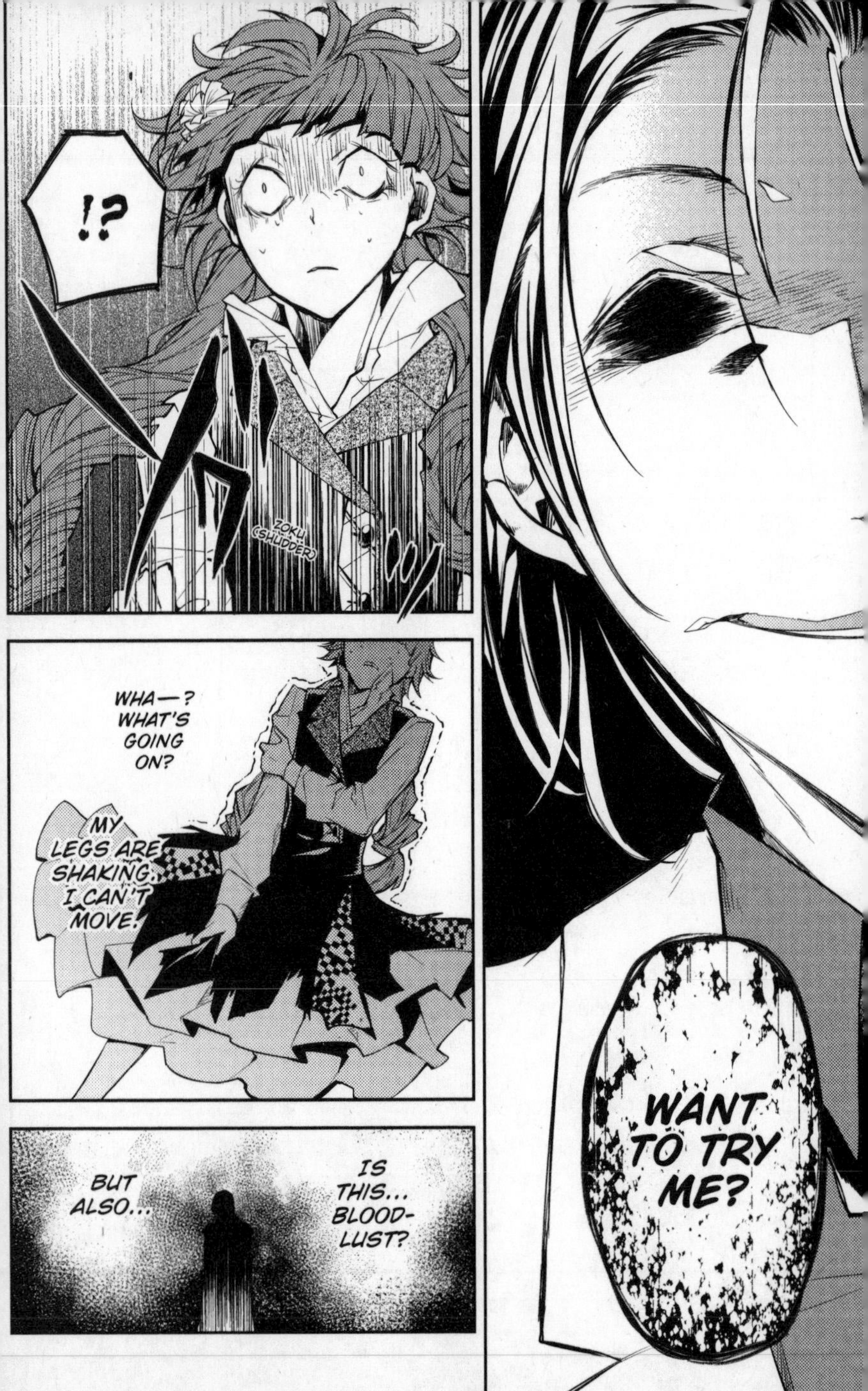
WANT TO TRY ME?
!?
ZOKU (SHUDDER)
WHA—? WHAT'S GOING ON?
MY LEGS ARE SHAKING. I CAN'T MOVE.
IS THIS... BLOOD-LUST?
BUT ALSO...

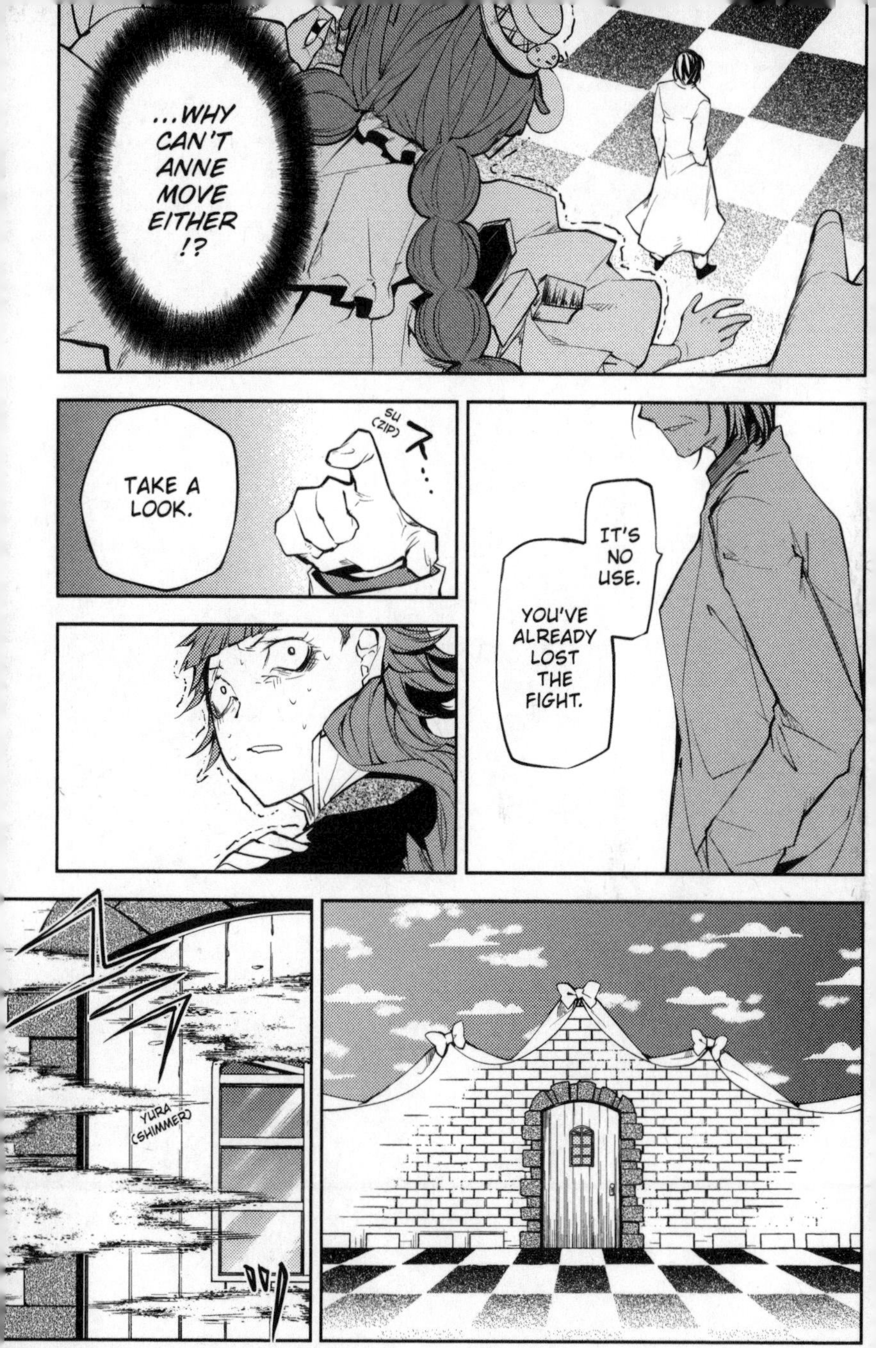
...WHY CAN'T ANNE MOVE EITHER!?
IT'S NO USE.
YOU'VE ALREADY LOST THE FIGHT.
SU (ZIP)
TAKE A LOOK.
YURA (SHIMMER)

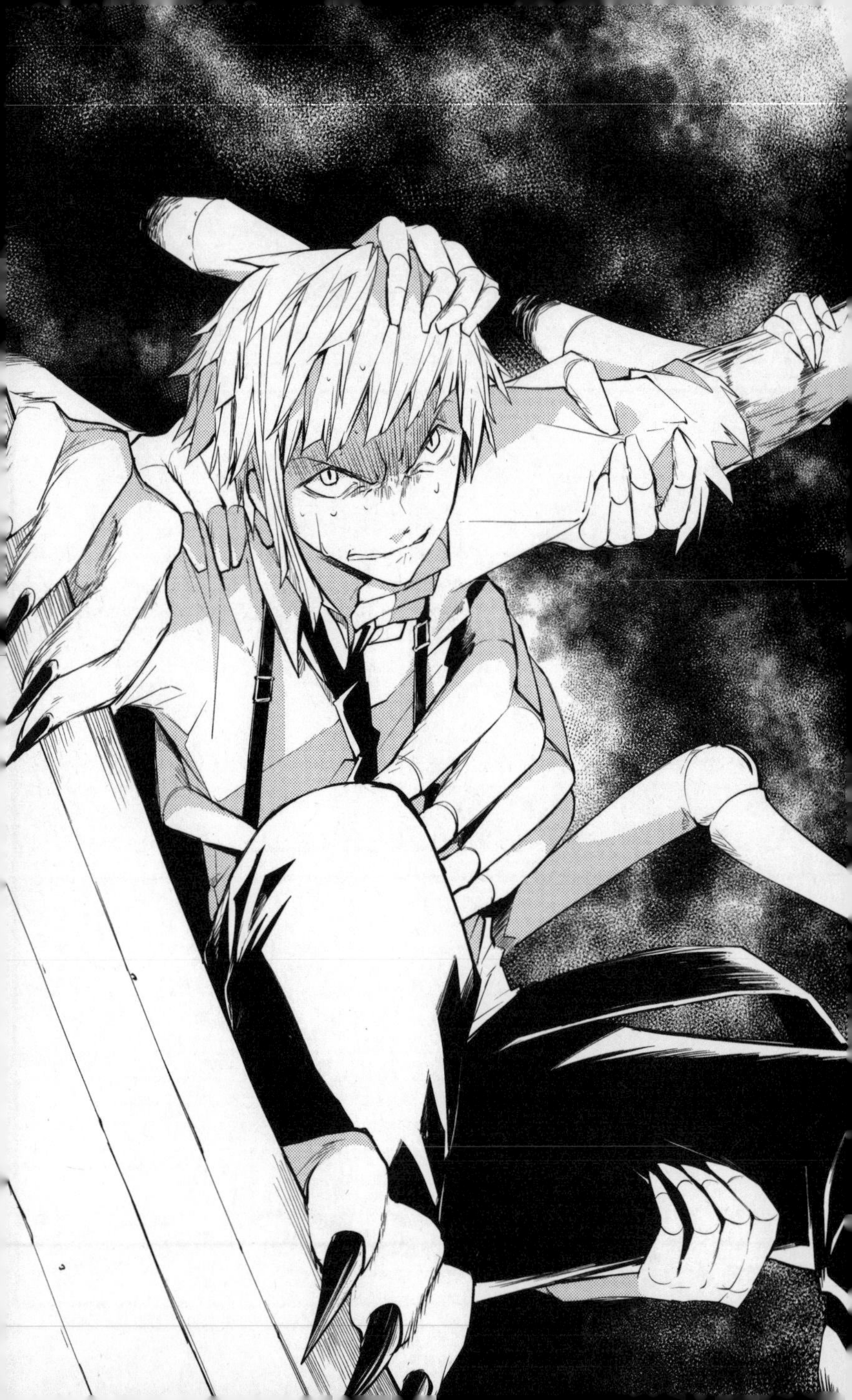

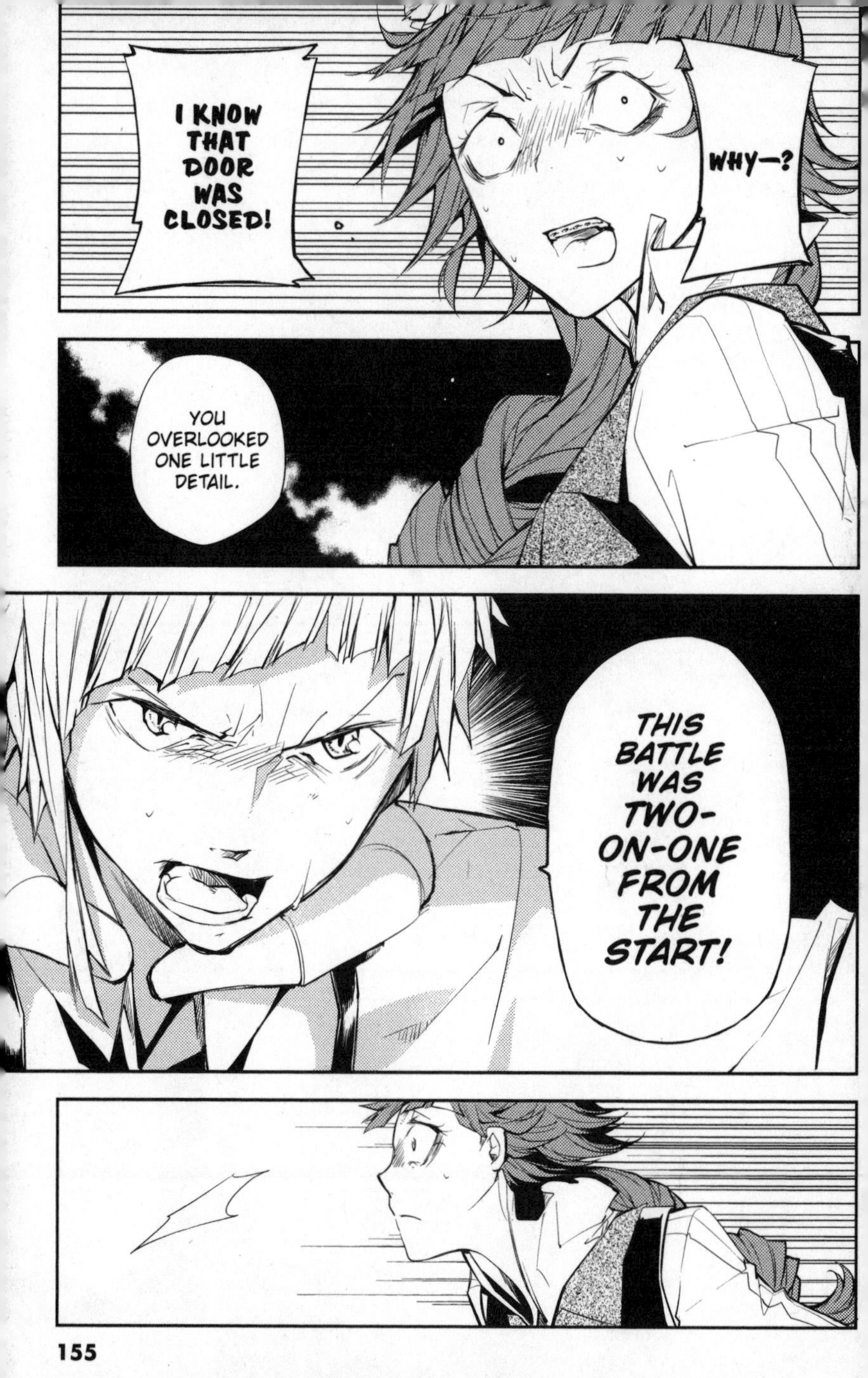
WHY—?
I KNOW THAT DOOR WAS CLOSED!
YOU OVERLOOKED ONE LITTLE DETAIL.
THIS BATTLE WAS TWO-ON-ONE FROM THE START!

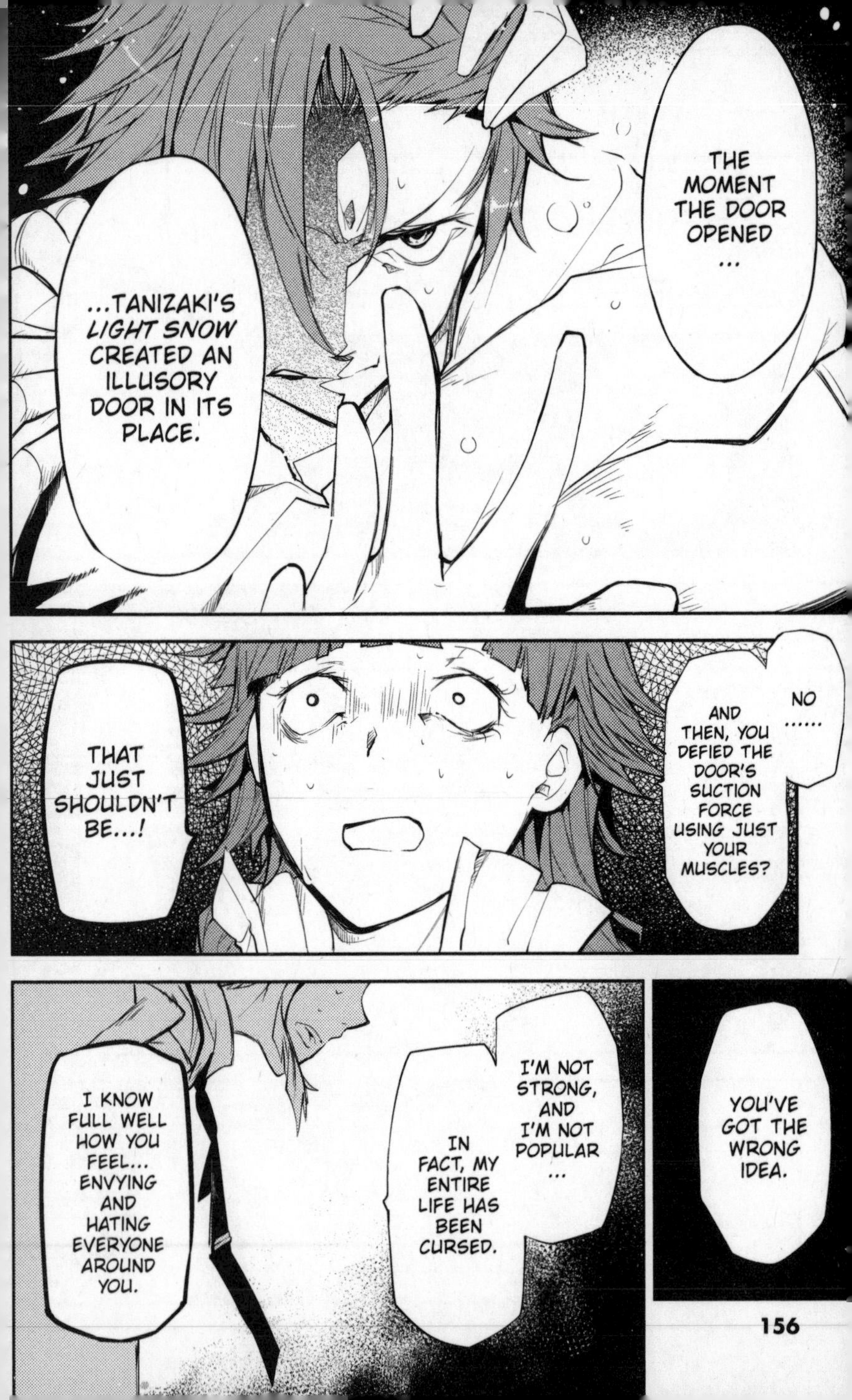
THE MOMENT THE DOOR OPENED ...
...TANIZAKI'S *LIGHT SNOW* CREATED AN ILLUSORY DOOR IN ITS PLACE.
NO ......
AND THEN, YOU DEFIED THE DOOR'S SUCTION FORCE USING JUST YOUR MUSCLES?
THAT JUST SHOULDN'T BE...!
YOU'VE GOT THE WRONG IDEA.
I'M NOT STRONG, AND I'M NOT POPULAR ...
IN FACT, MY ENTIRE LIFE HAS BEEN CURSED.
I KNOW FULL WELL HOW YOU FEEL... ENVYING AND HATING EVERYONE AROUND YOU.

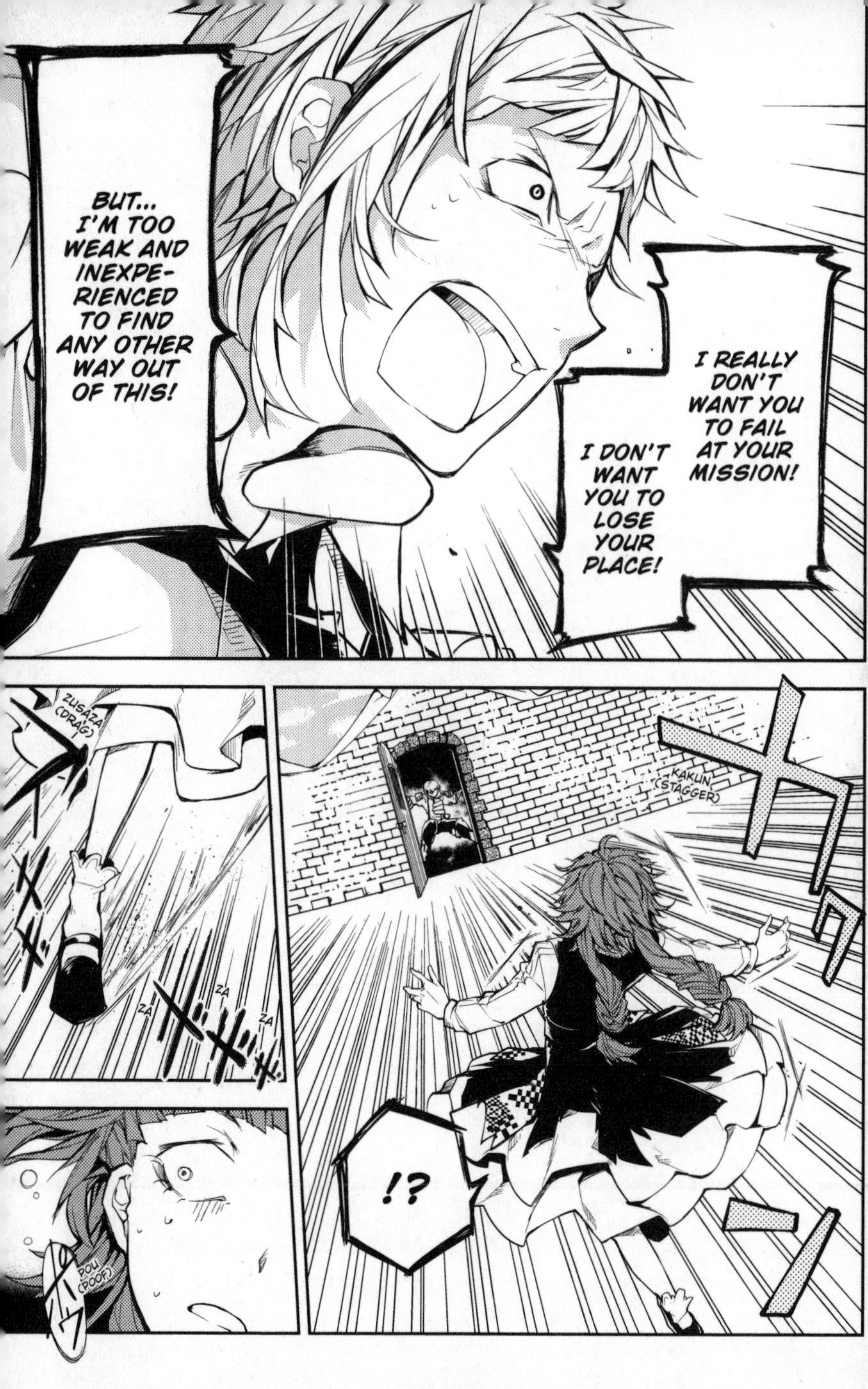
I REALLY DON'T WANT YOU TO FAIL AT YOUR MISSION!
I DON'T WANT YOU TO LOSE YOUR PLACE!
BUT... I'M TOO WEAK AND INEXPE- RIENCED TO FIND ANY OTHER WAY OUT OF THIS!
KAKUN (STAGGER)
!?
ZUSAZA (DRAG)
ZA
ZA
ZA
POU (POOF)

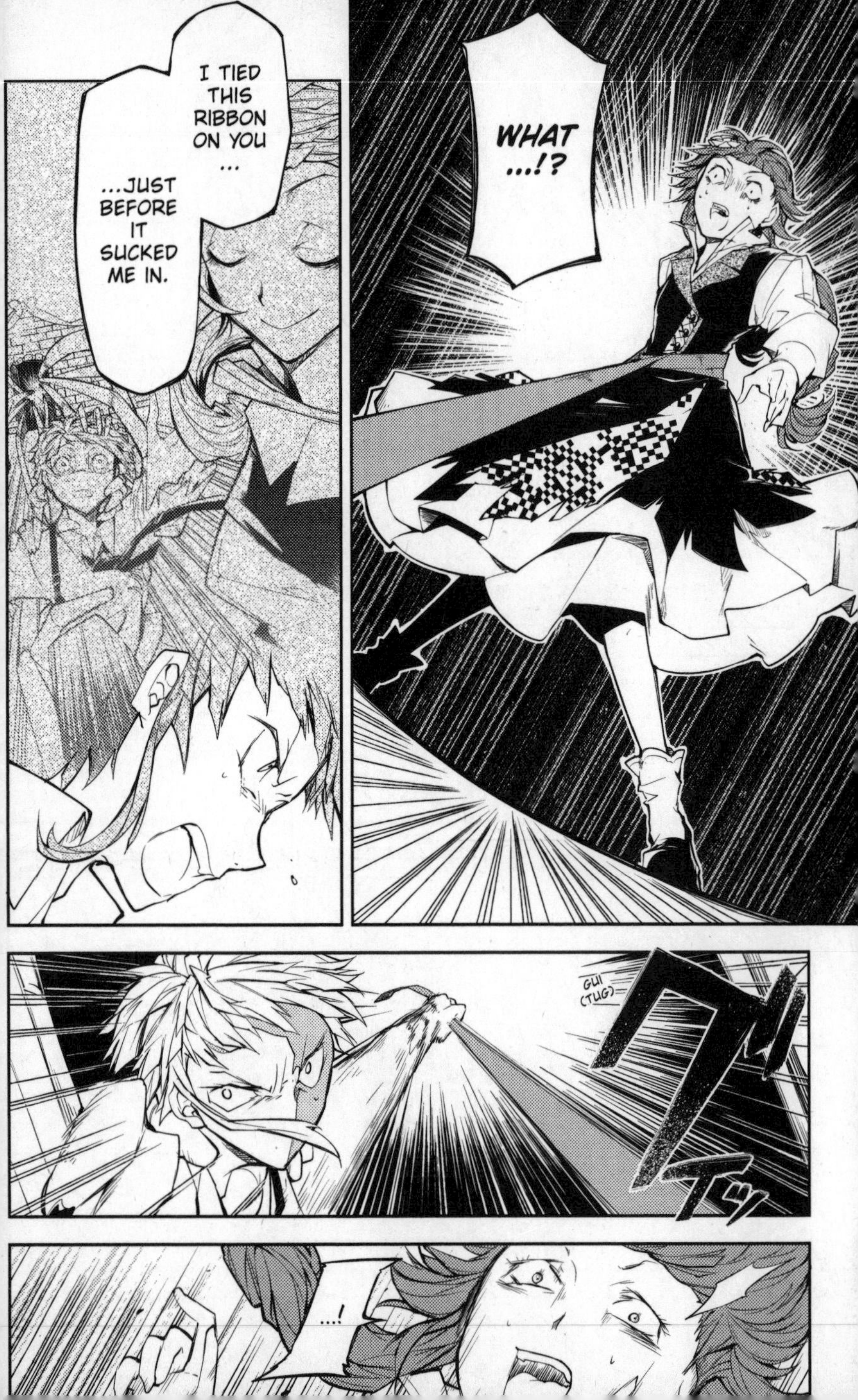
WHAT ...!?
I TIED THIS RIBBON ON YOU ...
...JUST BEFORE IT SUCKED ME IN.
GUI (TUG)
...!

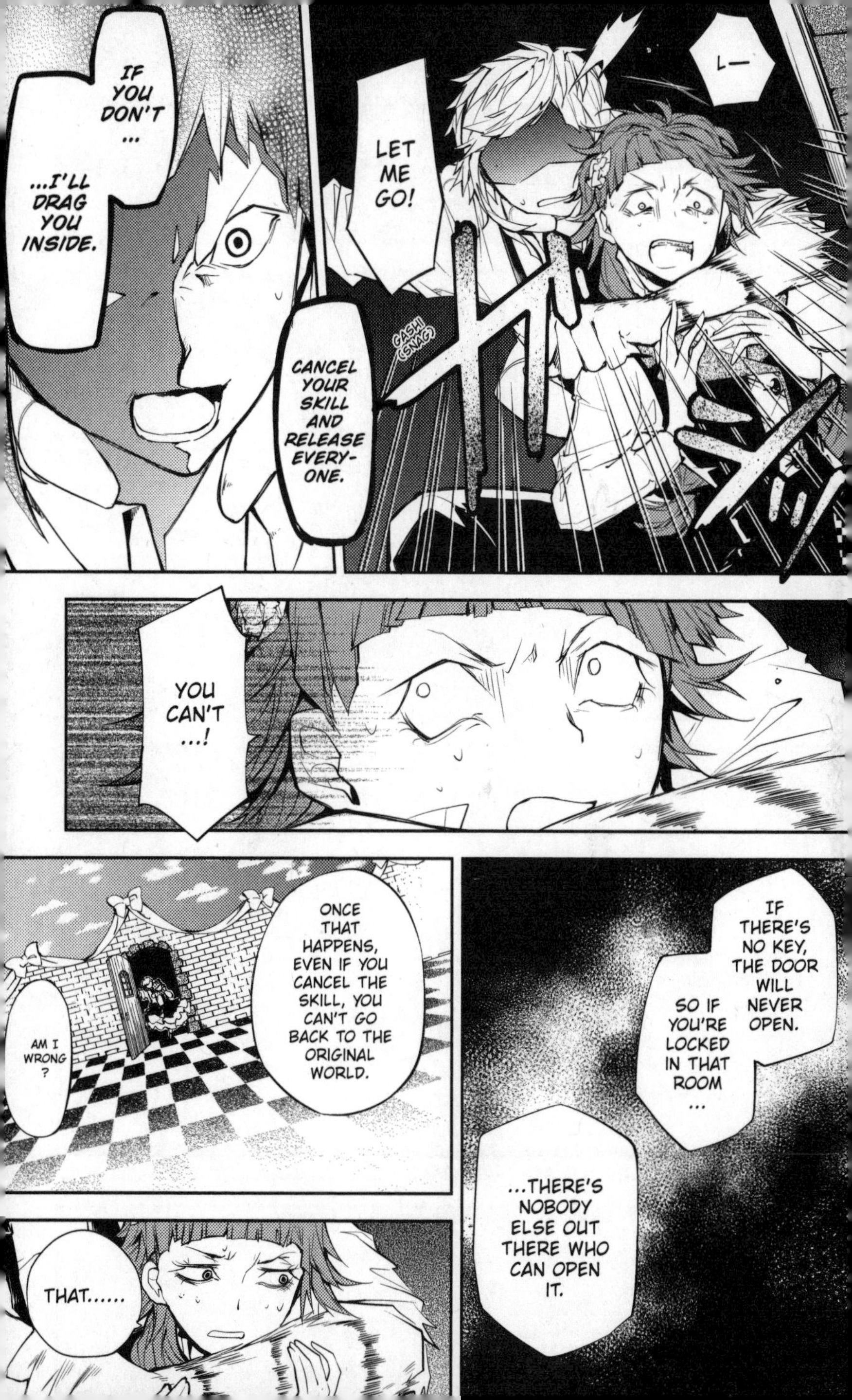
L—
LET ME GO!
GASHI (SNAG)
CANCEL YOUR SKILL AND RELEASE EVERY-ONE.
IF YOU DON'T ...
...I'LL DRAG YOU INSIDE.
YOU CAN'T ...!
IF THERE'S NO KEY, THE DOOR WILL NEVER OPEN.
SO IF YOU'RE LOCKED IN THAT ROOM ...
...THERE'S NOBODY ELSE OUT THERE WHO CAN OPEN IT.
ONCE THAT HAPPENS, EVEN IF YOU CANCEL THE SKILL, YOU CAN'T GO BACK TO THE ORIGINAL WORLD.
AM I WRONG?
THAT......

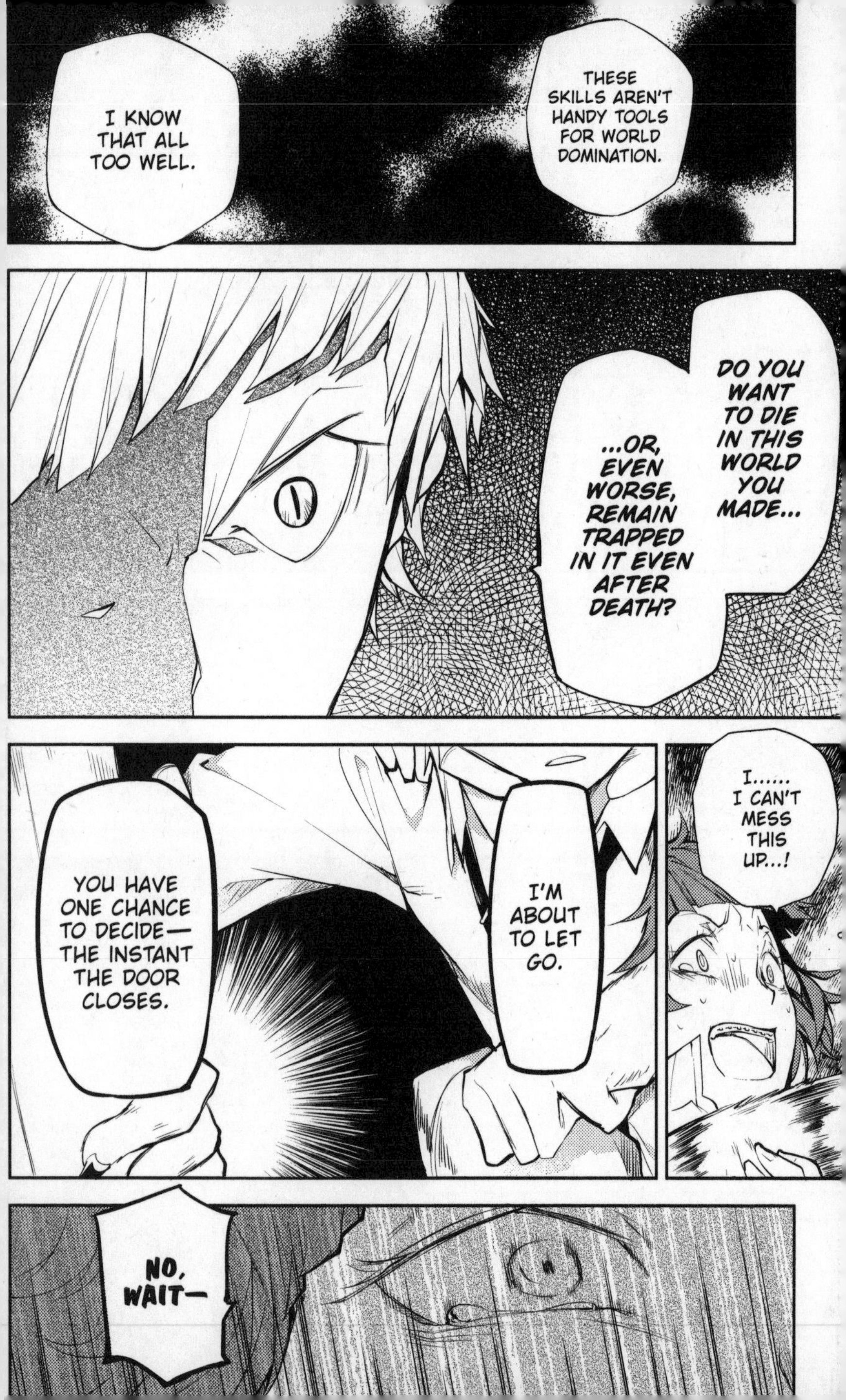
THESE SKILLS AREN'T HANDY TOOLS FOR WORLD DOMINATION.
I KNOW THAT ALL TOO WELL.
DO YOU WANT TO DIE IN THIS WORLD YOU MADE...
...OR, EVEN WORSE, REMAIN TRAPPED IN IT EVEN AFTER DEATH?
I...... I CAN'T MESS THIS UP...!
I'M ABOUT TO LET GO.
YOU HAVE ONE CHANCE TO DECIDE—THE INSTANT THE DOOR CLOSES.
NO, WAIT—

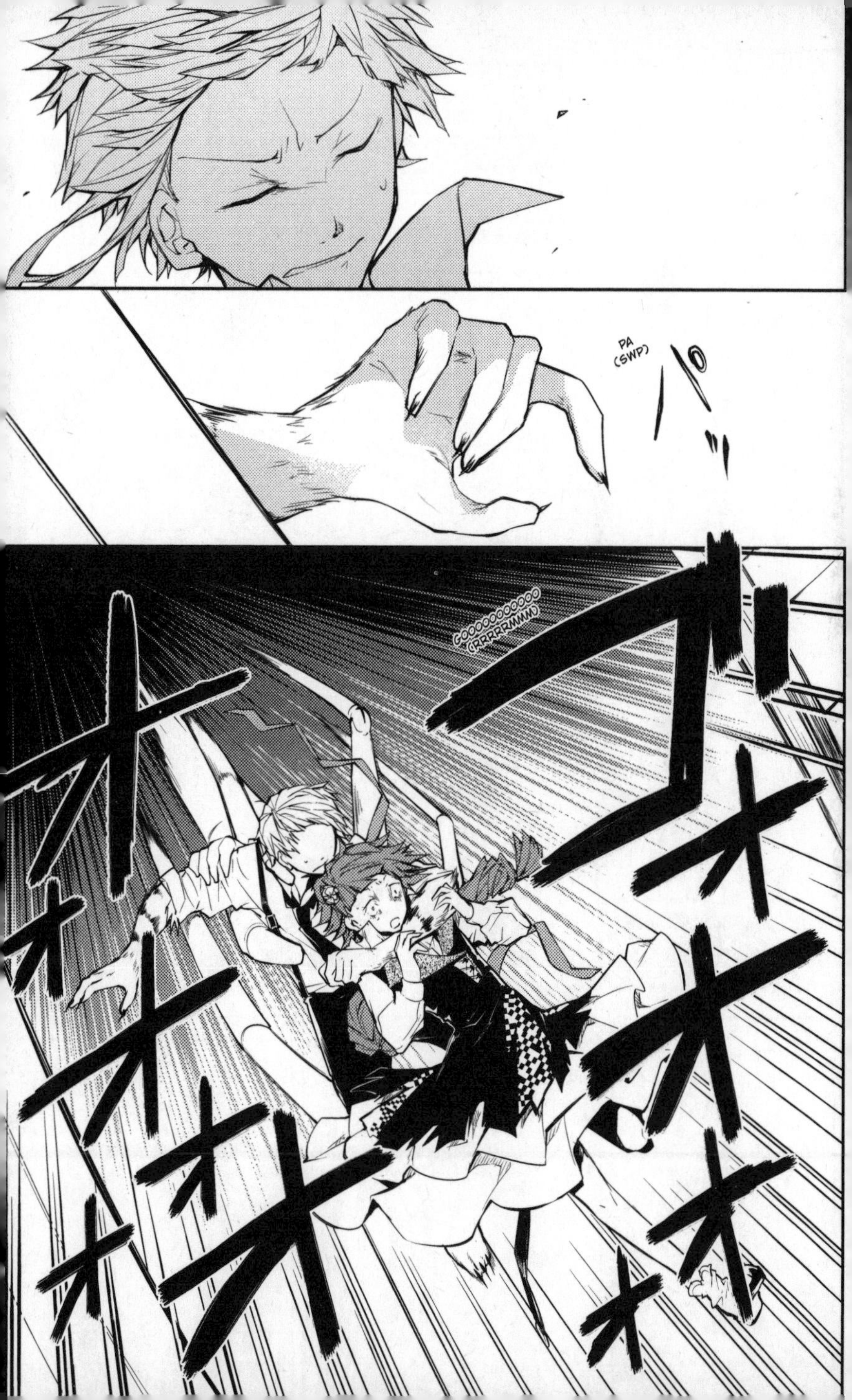
PA
(SWP)
GOOOOOOOOOOO
(RRRRRMMM)

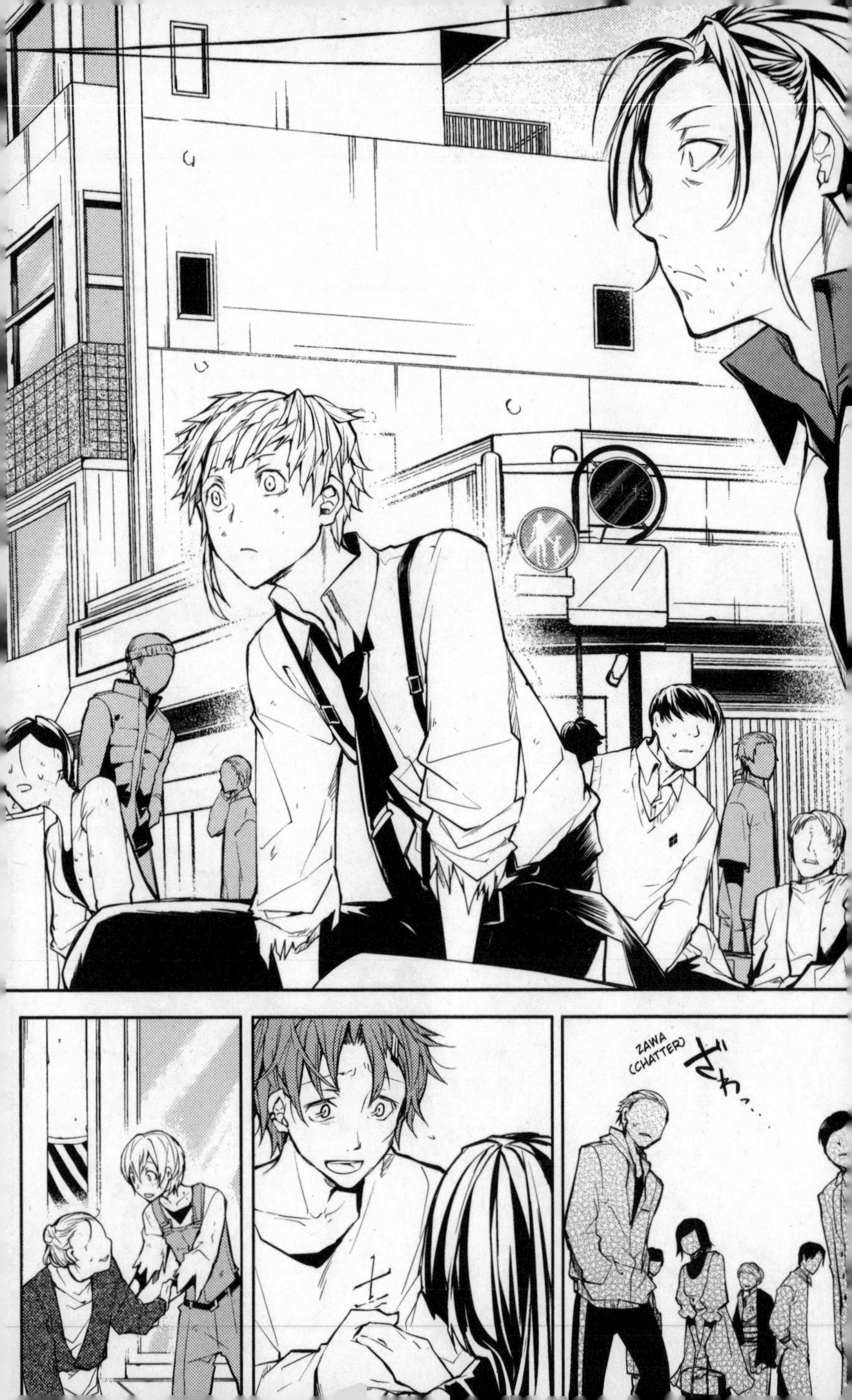
ZAWA (CHATTER)
ざわ…

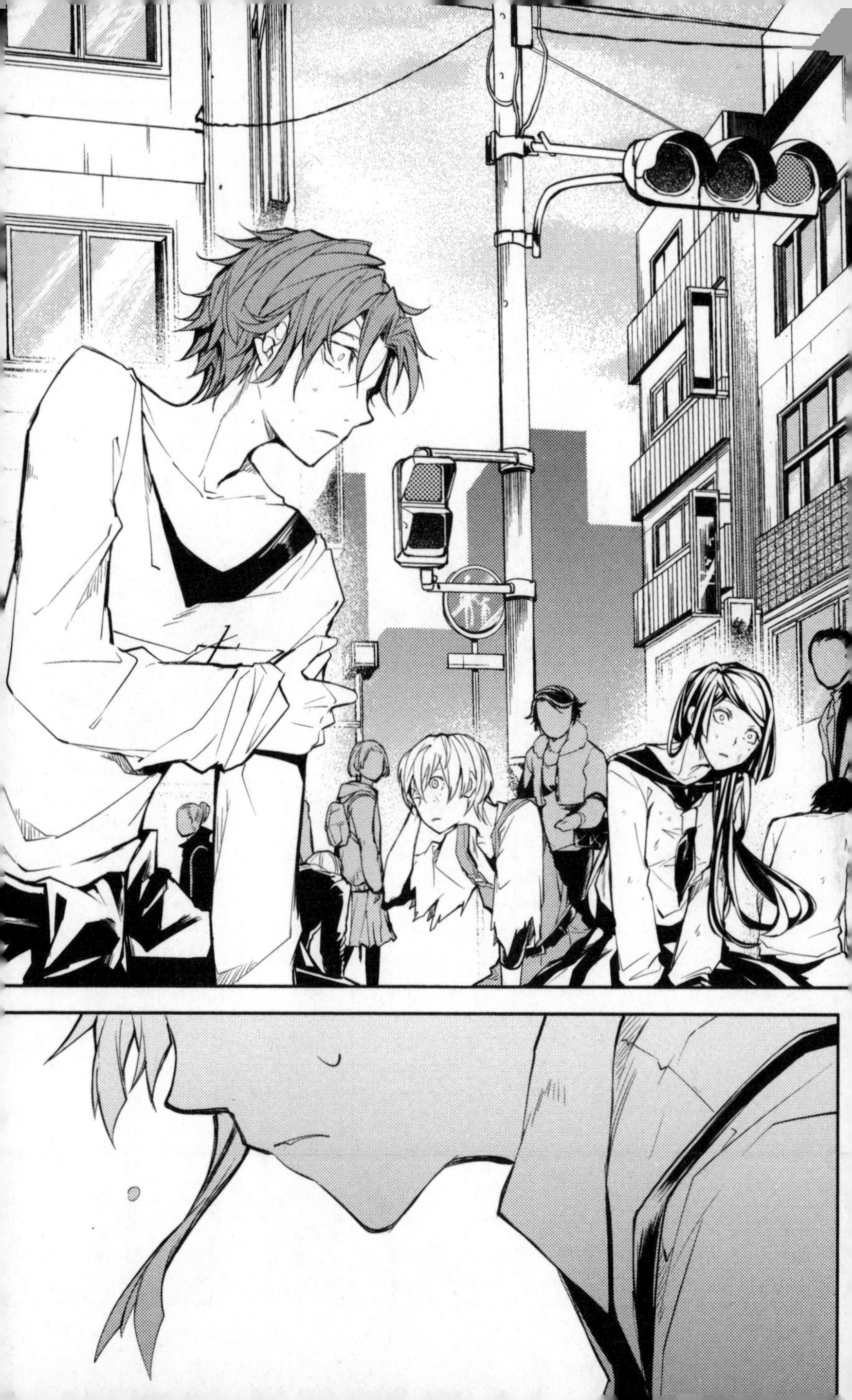

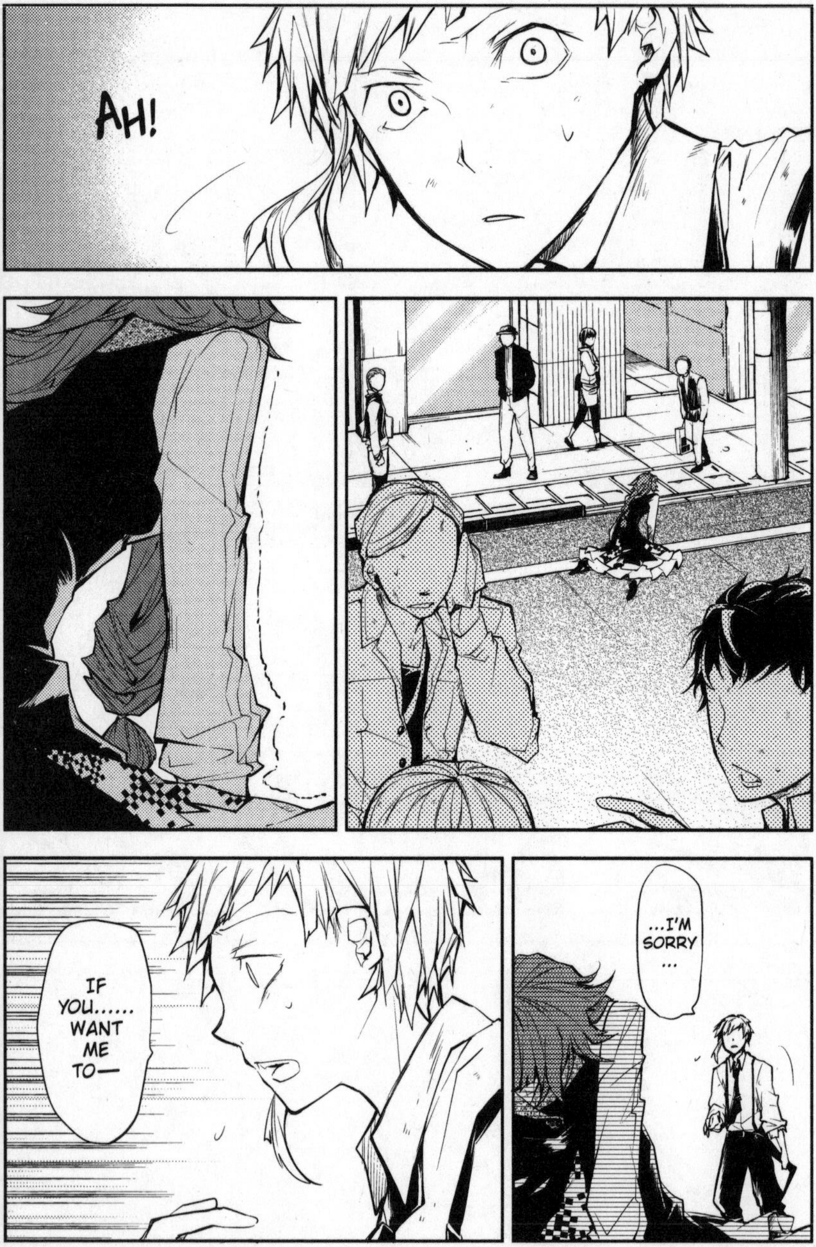

AH!
...I'M SORRY ...
IF YOU...... WANT ME TO—

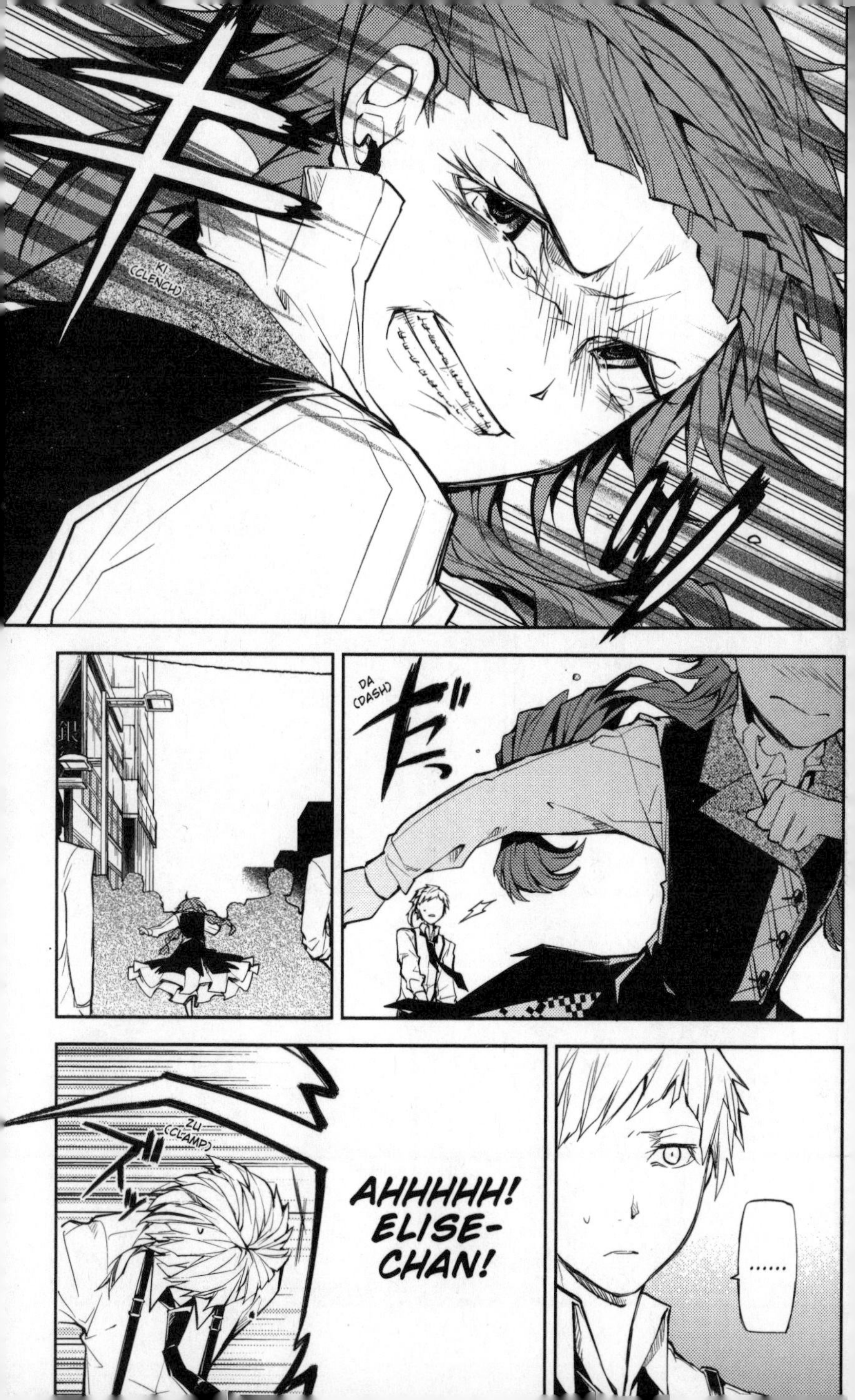
KI (CLENCH)
DA (DASH)
ZU (CLAMP)
AHHHHH! ELISE-CHAN!
......

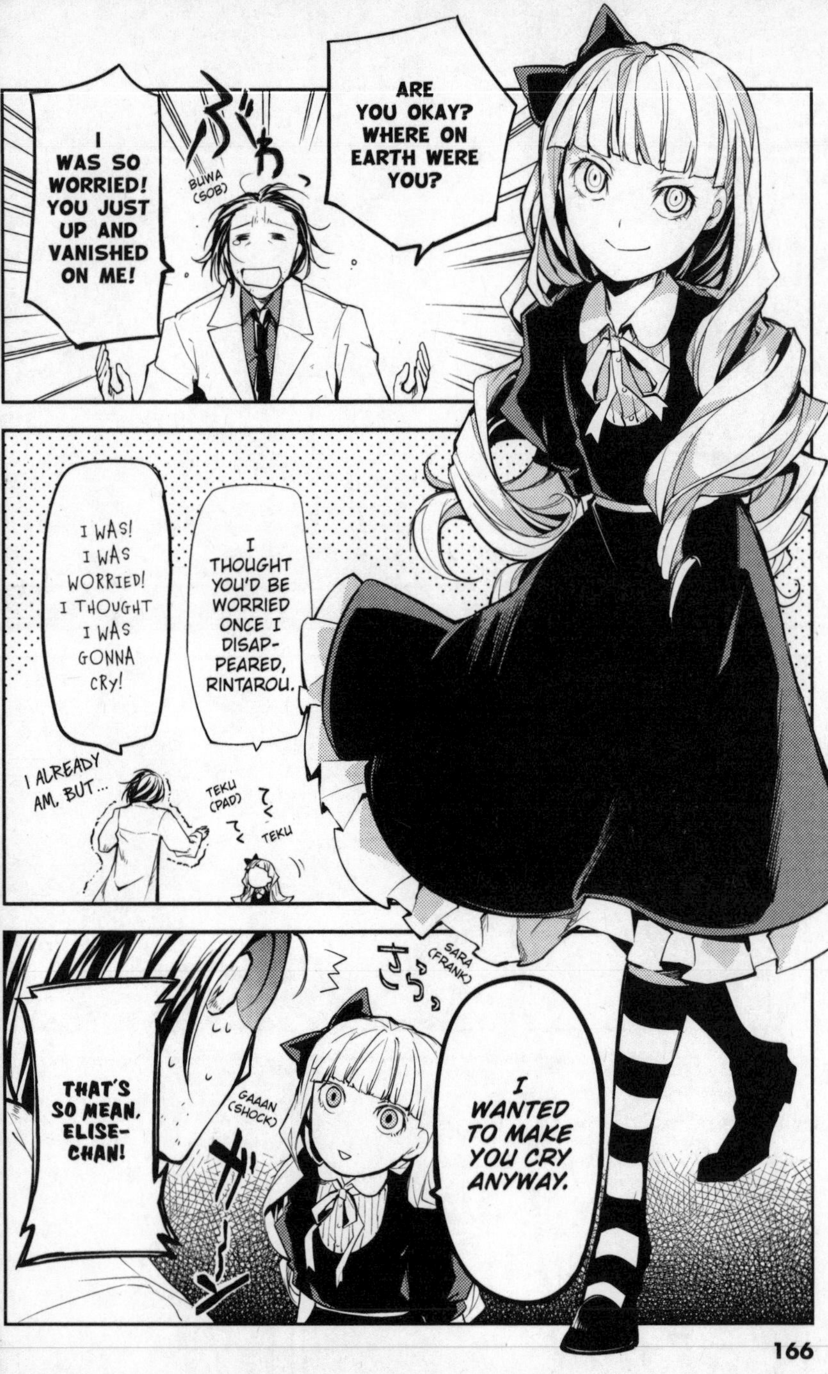
ARE YOU OKAY? WHERE ON EARTH WERE YOU?
BUWA (SOB)
I WAS SO WORRIED! YOU JUST UP AND VANISHED ON ME!
I THOUGHT YOU'D BE WORRIED ONCE I DISAP-PEARED, RINTAROU.
I WAS! I WAS WORRIED! I THOUGHT I WAS GONNA CRY!
TEKU (PAD)
TEKU
I ALREADY AM, BUT...
SARA (FRANK)
I WANTED TO MAKE YOU CRY ANYWAY.
GAAAN (SHOCK)
THAT'S SO MEAN, ELISE-CHAN!

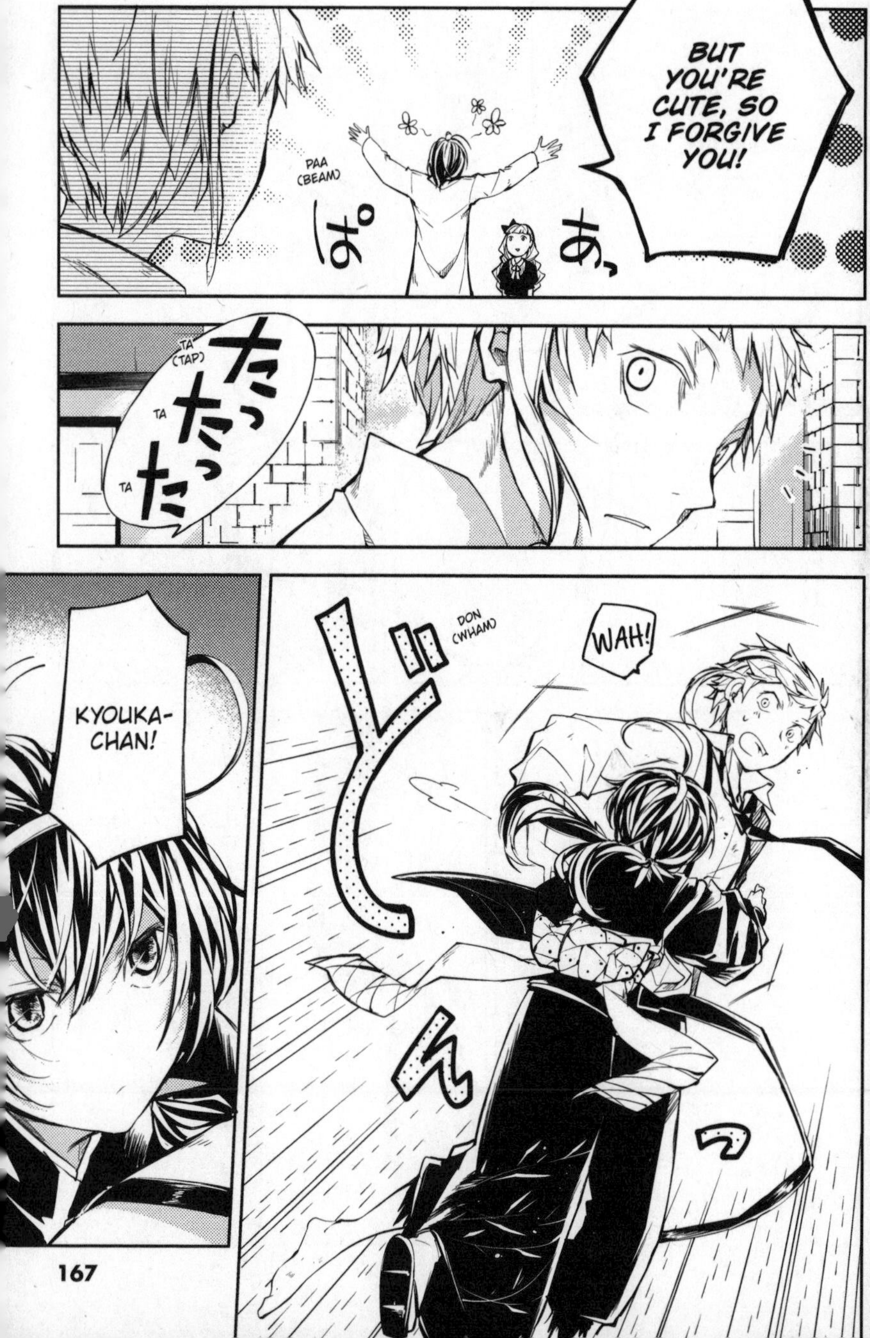
BUT YOU'RE CUTE, SO I FORGIVE YOU!
あっ
ぱ
PAA (BEAM)
たったった
TA (TAP) TA TA
WAH!
どんっ
DON (WHAM)
KYOUKA-CHAN!

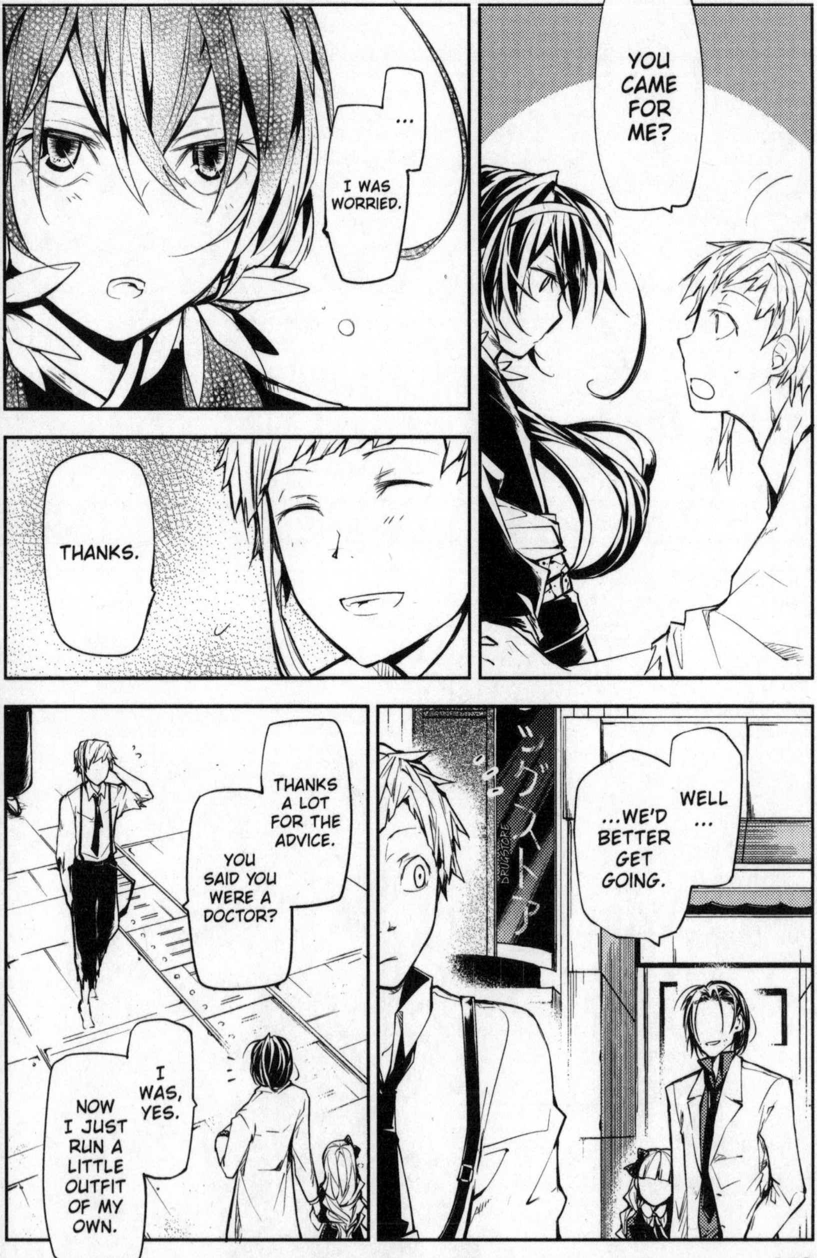
YOU CAME FOR ME?
...
I WAS WORRIED.
THANKS.
WELL ...
...WE'D BETTER GET GOING.
DRUGSTORE
THANKS A LOT FOR THE ADVICE.
YOU SAID YOU WERE A DOCTOR?
I WAS, YES.
NOW I JUST RUN A LITTLE OUTFIT OF MY OWN.

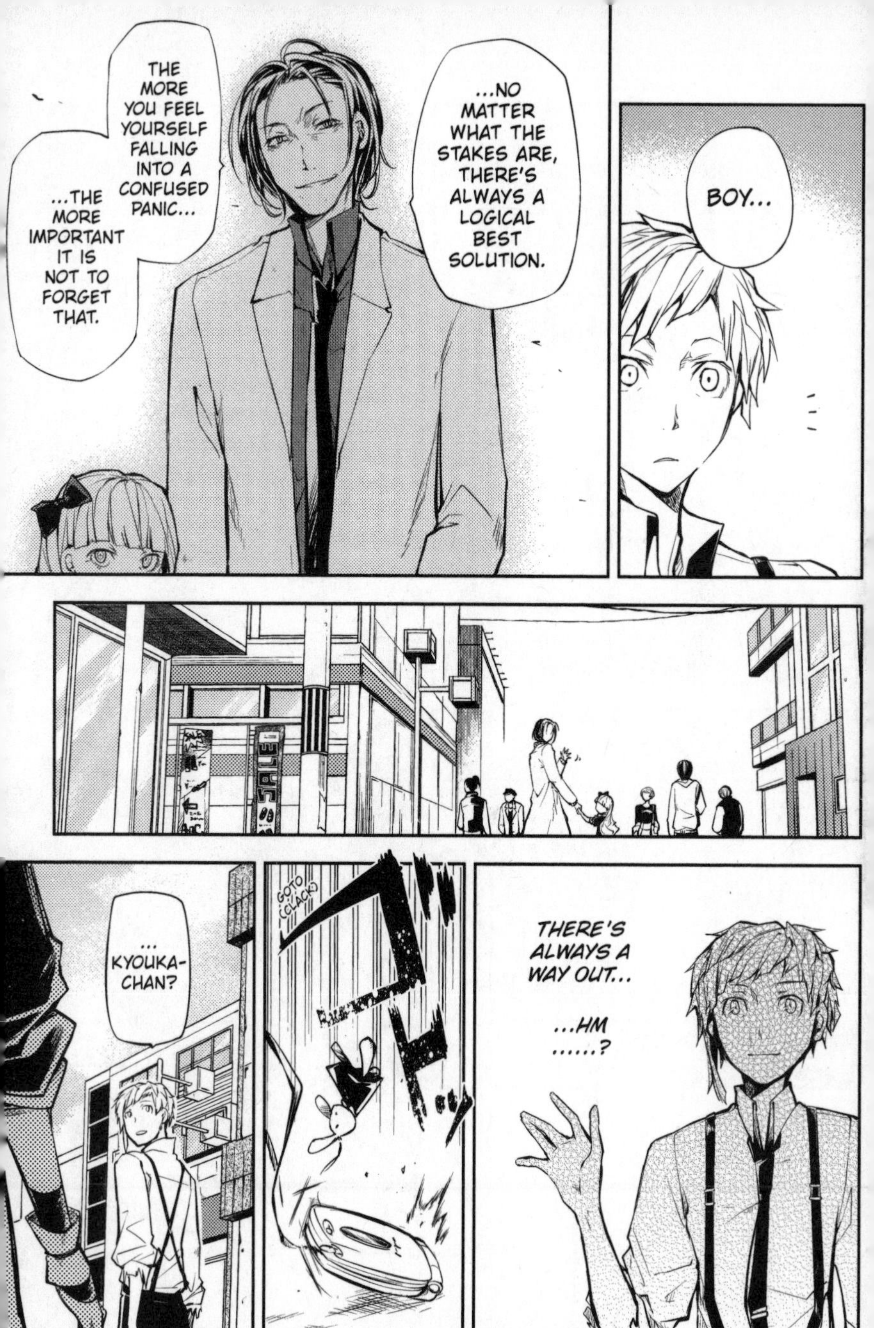
BOY...
...NO MATTER WHAT THE STAKES ARE, THERE'S ALWAYS A LOGICAL BEST SOLUTION.
THE MORE YOU FEEL YOURSELF FALLING INTO A CONFUSED PANIC...
...THE MORE IMPORTANT IT IS NOT TO FORGET THAT.
THERE'S ALWAYS A WAY OUT...
...HM ......?
GOTO (CLACK)
...KYOUKA-CHAN?

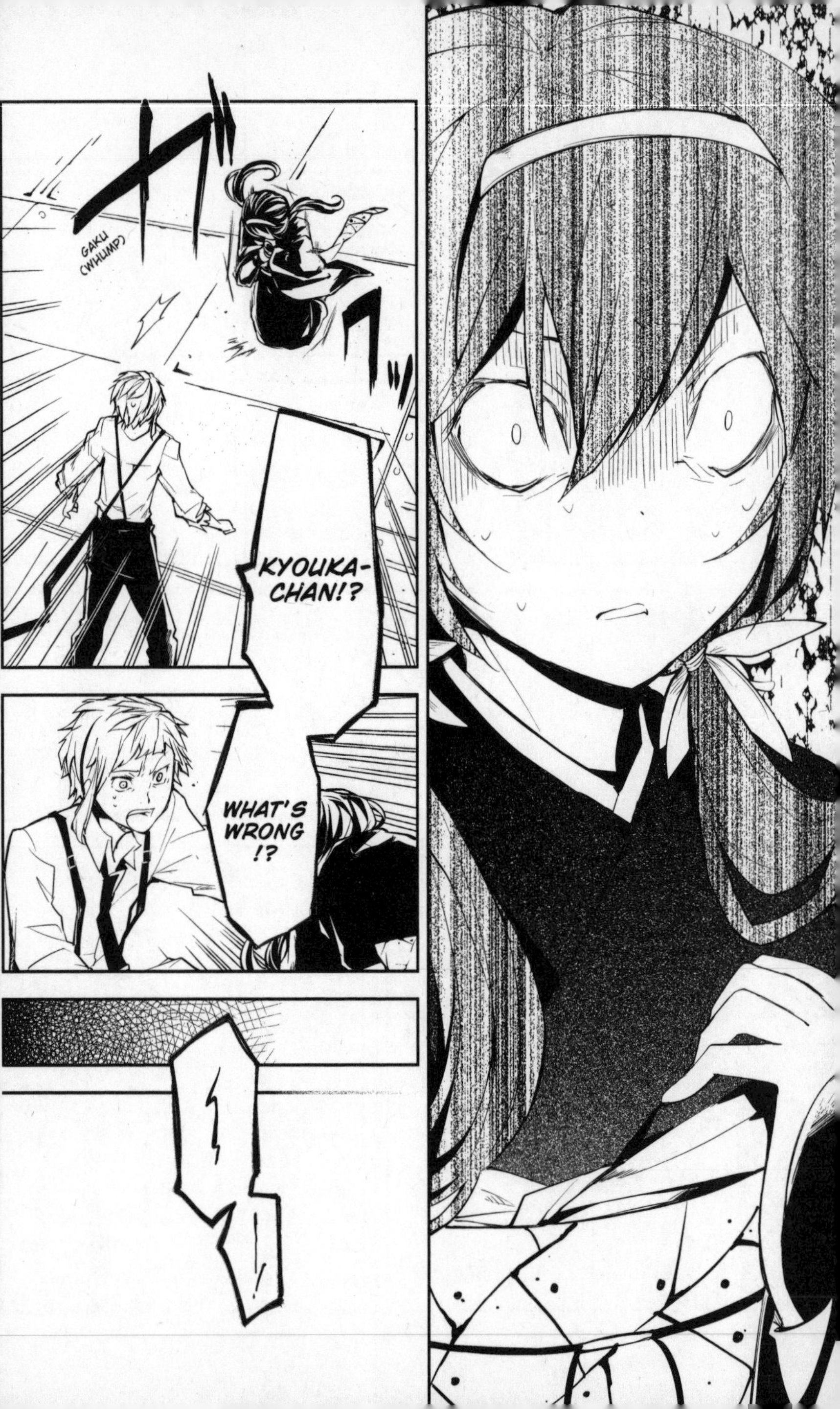
GAKU (WHUMP)
KYOUKA-CHAN!?
WHAT'S WRONG !?

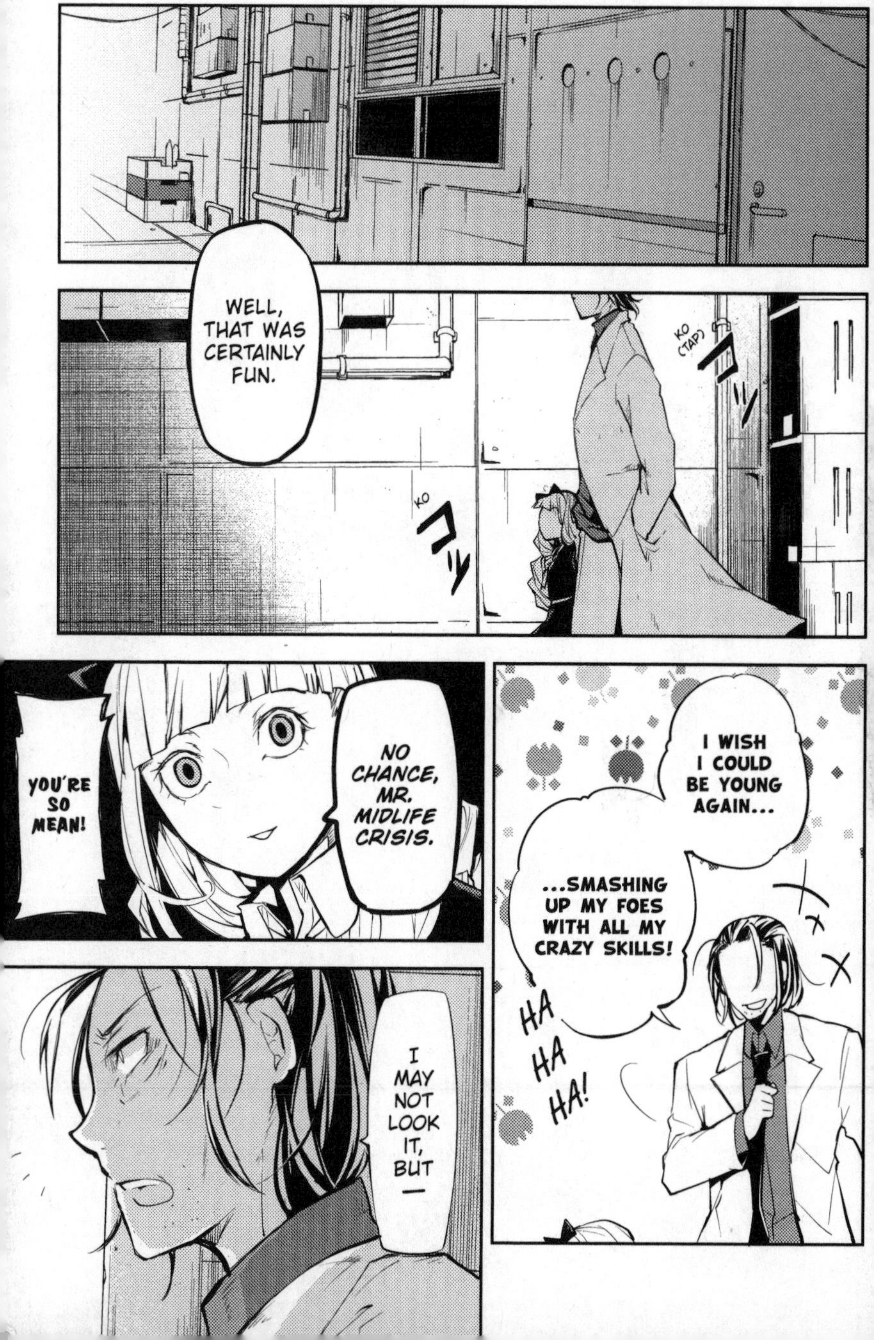
KO (TAP)
WELL, THAT WAS CERTAINLY FUN.
KO
I WISH I COULD BE YOUNG AGAIN...
...SMASHING UP MY FOES WITH ALL MY CRAZY SKILLS!
HA HA HA!
NO CHANCE, MR. MIDLIFE CRISIS.
YOU'RE SO MEAN!
I MAY NOT LOOK IT, BUT—

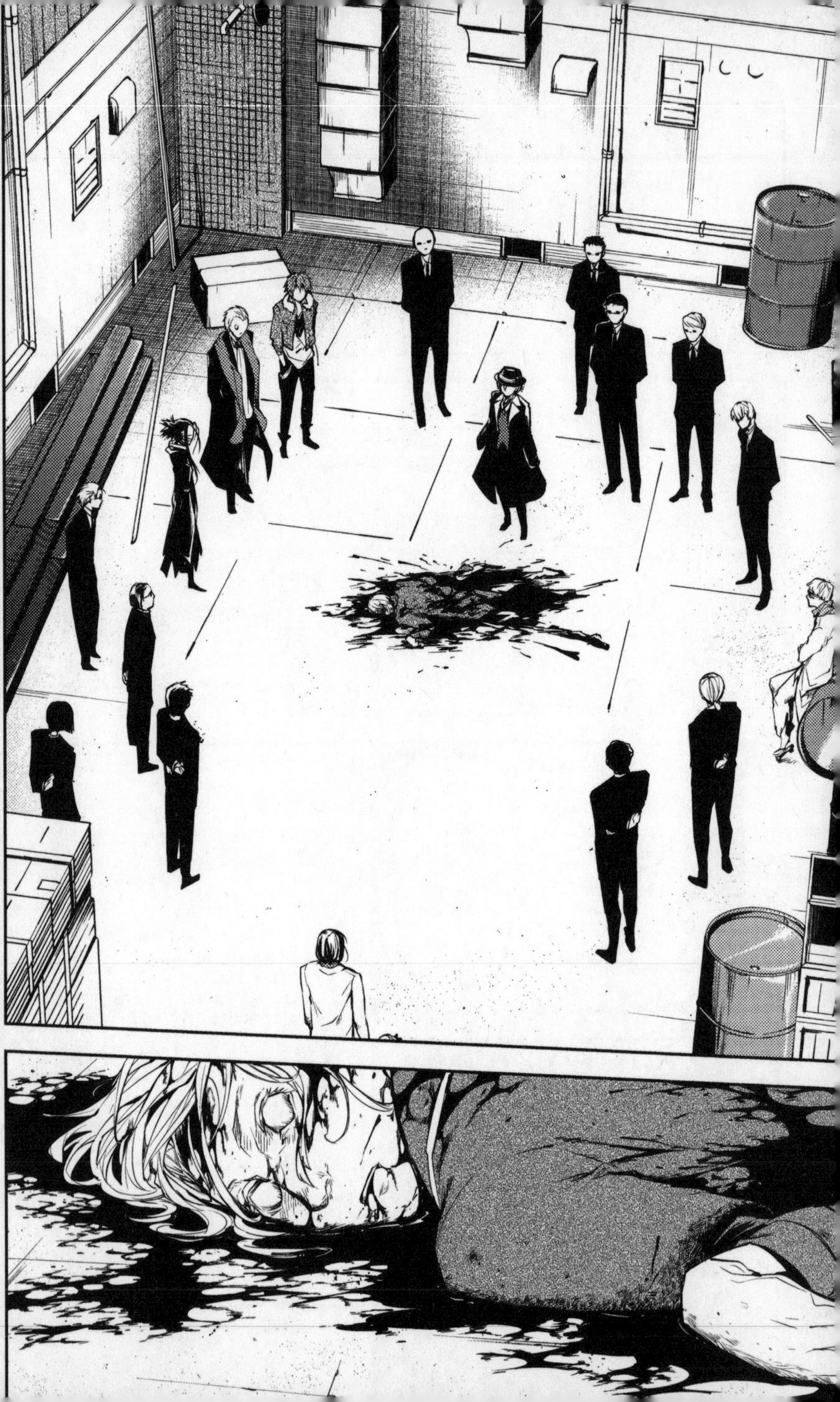

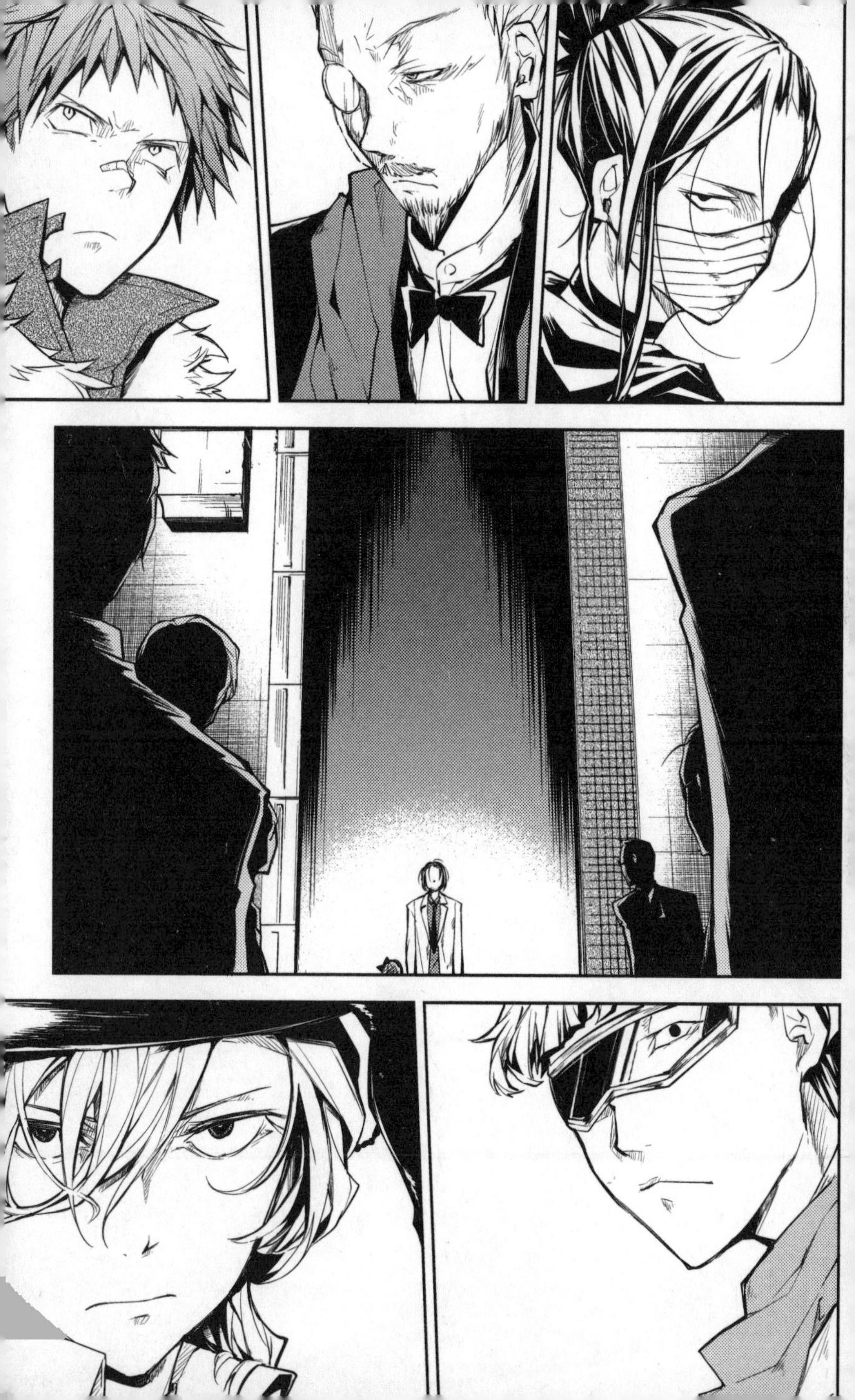

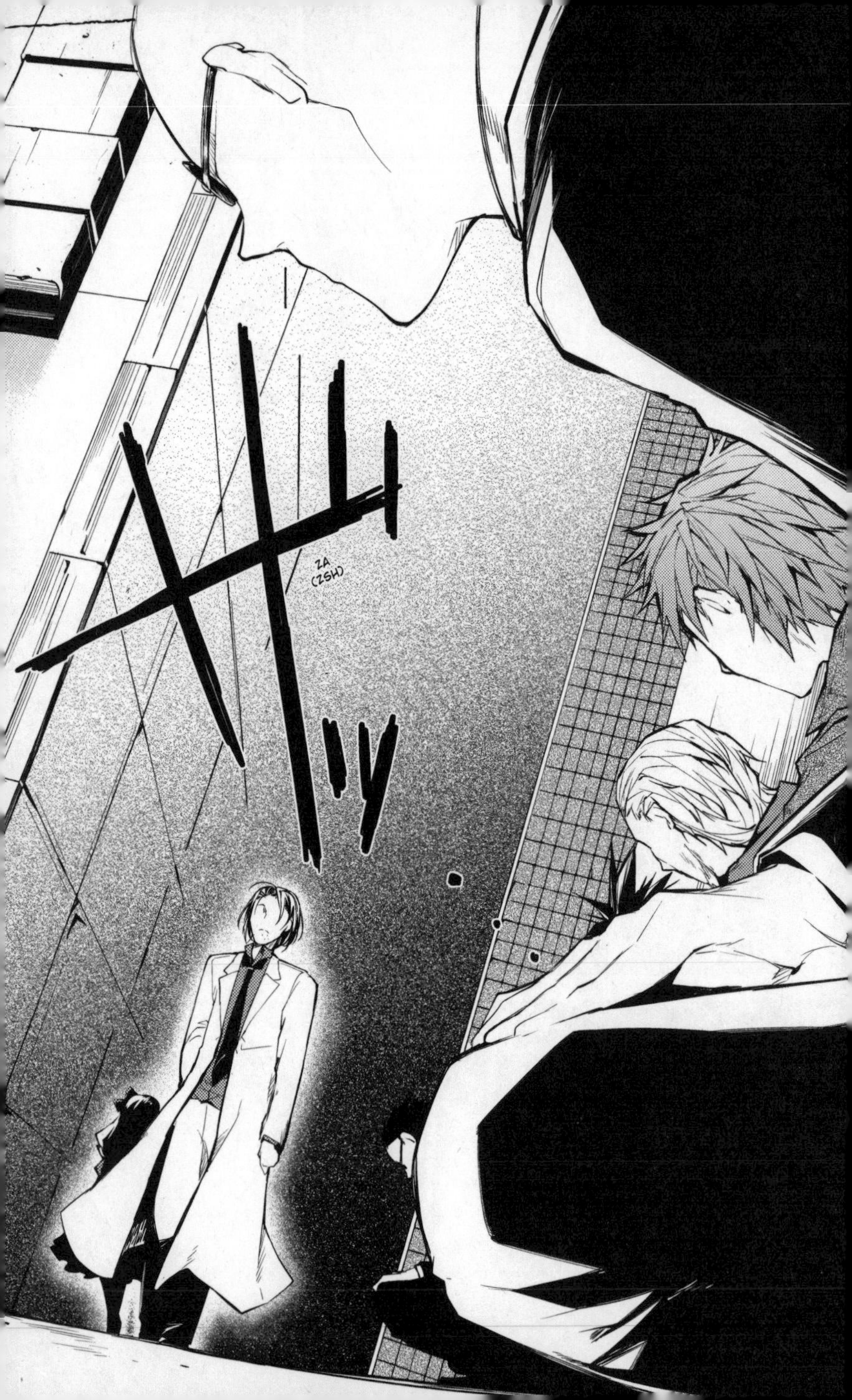
ZA
(ZSH)

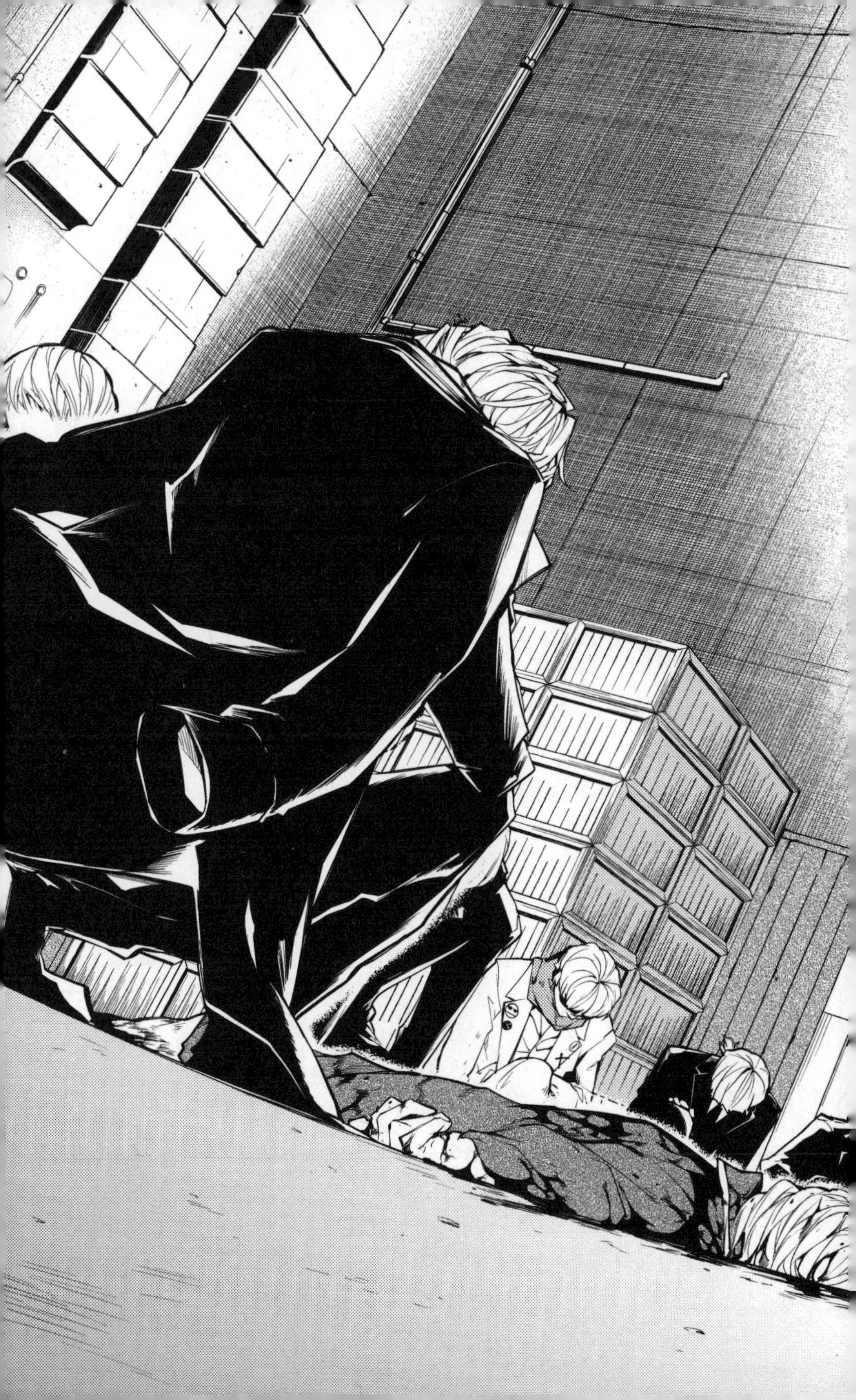

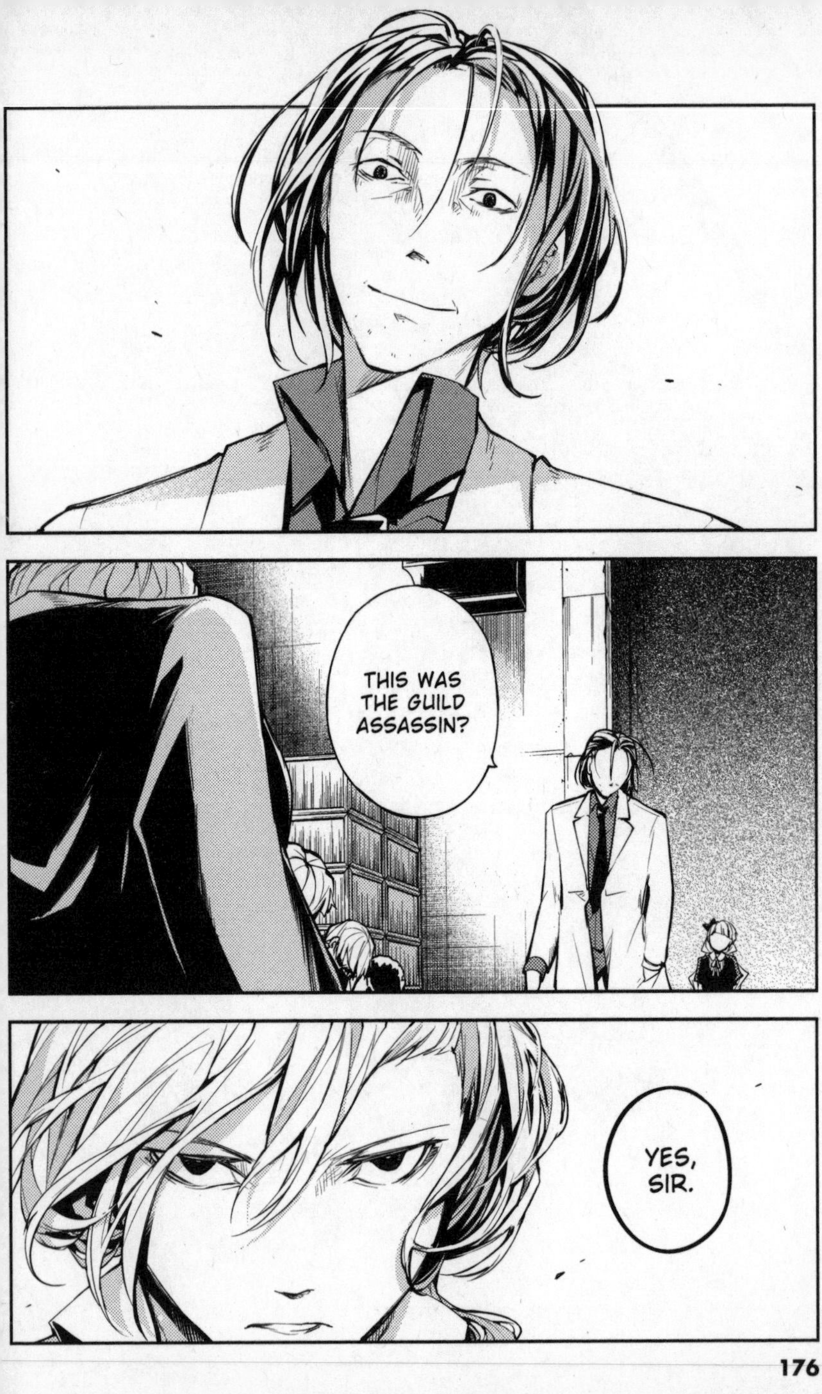
THIS WAS THE GUILD ASSASSIN?
YES, SIR.

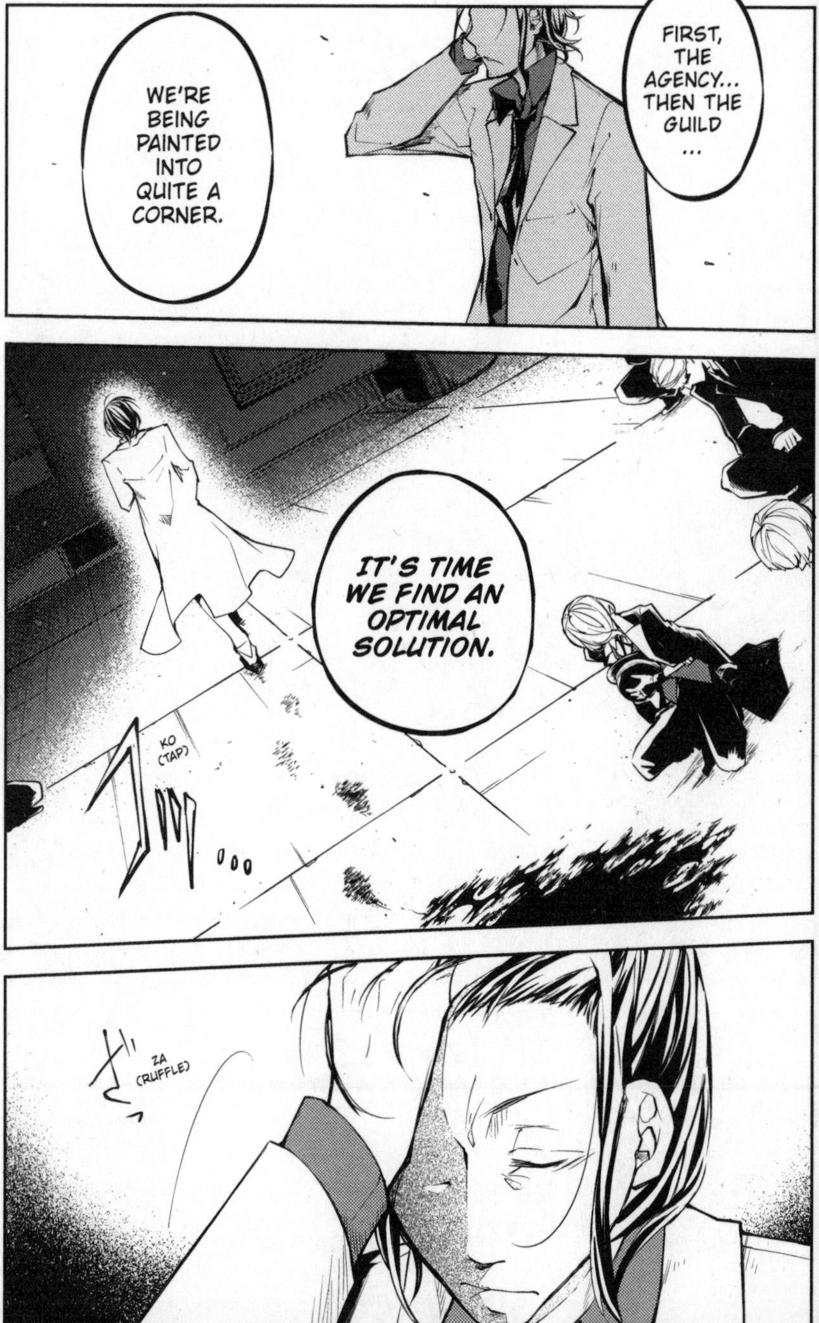
FIRST, THE AGENCY... THEN THE GUILD ...
WE'RE BEING PAINTED INTO QUITE A CORNER.
IT'S TIME WE FIND AN OPTIMAL SOLUTION.
KO (TAP)
ZA (RUFFLE)

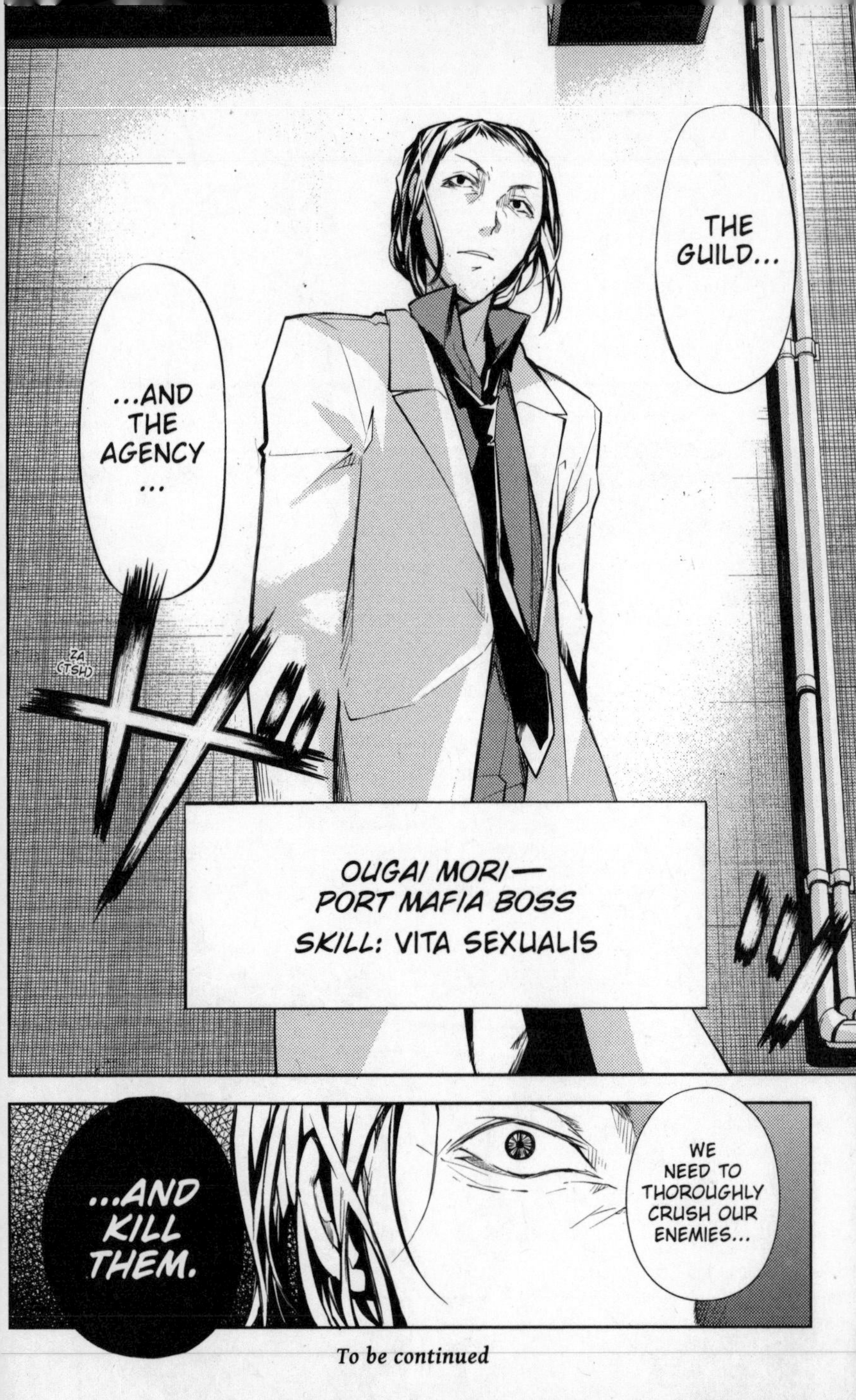
THE GUILD...
...AND THE AGENCY ...
ZA (TSH)
OUGAI MORI— PORT MAFIA BOSS
SKILL: VITA SEXUALIS
WE NEED TO THOROUGHLY CRUSH OUR ENEMIES...
...AND KILL THEM.

To be continued

KYOUKA IZUMI

SKILL: **Demon Snow**
Able to summon Demon Snow, an otherworldly form that wields a mighty weapon. It does not listen to Kyouka's orders, instead doing the bidding of a voice heard over a cell phone.

AGE: **14**

BIRTH DATE: *November 4*

HEIGHT: *148cm*

WEIGHT: *40kg*

BLOOD TYPE: *B*

LIKES: *Rabbits, tofu, hydrangeas, ghosts*

DISLIKES: *Dogs, thunder, gnats*

STRAY DOGS

Story: *Kafka Asagiri*   Art: *Sango Harukawa*

Translation: Kevin Gifford   †   Lettering: Bianca Pistillo

BUNGO STRAY DOGS Volume 4
©Kafka ASAGIRI 2014
©Sango HARUKAWA 2014
First published in Japan in 2014 by KADOKAWA CORPORATION, Tokyo.
English translation rights arranged with KADOKAWA CORPORATION, Tokyo through TUTTLE-MORI AGENCY, INC., Tokyo.

English translation © 2017 by Yen Press, LLC

Yen Press
1290 Avenue of the Americas
New York, NY 10104

Visit us at yenpress.com
facebook.com/yenpress
twitter.com/yenpress
yenpress.tumblr.com
instagram.com/yenpress

First Yen Press Edition: September 2017

Yen Press is an imprint of Yen Press, LLC.
The Yen Press name and logo are trademarks of Yen Press, LLC.

Library of Congress Control Number: 2016956681

ISBNs: 978-0-316-46816-9 (paperback)
       978-0-316-46830-5 (ebook)

10 9 8 7 6 5 4 3

WOR

Printed in the United States of America